15-
?

# Dr Z's NFL
# Guidebook

World Scientific Series
in FINANCE vol. 14

# Dr Z's NFL Guidebook

## William T. Ziemba
*University of British Columbia, Canada*
*London School of Economics, UK*

## Leonard C. MacLean
*Dalhousie University, Canada*

**World Scientific**

NEW JERSEY • LONDON • SINGAPORE • BEIJING • SHANGHAI • HONG KONG • TAIPEI • CHENNAI • TOKYO

*Published by*

World Scientific Publishing Co. Pte. Ltd.

5 Toh Tuck Link, Singapore 596224

*USA office:* 27 Warren Street, Suite 401-402, Hackensack, NJ 07601

*UK office:* 57 Shelton Street, Covent Garden, London WC2H 9HE

**British Library Cataloguing-in-Publication Data**
A catalogue record for this book is available from the British Library.

**World Scientific Series in Finance — Vol. 14**
**DR Z'S NFL GUIDEBOOK**

ISBN 978-981-3276-42-0
ISBN 978-981-3276-71-0 (pbk)

For any available supplementary material, please visit
https://www.worldscientific.com/worldscibooks/10.1142/11160#t=suppl

Desk Editor: Lum Pui Yee

Dedicated to the NFL players and TV announcers who gave us much enjoyment over the years.

Special thanks to Professor Lorne Switzer, Constantine Dzhabrov, and John Swetye for help preparing this guidebook.

# Contents

# Preface

NFL football is one of the most popular sports with a worldwide following. There are thirty-two teams, each vying to win the year's ultimate trophy — the Super Bowl. That spectacle moves from city to city in giant stadiums across the US, but what is consistent is its huge attendance at the game itself and the enormous worldwide following. The TV ads and halftime shows are shown around the world and are lavish productions. Many TV channels cover the run-up to the Super Bowl through the seventeen week season where each team plays sixteen games.

Ziemba and MacLean are professors, traders, financial analysts and sports enthusiasts. We cover ideas from the game's strategies, and much personal experience analyzing the regular season, the playoffs and the Super Bowls. The results of the actual betting for the 2009-10 to the 2017-18 seasons and information relevant for the upcoming 2018-2019 season are provided.

We start with some of the key points in the history of the NFL and discuss the greatest teams, coaches and players at various positions. We analyze important misconceptions by the announcers and coaches and the way statistics are evaluated. How are quarterbacks rated? What is the value of the field positions? What to do on a 4th down: whether to go for it or not including Bill Belichick's famous decision to go for it in the Indianapolis Colts-New England Patriots playoff game against Peyton Manning, and Pete Carroll's decision to pass in the Super Bowl against New England on the one yard line.

We discuss the ranking of the current and past great players according to the players and *Sports Illustrated*. We show how point spreads are determined and related to the chance of winning particular games. We determine the types of players that lead to game winning teams and surprisingly it is not the very best players.

We analyze actual betting for the 2009-2017 regular seasons plus playoffs and Super Bowls including the odds at key moments like the Super Bowl

51 when New England was 25 points behind in the third quarter with odds of 30-1 to win which they did over a high powered Atlanta Falcons team.

We discuss Super Bowl 52 which Philadelphia won when Tom Brady was stripped of the ball late in the game by one of the defensive ranked 80-100 players. Philadelphia benefited by a referee miscall that would have given New England another Super Bowl win. Many of the games are now decided by controversial referee calls which are mostly correct but not always.

Las Vegas odds provide the essentially efficient betting market so it is hard to win there without extreme skill. Biases including jet lag, home field advantage and the favorite-longshot bias are useful for the bettor. The odds prices move with the score so that one can create risk arbitrages on a regular basis particularly late in the games that then yield riskless profits.

We bet in off shore betting accounts such as Betfair in London and Pinnacle in the Caribbean. There one can go short or long on particular games and season outcomes and create successful hedging strategies. Risk arbitrage, mean reversion strategies are useful where you bet long on team A to win and then bet long on team B so that you are ahead on the betting regardless of whether A or B wins the games in the end. There are countless examples including the game for the ages — the 2012 New Orleans-San Francisco playoff game with four lead changes in the final three minutes of regular time.

We conclude with an analysis, prediction and results for the 2017-18 season and prepare for the 2018-19 season. Our discussion includes player injuries, player movements through free agency, retirement, trades, coaching changes, new players drafted from college and other aspects relevant for the season.

Many thanks to all involved who have helped over the years. Thanks to the publisher for producing and marketing the guidebook. We learned a lot from writing it.

William T Ziemba, Vancouver
Leonard C MacLean, Halifax
*July 2018*

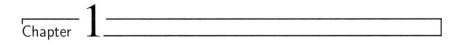

# Chapter 1

# Why NFL football is interesting & the plan for this book

What makes football interesting?[1]

The main reason it is a very good game of strategy that's fun to watch and bet on. So much happens so fast. We now discuss some of the components of the game.

**The Athletes**

The NFL is home to some of the best athletes in the world and their skill set varies so much from player to player and position to position.

You have wide receivers that can run 40 yards in a little over four seconds, and then you have linemen that can bench 250 pounds 30-plus times. You have quarterbacks that can sling a football 70 or 80 yards down the field right into the hands of a waiting receiver, and running backs that can carry defenders on their back as if they were small children. There are linebackers that can hit you hard enough to rattle your insides around, and kickers that can boot a ball through two posts from 50-plus yards away on a windy day.

The magic is that all of these athletes are on the same field at the same time.

At any point during a football game, you could see an athletic feat that you never expected. Who would have ever thought they'd see a wide receiver front flip over a defender into the end zone?

Other sports have great athletes as well, but none of them can match the variety that football brings to the table.

---

[1]We acknowledge help from AM, February 9, 2012 on the web

**Every Game is an event!**

Fans across the country and world watch the game whether or not it includes their own team. Of course, they will always take their home team
over any other game, but the interest in the sport overall is what makes it
so powerful. Any day a game is on, fans will be watching. Thanksgiving
Day in the US now features NFL games all day.

On Sundays, NFL fans watch pre-game coverage from morning to night.
There is also Monday Night Football and now Thursday and sometimes
Saturdays as well.

It works because every game matters. Each team only has 16 games every
season and one loss could cancel their hopes of making the playoffs. Each
week is just as important as the next adding to the interest and importance
to every week of football.

**Football is a game of ultimate strategy**.

A full week of game-planning goes into every game during the NFL season.
This involves breaking down game film to find trends and weaknesses in
the opposing team. Then a week's work of practice drilling the players on
what to expect and how to beat their rival.

No matter how much the teams prepare, it all comes down to execution on
game day. There is nothing more exciting than to see an offense driving
the ball downfield. Every one of the 11 players on the offense is doing their
job and it appears almost surgical at times how they move the ball. Some
quarterbacks are so good at this that it appears too easy. Other times you
have a vicious defense that uses physicality to win a game. Huge defenders
are flying in to the backfield, laying bone-crushing hits on opposing running
backs or quarterbacks. Wide receivers attempting to catch balls over the
middle often hear the footsteps of defenders closing in for a big hit.

A game can progress and end in so many different ways, but what you can
count on is that it will always be entertaining.

**The Super Bowl:** There is no bigger sporting event in the world.

Super Bowl 52 had a record 111.3 million viewers in addition to their record
breaking presence on social media sites such as Twitter and Facebook.
Whether an NFL fan or not, you are likely to watch the Super Bowl.

It is a major spectacle. It is preceded by two weeks of preparation with
many interviews and reports breaking down the game in every way possible.
Every analyst, celebrity and guest makes their prediction.

Recent Super Bowls have been amazing contests with every player putting it all on the line for this one game knowing that this is the last game of the year. The drama and magic of the game is unmatched. Players can instantly become legends that go down in NFL history or scapegoats that will never be forgiven by their home fans.

**The Drama:** The NFL tries to create parity in the league.

There are dominant teams and superstar players, but anyone can beat anyone in this league. The worst teams in the league can put together a performance that can beat the league's most elite any given week. Predictions are made, but you never know what will happen until two teams take the field. The drama that one game can bring is really what makes the sport unmatched. You could have a high-scoring game where two teams are going back and forth, making it appear as if the last team with the ball will win. Then there could be a defensive matchup that comes down to one big mistake by either team.

There is nothing more exciting than watching one of the league's best quarterbacks drive his team down the field with only seconds remaining on the clock. Millions of fans hold their breath each week as the ball is snapped and the kicker approaches it for the game-winning filed goal. Countless times fans have slowly stood up as the Hail Mary pass tumbles down in to a crowd of players in the end zone to win the game.

There are problems with NFL football, but it is still one of the greatest sports.

**The plan of this book**

We do several things which we hope are useful to fans, players, coaches, bettors and others who watch or participate in NFL games. We start with a bit of history in chapter 2 which covers past great players and teams from 1950 to current. The period from 2010 to 2018 is discussed in more detail in chapters 7-17. There we discuss what happened in major games in those years and our betting on these games throughout the season, the playoffs and the Super Bowl.

Chapter 3 presents the greatest teams, coaches and players at various positions and one ranking of the 100 best current players. The rest of the top 400 current players are in an appendix. We use one rating by *Sports Illustrated* and later discuss another ranking by the players themselves and compare these two ratings. Both are subjective but made with good knowledge of the game. We determine which teams have the best players and which players are most important to actually win NFL games.

We find that the players ranked 80-100 are crucial. Many are defensive players. A leading example is Super Bowl 52 where both offensive and defensive players in this category won the game for the Philadelphia Eagles over the New England Patriots.

In chapter 4 we begin our analysis of the game and discuss the chance of winning, odds spreads, quarterback ratings, the crucial 4th down and short yardage decision to go for it or punt or run or pass, the effect of jet lag, home field advantage and the decision to go for two or one extra points after a touchdown.

Chapter 5 discusses one way to rank the teams. The Elo is computed two ways: one way is to start afresh each year and the other way is to partially utilize the standings of the previous year. The Elo rankings evolve by which teams win or lose, home and away against another team. The ratings are useful to give a suggestion of who might be winners in particular games. In chapter 17 we evaluate how good these Elo ratings were at picking the winners and beating the spreads. This chapter also does the same things for a Montreal handicapper called the Radcliffe Rebel.

In chapter 6 we cover some topics useful largely for the bettor, namely, how arbitrage and risk arbitrage work, the favorite-longshot bias, and some literature on NFL score predictions. The Las Vegas odds measured by the spread are more or less the fair price, namely, an efficient market. Trying to bet and win on these games is difficult unless you are an expert or have spread knowledge. The scores move up and down frequently and often violently during the game. Making use of this leads to a winning strategy of mean reversion risk arbitrage The idea is you bet on team A who you think is the better team and later try to lock in a riskless arbitrage by betting on Team B at a good price when A is ahead. It does not always work but does happen in most games.

In the betting chapters 7-17 there are many such examples and they occur frequently. The structure of the playoffs is discussed in chapter 7. In general, the teams with the better record are given home advantage and play the weaker teams. This way, they are given an advantage for doing well during the regular season.

There is some literature on sports betting and prediction. Sauer (2008) and Ziemba (2018) review efficiency of wagering strategies. NFL football forecasting was reviewed by Stekler, Sendor and Verlander (2010). Baker and McHale (2013) try to predict the exact scores of NFL games during 2001-2008. Harville (1980), Brajer, Ferris and Marr (1988), Zuber, Gander and Bowers (1985), Glickman and Stern (1988) try to predict the point difference between the two teams. Cain, Law and Peel (2000) show using the non-normality of the forecast errors, that the over-under and point spread markets are essentially efficient. Stekler (2003) uses various approaches to predict game winners. All of these are interesting but just like the Elos and the Radcliffe Rebel picks, are essentially efficient markets where bettors cannot make excess profits. The goal in this book is to use a new approach of mean reversion risk arbitrage which we show does lead to risk adjusted gains most of the time. The only prior literature that suggests a way to win is in the Levitt (2004) paper where he demonstrates that bookmakers take positions themselves based on their superior ability to predict game outcomes and a knowledge of bettor preferences for local teams to obtain higher returns than would be if they cleared the market by accepting equal amounts of money on both sides of the point spread to lock in a riskfree return defined by the vig.

To understand our approach to uncertainty and risk, we suggest you look at our book which we wrote along with Blackjack and hedge fund legend Ed Thorp, (MacLean, Thorp and Ziemba (2010, 2011). There you will find what we think are the key papers on the theory of Kelly investment optimization as well as many applications and responses to critics. Our treatment is at a high level and supplements the casual treatment of this important subject by William Poundstone in his 2005 book *Fortune's Formula*. We recommend this book as a great read with a good account of Ed Thorp's blackjack contributions. Some easy to read Kelly papers are in Ziemba (2016) *Great Investment Ideas* which includes various simulations and a response to Paul Samuelson's letters to Ziemba on Kelly overbetting.

Chapters 15-17 consider the 2017-2018 season, playoffs and Super Bowl. In addition to the analysis and bets we made, we evaluate the Elo and Radcliffe Rebel predictions to see how good they were. Again, hedging and mean reversion risk arbitrage are the best strategies.

We end the book in chapter 18 with a forecast and preparation for the 2018-2019 season. This includes coaching and player changes, a list of the current top 25 players, a discussion of the NFL draft of new players and other issues such as injuries, retirements and free agencies.

# Chapter 2

# The basics of NFL games, strategies and wagering

What is now the NFL was established in 1920 as the American Professional Association with ten teams from four states. Jim Thorpe, one of the most famous athletes of all time, was president. It became the NFL in 1922. The Chicago Bears and the Arizona Cardinals can trace their roots back to two of the original ten teams. The Green Bay Packers is the oldest NFL team which has had the same name and location since joining the NFL in 1921.

In the first half of the twentieth century America's national game was base-ball, with boxing also enjoying great interest. Both those sports translated well to radio and that helped develop a national following. At mid century things started coming together for the NFL. Also television took hold in every household in the 1950's. Football was made for television and the future looked bright. The 1958 championship game between the Colts and Giants was an exciting TV event, featuring the great Johnny Unitas.

The American Football League was founded in 1960 and merged with the NFL in 1966 and created the Super Bowl which has become the most-watched annual sporting event in the US.

The early decades were somewhat unstable, with changes in teams and locations. Originally, college football was dominant. Of course legends were born in the professional game. The names Red Grange, Jim Thorpe, Curly Lambeau, Bronko Nagurski, George Halas, Don Hudson, Sammy Baugh and Sid Luckman are familiar to most sports fans.

The league continued to expand to its current size of 32 teams. A series of labor agreements during the 1990s and large television contracts have made the NFL one of the most profitable sports business in the US.

We start with some pivotal events and then discuss the evolution of the NFL. Kenneth Shouler (2017) was useful for this list of pivotal events. Then we review teams and players in the NFL from 1950 forward.

## Decade 1950–1959

Highlights

- 1950: Unlimited free substitution was restored in 1950, opening the way for the era of two platoons and specialization in pro football. The Los Angeles Rams became the first NFL team to have all of its games — both home and away — televised.

- A rule was passed in 1951 that no tackle, guard, or center would be eligible to catch a forward pass. The NFL Championship Game was televised coast-to-coast for the first time, December 23.

- In 1952 the Pittsburgh Steelers abandoned the Single-Wing for the T-formation, the last pro team to do so.

- Fullback Joe Perry of the 49ers became the first player in league history to gain 1,000 yards rushing in consecutive seasons, 1953-54.

- The sudden-death overtime rule was used for the first time in 1955. A rule change declared the ball dead immediately if the ball carrier touched the ground with any part of his body except his hands or feet while in the grasp of an opponent.

- In 1955 the Baltimore Colts made an 80-cent phone call to Johnny Unitas and signed him as a free agent. Another quarterback, Otto Graham, played his last game as the Browns defeated the Rams 38-14 in the NFL Championship Game. Graham had quarterbacked the Browns to 10 championship-game appearances in 10 years.

- The NFL Players Association was founded in 1956. CBS became the first network to broadcast some NFL regular-season games to selected television markets across the nation.

- Jim Brown of Cleveland gained an NFL-record 1,527 yards rushing in 1958.

- Vince Lombardi was named head coach of the Green Bay Packers, January 28, 1959.

The All Decade players for the 1950's are listed by position in Table 2.1. Although it was a different game back then, players like Otto Graham,

Table 2.1: All Pro Players: 1950-59

| Rotation | Position | Player | |
|---|---|---|---|
| Offense | QB | Bobby Layne, Lions | Otto Graham, Browns |
| | | Norm Van Brocklin, Eagles | |
| | RB | Ollie Matson | Frank Gifford |
| | | Hugh McElhenny | Lenny Moore |
| | | Joe Perry | Alan Ameche |
| | R | Elroy Hirsch | Raymond Berry |
| | | Tom Fears | Bobby Walston |
| | OL | Rosey Brown | Bob St. Clair |
| | | Dick Stanfel | Jim Parker |
| | | Dick Barwegen | Chuck Bednarik |
| Defense | DL | Len Ford | Gino Marchetti |
| | | Leo Nomellini | Art Donovan |
| | | Ernie Stautner | |
| | LB | Bill George | Sam Huff |
| | | Joe Schmidt | Joe Fortunato |
| | DB | Night Train Lane | Jack Butler |
| | | Jack Christiansen | Emlen Tunnell |
| | | Yale Lary | |

Rosey Brown, and Night Train Lane are considered among the best ever at their positions. Of course the name "Crazy Legs" Hirsch is hard to forget.

Football is a team game, and weakness at any offensive or defensive position can be exploited. Successful teams have strength on both sides of the ball. The top team in the 1950's was the Cleveland Browns, led by Otto Graham and Jim Brown. See Table 2.2.

Table 2.2: NFL Championship Teams: 1950-59

| Year | Winner | Loser | Score |
|---|---|---|---|
| 1950 | Cleveland Browns | Los Angeles Rams | 30-28 |
| 1951 | Los Angeles Rams | Cleveland Browns | 24-17 |
| 1952 | Detroit Lions | Cleveland Browns | 17-7 |
| 1953 | Detroit Lions | Cleveland Browns | 17-16 |
| 1954 | Cleveland Browns | Detroit Lions | 56-10 |
| 1955 | Cleveland Browns | Los Angeles Rams | 38-14 |
| 1956 | NY Giants | ChicagoBears | 47-7 |
| 1957 | Detroit Lions | Cleveland Browns | 59-14 |
| 1958 | Baltimore Colts | NY Giants | 23-17 |
| 1959 | Baltimore Colts | NY Giants | 31-16 |

## Decade 1960–1969

Highlights

- In 1960 Pete Rozelle was elected NFL Commissioner .

- The AFL began play in competition with the NFL. The Denver Broncos defeated the Patriots 13-10 before 21,597 at Boston in the first AFL regular-season game.

- Canton, Ohio, where the league that became the NFL was formed in 1920, was chosen as the site of the Pro Football Hall of Fame.

- Both leagues prohibited grabbing any player's facemask in 1962. The AFL voted to make the scoreboard clock the official timer of the game.

- In 1963 Rozelle suspended Green Bay halfback Paul Hornung and Detroit defensive tackle Alex Karras for placing bets on their own teams and on other NFL games.

- Jim Brown of Cleveland rushed for an NFL single-season record 1,863 yards in 1963.

- In 1964 Pete Gogolak of Cornell signed a contract with Buffalo, becoming the first soccer-style kicker in pro football.

- In 1965 Field Judge Burl Toler became the first black official in NFL history, September 19. According to a Harris survey, sports fans chose professional football (41 percent) as their favorite sport, overtaking baseball (38 percent) for the first time,

- A series of secret meetings regarding a possible AFL-NFL merger were held. Rozelle announced the merger, June 8. The leagues agreed to play an annual AFL-NFL World Championship Game (Super Bowl).

- The *sling-shot* goal post and a six-foot-wide border around the field were made standard in the NFL in 1968 February 22.

- Defensive back Emlen Tunnell of the New York Giants became the first black player to enter the Pro Football Hall of Fame.

- Vince Lombardi resigned as head coach of the Packers, but remained as general manager.

- In 1969 the movie Heidi became a footnote in sports history when NBC did not show the last :50 of the Jets-Raiders game in order to permit the children's special to begin on time.

- An AFL team won the Super Bowl for the first time, as the Jets defeated the Colts 16-7 Super Bowl III.

With the soaring popularity of football, many of the star players became sports icons. The great running back Jim Brown seamlessly moved from football to the movie screen. He was a few days late for the season's practice because of the filming of the movie *The Dirty Dozen* with Lee Marvin. Instead of facing a fine or suspension, he retired at the height of this career as the best running back and never returned to football and had a 40 year movie career. Bart Starr, Paul Horning, Jim Taylor, Ray Nitschke and other Packers epitimized team play. Table 2.3 lists the All Decade players.

The Green Bay Packers were the dominant team in the 1960's. Their coach Vince Lombardi was considered a great motivator and his team first approach spread to other domains. He is known for saying "winning is not the most important thing, it is the only thing." See Table 2.4.

Table 2.3: All Pro Players: 1960-69

| Rotation | Position | Player | |
|---|---|---|---|
| Offense | QB | Bart Starr | Sonny Jurgensen |
| | | Johnny Unitas | |
| | RB | Leroy Kelly | Gale Sayers |
| | | John David Crow | Paul Hornung |
| | | Jim Brown | Jim Taylor |
| | R | Gary Collins | Boyd Dowler |
| | | Charley Taylor | Del Shofner |
| | | John Mackey | |
| | OL | Ralph Neely | Bob Brown |
| | | Forrest Gregg | Gene Hickerson |
| | | Jerry Kramer | Howard Mudd |
| | | Jim Ringo | |
| Defense | DL | Willie Davis | Deacon Jones |
| | | Doug Atkins | Bob Lilly |
| | | Merlin Olsen | Alex Karras |
| | LB | Dave Robinson | Larry Morris |
| | | Dick Butkus | Ray Nitschke |
| | | Tommy Nobis | |
| | DB | Bobby Boyd | Herb Adderley |
| | | Lem Barney | Larry Wilson |
| | | Willie Wood | Eddie Meador |

Table 2.4: NFL Championship Teams: 1960-69

| Year | Winner | Loser | Score |
|------|--------|-------|-------|
| 1960 | Philadelphia | Green Bay | 17-13 |
| 1961 | Green Bay | NY Giants | 37-0 |
| 1962 | Green Bay | NY Giants | 16-7 |
| 1963 | Chicago | NY Giants | 14-10 |
| 1964 | Cleveland | Baltimore | 27-0 |
| 1965 | Green Bay | Cleveland | 23-12 |
| 1966 | Green Bay | Kansas City | 35-10 |
| 1967 | Green Bay | Oakland | 33-14 |
| 1968 | NY Jets | Indianapolis | 16-7 |
| 1969 | Kansas City | Minnesota | 23-7 |

## Decade 1970–1979

Highlights

- Baltimore, Cleveland, and Pittsburgh agreed to join the AFL teams to form the 13-team American Football Conference of the NFL in 1970.

- In 1970 the NFL agreed on a playoff format that would include one *wild-card* team per conference — the second-place team with the best record.

- The merged 26-team league adopted rules changes putting names on the backs of players' jerseys, making a point after touchdown worth only one point, and making the scoreboard clock the official timing device of the game.

- Tom Dempsey of New Orleans kicked a game-winning NFL-record 63-yard field goal against Detroit, on November 8, 1970.

- In 1971 Garo Yepremian kicked a 37-yard field goal for the Dolphins after 22 minutes, 40 seconds of overtime, as the game lasted 82 minutes, 40 seconds overall, making it the longest game in history.

- The inbounds lines or hashmarks were moved nearer the center of the field, 23 yards, 1 foot, 9 inches from the sidelines in 1972.

- Franco Harris's *Immaculate Reception* gave the Steelers their first postseason win ever, 13-7 over the Raiders, on December 23, 1972.

- A jersey numbering system was adopted in 1973: 1-19 for quarterbacks and specialists, 20-49 for running backs and defensive backs, 50-59 for centers and linebackers, 60-79 for defensive linemen and interior offensive linemen other than centers, and 80-89 for wide receivers and tight ends.

- O.J. Simpson of Buffalo became the first player to rush for more than 2,000 yards in a season, gaining 2,003.

- In 1974 sweeping rules changes were adopted to add action and tempo to games: one sudden-death overtime period was added for preseason and regular-season games; the goal posts were moved from the goal line to the end lines; kickoffs were moved from the 40- to the 35-yard line; after missed field goals from beyond the 20, the ball was to be returned to the line of scrimmage; restrictions were placed on members of the punting team to open up return possibilities; roll-blocking and cutting of wide receivers was eliminated; the extent of downfield contact a defender could have with an eligible receiver was restricted; the penalties for offensive holding, illegal use of the hands, and tripping were reduced from 15 to 10 yards; wide receivers blocking back toward the ball within three yards of the line of scrimmage were prevented from blocking below the waist.

- The divisional winners with the highest won-loss percentage were made the home team for the divisional playoffs, and the surviving winners with the highest percentage made home teams for the championship games in 1975.

- The Steelers joined Green Bay and Miami as the only teams to win two Super Bowls.

- On March 16, 1976, the league adopted the use of two 30-second clocks for all games, visible to both players and fans to note the official time between the ready-for-play signal and snap of the ball.

- In 1977 The NFL Players Association and the NFL Management Council ratified a collective bargaining agreement extending until 1982.

- The 16-game regular season and 4-game preseason was adopted beginning in 1978. A second wild-card team was added for the playoffs beginning in 1978, with the wild-card teams to play each other and the winners advancing to a round of eight postseason series.

- Rules changes were adopted to open up the passing game and to cut down on injuries. Defenders were permitted to make contact with

Table 2.5: All Pro Players: 1970-79

| Rotation | Position | Team 1 | Team 2 |
|---|---|---|---|
| Offense | QB | Roger Staubach | Ken Stabler |
| | | | Terry Bradshaw |
| | RB | Walter Payton | Franco Harris |
| | | O.J. Simpson | Earl Campbell |
| | R | Lynn Swann | Paul Warfield |
| | | Drew Pearson | Harold Carmichael |
| | | Dave Casper | Charlie Sanders |
| | OL | Art Shell | Dan Dierdorf |
| | | Rayfield Wright | Ron Yary |
| | | Larry Little | John Hannah |
| | | Joe DeLamielleure | Gene Upshaw |
| | | Jim Langer | Mike Webster |
| Defense | DL | Carl Eller | L.C. Greenwood |
| | | Jack Youngblood | Harvey Martin |
| | | Bob Lilly | Merlin Olsen |
| | | Joe Greene | Alan Page |
| | LB | Jack Ham | Robert Brazile |
| | | Dick Butkus | Jack Lambert |
| | | Ted Hendricks | Bobby Bell |
| | DB | Willie Brown | Roger Wehrli |
| | | Jimmy Johnson | Louis Wright |
| | | Ken Houston | Dick Anderson |
| | | Cliff Harris | Larry Wilson |

eligible receivers only once; the head slap was outlawed; offensive linemen were prohibited from thrusting their hands to an opponent's neck, face, or head; and wide receivers were prohibited from clipping, even in the legal clipping zone.

- Chicago's Walter Payton set a single-game rushing record with 275 yards (40 carries) against Minnesota, November 20, 1977.

- According to a Louis Harris Sports Survey in 1978, 70 percent of the nation's sports fans said they followed football, compared to 54 percent who followed baseball.

- The NFL continued a trend toward opening up the game. Rules changes permitted a defender to maintain contact with a receiver within five yards of the line of scrimmage, but restricted contact beyond that point. The pass-blocking rule was interpreted to permit the extending of arms and open hands.

- In 1979 NFL rules changes emphasized additional player safety. The changes prohibited players on the receiving team from blocking below the waist during kickoffs, punts, and field-goal attempts; prohibited the wearing of torn or altered equipment and exposed pads that could be hazardous; extended the zone in which there could be no crackback blocks; and instructed officials to quickly whistle a play dead when a quarterback was clearly in the grasp of a tackler.

Football is a rugged game and many rules changes were implemented in the 1970's to open up the game and increase player safety. The Steelers were possibly the toughest team ever, and players like "Mean" Joe Green were feared. Smooth players like Walter Payton and Lynn Swann were beautiful to watch, but defense was dominant. The All Decade Team is given in Table 2.5.

The Pittsburgh Steelers were the dominant team of the 1970s. The "Steel Curtain" defense set the tone in many games, and the team won 4 championships in 6 years. Table 2.6 gives the results of Super Bowls in the 70's.

Table 2.6: NFL Championship Games: 1970-79

| Year | Winner | Loser | Score |
|------|--------|-------|-------|
| 1970 | Baltimore | Dallas | 16-13 |
| 1971 | Dallas | Miami | 24-3 |
| 1972 | Miami | Washington | 14-7 |
| 1973 | Miami | Minnesota | 24-7 |
| 1974 | Pittsburgh | Minnesota | 16-6 |
| 1975 | Pittsburgh | Dallas | 21-17 |
| 1976 | Oakland | Minnesota | 32-14 |
| 1977 | Dallas | Denver | 27-10 |
| 1978 | Pittsburgh | Dallas | 35-31 |
| 1979 | Pittsburgh | Los Angeles | 31-19 |

# Decade 1980–1989

Highlights

- Rules changes placed greater restrictions on contact in the area of the head, neck, and face. Under the heading of *personal foul*, players were prohibited from directly striking, swinging, or clubbing on the head, neck, or face. Starting in 1980, a penalty could be called for such contact whether or not the initial contact was made below the neck area.

- A CBS-New York Times poll showed that 48 percent of sports fans preferred football to 31 percent for baseball.

- The NFL teams hosted 167 representatives from 44 predominantly black colleges during training camps for a total of 289 days.

- The NFL signed a five-year contract with the three television networks (ABC, CBS, and NBC) to televise all NFL regular-season and postseason games starting with the 1982 season.

- The 1982 season was reduced from a 16-game schedule to nine as the result of a 57-day players' strike. The strike was called by the NFLPA at midnight on Monday, September 20, 1982. Because of the shortened season, the NFL adopted a format of 16 teams competing in a Super Bowl Tournament for the 1982 playoffs. Since 1990, the NFL is the only major US league to have avoided the loss of regular-season games due to work stoppages.

- George Halas, the owner of the Bears and the last surviving member of the NFL's second organizational meeting, died at 88, October 31, 1983.

- Many all-time records were set in 1984: Dan Marino of Miami passed for 5,084 yards and 48 touchdowns; Eric Dickerson of the Los Angeles Rams rushed for 2,105 yards; Art Monk of Washington caught 106 passes; and Walter Payton of Chicago broke Jim Brown's career rushing mark, finishing the season with 13,309 yards.

- The league-wide conversion to videotape from movie film for coaching study was approved in 1985.

- Chicago defeated New England 46-10 in Super Bowl XX at the Louisiana Superdome, January 26, 1986. The NBC telecast replaced the final episode of M*A*S*H as the most-viewed television program in history, with an audience of 127 million viewers, according to A.C. Nielsen figures. NBC Radio figures indicated an audience of 10 million for the game.

- On March 11, 1987, the owners adopted limited use of instant replay as an officiating aid, prohibited players from wearing or otherwise displaying equipment, apparel, or other items that carry commercial names, names of organizations, or personal messages of any type.

- In 1987 a special payment program was adopted to benefit nearly 1,000 former NFL players who participated in the League before the current Bert Bell NFL Pension Plan was created and made retroactive to the 1959 season. Players covered by the new program spent at least five years in the League and played all or part of their career prior to 1959. Each vested player would receive $60 per month for each year of service in the League for life. Over 400 former NFL players from the pre-1959 era received first payments from NFL owners.

- On July 1, 1988, owners voted to continue the instant replay system for the third consecutive season with the Instant Replay Official to be assigned to a regular seven-man, on-the-field crew. A 45-second clock was also approved to replace the 30-second clock. For a normal sequence of plays, the interval between plays was changed to 45 seconds from the time the ball is signaled dead until it is snapped on the succeeding play.

- Johnny Grier became the first African-American referee in NFL history, September 4 1988.

- A strengthened policy regarding anabolic steroids and masking agents was announced by Commissioner Rozelle. NFL clubs called for strong disciplinary measures in cases of feigned injuries and adopted a joint proposal by the Long-Range Planning and Finance committees regarding player personnel rules, March 1989.

- Art Shell was named head coach of the Los Angeles Raiders making him the NFL's first black head coach since Fritz Pollard coached the Akron Pros in 1921.

- San Francisco joined Pittsburgh as the NFL's only teams to win four Super Bowls.

Table 2.7 lists the All Decade Team. "Joe Cool" Montana was the offensive star, with Jerry Rice the recipient of many of his clutch passes. Montana had 16 TDs and no interceptions in his four Super Bowl appearances and he won all of them. Defense was still prominent, with the "Minister of Defense" (Reggie White), LT (Lawrence Taylor) and Mike Singletary dominanting games.

The dominant team of the 80's was the San Francisco 49ers. The "West Coast" offense designed by coach Bill Walsh influenced play in future decades. See Table 2.8.

Table 2.7: All Pro Players: 1980-89

| Rotation | Position | Team 1 | Team 2 |
|----------|----------|--------|--------|
| Offense | QB | Joe Montana | Dan Fouts |
| | RB | Walter Payton | Roger Craig |
| | | Eric Dickerson | John Riggins |
| | R | Jerry Rice | James Lofton |
| | | Steve Largent | Art Monk |
| | | Kellen Winslow | Ozzie Newsome |
| | OL | Anthony Munoz | Joe Jacoby |
| | | Jimbo Covert | Gary Zimmerman |
| | | John Hannah | Bill Fralic |
| | | Russ Grimm | Mike Munchak |
| | | Dwight Stephenson | Mike Webster |
| Defense | DL | Howie Long | Bruce Smith |
| | | Reggie White | Lee Roy Selmon |
| | | Dan Hampton | Dave Butz |
| | | Randy White | Keith Millard |
| | LB | Lawrence Taylor | Andre Tippett |
| | | Ted Hendricks | John Anderson |
| | | Mike Singletary | Carl Banks |
| | | | Jack Lambert |
| | DB | Mel Blount | Frank Minnifield |
| | | Mike Haynes | Lester Hayes |
| | | Kenny Easley | Deron Cherry |
| | | Ronnie Lott | Joey Browner |
| | | | Nolan Cromwell |

Table 2.8: NFL Championship Teams: 1980-89

| Year | Winner | Loser | Score |
|------|--------|-------|-------|
| 1980 | Oakland | Philadelphia | 27-10 |
| 1981 | San Francisco | Cincinnati | 26-21 |
| 1982 | Washington | Miami | 27-17 |
| 1983 | Los Angeles | Washington | 38-9 |
| 1984 | San Francisco | Miami | 38-16 |
| 1985 | Chicago | New England | 46-10 |
| 1986 | New York Giants | Denver | 39-20 |
| 1987 | Washington | Denver | 42-10 |
| 1988 | San Francisco | Cincinnati | 20-16 |
| 1989 | San Francisco | Denver | 55-10 |

## Decade 1990–2000

Highlights

- The NFL announced revisions in its 1990 draft eligibility rules. College juniors became eligible but must renounce their collegiate football eligibility before applying for the NFL Draft.

- The NFL revised its playoff format to include two additional wild-card teams (one per conference), which raised the total to six wild-card teams.

- NFL International Week was celebrated with four preseason games in seven days in Tokyo, London, Berlin, and Montreal.

- In 1991 the NFL launched the World League of American Football, the first sports league to operate on a weekly basis on two separate continents.

- In a Harris Poll taken during the NFL offseason, professional football again was declared the nation's most popular sport.

- The Dallas Cowboys defeated the Buffalo Bills 52-17 in Super Bowl XXVII to capture their first NFL title since 1978. The NBC broadcast of the game was the most watched program in television history and was seen by 133,400,000 people in the United States. The game also was seen live or taped in 101 other countries. NFL announced plans to allow fans, for the first time ever, to join players and coaches in selecting the annual AFC and NFC Pro Bowl teams.

- On November 14, 1993 Don Shula became the winningest coach in NFL history when Miami beat Philadelphia to give Shula his 325th victory, one more than George Halas.

- In a move to increase offensive production, NFL clubs at the league's annual meeting in 1994 adopted a package of changes, including modifications in line play, chucking rules, and the roughing-the-passer rule, plus the adoption of the two-point conversion and moving the spot of the kickoff back to the 30-yard line.

- The NFL Management Council and the NFL Players Association announced an agreement on the formulation and implementation of the most comprehensive drug and alcohol policy in sports, October 28, 1994.

- The San Francisco 49ers became the first team to win five Super Bowls when they defeated the San Diego Chargers 49-26 in Super Bowl XXIX.

- A series of safety-related rules changes were adopted at a league meeting in Phoenix, primarily related to the use of the helmet against defenseless players, March 14, 1995.

- In 1995, many significant records and milestones were achieved: Miami's Dan Marino surpassed Pro Football Hall of Famer Fran Tarkenton in four major passing categories — attempts, completions, yards, and touchdowns-to become the NFL's all-time career leader. San Francisco's Jerry Rice became the all-time reception and receiving-yardage leader with career totals of 942 catches and 15,123 yards. Dallas' Emmitt Smith scored 25 touchdowns, breaking the season record of 24 set by Washington's John Riggins in 1983.

- Points scored totaled 762 and NFL paid attendance totaled 964,079 for 15 games in Week 11, 1996, the highest weekend totals in either category in the league's 77-year history.

- The 10,000th regular-season game in NFL history was played when the Seattle Seahawks defeated the Tennessee Oilers 16-13 at the Kingdome in Seattle, October 5, 1997.

- The World League was renamed the NFL Europe League, January 22, 1998. The Rhein Fire defeated the Frankfurt Galaxy 34-10 to win the 1998 World Bowl in front of 47,846 fans in Frankfurt's Waldstadion.

- NFL paid attendance of 19,741,493 for all games played during the 1998 season was the highest in league history.

- By a vote of 28-3, the owners adopted an instant replay system as an officiating aid for the 1999 season.

- In 1999, Walter Payton, the NFL's all-time leading rusher, died of liver cancer at the age of 45. Payton played for the Chicago Bears from 1975-1987 and rushed for an NFL-record 16,726 yards.

- Paid attendance for all NFL games increased in 1999 for the third year in a row and was the highest ever in the 80-year history of the league. The prestigious Walter Payton Man of the Year honors Payton's memory and rewards off the field community service.

- Cincinnati's Corey Dillon set a single-game rushing record with 278 yards (22 carries) against Denver, breaking the previous record of 275 yards by Chicago's Walter Payton in 1977, October 22, 1999. Minnesota's Gary Anderson converted a 21-yard field goal against Buffalo to pass George Blanda as the NFL's all-time scoring leader with 2,004 points, October 22. On December 17 San Francisco's

Terrell Owens set a single-game receiving record with 20 receptions (283 yards) against Chicago, surpassing the previous mark of 18 by Tom Fears of the Los Angeles Rams in 1950.

The 1990s All Decade Teams are listed in Table 2.9. Changes in rules saw the rise of offensive stars. The straight ahead Emmitt Smith and the elusive Barry Sanders brought the running game to the forefront. Not to be outdone, Jerry Rice continued his outstanding receiving, with Steve Young the San Francisco 49ers QB.

The top team of the 90's was the Dallas Cowboys. The team was solid in all positions, although only Emmitt Smith, Michael Irving, Mark Stepnoski and Deion Sanders are All Decade. Their triple threat of Troy Aikman QB, Emmitt Smith running back and Michael Irving wide receiver led them to three Super Bowl wins and entry in the Hall of Fame. See Table 2.10.

Table 2.9: All Pro Players: 1990-99

| Rotation | Position | Team 1 | Team 2 |
|----------|----------|--------|--------|
| Offense | QB | John Elway | Brett Favre |
| | RB | Emmitt Smith | Terrell Davis |
| | | Barry Sanders | Thurman Thomas |
| | R | Jerry Rice | Michael Irvin |
| | | Cris Carter | Tim Brown |
| | | Shannon Sharpe | Ben Coates |
| | OL | Gary Zimmerman | Tony Boselli |
| | | Willie Roaf | Richmond Webb |
| | | Bruce Matthews | Steve Wisniewski |
| | | Randall McDaniel | Larry Allen |
| | | Dermontti Dawson | Mark Stepnoski |
| Defense | DL | Reggie White | Neil Smith |
| | | Bruce Smith | Chris Doleman |
| | | Cortez Kennedy | Warren Sapp |
| | | John Randle | Bryant Young |
| | LB | Derrick Thomas | Hardy Nickerson |
| | | Junior Seau | C |
| | | Kevin Greene | Levon Kirkland |
| | DB | Deion Sanders | Darrell Green |
| | | Rod Woodson | Aeneas Williams |
| | | LeRoy Butler | Ronnie Lott |
| | | Steve Atwater | Carnell Lake |

Table 2.10: NFL Championship Game: 1990-99

| Year | Winner | Loser | Score |
|------|--------|-------|-------|
| 1990 | New York Giants | Buffalo | 20-19 |
| 1991 | Washington | Buffalo | 37-24 |
| 1992 | Dallas | Buffalo | 52-17 |
| 1993 | Dallas | Buffalo | 30-13 |
| 1994 | San Francisco | San Diego | 49-26 |
| 1995 | Dallas | Pittsburgh | 27-17 |
| 1996 | Green Bay | New England | 35- 21 |
| 1997 | Denver | Green Bay | 31- 24 |
| 1998 | Denver | Atlanta | 34-19 |
| 1999 | St. Louis | Tennessee | 23-16 |

## Decade 2000–2010

Highlights

- In 2001 the Washington Redskins set an all-time NFL regular-season home paid attendance record with a total of 656,599 for eight games, breaking the record of 634,204 held by the 1980 Detroit Lions.

- In the wake of the September 11, 2001 terrorist attacks, Commissioner Paul Tagliabue postponed the games scheduled for September 16-17, September 13. The league's 16-game regular season was retained when the postponed Week 2 games were re-scheduled for the weekend of January 6-7.

- President Bush designated Super Bowl XXXVI as a *National Special Security Event*, allowing all security for the game to be coordinated by the Secret Service.

- The New England Patriots won their first Super Bowl by defeating the NFC champion St. Louis Rams 20-17 in Super Bowl XXXVI at the Louisiana Superdome in New Orleans. The game marked the first time in Super Bowl history that the winning points came on the final play, a 48-yard field goal by Patriots kicker Adam Vinatieri.

- In 2001 NFL Europe kicked off its 10th season with a record 254 players allocated by NFL clubs.

- For the first time, the NFL season kicked off on a Thursday night in prime time as the San Francisco 49ers defeated the New York Giants 16-13 at Giants Stadium. Johnny Unitas, the legendary quarterback for the Baltimore Colts and a Pro Football Hall of Fame member, died of a heart attack at the age of 69, September 11, 2001. Oakland Raiders wide receiver Jerry Rice became the all-time leader in yards from scrimmage, surpassing Pro Football Hall of Fame running back Walter Payton (21,281 yards).

- Baltimore Ravens cornerback Chris McAlister set an NFL record for the longest scoring play with a 107-yard touchdown return of an errant 57-yard field goal attempt by Denver Broncos kicker Jason Elam, September 30, 2001.

- Dallas Cowboys running back Emmitt Smith became the NFL's all-time rushing leader, surpassing Pro Football Hall of Fame running back Walter Payton (16,726 yards), October 27, 2001. Indianapolis Colts wide receiver Marvin Harrison set the NFL single-season record for pass receptions with 143, surpassing Herman Moore (123), December 29, 2001.

- The 2002 season concluded with 25 overtime games, the most in NFL history.

- The NFL Network will be the first television programming service fully dedicated to the NFL and the sport of football in 2003.

- The NFL set an all-time paid attendance record in 2002 with 21,505,138, the first time paid attendance topped 21- million.

- Otto Graham, the legendary quarterback of the Cleveland Browns and a member of the Pro Football Hall of Fame, died at the age of 82, December 17, 2003.

- The New England Patriots defeated the New York Jets 13-7 for their NFL-record 18th consecutive regular-season victory, October 24, 2004.

- Indianapolis Colts quarterback Peyton Manning set the NFL single-season record with 49 touchdown passes in 2004.

- In 2005 the NFL strengthened its steroids program by adopting the Olympic testosterone testing standard, tripling the number of times a player can be randomly tested during the offseason from two to six, adding substances to the list of banned substances, and putting new language in the policy to allow for testing of designer drugs and other substances that may have evaded detection.

- The Steelers won their fifth Super Bowl, defeating the Seattle Seahawks 21-10 in Super Bowl XL at Ford Field in Detroit, Michigan.

Table 2.11: All Pro Players: 2000-09

| Rotation | Position | Team 1 | Team 2 |
|----------|----------|--------|--------|
| Offense | QB | Tom Brady | Peyton Manning |
| | RB | LaDainian Tomlinson | Jamal Lewis |
| | | Edgerrin James | Shaun Alexander |
| | | Lorenzo Neal | Tony Richardson |
| | R | Marvin Harrison | Torry Holt |
| | | Randy Moss | Terrell Owens |
| | | Tony Gonzalez | Antonio Gates |
| | OL | Walter Jones | Orlando Pace |
| | | Jonathan Ogden | Willie Roaf |
| | | Alan Faneca | Larry Allen |
| | | Steve Hutchinson | Will Shields |
| | | Kevin Mawae | Olin Kreutz |
| Defense | DL | Dwight Freeney | Jason Taylor |
| | | Michael Strahan | Julius Peppers |
| | | Warren Sapp | La'Roi Glover |
| | | Richard Seymour | Kevin Williams |
| | LB | Derrick Brooks | DeMarcus Ware |
| | | Ray Lewis | Joey Porter |
| | | Brian Urlacher | Zach Thomas |
| | DB | Charles Woodson | Ronde Barber |
| | | Champ Bailey | Ty Law |
| | | Ed Reed | Darren Sharper |
| | | Brian Dawkins | Troy Polamalu |

- In total, the NFL, its owners, teams, players, and fans contributed $21 million to aid the Hurricane Katrina rebuilding effort.

- Chicago Bears cornerback Nathan Vasher set an NFL record for the longest scoring play with a 108-yard touchdown return of an errant field goal by San Francisco kicker Joe Nedney in Chicago, November 13, 2005.

- Seattle Seahawks running back Shaun Alexander set the NFL single-season record for touchdowns with 28, in 2005.

- The NFL set an all-time paid attendance record in 2005 for the fourth consecutive season.

- In 2007 the Patriots go undefeated- 16-0 in the regular season but lost the Super Bowl the the NY Giants. Recall that in 1973 the Miami Dolphins were undefeated Super Bowl champions.

- Winner Indianapolis Colts quarterback Peyton Manning wins his 4th MVP in 2008.

- Brett Favre became the first NFL quarterback to pass for 500 touchdowns, throw for 70,000 yards, complete 6,000 passes, and attempt 10,000 passes.

All time great quarterbacks were on display in this decade. Tom Brady and Peyton Manning are in the discussion for GOAT. Brady's winning percentage is unmatched. Not surprising, passing was more prominent than ever. The All Decade team is shown in Table 2.11.

The New England Patriots were the team of the Decade. Tom Brady had an uncanny ability to bring his team downfield late in a game, often to be won on an Adam Viniteri field goal. Coach Belichick stands with Vince Lombardi for an ability to engender team discipline. Brady, Richard Seymour, and Ty Law are on the All decade list, but success for the Patriots is achieved by contributions from all players. See Table 2.12.

Table 2.12: NFL Championship Game: 2000-2009

| Year | Winner | Loser | Score |
|------|--------|-------|-------|
| 2000 | Baltimore | NY Giants | 34-7 |
| 2001 | New England | St. Louis | 20-17 |
| 2002 | Tampa Bay | Oakland | 48-21 |
| 2003 | New England | Carolina | 32-29 |
| 2004 | New England | Philadelphia | 24-21 |
| 2005 | Pittsburgh | Seattle | 21-10 |
| 2006 | Indianapolis | Chicago | 29-17 |
| 2007 | NY Giants | New England | 17-14 |
| d2008 | Pittsburgh | Arizona | 27-23 |
| 2009 | New Orleans | Indianapolis | 31, 17 |

## Decade 2010–2018

The highlights in this past decade are detailed in the strategy and betting chapters 7-17.

## Stadiums

Stadiums are now built for luxury and an experience which includes the football game.

## Table 2.13: Stadiums that have held the Super Bowl

| # | Date | Site | Result |
|---|------|------|--------|
| I | Jan 15, 1967 | Los Angeles Memorial Coliseum | Green Bay 35, Kansas City 10 |
| II | Jan 14, 1968 | Orange Bowl (Miami) | Green Bay 33, Oakland 14 |
| III | Jan 12, 1969 | Orange Bowl (Miami) | New York Jets 16, Baltimore 7 |
| IV | Jan 11, 1970 | Tulane Stadium (New Orleans) | Kansas City 23, Minnesota 7 |
| V | Jan 17, 1971 | Orange Bowl (Miami) | Baltimore 16, Dallas 13 |
| VI | Jan 16, 1972 | Tulane Stadium (New Orleans) | Dallas 24, Miami 3 |
| VII | Jan 14, 1973 | Los Angeles Memorial Coliseum | Miami 14, Washington 7 |
| VIII | Jan 13, 1974 | Rice Stadium (Houston) | Miami 24, Minnesota 7 |
| IX | Jan 12, 1975 | Tulane Stadium (New Orleans) | Pittsburgh 16, Minnesota 6 |
| X | Jan 18, 1976 | Orange Bowl (Miami) | Pittsburgh 21, Dallas 17 |
| XI | Jan 9, 1977 | Rose Bowl (Pasadena, Calif.) | Oakland 32, Minnesota 14 |
| XII | Jan 15, 1978 | Superdome (New Orleans) | Dallas 27, Denver 10 |
| XIII | Jan 21, 1979 | Orange Bowl (Miami) | Pittsburgh 35, Dallas 31 |
| XIV | Jan 20, 1980 | Rose Bowl (Pasadena) | Pittsburgh 31, Los Angeles 19 |
| XV | Jan 25, 1981 | Superdome (New Orleans) | Oakland 27, Philadelphia 10 |
| XVI | Jan 24, 1982 | Silverdome (Pontiac) | San Francisco 26, Cincinnati 21 |
| XVII | Jan 30, 1983 | Rose Bowl (Pasadena) | Washington 27, Miami 17 |
| XVIII | Jan 22, 1984 | Tampa (Fla.) Stadium | Los Angeles 38, Washington 9 |
| XIX | Jan 20, 1985 | Stanford Stadium | San Francisco 38, Miami 16 |
| XX | Jan 26, 1986 | Superdome (New Orleans) | Chicago 46, New England 10 |
| XXI | Jan 25, 1987 | Rose Bowl (Pasadena) | New York Giants 39, Denver 20 |
| XXII | Jan 31, 1988 | Jack Murphy Stadium (San Diego) | Washington 42, Denver 10 |
| XXIII | Jan 22, 1989 | Joe Robbie Stadium (Miami) | San Francisco 20, Cincinnati 16 |
| XXIV | Jan 28, 1990 | Superdome (New Orleans) | San Francisco 55, Denver 10 |
| XXV | Jan 27, 1991 | Tampa Stadium | New York Giants 20, Buffalo 19 |
| XXVI | Jan 26, 1992 | Metrodome (Minneapolis) | Washington 37, Buffalo 24 |
| XXVII | Jan 31, 1993 | Rose Bowl (Pasadena) | Dallas 52, Buffalo 17 |
| XXVIII | Jan 30, 1994 | Georgia Dome (Atlanta) | Dallas 30, Buffalo 13 |
| XXIX | Jan 29, 1995 | Joe Robbie Stadium (Miami) | San Francisco 49, San Diego 26 |
| XXX | Jan 28, 1996 | Sun Devil Stadium (Tempe) | Dallas 27, Pittsburgh 17 |
| XXXI | Jan 26, 1997 | Superdome (New Orleans) | Green Bay 35, New England 21 |
| XXXII | Jan 25, 1998 | Qualcomm Stadium (San Diego) | Denver 31, Green Bay 24 |
| XXXIII | Jan 31, 1999 | Pro Player Stadium (Miami) | Denver 34, Atlanta 19 |
| XXXIV | Jan 30, 2000 | Georgia Dome (Atlanta) | St. Louis 23, Tennessee 16 |
| XXXV | Jan 28, 2001 | Raymond James Stadium (Tampa) | Baltimore 34, New York Giants 7 |
| XXXVI | Feb 3, 2002 | Superdome (New Orleans) | New England 20, St. Louis 17 |
| XXXVII | Jan 26, 2003 | Qualcomm Stadium (San Diego) | Tampa Bay 48, Oakland 21 |
| XXXVIII | Feb 1, 2004 | Reliant Stadium (Houston) | New England 32, Carolina 29 |
| XXXIX | Feb 6, 2005 | Alltel Stadium (Jacksonville) | New England 24, Philadelphia 21 |
| XL | Feb 5, 2006 | Ford Field (Detroit) | Pittsburgh 21, Seattle 10 |
| XLI | Feb 4, 2007 | Dolphin Stadium (Miami) | Indianapolis 29, Chicago 17 |
| XLII | Feb 3, 2008 | U of Phoenix Stadium (Glendale) | New York Giants 17, New England 14 |
| XLIII | Feb 1, 2009 | Raymond James Stadium (Tampa) | Pittsburgh Steelers 27, Arizona Cardinals 23 |
| XLIV | Feb 7, 2010 | Sun Life Stadium (Miami) | New Orleans Saints 31, Indianapolis Colts 17 |
| XLV | Feb 6, 2011 | Cowboys Stadium (Arlington) | Green Bay Packers 31, Pittsburgh Steelers 25 |
| XLVI | Feb 5, 2012 | Lucas Oil Stadium (Indianapolis) | New York Giants 21, New England Patriots 17 |
| XLVII | Feb 3, 2013 | Mercedes-Benz Superdome (New Orleans) | Baltimore Ravens 34, San Francisco 49ers 31 |
| XLVIII | Feb 2, 2014 | MetLife Stadium (E.Rutherford) | Seattle Seahawks 43, Denver Broncos 8 |
| XLIX | Feb 1, 2015 | U of Phoenix Stadium (Glendale) | New England Patriots 28, Seattle Seahawks 24 |
| L | Feb 7, 2016 | Levi's Stadium (Santa Clara) | Denver Broncos 24, Carolina Panthers 10 |
| LI | Feb 5, 2017 | NRG Stadium (Houston) | New England Patriots 34, Atlanta Falcons 28 |
| LII | Feb 4, 2018 | US Bank Stadium (Minneapolis) | Philadelphia Eagles 41, New England Patriots 33 |

## Table 2.14: Where are future Super Bowls to be held?

| # | Date | City | Cost | Year Opened |
|---|------|------|------|-------------|
| LII | 2018 | Minneapolis | $1.1 billion | 2016 |
| LIII | 2019 | Atlanta | $1.6 billion | 2017 |
| LIV | 2020 | Miami | $500 million reno | 2018 |
| LV | 2021 | Tampa | | |
| LVI | 2022 | Los Angeles | $2.6 billion | 2021 |

Given Minnesota's very cold climate, the roof of the US Bank Stadium in Minneapolis has a special lightweight but durable plastic (ETFE: ethylene tetra fluoroethylene). It is so transparent it lets in a large amount of natural light so one needs sunglasses. During warm weather, large glass doors open the stadium.

The Mercedes-Benz Stadium in Atlanta was modeled after Rome's Pantheon, with eight ETFE panels in the shape of falcon wings expand and contract inside the oculus like the aperture of a camera. They have the lowest food and drink prices of any sports venue.

The Hard Rock Stadium in Miami is the renovation of the old Joe Robbe Stadium. The canopy is made with ETFE and steel so that 90% of the seats are in the shade so temperatures are reduced by 20-30 degrees F.

The LA Stadium complex have a 70,000 seat football stadium, a 6000 seat performance center, 1.5 million square feet of office and retail space, 300 hotel rooms and 2500 residences. The 18 acre wave length canopy will be made with EFTE with the sides of the building open. LA now has both the Rams and the Chargers who moved from St Louis and San Diego, respectively.

The stadiums hosting Super Bowls are listed in Table 2.13. Planned future Super Bowl/ venues are shown in Table 2.14.

# Chapter 3

# Team Composition – Are the Best Players on the Best Teams?

## Introduction

In team sports the individual players occupy defined positions in the field of play. If a team has superior players at every position or even most positions then success is likely. There are team dynasties which attest to this fact — the Montreal Canadiens in ice hockey, the New York Yankees in baseball, the Boston Celtics in basketball, and the Green Bay Packers in football were all dominant over a period of time. We are focusing on football and note that the Pittsburgh Steelers, San Francisco 49ers, Dallas Cowboys and New England Patriots have also achieved periods of dominance. It is also true that the players "Hall of Fame" for each of the major North American sports is crowded with players from these legendary teams. At the same time there are teams with modest success which have one or more great players at their designated position. The running back Jim Brown is in many minds the greatest football player ever, but had a single championship. The great Ted Williams never played on a championship baseball team. Wilt Chamberlain won two NBA championships but that did not reflect his dominance in basketball. Even Bobby Orr only won two hockey Stanley Cup championships with the Boston Bruins.

## The greatest teams, coaches and players at various positions

Confounding the team versus individual accomplishment is the impact of coaching and game strategy on team results. We consider the great player-great team connection in football. For individual players we use the rating determined by NFL players and/or expert rankers. The Team rating is defined by the win percentage in games. We analyze the 2017 NFL season, with the player ratings before the season began and the win percentage at the end of the season. Many events during the course of the season are critical to success. The loss of a key player (Aaron Rogers), the unanticipated emergence of a star (Carson Wentz) do not factor into preseason ratings, but have a major impact on team success.

The role of the coach in NFL football: The owners control the money for the NFL teams but the major decisions are usually made by the coaches and sometimes the general managers. The coaches have the ultimate authority. Helping them they have various assistants including defensive and offensive coordinators, special team and quarterback coaches. In some cases the coach is extremely dominant. A leading example is New England where Belichick exercises tight control over his team. At times he has traded or gotten rid of players even some with excellent performance once they become expensive or do not follow his rules. This formula has been very successful in team building and has led to many Super Bowl appearances and victories. Other coaches in the list that follows have different styles, and sometimes the general manager (who can be the coach as well) or the owners are the dominant decision maker. Some owners such as those of the Pittsburgh Steelers, have had very few coaches over time. Other teams have many coaching changes with quite a few being fired when performance is not good. In chapter 18 we discuss some of the changes for the 2018-9 season.

## Number of Top 400 players by Team in 2017 by Sports Illustrated

Sports Illustrated publishes a ranking of the top 400 NFL players at the start of each season, compiled by Andy Benoit. The ranking is based on player comparisons using films of games from the previous season. The stated criterion is "Does player A do his job better than player B?" There are algorithms for generating a ranking of players from pairwise comparisons (Negahban and Shah, 2012). The SI rankings are subjective rather than algorithmic based.

An interesting question is who is the greatest player which can be extended to who is the greatest person. In sports this is often measured in MVP outcomes. But there are many other measures. For example, Tom Brady's recent fifth Super Bowl win makes him the winningest Super Bowl quarterback in NFL history. All measures have advantages and limitations.

## Some of the greatest coaches

Don Shula (1963-1995)          Vince Lombardi (1959-1969)
Bill Walsh (1979-1988)         Bill Belichick (1994-current)
Paul Brown (1946-1975)         Chuck Noll (1969-1991)
George Halas (1920-1967)       Tom Landry (1960-1988)
Joe Gibbs (1981-1992; 2004-2007)   Bill Parcells (1983-2006)
John Madden (1969-1978)        Curly Lambeau (1921-1953)
Marv Levy (1978-1997)          Bud Grant (1967-1985)
Tony Dungy (1996-2008)         George Allen (1966-1977)

Jeff Fisher    George Seifert    Jason Garrett    Al Davis      Gary Kubiak    Marvin Lewis
                                                 1929-2011

Ron Rivera    Jack Del Rio    Tom Flores    Bruce Arians    Brian Billick    Bill O'Brien

Mike Zimmer    Dennis Green    Jim Caldwell
               1949-2016

## The 100 greatest current players

These are Andy Benoit's rankings published in *Sports Illustrated* in September 2017. Such rankings, even when using models and statistical performance measures are judgement calls. Benoit provides a rationale for his rankings, but in the end, the ranking is his judgement. In the main the rankings make sense and the top players ranked are surely the top players. Benoit ranks them by teams, listing each player and position in the top 400. Here we have arranged them in terms of the top 20 and then 21-100. The entire 101 to 400 are listed in Tables 3.17-3.19 at the end of the chapter.

1. Tom Brady (NE, QB)
2. JJ Watt (HOU, DE)
3. Von Miller (DEN, OLB)
4. Luke Kubchly (CAR, LB)
5. Le'Veon Bell (PIT, R)
6. Aaron Rodgers (GB, QB)
7. Rob Gronkowski (NE, TE)
8. Khalil Mack (OAK, DE)
9. Julio Jones (ATL, WR)
10. Antonio Brown (PIT, WR)
21. Travis Kelce (KC, TE)
22. Chris Harris (DEN, CB)
23. Odell Beckham Jr (NYG, WR)
24. Zack Martin (DAL, RG)
25. Trent Williams (WAS, T)

11. Tyron Smith (DAL, T)
12. Earl Thomas (SEA, FS)
13. Aaron Donald (LAR, DT)
14. Patrick Peterson (ARI, CB)
15. David Johnson (ARI, RB)
16. Ben Roethlisberger (PIT, QB)
17. Michael Bennett (SEA, DE)
18. Travis Frederick (DAL, C)
19. Bobby Wagner (SEA, LB)
20. Joey Bosa (LAC, OLB)
61. Ryan Shazier (PIT, LB)
62. Maurice Poucey (PIT, C)
63. David Bakhtiari (GB, T)
64. Whitney Mercilus (HOU, OLB)
65. Thomas Davis (CAR, LB)

26 Fletcher Cox (PHI, DT)
27 Eric Berry (KC, SS)
28 Matt Ryan (ATL, QB)
29 Sean Lee (DAL, LB)
30 Andrew Luck (IND, QB)
31 KJ Wright (SEA, LB)
32. Alex Mack (ATL, C)
33. AJ Green (CIN, WR)
34. Jordan Reed (WAS, TE)
35. Calais Campbell (JAK, DE)
36. Devin McCorty (NE, IS)
37. Drew Brees (NO, QB)
38. Joe Thomas (CLE, T)
39. Justin Houston (KC, OLB)
40. Harrison Smith (MIN, SS)
41. Jurrell Casey (TEN, DE)
42. Greg Olsen (CAR, TE)
43. Cam Chancellor (SEA, SS)
44. Desmond Trufant (ATL, CB)
45. Tyrann Mathieu (ARI, FS)
46. Cliff Avriel (SEA, DE)
47. Brandon Williams (BAL, NT)
48. Jadeveon Davarus Clowney (HOU, DE)
49. Gerald McCoy (TAM, DT)
50. David Decastro (PIT, G)
51. Ndamukong Sun (MIA, DT0
52. Lesean McCoy (BUF, RB)
53. Markus Peters (KC, CB)
54. Telvin Smith (JAK, LB)
55. Geno Atkins (CIN, DT)
56. Ezekiel Elliot (DAL, RB)
57. Olivier Vernon (NYG, DE)
58. Mike Daniels (GB, DE)
59. Kyle Long (CHI, G)
60. AJ Bouye (JAK, CB)

66. Kelechi Osmele (OAK, G)
67. Jason Verrett (LAC, CB)
68. Robert Quinn (LAR, DE)
69. Marshal Yanda (BAL, RG)
70. Mike Evans (TAM, WR)
71. Ryan Kalil (CAR, C)
72. Jimmy Graham (SEA, TE)
73. Byron Jones (DAL, FS)
74. Leonard Williams (NYJ, DE)
75. Dez Bryant (DAL, WR)
76. Aqib Talib (DEN, CB0
77. Kawaan Short (CAR, OT)
78. TJ Ward (DEN, SS)
79. Jason Witten (DAL, TE)
80. Mike Pouncey (MIA, C)
81. Josh Norman (WAS, CB)
82. Andrew Whitworth (LAR, LT)
83. Mitchel Schwartz (KC, T)
84. Lane Johnson (PHI, T)
85. Terrell Suggs (BAL, OLB)
86. Donta Hightower (NE, LB)
87. Xavier Rhodes (MIN, CB)
88. Philip Rivers (LAC, QB)
89. Alshon Jeffery (PHIL, WR)
90. Jandris Jenkins (NYG, CB)
91. Devin Coleman (ATL, RB)
92. Devonta Freeman (ATL, RB)
93. Muhammad Wilderson (NYJ, DE
94. Damon Harrison (NYG, DT)
95. Melvin Ingram (LAC, OLB)
96. Linval Joseph (MIN, DT)
97. Jordy Nelson (GB, WR)
98. Brandon Graham (PHI, DE)
99. Ziggy Ansah (DET, DE)
100. Vontae Davis (IND, CB)

Notable terrific players ranked above 100 include:
108 Larry Fitzgerald (ARI, WR)
130 Richard Sherman (SEA, CB)
132 DeSean Jackson (TAM, WR)
139 Russell Wilson (SEA, QB)
155 Carson Palmer (ARI, QB)
162 Cam Newton (CAR, QB)
164 Jameis Winston (TAM,QB)
169 Adrian Peterson ( NO, HB)

Table 3.1: Top 400 NFL players by Team

| Team | G1 | G2 | G3 | G4 | G5 | G6 | G7 | G8 |
|---|---|---|---|---|---|---|---|---|
| Arizona Cardinals | 3 | 0 | 2 | 1 | 2 | 0 | 2 | 1 |
| Atlanta Falcons | 4 | 2 | 3 | 2 | 2 | 2 | 0 | 1 |
| Baltimore Ravens | 1 | 2 | 4 | 0 | 0 | 2 | 2 | 1 |
| Buffalo Bills | 0 | 1 | 0 | 3 | 1 | 2 | 4 | 0 |
| Carolina Panthers | 2 | 3 | 0 | 1 | 1 | 4 | 3 | 2 |
| Chicago Bears | 0 | 1 | 1 | 0 | 4 | 1 | 0 | 1 |
| Cincinnati Bengals | 1 | 1 | 1 | 2 | 1 | 2 | 1 | 2 |
| Cleveland Browns | 1 | 0 | 2 | 1 | 2 | 1 | 1 | 1 |
| Dallas Cowboys | 4 | 4 | 0 | 0 | 3 | 0 | 1 | 2 |
| Denver Broncos | 2 | 2 | 2 | 2 | 0 | 2 | 2 | 3 |
| Detroit Lions | 0 | 1 | 2 | 3 | 1 | 4 | 3 | 2 |
| Green Bay Packers | 1 | 3 | 2 | 3 | 2 | 1 | 0 | 0 |
| Houston Texans | 2 | 1 | 0 | 2 | 0 | 1 | 3 | 2 |
| Indianapolis Colts | 1 | 1 | 1 | 0 | 1 | 1 | 1 | 4 |
| Jacksonville Jaguars | 1 | 2 | 0 | 3 | 1 | 1 | 0 | 0 |
| Kansas City Chiefs | 3 | 2 | 0 | 4 | 2 | 3 | 2 | 3 |
| Los Angeles Chargers | 1 | 3 | 1 | 2 | 1 | 0 | 2 | 1 |
| Los Angeles Rams | 1 | 2 | 3 | 0 | 1 | 0 | 1 | 1 |
| Miami Dolphins | 0 | 2 | 2 | 3 | 1 | 1 | 3 | 0 |
| Minnesota Vikings | 1 | 2 | 1 | 3 | 2 | 1 | 0 | 1 |
| New England Patriots | 3 | 1 | 5 | 1 | 1 | 3 | 5 | 1 |
| New Orleans Saints | 1 | 0 | 1 | 2 | 3 | 2 | 1 | 2 |
| New York Giants | 1 | 3 | 3 | 3 | 1 | 0 | 1 | 1 |
| New York Jets | 0 | 2 | 1 | 0 | 0 | 0 | 1 | 1 |
| Oakland Raiders | 1 | 1 | 4 | 1 | 3 | 2 | 0 | 1 |
| Philadelphia Eagles | 1 | 3 | 2 | 0 | 2 | 1 | 1 | 4 |
| Pittsburgh Steelers | 4 | 2 | 2 | 2 | 2 | 0 | 2 | 0 |
| San Francisco 49ers | 0 | 0 | 0 | 0 | 2 | 4 | 1 | 4 |
| Seattle Seahawks | 6 | 1 | 2 | 2 | 0 | 0 | 0 | 1 |
| Tampa Bay Buccaneers | 1 | 1 | 1 | 2 | 5 | 3 | 3 | 0 |
| Tennessee Titans | 1 | 0 | 0 | 1 | 2 | 3 | 3 | 4 |
| Washington Redskins | 2 | 1 | 2 | 1 | 1 | 2 | 0 | 0 |

Table 3.2: SI Count and Win % — 2017

| Team | Win PCT | Number |
|---|---|---|
| Arizona | 0.5000 | 11 |
| Atlanta | 0.6250 | 16 |
| Baltimore | 0.5620 | 12 |
| Buffalo | 0.5620 | 11 |
| Carolina | 0.6880 | 16 |
| Chicago | 0.3120 | 8 |
| Cincinnati | 0.4380 | 11 |
| Cleveland | 0.0322 | 9 |
| Dallas | 0.5620 | 14 |
| Denver | 0.3120 | 15 |
| Detroit | 0.5620 | 16 |
| Green Bay | 0.4380 | 12 |
| Houston | 0.2500 | 11 |
| Indianapolis | 0.2500 | 10 |
| Jacksonville | 0.6250 | 8 |
| Kansas City | 0.6250 | 19 |
| LA Chargers | 0.5620 | 11 |
| LA Rams | 0.6880 | 9 |
| Miami | 0.3750 | 12 |
| Minnesota | 0.8120 | 11 |
| New England | 0.8120 | 20 |
| New Orleans | 0.6880 | 12 |
| NY Giants | 0.1880 | 13 |
| NY Jets | 0.3120 | 5 |
| Oakland | 0.3750 | 13 |
| Philadelphia | 0.8120 | 14 |
| Pittsburgh | 0.8120 | 14 |
| San Francisco | 0.3750 | 11 |
| Seattle | 0.5620 | 12 |
| Tampa Bay | 0.3120 | 16 |
| Tennessee | 0.5620 | 14 |
| Washington | 0.4380 | 9 |

We consider the distribution of the "Top 400" players by team. There are 53 active players on a team roster, so we split the ranks into groups of 50. Under complete parity each team would expect to have a player in each rank group. The top players are well distributed across teams, but some teams are "stacked". Seattle has 6 top 50 players and Atlanta, Dallas and Pittsburgh have 4. The distribution of top players at the beginning of the 2017 season is in Table 3.1. The notation for rank group is as follows: G1: 1-50; G2:51-100; G3:101-150; G4:151-200; G5:201-250; G6:251-300; G7:301-350; G8:351-400.

A preliminary look at the team composition and team success is in Table 3.2. There is support for an association between team success and the number of top 400 players. The teams with the most top players generally have high win percentages, and teams with fewer top players have low win percentages. However, the correlation is only 0.392, so top players only explain 15% of the variation in the win percentage.

Jacksonville has only eight top players. Their strong showing in 2017 seems to be the result of a number of great players. New England has 20 and Kansas City has 19. They have the most top 400 players. Carolina, Detroit and Tampa Bay have 16 each. Pittsburgh has 14. Even the worst NFL team, Cleveland (0-16), has nine top players.

## NFL Top 100

There are other rankings of NFL players. The NFL Top 100 lists the top one hundred players as chosen by fellow NFL players. The rankings are based on an off-season poll organized by the NFL, where players vote on their fellow players based on their projected performance for the next NFL season. Only players that will be active in the next season are eligible for consideration. A strong case can be made that the best rating of players comes from other players. The tradition of experts and sports reporters ranking teams and players still rules the day. For comparison the top 100 from Sports Illustrated and the NFL are shown in Table 3.3.

The top 100 from the NFL ranking is split into deciles and the number of players in each decile by team is in Table 3.4. Teams with higher numbers are highlighted.

The connection of top 100 players to team winning percentage is in Table 3.5. The correlation is 0.292, reduced from the top 400 result as would be expected with fewer players per team. Again, the teams with more top 100 players have high win percentages and the teams with fewer top 100 players have low win percentages.

Table 3.3: Top 100 NFL Players in 2017 by Sports Illustrated and NFL Players

| | SI | | | | NFL | | |
|---|---|---|---|---|---|---|---|
| RANK | PLAYER | RANK | PLAYER | RANK | PLAYER | RANK | PLAYER |
| 1 | Tom Brady | 51 | Ndamukong Suh | 1 | Tom Brady | 51 | Andrew Luck |
| 2 | J.J. Watt | 52 | LeSean McCoy | 2 | Von Miller | 52 | Gerald McCoy |
| 3 | Von Miller | 53 | Marcus Peters | 3 | Julio Jones | 53 | Amari Cooper |
| 4 | Luke Kuechly | 54 | Telvin Smith | 4 | Antonio Brown | 54 | Janoris Jenkins |
| 5 | Le'Veon Bell | 55 | Geno Atkins | 5 | Khalil Mack | 55 | Ndamukong Suh |
| 6 | Aaron Rodgers | 56 | Ezekiel Elliott | 6 | Aaron Rodgers | 56 | Cliff Avril |
| 7 | Rob Gronkowski | 57 | Olivier Vernon | 7 | Ezekiel Elliott | 57 | Jameis Winston |
| 8 | Khalil Mack | 58 | Mike Daniels | 8 | Odell Beckham Jr. | 58 | Zack Martin |
| 9 | Julio Jones | 59 | Kyle Long | 9 | Le'Veon Bell | 59 | Josh Norman |
| 10 | Antonio Brown | 60 | A.J. Bouye | 10 | Matt Ryan | 60 | Dez Bryant |
| 11 | Tyron Smith | 61 | Ryan Shazier | 11 | Derek Carr | 61 | T.Y. Hilton |
| 12 | Earl Thomas | 62 | Maurkice Pouncey | 12 | David Johnson | 62 | Cameron Wake |
| 13 | Aaron Donald | 63 | David Bakhtiari | 13 | Eric Berry | 63 | Chris Harris Jr. |
| 14 | Patrick Peterson | 64 | Whitney Mercilus | 14 | Dak Prescott | 64 | Casey Hayward |
| 15 | David Johnson | 65 | Thomas Davis | 15 | Aaron Donald | 65 | Jordan Reed |
| 16 | Ben Roethlisberger | 66 | Kelechi Osemele | 16 | Drew Brees | 66 | Xavier Rhodes |
| 17 | Michael Bennett | 67 | Jason Verrett | 17 | A.J. Green | 67 | Greg Olsen |
| 18 | Travis Frederick | 68 | Robert Quinn | 18 | Tyron Smith | 68 | Geno Atkins |
| 19 | Bobby Wagner | 69 | Marshal Yanda | 19 | Patrick Peterson | 69 | Jay Ajayi |
| 20 | Joey Bosa | 70 | Mike Evans | 20 | Luke Kuechly | 70 | Kirk Cousins |
| 21 | Travis Kelce | 71 | Ryan Kalil | 21 | Richard Sherman | 71 | Julian Edelman |
| 22 | Chris Harris | 72 | Jimmy Graham | 22 | Ben Roethlisberger | 72 | Taylor Lewan |
| 23 | Odell Beckham Jr. | 73 | Byron Jones | 23 | Rob Gronkowski | 73 | Phillip Rivers |
| 24 | Zack Martin | 74 | Leonard Williams | 24 | Russell Wilson | 74 | Harrison Smith |
| 25 | Trent Williams | 75 | Dez Bryant | 25 | Joe Thomas | 75 | Delanie Walker |
| 26 | Fletcher Cox | 76 | Aqib Talib | 26 | Travis Kelce | 76 | Justin Houston |
| 27 | Eric Berry | 77 | Kawann Short | 27 | LeSean McCoy | 77 | Ha Ha Clinton-Dix |
| 28 | Matt Ryan | 78 | T.J. Ward | 28 | Landon Collins | 78 | Brian Orakpo |
| 29 | Sean Lee | 79 | Jason Witten | 29 | Mike Evans | 79 | Sean Lee |
| 30 | Andrew Luck | 80 | Mike Pouncey | 30 | Earl Thomas | 80 | LeGarrette Blount |
| 31 | K.J. Wright | 81 | Josh Norman | 31 | Matthew Stafford | 81 | Alex Smith |
| 32 | Alex Mack | 82 | Andrew Whitworth | 32 | Marcus Peters | 82 | Clay Matthews |
| 33 | A.J. Green | 83 | Mitchell Schwartz | 33 | DeMarco Murray | 83 | Calais Campbell |
| 34 | Jordan Reed | 84 | Lane Johnson | 34 | Kam Chancellor | 84 | Mike Daniels |
| 35 | Calais Campbell | 85 | Terrell Suggs | 35 | J.J. Watt | 85 | Chandler Jones |
| 36 | Devin McCourty | 86 | Dont'a Hightower | 36 | Tyreek Hill | 86 | Jurrell Casey |
| 37 | Drew Brees | 87 | Xavier Rhodes | 37 | Aqib Talib | 87 | Travis Frederick |
| 38 | Joe Thomas | 88 | Philip Rivers | 38 | Fletcher Cox | 88 | Doug Baldwin |
| 39 | Justin Houston | 89 | Aishon Jeffery | 39 | Bobby Wagner | 89 | Thomas Davis |
| 40 | Harrison Smith | 90 | Janoris Jenkins | 40 | Vic Beasley | 90 | Malcolm Jenkins |
| 41 | Jurrell Casey | 91 | Tevin Coleman | 41 | Devonta Freeman | 91 | Lorenzo Alexander |
| 42 | Greg Olsen | 92 | Devonta Freeman | 42 | Jarvis Landry | 92 | Everson Griffen |
| 43 | Kam Chancellor | 93 | Muhammad Wilkerson | 43 | Marshal Yanda | 93 | Brandon Graham |
| 44 | Desmond Trufant | 94 | Damon Harrison | 44 | Cam Newton | 94 | Dont'a Hightower |
| 45 | Tyrann Mathieu | 95 | Melvin Ingram | 45 | Larry Fitzgerald | 95 | Kelechi Osemele |
| 46 | Cliff Avril | 96 | Linval Joseph | 46 | Michael Bennett | 96 | Damon Harrison |
| 47 | Brandon Williams | 97 | Jordy Nelson | 47 | Trent Williams | 97 | David DeCastro |
| 48 | Jadeveon Clowney | 98 | Brandon Graham | 48 | Jordy Nelson | 98 | Adrian Peterson |
| 49 | Gerald McCoy | 99 | Ziggy Ansah | 49 | Jadeveon Clowney | 99 | Malcolm Butler |
| 50 | David DeCastro | 100 | Vontae Davis | 50 | Marcus Mariota | 100 | Joey Bosa |

Table 3.4: NFL Top 100 by Team and Decile

| Team | D1 | D2 | D3 | D4 | D5 | D6 | GD7 | D8 | D9 | D10 | All |
|------|----|----|----|----|----|----|-----|----|----|-----|-----|
| Arizona | 0 | 2 | 0 | 0 | 1 | 0 | 0 | 0 | 1 | 0 | 4 |
| Atlanta | 2 | 0 | 0 | 1 | 1 | 0 | 0 | 0 | 0 | 0 | 4 |
| Baltimore | 0 | 0 | 0 | 0 | 1 | 0 | 0 | 0 | 0 | 0 | 1 |
| Buffalo | 0 | 0 | 1 | 0 | 0 | 0 | 0 | 0 | 0 | 1 | 2 |
| Carolina | 0 | 1 | 0 | 0 | 1 | 0 | 1 | 0 | 1 | 0 | 4 |
| Chicago | 0 | 0 | 0 | 0 | 0 | 0 | 0 | 0 | 0 | 0 | 0 |
| Cincinnati | 0 | 1 | 0 | 0 | 0 | 0 | 1 | 0 | 0 | 0 | 2 |
| Cleveland | 0 | 0 | 1 | 0 | 0 | 0 | 0 | 0 | 0 | 0 | 1 |
| **Dallas** | **1** | **2** | **0** | **0** | **0** | **2** | **0** | **1** | **1** | **0** | **7** |
| Denver | 1 | 0 | 0 | 1 | 0 | 0 | 1 | 0 | 0 | 0 | 3 |
| Detroit | 0 | 0 | 0 | 1 | 0 | 0 | 0 | 0 | 0 | 0 | 1 |
| Green Bay | 1 | 0 | 0 | 0 | 1 | 0 | 0 | 1 | 2 | 0 | 5 |
| Houston | 0 | 0 | 0 | 1 | 1 | 0 | 0 | 0 | 0 | 0 | 2 |
| Indianapolis | 0 | 0 | 0 | 0 | 0 | 1 | 1 | 0 | 0 | 0 | 2 |
| Jacksonville | 0 | 0 | 0 | 0 | 0 | 0 | 0 | 0 | 1 | 0 | 1 |
| **Kansas City** | **0** | **1** | **1** | **2** | **0** | **0** | **0** | **1** | **1** | **0** | **6** |
| LA Chargers | 0 | 0 | 0 | 0 | 0 | 0 | 1 | 1 | 0 | 1 | 3 |
| LA Rams | 0 | 1 | 0 | 0 | 0 | 0 | 0 | 0 | 0 | 0 | 1 |
| Miami | 0 | 0 | 0 | 0 | 1 | 1 | 2 | 0 | 0 | 0 | 4 |
| Minnesota | 0 | 0 | 0 | 0 | 0 | 0 | 1 | 1 | 0 | 1 | 3 |
| **New England** | **1** | **0** | **1** | **0** | **0** | **0** | **0** | **2** | **0** | **2** | **6** |
| New Orleans | 0 | 1 | 0 | 0 | 0 | 0 | 0 | 0 | 0 | 1 | 2 |
| NY Giants | 1 | 0 | 1 | 0 | 0 | 1 | 0 | 0 | 0 | 1 | 4 |
| NY Jets | 0 | 0 | 0 | 0 | 0 | 0 | 0 | 0 | 0 | 0 | 0 |
| Oakland | 1 | 1 | 0 | 0 | 0 | 1 | 0 | 0 | 0 | 1 | 4 |
| Philadelphia | 0 | 0 | 0 | 1 | 0 | 0 | 0 | 0 | 1 | 1 | 3 |
| Pittsburgh | 2 | 0 | 1 | 0 | 0 | 0 | 0 | 0 | 0 | 1 | 4 |
| San Francisco | 0 | 0 | 0 | 0 | 0 | 0 | 0 | 0 | 0 | 0 | 0 |
| **Seattle** | **0** | **0** | **3** | **2** | **1** | **1** | **0** | **0** | **1** | **0** | **8** |
| Tampa Bay | 0 | 0 | 1 | 0 | 0 | 2 | 0 | 0 | 0 | 0 | 3 |
| **Tennessee** | **0** | **0** | **0** | **1** | **1** | **0** | **0** | **3** | **1** | **0** | **6** |
| Washington | 0 | 0 | 0 | 0 | 1 | 1 | 2 | 0 | 0 | 0 | 4 |

Table 3.5: Number of Top 100 NFL Players and Win %

| Team | Win PCT | Number |
|---|---|---|
| Arizona | 0.5000 | 4 |
| Atlanta | 0.6250 | 4 |
| Baltimore | 0.5620 | 1 |
| Buffalo | 0.5620 | 2 |
| Carolina | 0.6880 | 4 |
| Chicago | 0.3120 | 0 |
| Cincinnati | 0.4380 | 2 |
| Cleveland | 0.0322 | 1 |
| Dallas | 0.5620 | 7 |
| Denver | 0.3120 | 3 |
| Detroit | 0.5620 | 1 |
| Green Bay | 0.4380 | 5 |
| Houston | 0.2500 | 2 |
| Indianapolis | 0.2500 | 2 |
| Jacksonville | 0.6250 | 1 |
| Kansas City | 0.6250 | 6 |
| LA Chargers | 0.5620 | 3 |
| LA Rams | 0.6880 | 1 |
| Miami | 0.3750 | 4 |
| Minnesota | 0.8120 | 3 |
| New England | 0.8120 | 6 |
| New Orleans | 0.6880 | 2 |
| NY Giants | 0.1880 | 4 |
| NY Jets | 0.3120 | 4 |
| Oakland | 0.3750 | 0 |
| Philadelphia | 0.8120 | 3 |
| Pittsburgh | 0.8120 | 4 |
| San Francisco | 0.3750 | 0 |
| Seattle | 0.5620 | 8 |
| Tampa Bay | 0.3120 | 3 |
| Tennessee | 0.5620 | 6 |
| Washington | 0.4380 | 4 |

## Comparison of Sports Illustrated and NFL Rankings

How does the top 100 from Sports Illustrated compare to that provided by the NFL players? The players on both lists are shown in Table 3.6 About two-thirds of the top 100 are on both lists. However, the rankings are quite mixed. The correlation between ranks is only 0.456, so there is much disagreement. Some notable examples of very different rankings are Russell Wilson in Seattle and J. J. Watt in Houston.

Table 3.6: Comparison of Rankings

| SI RANK | SI PLAYER | NFL RANK | NFL PLAYER_1 | SI RANK | SI PLAYER | NFL RANK | NFL PLAYER |
|---|---|---|---|---|---|---|---|
| 13 | Aaron Donald | 15 | Aaron Donald | 9 | Julio Jones | 3 | Julio Jones |
| 6 | Aaron Rodgers | 6 | Aaron Rodgers | 41 | Jurrell Casey | 86 | Jurrell Casey |
| 30 | Andrew Luck | 51 | Andrew Luck | 39 | Justin Houston | 76 | Justin Houston |
| 10 | Antonio Brown | 4 | Antonio Brown | 43 | Kam Chancellor | 34 | Kam Chancellor |
| 76 | Aqib Talib | 37 | Aqib Talib | 66 | Kelechi Osemele | 95 | Kelechi Osemele |
| 16 | Ben Roethlisberger | 22 | Ben Roethlisberger | 8 | Khalil Mack | 5 | Khalil Mack |
| 19 | Bobby Wagner | 38 | Bobby Wagner | 5 | Le'Veon Bell | 70 | Kirk Cousins |
| 98 | Brandon Graham | 93 | Brandon Graham | 74 | Leonard Williams | 9 | Le'Veon Bell |
| 35 | Calais Campbell | 88 | Calais Campbell | 52 | LeSean McCoy | 27 | LeSean McCoy |
| 22 | Chris Harris | 63 | Chris Harris Jr. | 4 | Luke Kuechly | 20 | Luke Kuechly |
| 46 | Cliff Avril | 56 | Cliff Avril | 53 | Marcus Peters | 32 | Marcus Peters |
| 94 | Damon Harrison | 96 | Damon Harrison | 69 | Marshal Yanda | 43 | Marshal Yanda |
| 15 | David Johnson | 12 | David Johnson | 28 | Matt Ryan | 10 | Matt Ryan |
| 92 | Devonta Freeman | 41 | Devonta Freeman | 17 | Michael Bennett | 46 | Michael Bennett |
| 75 | Dez Bryant | 60 | Dez Bryant | 58 | Mike Daniels | 84 | Mike Daniels |
| 86 | Dont'a Hightower | 94 | Dont'a Hightower | 70 | Mike Evans | 29 | Mike Evans |
| 37 | Drew Brees | 16 | Drew Brees | 51 | Ndamukong Suh | 55 | Ndamukong Suh |
| 12 | Earl Thomas | 30 | Earl Thomas | 23 | Odell Beckham Jr. | 8 | Odell Beckham Jr. |
| 27 | Eric Berry | 13 | Eric Berry | 14 | Patrick Peterson | 19 | Patrick Peterson |
| 56 | Ezekiel Elliott | 7 | Ezekiel Elliott | 88 | Philip Rivers | 73 | Philip Rivers |
| 26 | Fletcher Cox | 38 | Fletcher Cox | 7 | Rob Gronkowski | 23 | Rob Gronkowski |
| 55 | Geno Atkins | 68 | Geno Atkins | 68 | Robert Quinn | 24 | Russell Wilson |
| 49 | Gerald McCoy | 52 | Gerald McCoy | 29 | Sean Lee | 79 | Sean Lee |
| 42 | Greg Olsen | 67 | Greg Olsen | 65 | Thomas Davis | 89 | Thomas Davis |
| 40 | Harrison Smith | 74 | Harrison Smith | 1 | Tom Brady | 1 | Tom Brady |
| 48 | Jadeveon Clowney | 48 | Jadeveon Clowney | 18 | Travis Frederick | 87 | Travis Frederick |
| 90 | Janoris Jenkins | 54 | Janoris Jenkins | 21 | Travis Kelce | 26 | Travis Kelce |
| 38 | Joe Thomas | 25 | Joe Thomas | 25 | Trent Williams | 47 | Trent Williams |
| 20 | Joey Bosa | 100 | Joey Bosa | 11 | Tyron Smith | 18 | Tyron Smith |
| 34 | Jordan Reed | 65 | Jordan Reed | 3 | Von Miller | 2 | Von Miller |
| 97 | Jordy Nelson | 48 | Jordy Nelson | 87 | Xavier Rhodes | 66 | Xavier Rhodes |
| 81 | Josh Norman | 59 | Josh Norman | 24 | Zack Martin | 58 | Zack Martin |

## Modeling the Dependence of Team Win percentage on Top Players

We would expect that having elite players would translate into better team performance. However, the correlations between team win percentage and number of top players is rather low. Of course the player rankings are from performance in prior seasons, not 2017. So this is an attempt to anticipate performance based on team composition at the start of the 2017 season. Team composition is much more complex than a simple count of top players, but we explore the relationship.

## Number of Top Players from Sports Illustrated

If we consider the number of top players, without taking into account player position, the relationship between team win percentage and team top players can be analyzed. Consider the breakdown of SI's top 400. Let

$T_1$ = number of top 50 players at the start of 2017

$T_2$ = number of top 100 players at the start of 2017

$T_3$ = number of top 150 players at the start of 2017

$T_4$ = number of top 200 players at the start of 2017

$T_5$ = number of top 250 players at the start of 2017

$T_6$ = number of top 300 players at the start of 2017

$T_7$ = number of top 350 players at the start of 2017

$T_8$ = number of top 400 players at the start of 2017.

So $T_j, j = 1, \ldots, 8$ captures the accumulation of top players in descending rank.

With $P$ = team win percentage in 2017, let

$$Y = \ln\left(\frac{P}{1-P}\right).$$

$Y$ is the logarithm of the odds ratio and is called the logit. The logit linearizes the usual Bradley-Terry model for probability.

The model $Y = \beta_0 + \beta_1 T_j + \varepsilon$ is equivalent to

$$P = \frac{e^{\beta_0 + \beta_1 T_j + \varepsilon}}{1 + e^{\beta_0 + \beta_1 T_j + \varepsilon}}.$$

Then the relationships between win percentage and number of top players are given in Table 3.7.

Table 3.7: Fitted logistic model for win%

| Variable | $R^2$ | $\beta_1$ | $t$ | $P$ |
|----------|-------|-----------|-----|-----|
| $T_1$ | 10.41 | 0.045 | 1.87 | 0.072 |
| $T_2$ | 15.03 | 0.041 | 2.30 | 0.028 |
| $T_3$ | 11.72 | 0.028 | 2.00 | 0.055 |
| $T_4$ | 12.20 | 0.026 | 2.04 | 0.050 |
| $T_5$ | 11.94 | 0.025 | 2.02 | 0.053 |
| $T_6$ | 14.94 | 0.028 | 2.30 | 0.028 |
| $T_7$ | 15.66 | 0.025 | 2.36 | 0.025 |
| $T_8$ | 15.38 | 0.025 | 2.33 | 0.026 |

The effect of top ranked players on performance is significant, but rather small. We previously noted that the top 400 accounted for around 15% of the variation in win% P. $T_8$ confirms that effect. The number of top 100 players ($T_2$) seems to have the most impact. Beyond the top 100 there is not an increase in $R^2$=percent explained. We concentrate on the top 100. It is not surprising that in a team game it is better to have a roster of many good players rather than a small subset of stars. This is similar to stud prices for thoroughbred stallions (Cameron, 2010; Ziemba, 2017). The price is determined by having many good offspring, not by having a few great ones.

## Weighting by Position — Top 100 from NFL Ranking

Football is a team game, but the importance of each position to success is not equal. Obviously the quarterback position is crucial, since the QB is "the player with the ball" most of the time, makes decisions on each down, and is the key factor in successful offense. Figure 3.1 summarizes the salary for top players at each position. We assume that salary is a proxy for the importance of the position to team success.

If the average salary of the top 10 at each position is taken as a player weight, then the weighted value for the top 100 players as determined by the NFL can be calculated. Let

$X_1$= players ranked from 1 to 10 weighted by average position salary

$X_2$= players ranked from 10 to 20 weighted by average position salary

$X_3$= players ranked from 21 to 30 weighted by average position salary

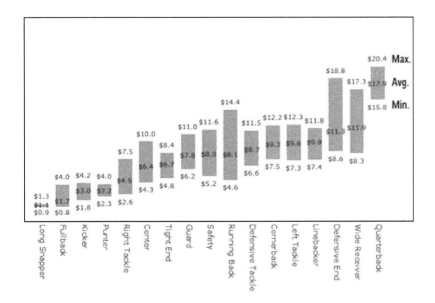

Figure 3.1: Salary of Top 10 Players by position — Source: Spotrac.com

$X_4$ = players ranked from 31 to 40 weighted by average position salary

$X_5$ = players ranked from 41 to 50 weighted by average position salary

$X_6$ = players ranked from 51 to 60 weighted by average position salary

$X_7$ = players ranked from 61 to 70 weighted by average position salary

$X_8$ = players ranked from 71 to 80 weighted by average position salary

$X_9$ = players ranked from 81 to 90 weighted by average position salary

$X_{10}$ = players ranked from 91 to 100 weighted by average position salary.

Table 3.8 shows the weighted score by ranking decile for each team. Some teams with high scores are flagged. It is important to keep in mind that these rankings and scores are before the actual 2017 season started. However, the marked teams were favorites in each division at the start of the season.

Table 3.8: Weighted score for top players by team

| Team | $X_1$ | $X_2$ | $X_3$ | $X_4$ | $X_5$ | $X_6$ | $X_7$ | $X_8$ | $X_9$ | $X_{10}$ |
|---|---|---|---|---|---|---|---|---|---|---|
| Arizona | 0.0 | 17.4 | 0.0 | 0.0 | 11.9 | 0.0 | 0.0 | 0.0 | 9.9 | 0.0 |
| Atlanta | 29.8 | 0.0 | 0.0 | 9.9 | 8.1 | 0.0 | 0.0 | 0.0 | 0.0 | 0.0 |
| Baltimore | 0.0 | 0.0 | 0.0 | 0.0 | 7.8 | 0.0 | 0.0 | 0.0 | 0.0 | 0.0 |
| Buffalo | 0.0 | 0.0 | 8.1 | 0.0 | 0.0 | 0.0 | 0.0 | 0.0 | 0.0 | 9.9 |
| Carolina | 0.0 | 9.9 | 0.0 | 0.0 | 17.9 | 0.0 | 6.7 | 0.0 | 9.9 | 0.0 |
| Chicago | 0.0 | 0.0 | 0.0 | 0.0 | 0.0 | 0.0 | 0.0 | 0.0 | 0.0 | 0.0 |
| Cincinnati | 0.0 | 11.9 | 0.0 | 0.0 | 0.0 | 0.0 | 8.7 | 0.0 | 0.0 | 0.0 |
| Cleveland | 0.0 | 0.0 | 8.7 | 0.0 | 0.0 | 0.0 | 0.0 | 0.0 | 0.0 | 0.0 |
| Dallas | 8.1 | 26.6 | 0.0 | 0.0 | 0.0 | 19.7 | 0.0 | 9.9 | 6.4 | 0.0 |
| Denver | 9.9 | 0.0 | 0.0 | 9.3 | 0.0 | 0.0 | 9.3 | 0.0 | 0.0 | 0.0 |
| Detroit | 0.0 | 0.0 | 0.0 | 17.9 | 0.0 | 0.0 | 0.0 | 0.0 | 0.0 | 0.0 |
| Green Bay | 17.9 | 0.0 | 0.0 | 0.0 | 11.9 | 0.0 | 0.0 | 8.0 | 18.6 | 0.0 |
| Houston | 0.0 | 0.0 | 0.0 | 11.3 | 11.3 | 0.0 | 0.0 | 0.0 | 0.0 | 0.0 |
| Indianapolis | 0.0 | 0.0 | 0.0 | 0.0 | 0.0 | 17.9 | 11.9 | 0.0 | 0.0 | 0.0 |
| Jacksonville | 0.0 | 0.0 | 0.0 | 0.0 | 0.0 | 0.0 | 0.0 | 0.0 | 11.3 | 0.0 |
| Kansas City | 0.0 | 8.0 | 6.7 | 21.2 | 0.0 | 0.0 | 0.0 | 9.9 | 17.9 | 0.0 |
| LA Chargers | 0.0 | 0.0 | 0.0 | 0.0 | 0.0 | 0.0 | 9.3 | 17.9 | 0.0 | 11.3 |
| LA Rams | 0.0 | 8.7 | 0.0 | 0.0 | 0.0 | 0.0 | 0.0 | 0.0 | 0.0 | 0.0 |
| Miami | 0.0 | 0.0 | 0.0 | 0.0 | 11.9 | 8.7 | 19.4 | 0.0 | 0.0 | 0.0 |
| Minnesota | 0.0 | 0.0 | 0.0 | 0.0 | 0.0 | 0.0 | 9.3 | 8.0 | 0.0 | 11.3 |
| New England | 17.9 | 0.0 | 6.7 | 0.0 | 0.0 | 0.0 | 0.0 | 20.0 | 0.0 | 19.2 |
| New Orleans | 0.0 | 17.9 | 0.0 | 0.0 | 0.0 | 0.0 | 0.0 | 0.0 | 0.0 | 8.1 |
| NY Giants | 11.9 | 0.0 | 8.0 | 0.0 | 0.0 | 9.3 | 0.0 | 0.0 | 0.0 | 8.7 |
| NY Jets | 0.0 | 0.0 | 0.0 | 0.0 | 0.0 | 0.0 | 0.0 | 0.0 | 0.0 | 0.0 |
| Oakland | 11.3 | 17.9 | 0.0 | 0.0 | 0.0 | 11.9 | 0.0 | 0.0 | 0.0 | 7.8 |
| Philadelphia | 0.0 | 0.0 | 0.0 | 8.7 | 0.0 | 0.0 | 0.0 | 0.0 | 8.0 | 11.3 |
| Pittsburgh | 20.0 | 0.0 | 17.9 | 0.0 | 0.0 | 0.0 | 0.0 | 0.0 | 0.0 | 7.8 |
| San Francisco | 0.0 | 0.0 | 0.0 | 0.0 | 0.0 | 0.0 | 0.0 | 0.0 | 0.0 | 0.0 |
| Seattle | 0.0 | 0.0 | 35.2 | 17.9 | 11.3 | 11.3 | 0.0 | 0.0 | 11.9 | 0.0 |
| Tampa Bay | 0.0 | 0.0 | 11.9 | 0.0 | 0.0 | 26.6 | 0.0 | 0.0 | 0.0 | 0.0 |
| Tennessee | 0.0 | 0.0 | 0.0 | 8.1 | 17.9 | 0.0 | 0.0 | 25.3 | 8.7 | 0.0 |
| Washington | 0.0 | 0.0 | 0.0 | 0.0 | 8.7 | 9.3 | 24.6 | 0.0 | 0.0 | 0.0 |

# Team Performance: Predicted and Actual

Can the team performance in 2017 be predicted based on the weighted player rankings from Table 3.8? We analyze team performance with the logistic model where

$$Y = ln\left(\frac{P}{1-P}\right) \text{ and } X = X_1, \ldots, X_{10}. \text{ So}$$

$$Y = B'X + \varepsilon,$$

for $P$ = team win percentage. The multiple linear regression of $Y$ on $X$ gives

$$Y = -0.746 + 0.0087X_1 + 0.0301X_2 - 0.0037X_3 + 0.0292X_4 + 0.0173X_5$$

$$-0.0254X_6 + 0.0192X_7 - 0.0026X_8 + 0.0426X_9 + 0.1088X_{10}.$$

The analysis of variation in $Y$ shows that almost 40% is accounted for by the relationship to $X$. So accounting for player position increases the explanatory power of top players. The data has the unusual result that the tenth decile values are the strongest predictors as shown in Table 3.9.

Table 3.9: Logistic Model — ANOVA

| Source | DF | Seq SS | Cont. % | Adj SS | F | P |
|--------|-----|--------|---------|--------|------|-------|
| Regression | 10 | 12.4513 | **39.87** | 12.4513 | 1.39 | 0.250 |
| $X_1$ | 1 | 0.9129 | 2.92 | 0.1245 | 0.14 | 0.713 |
| $X_2$ | 1 | 0.6561 | 2.10 | 1.0848 | 1.21 | 0.283 |
| $X_3$ | 1 | 0.0202 | 0.06 | 0.0134 | 0.01 | 0.904 |
| $X_4$ | 1 | 0.6596 | 2.11 | 0.7128 | 0.80 | 0.382 |
| $X_5$ | 1 | 0.0248 | 0.08 | 0.1979 | 0.22 | 0.643 |
| $X_6$ | 1 | 2.5340 | 8.11 | 0.6410 | 0.72 | 0.407 |
| $X_7$ | 1 | 0.3532 | 1.13 | 0.3025 | 0.34 | 0.567 |
| $X_8$ | 1 | 2.0209 | 6.47 | 0.0061 | 0.01 | 0.935 |
| $X_9$ | 1 | 0.3526 | 1.13 | 1.0288 | 1.15 | 0.296 |
| $X_{10}$ | 1 | **4.9170** | **15.74** | **4.9170** | **5.50** | **0.029** |
| Error | 21 | 18.7791 | 60.13 | 18.7791 | | |
| Total | 31 | 31.2303 | 100.00 | | | |

To pursue that effect we looked at all combinations of predictors. The best subsets of independent variables are in Table 3.10.

For the NFL player ranking data the 9th and 10th deciles are sufficient to account for most of the variation in team performance. The model equation

Table 3.10: Best Subsets: Y versus $X$

| $p$ | $R^2$ | $adjR^2$ | $S$ | $X_1$ | $X_2$ | $X_3$ | $X_4$ | $X_5$ | $X_6$ | $X_7$ | $X_8$ | $X_9$ | $X_{10}$ |
|---|---|---|---|---|---|---|---|---|---|---|---|---|---|
| 1 | 19.2 | 16.5 | 0.91693 | | | | | | | | | | √ |
| **2** | **30.9** | **26.1** | **0.86265** | | | | | | | | | √ | √ |
| 3 | 33.1 | 26.0 | 0.86355 | | | | | | √ | | | √ | √ |
| 4 | 35.4 | 25.9 | 0.86420 | | √ | | | | √ | | | √ | √ |
| 5 | 37.1 | 25.0 | 0.86946 | | √ | √ | | | √ | | | √ | √ |
| 6 | 38.7 | 23.9 | 0.87540 | | √ | √ | | | √ | √ | | √ | √ |
| 7 | 39.4 | 21.7 | 0.88789 | | √ | √ | √ | √ | √ | | | √ | √ |
| 8 | 39.8 | 18.9 | 0.90397 | √ | √ | | √ | √ | √ | √ | | √ | √ |
| 9 | 39.8 | 15.2 | 0.92405 | √ | √ | √ | √ | √ | √ | √ | | √ | √ |
| 10 | 39.9 | 11.2 | 0.94564 | √ | √ | √ | √ | √ | √ | √ | √ | | √ |

with $X_9, X_{10}$ is

$$Y = -0.535 + 0.0627X_9 + 0.1015X_{10}.$$

The analysis of variance for the reduced model is in Table 3.11.

Table 3.11: Reduced Model

| *Source* | *DF* | *Seq SS* | *Cont. %* | *Adj SS* | *F* | *P* |
|---|---|---|---|---|---|---|
| Regression | 2 | 9.650 | 30.90 | 9.650 | 6.48 | 0.005 |
| $X_9$ | 1 | 1.608 | 5.15 | 3.642 | 4.89 | 0.035 |
| $X_{10}$ | 1 | **8.042** | **25.75** | **8.042** | **10.81** | **0.003** |
| *Error* | 29 | 21.581 | 69.10 | 21.581 | | |
| *Total* | 31 | 31.2303 | 100.00 | | | |

The fact that the 9th and 10th deciles are so important for team success is curious, so Table 3.12 lists the players involved. The players have above average position weight. The striking observation is that the defensive positions are prominent. Half the players are defensive ends or linebackers. It is well known that these positions are the key to disrupting quarterback play. The 2018 Super Bowl was decided by a quarterback strip of Tom Brady by the defensive end Brandon Graham.

In 2016 LaGarrette Blount (# 80) scored 18 TDs for the Patriots and was on their Super Bowl winning team. Most of the TDs were short 1 or 2 yard power runs by the 250 back. He was instrumental in New England winning the Super Bowl. While Bill Belichick is widely considered the smartest coach in football, the decision not to give Blount a new contract for the same salary was a dubious decision. Blount was instrumental in Philadelphia beating New England in Super Bowl 52 in February 2018 with a number of good runs.

Table 3.12: 9th and 10th Decile Players — NFL Ranking

| Rank | Player | Position | Team | Weight |
|------|--------|----------|------|--------|
| 80 | LeGarrette Blount | RB | Patriots | 8.1 |
| 81 | Alex Smith | QB | Chiefs | 17.9 |
| 82 | Clay Matthews | LB | Packers | 9.9 |
| 83 | Calais Campbell | DE | Jaguars | 11.3 |
| 84 | Mike Daniels | DT | Packers | 8.7 |
| 85 | Chandler Jones | LB | Cardinals | 9.9 |
| 86 | Jurrell Casey | DT | Titans | 8.7 |
| 87 | Travis Frederick | C | Cowboys | 6.4 |
| 88 | Doug Baldwin | WR | Seahawks | 11.9 |
| 89 | Thomas Davis | LB | Panthers | 9.9 |
| 90 | Malcolm Jenkins | S | Eagles | 8.0 |
| 91 | Lorenzo Alexander | LB | Bills | 9.9 |
| 92 | Everson Griffen | DE | Vikings | 11.3 |
| 93 | Brandon Graham | DE | Eagles | 11.3 |
| 94 | Dont'a Hightower | LB | Patriots | 9.9 |
| 95 | Kelechi Osemele | G | Raiders | 7.8 |
| 96 | Damon Harrison | DT | Giants | 8.7 |
| 97 | David DeCastro | G | Steelers | 7.8 |
| 98 | Adrian Peterson | RB | Saints | 8.1 |
| 99 | Malcolm Butler | CB | Patriots | 9.3 |
| 100 | Joey Bosa | DE | Chargers | 11.3 |

## Model Predictions

There is a lot of unexplained variation, but the reduced model is significant. The observed and predicted win percentages (from the reduced model) are in Table 3.13.

The highlighted teams have reasonable predictions from the reduced model. If we go back to the data on deciles, the predicted poor performance is from teams with no players in the bottom deciles of the top 100, and the strong performers had multiple players in the bottom deciles.

Table 3.13: Model Predictions

| Team | Observed Win Rate | Predicted Win Rate |
|---|---|---|
| Arizona | 0.5000 | 0.5215 |
| Atlanta | 0.6250 | 0.3694 |
| Baltimore | 0.5620 | 0.3694 |
| Buffalo | 0.5620 | 0.6154 |
| Carolina | 0.6880 | 0.5215 |
| Chicago | 0.3120 | 0.3694 |
| Cincinnati | 0.4380 | 0.3694 |
| Cleveland | 0.0322 | 0.3694 |
| Dallas | 0.5620 | 0.4666 |
| Denver | 0.3120 | 0.3694 |
| Detroit | 0.5620 | 0.3694 |
| Green Bay | 0.4380 | 0.6527 |
| Houston | 0.2500 | 0.3694 |
| Indianapolis | 0.2500 | 0.3694 |
| Jacksonville | 0.6250 | 0.5431 |
| Kansas City | 0.6250 | 0.6427 |
| LA Chargers | 0.5620 | 0.6484 |
| LA Rams | 0.6880 | 0.3694 |
| Miami | 0.3750 | 0.3694 |
| Minnesota | 0.8120 | 0.6484 |
| New England | 0.8120 | 0.8042 |
| New Orleans | 0.6880 | 0.5713 |
| NY Giants | 0.1880 | 0.5861 |
| NY Jets | 0.3120 | 0.3694 |
| Oakland | 0.3750 | 0.5639 |
| Philadelphia | 0.8120 | 0.7527 |
| Pittsburgh | 0.8120 | 0.5639 |
| San Francisco | 0.3750 | 0.3694 |
| Seattle | 0.5620 | 0.5526 |
| Tampa Bay | 0.3120 | 0.3694 |
| Tennessee | 0.5620 | 0.5025 |
| Washington | 0.4380 | 0.3694 |

## The Sports Illustrated List — top 100

We used the NFL list of top 100 players for the analysis of team performance. The top 100 from the SI list had an overlap of about 2/3rds of players with the NFL list, but the ranking of individual players in the lists differed. Although we lean towards the NFL list, it is informative to analyze the deciles from the Sports Illustrated list for their effect on Y.

Let $Z_1$ = players ranked from 1 to 10 by SI, weighted by average position salary

$Z_2$ = players ranked from 10 to 20 by SI, weighted by average position salary

$Z_3$ = players ranked from 21 to 30 by SI, weighted by average position salary

$Z_4$ = players ranked from 31 to 40 by SI, weighted by average position salary

$Z_5$ = players ranked from 41 to 50 by SI, weighted by average position salary

$Z_6$ = players ranked from 51 to 60 by SI, weighted by average position salary

$Z_7$ = players ranked from 61 to 70 by SI, weighted by average position salary

$Z_8$ = players ranked from 71 to 80 by SI, weighted by average position salary

$Z_9$ = players ranked from 81 to 90 by SI, weighted by average position salary

$Z_{10}$ = players ranked from 91 to 100 by SI, weighted by average position salary.

The logistic regression equation is

$$Y = -0.805 + 0.0486Z_1 + 0.0236Z_2 - 0.0201Z_3 + 0.0426Z_4 + 0.0211Z_5$$

$$+ 0.0194Z_6 + 0.0046Z_7 + 0.0171Z_8 + 0.0804Z_9 + 0.0182Z_{10}.$$

The model has less predictive power. Of course, since most of the same players are on both lists the results have comparable $R^2$ with the 10 deciles included . However, the contrasting rankings produce a different important decile. In the SI list it is the players ranked from 81 to 90 who have the big impact. Those players are listed in Table 3.15. There is a split between offensive and defensive players. The defense positions (LB, CB) have high weights.

Table 3.14: Fitted Logistic Model — SI Rankings

| Source | DF | Seq SS | Cont. % | Adj SS | F | P |
|---|---|---|---|---|---|---|
| Regression | 10 | 10.5145 | 33.67 | 10.5145 | 1.07 | 0.428 |
| $Z_1$ | 1 | 2.4480 | 7.84 | 2.1031 | 2.13 | 0.159 |
| $Z_2$ | 1 | 1.1373 | 3.64 | 0.5941 | 0.60 | 0.446 |
| $Z_3$ | 1 | 0.0316 | 0.10% | 0.3124 | 0.32 | 0.580 |
| $Z_4$ | 1 | 0.9206 | 2.95% | 1.0219 | 1.04 | 0.320 |
| $Z_5$ | 1 | 0.0099 | 0.03% | 0.2122 | 0.22 | 0.648 |
| $Z_6$ | 1 | 0.0055 | 0.02% | 0.1944 | 0.20 | 0.662 |
| $Z_7$ | 1 | 0.3164 | 1.01% | 0.0080 | 0.01 | 0.929 |
| $Z_8$ | 1 | 0.1387 | 0.44% | 0.2546 | 0.26 | 0.617 |
| $Z_9$ | **1** | **5.3247** | **17.05%** | **4.8768** | **4.94** | **0.037** |
| $Z_{10}$ | 1 | 0.1817 | 0.58% | 0.1817 | 0.18 | 0.672 |
| Error | 21 | 20.7158 | 66.33% | 20.7158 | | |
| Total | 31 | 31.2303 | 100.00 | | | |

Table 3.15: Best Subsets: $Y$ versus $Z$

| $p$ | $R^2$ | $adjR^2$ | $S$ | $Z_1$ | $Z_2$ | $Z_3$ | $Z_4$ | $Z_5$ | $Z_6$ | $Z_7$ | $Z_8$ | $Z_9$ | $Z_{10}$ |
|---|---|---|---|---|---|---|---|---|---|---|---|---|---|
| 1 | 14.1 | 11.2 | 0.94586 | | | | | | | | | √ | |
| 2 | 22.8 | 17.5 | 0.91163 | √ | | | | | | | | √ | |
| 3 | 27.9 | 20.2 | 0.89667 | √ | √ | | | | | | | √ | |
| **4** | **31.5** | **21.4** | **0.88991** | √ | √ | | √ | | | | | √ | |
| 5 | 31.9 | 18.8 | 0.90424 | √ | √ | √ | √ | | | | | √ | |
| 6 | 32.4 | 16.1 | 0.91922 | √ | √ | √ | √ | | | | √ | √ | |
| 7 | 32.7 | 13.1 | 0.93554 | √ | √ | √ | √ | √ | | | √ | √ | |
| 8 | 33.1 | 9.8 | 0.95339 | √ | √ | √ | √ | √ | √ | | √ | √ | |
| 9 | 33.6 | 6.5 | 0.97056 | √ | √ | √ | √ | √ | √ | | √ | √ | √ |
| 10 | 33.7 | 2.1 | 0.99321 | √ | √ | √ | √ | √ | √ | √ | √ | √ | √ |

Table 3.16: 9th Decile of SI Top 100 Players

| Rank | Player | Position | Team | Weight |
|---|---|---|---|---|
| 81 | Josh Norman | CB | Red Skins | 9.3 |
| 82 | Andrew Whitworth | LT | Rams | 8.7 |
| 83 | Mitchell Schwartz | RT | Chiefs | 8.7 |
| 84 | Lane Johnson | RT | Eagles | 8.7 |
| 85 | Terrell Suggs | LB | Ravens | 9.9 |
| 86 | Dont'a Hightower | LB | Patriots | 9.9 |
| 87 | Xavier Rhodes | CB | Vikings | 9.3 |
| 88 | Philip Rivers | QB | Chargers | 17.9 |
| 89 | Alshon Jeffery | WR | Eagles | 11.9 |
| 90 | Janoris Jenkins | CB | Giants | 9.3 |

It is again the case that a reduced model accounts for most of the variation. The model with $Z_1, Z_2, Z_4, Z_9$ is identified in Table 3.16.

## Conclusion

The data on pre-season player rankings and team success in 2017 yielded the following conclusions:

- An association exists between team success and the number of top 400 players. However, the correlation is 0.392 so top players only explain 15% of the variation in win percentage.

- The teams with the most top players generally have high win percentages, and teams with fewer top players have low win percentages.

- The connection of top 100 players to team winning percentage is most important. The correlation is 0.292, reduced from the top 400 result as would be expected with fewer players per team.

- The correlation between ranks of top 100 players on the Sports Illustrated list and the NFL players list is 0.456, so there is quite bit of disagreement.

- Weighting players by position value increases the explanatory power of top players.

- For the NFL player ranking data the lower deciles 9 and 10 are sufficient to account for most of the variation in team performance. These deciles emphasize the defensive positions, and they are key factors in team success.

# 4

# Misconceptions of the media and the value of proper analysis

In this chapter we discuss a number of interesting ideas including some from the class notes of our late colleague Tom Cover, a Professor of Statistics and Electrical Engineering at Stanford University. Tom took ill and died at the age of 73 in 2016. He taught a course in Sports Statistics and interested numerous students in the topic. Analytics is popular in today's sports analysis, and Tom was ahead of his time in bringing mathematics and statistics to decision making in sports.

## Expected Value of Field Position in Football

In American football the playing field is 100 yards long. When the offense takes possession of the ball at the $x$ yard line, there is $100 - x$ yards to cross the goal line for a touchdown. For strategy purposes it is important to understand the chance $p(x)$ of a touchdown on that possession starting at the $x$ yard line. Assuming the convert is automatic, the outcomes on that possession drive are: 7 points with probability $p(x)$ or 0 points with probability $(1 - p(x))$.

The expected number of points $= 7 \times p(x)$.

Figure 4.1 displays the average number of points for starting positions during NCAA football games in the Big Ten Conference over the 2013-14 seasons. Similar plots exist for NFL games.

The remarkable feature of the plot is the simple pattern. If a line is drawn as shown from the 0-yard line (a touchback costing $-2$ points) to the 100 yard line (a touchdown paying $+7$ points) the straight line almost passes

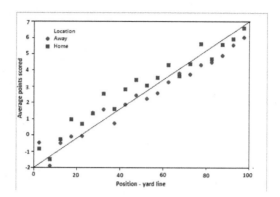

Figure 4.1: Field position and points scored

through the middle of the points. With this observation the expected value of field position $V(x)$, is approximately

$$V(x) = -2 + 0.09x.$$

This formula can be used to support decision making by the offensive team depending on field position. (See: Carter and Macholl (1978), Carroll, Palmer, and Thorn (1988), and Quinn (2012)).We illustrate this with some examples.

1. Kicking — It is 4th down and 5 yards to a first down on the opponents 30 yard line. The options are to kick a field goal for 3 points or attempt to advance the ball at least to the 25 yard line for a first down. It is estimated that the chance of a successful field goal from the 30 (actually a 47 yard kick) is 0.5. The chance of a first down $x$ yards past the 25 yard line is 0.4 and the chance of falling $y$ yards short of the 25 is 0.6.

   Assume if the field goal is missed the opponent takes over at their 30 yard line, and if the field goal is successful the ball is placed at the 20 (a touchback). The expected value of kicking the field goal is

   $$EV = 0.5 \times (3 - V(20) + 0.5 \times (-V(30)) = 1.25.$$

   The expected value of going for the first down is

   $$EV(x, y) = 0.4 \times V(75 + x) + 0.6 \times V(100 - (70 + y)) = 1.48.$$

   So the best option is to go for the first down.

2. Passing — A team has first down at the $x$ yard line and they are
   interested in the distance an intercepted pass needs to be thrown
   (assuming it is downed immediately) so that the expected value field
   position of the offense at $x$ yards equals the expected value of the
   opposition from intercepting the pass at $y$ yards. The distance the
   ball was thrown is $y - x$. The change in value from the interception is

$$\Delta = V(x) - (-V(100 - y)) = 5 - 0.09(y - x).$$

If $\Delta = 0$, then $y - x \approx 55$.

Of course that is quite a throw and equal to the distance of a good
punt. Most passes are much shorter and the value of an interception is
negative. The chance of a completion, incompletion or interception for
passes of each distance would would be used to calculate the expected
value of a pass attempt of $y - x$ yards.

## Chance of Winning: Combining Odds Ratios

A popular model for the probability of an event is the Bradley-Taylor model.
Let $p = Pr\,[A]$ for event $A$. Then $p$ is defined by the formula

$$p = \frac{e^\beta}{1 + e^\beta} = \frac{1}{1 + e^{-\beta}}.$$

As $\beta$ ranges from $-\infty$ to $+\infty$ we have $p$ moving from 0 to 1. For the param-
eter $\beta$ we have $\beta = \ln\left(\frac{p}{1-p}\right)$, where $\frac{p}{1-p}$ is the odds ratio and $\ln\left(\frac{p}{1-p}\right)$ is
called the logit. The logit transformation has the effect of linearizing prob-
ability and a linear model for logits is justified. Consider a simple 2-factor
linear model for logits

Table 4.1: Logit Model

|                | $B$ | $\bar{B}$ |
| -------------- | --- | --------- |
| $A$            |     |           |
| $\bar{A}$      |     |           |

Then in expectation $\beta_{AB} = \beta_{A.} + \beta_{.B} - \beta_{..}$. In terms of logits

$$\ln\left(\frac{p_{AB}}{1 - p_{AB}}\right) = \ln\left(\frac{p_{A.}}{1 - p_{A.}}\right) + \ln\left(\frac{p_{.B}}{1 - p_{.B}}\right) - \ln\left(\frac{p_{..}}{1 - p_{..}}\right)$$

and for odds ratios

$$\frac{p_{AB}}{1 - p_{AB}} = \frac{p_{A\cdot}}{1 - p_{A\cdot}} \times \frac{p_{\cdot B}}{1 - p_{\cdot B}} \times \frac{1 - p_{\cdot\cdot}}{p_{\cdot\cdot}}.$$

In these expressions, $p_{AB}$ is the joint probability for $A$ and $B$, $p_{A\cdot}$ is the marginal probability for $A$, $p_{\cdot B}$ is the marginal probability for $B$, and $p_{\cdot\cdot}$ is the overall probability. The odds ratios for the margins generate the odds ratio for the specific $AB$ event. Obviously there are many ways to combine odds ratios based on the Bradley-Taylor model and linear factor models. This is a general and powerful method for developing the chance for an particular outcome from a competition.

As an example of the use of a 2-factor model, let $p_{AB}$ = win probability of team $A$ against team $B$. Then $p_{A\cdot}$ =the win probability of $A$ against all teams, $p_{\cdot B}$ = the win probability of all teams against team $B$, and $p_{\cdot\cdot}$ = the average win probability overall. If team $A$ is facing team $B$, then the chance of winning in the game can be determined from the knowledge of the average win probability of $A$, the average win probability against $B$ and the league average win probability, statistics which are known.

For illustration consider a good team with $p_{A\cdot}$ = .750 facing a poor team with $p_{\cdot B}$ = .68, and a league average $p_{\cdot\cdot}$ = .50. Then

$$\frac{p_{AB}}{1 - p_{AB}} = \frac{.75}{.25} \times \frac{.68}{.32} \times \frac{.50}{.50} = 6.375,$$

and $p_{AB}$ = .864.

This use of marginal probabilities to generate probabilities for specific scenarios can be used to calculate the chance for an outcome from any head to head competition, where the characteristics of the competitors is known.

## Game Point Spread — Predicting Success

Leading up to a sporting competition there is a lot of "expert" opinion expressed about the eventual outcome of the competition. One type of opinion or judgement is manifest in betting on the outcome, a very popular activity worldwide. In a sporting event almost every game has a favorite and an underdog. Let $F$ = the number of points scored by the favorite, and $U$ = the number of points scored by the underdog. Then the point spread is

$$P = F - U.$$

The general purpose of spread betting is to create an active market for both sides of a binary wager. The point spread is essentially a handicap towards the underdog and the wager becomes "Will the favorite win by more than the point spread?" The point spread is set at a level to create an equal number of participants on each side of the wager. This allows a bookmaker to act as a market maker by accepting wagers on both sides of the spread. Spread betting is a judgement on the likely outcome of a game.

The points by the favorite and underdog are uncertain and the margin of victory over/under the point spread is a variable. Let $M$ be the margin over the posted point spread

$$M = F - U - p.$$

Figure 4.2 displays an empirical distribution of $M$ for NFL games covering 1981-84. (Stern, 1991).

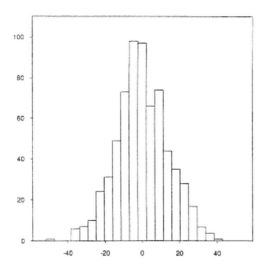

Figure 4.2: Margin over point spread

The shape of the distribution is very close to a normal, and normality is supported by statistical tests. The mean of the distribution is $\overline{M} = 0.07$, and the standard deviation is $s_M = 13.86$.

We assume that

$$M \propto N(0, 14).$$

With a given point spread $P = p$, the chance of the favorite winning can be calculated as

$$Pr\left[F > U \mid P = p\right] = Pr\left[M > -P \mid P = p\right] = 1 - \Phi\left(\frac{-p}{14}\right),$$

where $\Phi$ is the normal cumulative distribution.

For example in a game between San Francisco 49ers and Oakland Raisers, the 49ers are favored by 4 points. Then the chance of the 49ers winning the contest is $1 - \Phi(-0.2857) = 0.6124$.

So the spread is converted into a chance of winning. Around 30% of NFL games are decided by 3 or 7 points. This means that -2.5, +3.5, -6.5, and +7.5 are important numbers in handicap betting. So the spread and probability of winning are matched. The odds = pr(win)/pr(not win) are also reported for the games.

If you are betting against a bookmaker or Las Vegas where the commission markup is taken, then we can compute the probability of winning as follows: If the odds for competing teams are given and the profit margin is known, then the probabilities of winning for the teams can be estimated. Suppose the posted odds for the favorite are $o_f$ and the markup is $\delta$ then

$$o_f = \frac{p + \delta}{q + \delta} = \frac{p + \delta}{(1 - p) + \delta}$$

and solving for $p$ gives

$$p = \frac{o_f}{(1 + o_f) - \delta}$$

As an example, if $o_f = 7/3$, $\delta = 0.1$, then $p = 0.6$.

## Aggregation of Performance Measures

The overall evaluation of a player in a sport such as football is an aggregation of performance statistics across seasons. When highlighting Hall of Fame performers it is usual to emphasize aggregate career statistics. The aggregation is more complicated than a simple average of season statistics. Consider data on catch percentage (completions) in football for 2 seasons in Table 4.2. Catch percentage is a performance measure for receivers, indicating "great hands".

Table 4.2: Aggregation

| | Season 1 | Season 2 |
|---|---|---|
| Catch percentage: A | $p_{A1}$ | $p_{A2}$ |
| Targets: A | $n_{A1}$ | $n_{A2}$ |
| Catch percentage: B | $p_{B1}$ | $p_{B2}$ |
| Targets: B | $n_{B1}$ | $n_{B2}$ |

The aggregate average for $A$ is

$$p_A = \frac{n_{A1}}{n_{A1} + n_{A2}} \times p_{A1} + \frac{n_{A2}}{n_{A1} + n_{A2}} \times p_{A2},$$

and the aggregate for $B$ is

$$p_B = \frac{n_{B1}}{n_{B1} + n_{B2}} \times p_{B1} + \frac{n_{B2}}{n_{B1} + n_{B2}} \times p_{B2}.$$

It is possible that $p_{A1} > p_{B1}$ and $p_{A2} > p_{B2}$ but $p_A < p_B$. That is, player $A$ has a better percentage in both seasons but a lesser percentage in the combined seasons. This effect is an example of Simpsons (1951) paradox and is generated by the disparity in targets between players.

To observe the paradox consider the data in Table 4.3.

Table 4.3: Simpsons Paradox: Completion Percentage

| | Season 1 | Season 2 |
|---|---|---|
| Catch percentage: A | .667 | .50 |
| Targets: A | 30 | 100 |
| Catch percentage: B | .65 | .40 |
| Targets: B | 30 | 10 |

Then combining seasons we have

$$p_A = \frac{30}{130} \times .667 + \frac{100}{130} \times .50 = .539$$

and

$$p_B = \frac{30}{40} \times .65 + \frac{10}{40} \times .40 = .588.$$

So $(p_{A1}, p_{A2}) > (p_{B1}, p_{B2})$ and $p_A < p_B$. Although this example is based on modest numbers of targets, it is possible to find the same effect for large numbers if the targets are disproportionate.

The same analysis can be seen with another statistic for receivers, $\overline{X}$ =average yards per catch. This is a "legs" measure since it reflects speed. Consider average yards per catch in Table 4.4.

Table 4.4: Simpsons Paradox: Yds per Catch

| | *Season 1* | *Season 2* |
|---|---|---|
| *Yds per catch:A* | 15 | 8 |
| *Catches: A* | 20 | 50 |
| *Yds per catch: B* | 14 | 7 |
| *Catches: B* | 19 | 4 |

Then $\overline{X}_A = \frac{20}{70} \times 15 + \frac{50}{70} \times 8 = 10$ and $\overline{X}_B = \frac{19}{23} \times 14 + \frac{4}{23} \times 7 = 12.78$. Although receiver $A$ has more yards per catch in each season, in aggregate receiver $B$ is better.

## Performance Measures — QB Rating

A sports contest (game) is composed of many events or individual contests, with the result of each contest being a failure or a success. The failure/success can have a variety of consequences. Consider, for example, an attempt (down) in football. The offensive team has possession of the ball and seeks to advance the ball at each attempt. The critical offensive player is the quarterback, since he takes possession of the ball and manages the forward thrust. About half of the attempts involve moving the ball through passing to an eligible receiver. The passing game has come to dominate football. The quarterback performance is measured by successes and failures of passing attempts. The simplest classification has a success as: completed pass of $x$ yards or completed pass for a touchdown (score). A failure is classified as: an incomplete pass or an interception by the defense.

In the NFL the aggregate passing performance over games is measured by four variables: $x_1$ = completions per attempt, $x_2$ = yards per attempt, $x_3$ = touchdowns per attempt, and $x_4$ = interceptions per attempt. The multidimensional score $X = (x_1, x_2, x_3, -x_4)$ is the basis of performance measurement. (Note that $x_4$ is a failure statistic and is negative in ranking $X$.)

In addition to reporting performance on each of the 4 dimensions, a combined passer rating score is completed. First, each of the $x_i$ variables is scaled to a value between 0 and 2.375, with 1.0 being statistically average (based on league data between 1960-1970). The four separate calculations can be expressed by the following equations:

$$z_1 = max\left\{min\left\{(x_1 - .3) \times 5, 2.375\right\}, 0\right\}$$

$$z_2 = max\left\{min\left\{(x_2 - 3) \times .25, 2.375\right\}, 0\right\}$$

$$z_3 = max\left\{min\left\{x_3 \times 20, 2.375\right\}, 0\right\}$$

$$z_4 = max\left\{min\left\{2.375 - (x_4 \times 25), 2.375\right\}, 0\right\}.$$

Second, the separate scores are aggregated with the formula:

$$Y = \frac{100}{6}(z_1 + z_2 + z_3 + z_4).$$

A perfect passer rating (158.3) requires at least: 77.5% completion percentage, 12.5 yards per attempt, 11.875% touchdown percentage, and no interceptions.

The rating score $Y$ reduces the 4 dimensional representation to a single dimension. The rating is from the pro football Hall of Fame official site. The formula does not include rushing statistics or fumbles, nor does it put added weight on performance in situations like third downs or fourth-quarter scoring tries. The rating does not account for the quality of receivers or protection from the offensive line. The rating does not measure a quarterback's contributions to team wins. The highest career passing rating is 104.0 by Aaron Rodgers, 2005-2016. He also holds the one-season highest rating of 122.5 in 2011. Peyton Manning holds the record for the most games (4) with a perfect passer rating. Phil Simms holds the record for the highest passer rating in a Super Bowl of 150.92 in Super Bowl 21. Ben Roethinsberger holds the record for the lowest passer rating to win a Super Bowl at 22.6 in Super Bowl 40.

There are desired properties of any aggregate rating score and we will mention three.

1. Consistency: Any ranking by $Y$ should be consistent with the partial ranking by $X = (x_1, x_2, x_3, -x_4)$ That is if $X_1 \leq X_2$ then $Y_1 \leq Y_2$.

2. Order Preserving: If $Y_1 \leq Y_2$ and $Y_2 \leq Y_3$, then $Y_1 \leq Y_3$

3. Distance: If $d$ is a distance function, then $d(X_1, X_2) \leq d(X_2, X_3) \Rightarrow d(Y_1, Y_2) \leq d(Y_2, Y_3)$

Table 4.5: Quarterback Performance

|   | $x_1$ | $x_2$ | $x_3$ | $x_4$ |
|---|-------|--------|-------|-------|
| A | 9/10  | 300/10 | 3/10  | 1/10  |
| B | 9/11  | 300/11 | 3/11  | 2/11  |

Table 4.6: Quarterback Rating

|   | $z_1$ | $z_2$ | $z_3$ | $z_4$ | $Y$ |
|---|-------|-------|-------|-------|--------|
| A | 2.375 | 2.375 | 2.375 | 0     | 118.75 |
| B | 2.375 | 2.375 | 2.375 | 1.7   | 120.45 |

The passer rating score $Y$ actually fails the consistency property. Consider game data on two quarterbacks in Table 4.5.

So quarterback B threw an extra pass which was intercepted. The scoring for dimensions and the combined rating are in Table 4.6.

The anomaly in rating where $X_A > X_B$ whereas $Y_A \leq Y_B$ is created by the benchmark figure 2.375.

There has been much criticism of the QB rating formula. (Byrne, 2011). Consider a quarterback who is 3/10 for 30 yards, with 0 touchdowns and 1 interception. At that point, with $x_1 = 0.3,$, $x_2 = 3.0,$, $x_3 = 0,$, and $x_4 = 0.1$,

the rating is $Y = 0$.

Suppose the quarterback then throws an incomplete pass. The statistics are $x_1 = 0.272,$, $x_2 = 2.272$, $x_3 = 0,$, $x_4 = 0.09$, and $Y = 1.705$.

The rate has improved by throwing an incompletion, because the interception rate improved.

A recent illustration of the quarterback rating shortcomings come from the 2017 Super Bowl. (Ziemba, 2017). Some Super Bowl statistics: Tom Brady was 43 of 62 for 466 yards with two TDs, one interception, and a 95.2 rating. Matt Ryan was 17 of 23 for 284 yards with two TDs, no interceptions, five sacks, and one fumble for a 144.1 rating. The reason Ryan's rating was so much more than Brady's can be seen from the rating formula and the statistics counted in the formula. Of course, statistics can lie. Performance in crucial game situations by Brady is missed with the total game statistics. Brady is pleased and Ryan is not with the outcome of the game.

Wikipedia lists a number of attempts at alternative rating formulas for quarterbacks, but none of them seem to capture the full essence of the quarterback concept, which is very complex. We will add our contribution to a more complete QB rating formula in MacLean and Ziemba (2019) *Sports Statisitcs.*

## Blunder or correct decision? The Belichick decision to go for it on 4th down

*An interesting sports decision situation — namely, an analysis of a crucial play that lost the top NFL game of the year by New England coach Bill Belichick.*

As I write on Sunday November 22, 2010, I am watching the TV analysts discuss this controversial decision on Sunday, November 15. They are all ex-NFL star players together with an announcer. Their analysis is seat of the pants. But is that the right way to analyze complex decision situations? So it is a good example for us to look at.

The setting was the showdown of the year, pitting the two "best" quarterbacks, Peyton Manning of the 9-0 Indianapolis Colts at home versus Tom Brady of the 6-2 New England Patriots and winner of three Super Bowls. Between them they have won most of the recent MVP honors. Manning has won the MVP of the season four times. Both teams have very good receivers and plenty of them for these superb quarterbacks to run down the field with.

Dr Z's bets were long New England at match odds - Indianapolis was favored and New England $+2\frac{1}{2}$ and $+3\frac{1}{2}$ points on Betfair in London. The Colts got a fast touchdown then New England got three touchdowns plus a field goal so moved out to a 24-7 lead. I then hedged my match odds bets, the larger ones to lock in a sure profit no matter who wins.

See Lane and Ziemba (2008) for an analysis of these types of bets where you can lock in odds on A then on B to guarantee a profit on a sports betting and some financial market situations. See Hausch and Ziemba (2008) and Hausch, Lo and Ziemba (2008) for many studies of sports betting analyses.

I kept the $+2\frac{1}{2}$ and $+3\frac{1}{2}$ bets as 17 points seemed a huge lead. But I knew from past Patriots-Colts games that mean reversion comebacks are frequent. Indeed, the Colts rallied. With 2.08 left to play, the Patriots were ahead by 6 points (34-28) on their 28 yard line with 4th down. Normally it is conservative football wisdom with a 6-point lead to kick and move the ball down the field to say the Indianapolis 25 yard line. But the Patriots pass defense was not effective against Manning's fast accurate passes so they could easily move down the field and win the game. The Patriots traded two great defensive players Richard Seymour and Mike Vrabel plus some other key defense players including Teddy Bruski and Junior Sean had retired. So the Patriots were weaker on defense than usual. They had just seen Manning run through the defense for two long touchdowns.

Should the Patriots go for it and get the first down they likely could run out the clock or get a field goal to go ahead by an insurmountable 9 points. What to do?

The play was similar to a 2-point conversion after a touchdown but with a longer field. Coach Belichick was familiar with and accepted the conclusions of a paper by Berkeley Economics Professor David Romer (2006) which argues that going for it on 4th down is optimal much more frequently than coaches actually go for it.[1] And indeed Belichick has gone for it much more then the league average. So Belichick ordered Brady to try to pass for a 3 yard gain to get the first down 2 yards away.

Brady delivered a good pass to Kevin Faulk but Faulk bobbled the ball and was then pushed back so he did not gain the needed 2 yards when he hit the ground. Manning, of course, drove the Colts in 4 plays from the New England 29 with 1.57 to go. With all 3 timeouts available, this is an eternity for the 3 time MVP to a score using up all the time left except a few (13) seconds. So Brady had no time to rally back for a game winning field goal. To use the clock Manning ran on three plays then hit favorite target Reggie Wayne for the winning touchdown. Belichick had used up 2 of his 3 time outs prior to the 4th down failed play.

---

[1]Romer looks at extensive data and does a good analysis recognizing that these decisions are really the first step of a dynamic situation so Bellman dynamic programming is involved. But it is complex with the number of things that can happen in the future and future decisions. With great players such as Brady and Manning involved it is even more complex to get the data right. We are reminded why Wayne Gretzy was essentially the only player four standard deviation sports better than average. He knew where the opposing player was going even before the player did. Here you are facing the greatest fast passing quarterback in history, Manning. So no matter where you leave him timewise and on the field, his chances of scoring are high. And as we see below, he managed the clock perfectly to not give Brady a chance to win the game with a field goal or touchdown.

So the Colt's won 35-34. Manning said "we were preparing to go 60, 70 yards. It was a great play by the defense, shortened our field." I won all my bets. But the big issue is the criticism leveled against Belichick for a so-called stupid decision. One coach, Brian Billick, fired last year as Baltimore coach, said "it's 50-50" you either make it or not. Other coaches pooh-poohed the Romer analysis saying they flunked calculus in college.

Of course, the analysis is very simple. It is just expected value arithmetic in this application.

For example, Brian Burke of Advanced NFL Statistics calculated that there was a 70% probability that the Patriots would win if they punted. But it was 79% if they went for it assuming that the chance that the Patriots get the first down was 60%.

> [Burke writes]: A team picks up 4th and 2 about 60 percent of the time – and we all know that a fourth down conversion in this case means certain victory. On the flip side: A team would score a game-winning touchdown from the 30 about 53 percent of the time. This leads to this formula – the first part is the 60 percent multiplied by 1 (1 signifying the certain victory if the play is converted). The second part is 40 percent multiplied by the chance of winning the game if the 4th down play fails:
>
> $(.60 * 1) + (.40 * (1 - .53)) = 78.8\%$ chance of winning.
>
> ... Burke then estimates the chance of winning if Belichick punts – that is the chance of a team going 66 yards for a touchdown in the final two minutes. He says, historically, teams get that about 30 percent of the time. So a punt gives the Patriots a 70 percent chance of winning.
>
> ... Now, you probably are saying the numbers do not sound all that authentic. The Peyton Manning Colts would have a much better than 53 percent chance of scoring from the 30 (and, as it played out, the Colts scored so easily and left so little time on the clock it seemed just about automatic). But, you have to figure the Colts also had a much better than 30 percent chance of scoring had the Patriots punted – no doubt this was weighing on Belichick's mind. And for that matter, you have to figure that Brady has a better chance than 60 percent chance of converting on fourth down and two.

Really, no matter how you play with the numbers, it will come out about the same. Try it. There is almost no way – without suppressing the numbers – to make the percentages even out. The Patriots' best percentage chance was to go for it on fourth down. Of course, football is not really a percentage game for most of us, is it? No, it's a game about emotion and passion and momentum.

When the game ended and Belichick's gamble failed, people lined up to bash him – and normally I'd be all for this. Former Patriots player Rodney Harrison called it the worst coaching move Belichick ever made. Former Patriots player Teddy Bruski wrote that Belichick dissed his defense by not believing they could stop the Colts over 70 yards. Tony Dungy said, "You have to punt there. You just have to punt there."

More or less, this analysis is ok but it is possible for the Pats to get the first down and still lose and the 53% versus 30% chances under these circumstances are likely much closer. And the situation is dynamic. Still it looks like Belichick made the right decision.

A Vancouver friend of mine who is a professional sports bettor related the following to me:

There was a big bet in NYC late overnight on the "correctness" of the call. a jury of five top poker players/sports bettors gave their probability estimates for four questions:

- probability of NE fourth-down conversion

- Colts win probability after successful conversion

- Colts win probability after failed conversion

- Colts win probabilty after punt

A friend of mine laid -1000, to win 100k, that the jury would return a verdict, based on their inputs above, of "correct to go for it". The estimates were varied, especially for item two, but all five supported the call. They are doing a second round of west-coast jurors today. I already voted (62%, 6%, 58%, 33%, respectively).

His 56%=62%-6% is more than 50% so with essentially any reasonable utility function, the decision to go for it is optimal. Observe that since we are so close to the end of the game, so this two-stage modeling approach approximates the dynamic situation. One could add the probability that the Colts score with the Pats having enough time left to win with a field goal or touchdown.

My friend adds:

> Yes, what all the talking heads don't understand is that all of Indy's wins come off the second leg of a parlay, if NE goes for it, and that they're a solid underdog on the first leg. (Parlay = NE fail to convert, Indy score TD, NE fail to kick FG). Yes and indy gets PAT. They just look at the gap between prob(score from NE28) and prob(score from Indy25), without realising it's conditioned on NE not converting, in which case NE wins outright. Yes and Prob(score from Indy25) might be close to Prob(score from NE28). It's a trivial problem, but it's funny to see how much sound and fury is expended by folks thinking the (trivially) correct choice is a punt. Yes former Indy coach Tony Dungy said that so did Rodney Harrison former Patriot player on the commentary after the game. There might be as much as a 8-9% swing in overall win probability by going for it, which is huge.

The goal is to win the Super Bowl and making the playoffs with a first week bye, and having home field advantage throughout the playoffs is paramount. At 6-3, New England is leading their division so are on track to have a chance to get the bye and one home field advantage but 9-0 Indianapolis looks poised to have an easy trip to the Super Bowl with a bye and home field advantage till the Super Bowl. Should both teams so progress, they would meet for the American Conference final in Indianapolis and not in the snow of Foxboro. Both teams won the following Sunday so the Patriots were 7-3 and the Colts 10-0.

The debate continues with most of the commentary and former football player stars who are experts on TV still blaming Belichick for a bad decision. Indeed they did lose the game. However, essentially all the sports bettors and sophisticated fans favored Belichick's decision. Again, getting the mean right is crucial and the key is the probability of getting the first down.

The league average for two-point conversions is about 45%. But on the 28th yard line, with Brady passing, it is at least 55-60% with 65% likely the upper bound.

It is too bad with the billions at stake that professional sports teams do not use statistical and economic analysis more. Billy Ball as it is called, is a notable exception where the Oakland A's usually have a top team with a low budget. But they have not won a World Series. See Lewis (2003) and the Brad Pitt movie, *Moneyball*, which discusses Billy Bean's strategy. The strategy is basically to assemble players that produce runs assuming that the more runs you have, the more games you will win. This means instead of batting average go for players who were on base very often. The Yankees, who have won by far the most World Series, have a simple formula for success: buy the best players. But this approach can lead to suboptimal behavior because the best players may not be the ones producing the most runs. In the Oakland A's application they put together less expensive players who together produce a lot of runs. Ziemba found similar behavior in lotteries where he consulted for 30+years. Most games are designed by non-analysts but when there are bugs they call on us.

## The jet lag effect

There are many edges that can be used to successfully wager on NFL games. A powerful edge is mean reversion and risk arbitrage. This we show in multiple seasons of the NFL throughout the season, playoffs and Super Bowl. Here we discuss the jet lag effect.

We all face jet lag when we travel. We know also that the home team very often has an advantage. For example, the Seattle Seahawks are often undefeated at home. During the 2016 season, they were 8-0 but yet they lost many games on the road. It is often said that the stadiums are built to help the home team and in the case of Seattle the loud crowd, one of the very loudest in the NFL along with Kansas City and Denver, is known as the 13th player. Why then do they lose more often on the road? Foder (2014) show for the 2005-2010 regular seasons that there is a significant jet lag effect. What they find is that the effect is strongest when teams go from west to east over several time zones and then play and wind up losing those games. A Seattle example was in the 2017 playoffs when they went to Atlanta and lost.

The effect is strongest during afternoon games and when teams are in different divisions. However the effect does not seem to be there if it is a night game and it is less when the teams go east to west and when they are in the same division.

## How to calculate the home field advantage

I have mostly worked with simple models. Complicated models do not necessarily improve prediction accuracy. I used a simple model focusing on home advantage to win 74% in the NHL against Roxys 50-50 line and used it to set the line for the BC lotto corp. But keeping track of some other things can be useful.

We use the following formulas to get our probabilities that a given team wins adjusting for the home field advantage. This probability can be compared to the probability of winning based on the odds makers spread, which is discussed below.

If Team A has true strength $R_A$ and Team B has true strength $R_B$, the exact formula (using the logistic curve) for the chance of winning for Team A is

$$p_A = \frac{1}{1 + 10^{(R_B - R_A)/200}}.$$

Similarly the expected score for Team B is

$$p_B = \frac{1}{1 + 10^{(R_A - R_B)/200}}.$$

yielding

$$p_A = \frac{Q_A}{Q_A + Q_B}$$

and

$$p_B = \frac{Q_B}{Q_A + Q_B}$$

where $Q_A = 10^{R_A/200}$ and $Q_B = 10^{R_B/200}$ and $p_A + p_B = 1$. In the latter case, the same denominator applies to both expressions. This means that by studying only the numerators, we find out that the expected chance of winning for Team A is $Q_A/Q_B$ times greater than the expected chance of winning for Team B. It then follows that for each 200 rating points of advantage over the opponent, the chance of winning is magnified ten times in comparison to the opponent's chance of winning.

Since the true strength of each team is unknown, the forecasted probabilities are calculated using the team's current ratings.

## The decision on what to do on fourth down on the one yard line

In 2017 La Garette Blount of the New England Patriots scored 18 TDs and many of these were one or two yard plunges to the end zone to score these TDs. During the off season, the 250 pound Blount went from New England to the Philadelphia Eagles, the highest rated team. Previously he had gone to New England after being cut by Pittsburgh. In the 2017-18 year, Blount had a very good running game, sharing duties on the Eagles with Jay Ajai and he has had more of these one yard TDs.

In many cases, the decision on what to do on fourth on one is crucial to winning or losing a close game. Tom Brady, of New England, has a high effect rate nearing 90% and he has used the play some of the time. The classic case in the 2015 Super Bowl with Seattle on the one yard line on the first down with the possibility to run three times the powerful running back Marshan Lynch, who excels at this. The coaches elected not to do this and Russell Wilson's pass was intercepted and lost the game. Why did they do this when it seems non-optimal.

Another example was 2018 in the Pittsburgh home playoff game against Jacksonville. Twice the Steelers had the ball on the one yard line on the fourth down. Their QB, Big Ben Roethinsberger, at 250 pounds, is a good candidate to QB sneak the ball. He is 18 of 19 in fourth and one rush attempts in his career. This is the highest success rate (94.7%) for any player with over ten attempts in his career including the playoffs. But Big Ben is not allowed to change the plays designed by the offensive coordinator and coach Mike Tomlin. In this game, in the two times they were on the one yard line on fourth down, the decision was to run LéVeon Bell, who failed and to have Ben pass, which also failed. This cost them the game and a chance to meet New England in the AFC championship. One wonders why the Pittsburgh coaches do this.

There were also other dubious coaching decisions that did not seem optimal that cast doubt on the Pittsburgh management. For example, the final 47 seconds against the Jaguars in 2018 were basically wasted although they almost pulled out a victory. There have been other instances of wasted time in Pittsburgh games.

There are rumblings from some minor Steelers owners about this alleged poor coaching, but the major owner, Art Rooney II, likely will not make any coaching changes since historically Pittsburgh coaches have long, 10+ year contracts. One source argued that Pittsburgh would be undefeated if Belichick were the coach given the talent on the bench.

## The two versus one extra point fallacy

Walker et al (2018) describe a behavioral finance fallacy where coaches focus too much on the possibility of an immediate loss. They avoid risking instant defeat even when taking that risk offers the best chance to win the game. This is highly related to the previous section on going for it on fourth and one. The authors used ten years of NFL data focusing on a last minute TD with the scoring team being one point behind with little time left in the game. The choice is to kick a field goal to send the game into overtime or attempt a two point conversion by running or passing.

What is optimal? And what do coaches actually do? In 47 such incidences over the 10 years, the team kicked 42 times, which is 89% of the time. Teams who kicked won 40% of the games, which is below the average success rate for two point conversions which would have won the game rather than go into overtime. Of course, Some players like Brady and Big Ben are 90% which is much higher than the about 50% for two point conversions in the league.

The authors show that the ad hoc bias is also in NBA basketball. It is similar to the Belichick fourth down situation discussed above. They argue that the bias is involved with the tendency to treat problems in isolation rather than as part of a larger whole, that is, they are myopic. In lab experiments they found that decisions were uncorrelated with how teams would perform in overtime. The idea is to minimize the chance of losing now.

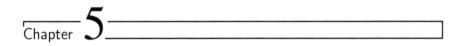
# Elo Team Strength Ratings: Two Versions

**The Swetye Elo Method: which team will win a given football game?**

Most sports have a significant home field advantage. It has to do with the shape of the playing surface, the players, not having to travel, the jet lag on the opponent and crowd noise. The last factor is extremely important as the loudness is extreme.

Our colleague John Swetye computes the Elo ratings. These are based on actual scores of team $i$ playing team $j$ adjusting for a home field bias and the final score. When favorites win, their ratings go up slowly, but when longshots win, their ratings improve more. Winning by a lot does not improve the score much above just winning. The idea comes from a chess rating system and 1000 is the base. Table 7.1 has these ratings for all the NFL teams as of December 22, 2009 and at 14 weeks, 17 weeks (end of regular season) and at the final post season. Both Indianapolis (14-0 in the AFC) and New Orleans (14-0 in the NFC) were undefeated after week 14. There were lots of discussions regarding two undefeated teams in the Super Bowl. Plus the fame to join the 1972 Miami Dolphins as a 17-0 undefeated Super Bowl winner — the only undefeated team in the full season through the Super Bowl. The argument is: do you rest players to go for a higher chance of winning the Super Bowl, assuming that resting helps more than not staying sharp, or go for greatness of an undefeated season?

Undefeated at the top level is very rare in all sports. Almost all the greatest competitors have had some losses. Yogi Berra, commenting on famed Dodger pitcher Sandy Koufax, said "I understand why he won 25 games but don't understand why he lost 3 games." Well, some opposing pitcher might have been better that day or he was off form or his team made errors or his team did not get enough runs. It is easy to lose. In horse racing it is similar. The two greatest race horses since 1900 in the US were Man O'War and Secretariat. Man O'War had all wins except one fluke loss. In that race he was not ready for the start and situated 4 lengths behind the starting position. A horse called Upset beat him by a nose. In all his 3-year-old races he either set the track record or world record in almost every race. Secretariat was horse of the year at two and three. In the Triple Crown he broke the track record in all three races and no horse has beaten his 1973 times since, yet he lost 5 of his 21 races. Tesio had three undefeated horses in Europe. Those plus Frankel, who ran recently, are all the undefeated horses in Europe if you use my rule: after 1900, at least ten races at the top level. The US had two undefeated horses, namely Colin in 1907 and Personal Ensign in 1988. Australia had one: the sprinter Black Cavier. See Ziemba (2018).

In the 2007-08 season, the New England Patriots started 16-0 not resting players. Tom Brady set the record with 50 touchdown passes and receiver Randy Moss caught 23 touchdown passes, also a record. With other great players on offense and defense, they looked invincible (much more impressive than Indianapolis and New Orleans that year). At the end of the season, the New York Giants, a good but not as impressive a team, instead of letting the Patriots swamp them they put up a strong fight but did lose in the end. So the Patriots were 16-0 and looked simply unbeatable. Nonetheless, they lost the Super Bowl to the Giants. Granted, it took a miraculous play but with rested players, the outcome might have been different as New England was not sharp at all.

Indianapolis and New Orleans rested players after they had clinched home field advantage throughout the playoffs and ended up 14-2 and 13-3, respectively. New Orleans, a dream team, was trying to undo the impact of Hurricane Katrina which destroyed much of New Orleans. We present the various estimates of the outcome of the game.

Indianapolis and New Orleans were the highest rated teams if you do not count the last three weeks. San Diego had the highest rating over the 17-week full regular season. They had 11 straight wins and were a major force but were eliminated when their pro-bowl nominated kicker, who was a perfect 16/16 in field goals under 40 yards, actually missed three field goals. These errors and bad scenarios were all over the playoffs. In the New Orleans-Minnesota game, Minnesota greatly outplayed New Orleans but five turnovers gave the game to New Orleans. Drew Brees, the great New Orleans quarterback, was not as sharp as usual. Meanwhile, Brett Farve, the 40-year-old Minnesota quarterback, outplayed him but in the end made an error. He was in position to go out of bounds and leave their kicker with an easy game winning field goal, but the punishment of the New Orleans defense wore him down physically and mentally so he regressed to a cowboy pass, which was intercepted. The New Orleans defensive players continually drove him to the ground so his was visibly tired near the end of the game. He is a very durable player but it seems that he should use the Peyton Manning approach to simply drop to the ground immediately after a pass is thrown so a running play executed. Then if he is hit which is less likely its a 15-yard roughing the passes penalty. That led to overtime and New Orleans won the coin toss then won the game on a field goal.

## The Swetye Elo Power Ratings for NFL teams

Empirical evidence suggests that the Swetye Elos are useful but do not predict as well as the 538 Elos which contains information from the previous year's results. These ratings are similar to Sagarin ratings. They are based on the physicist Arpad Elo's Chess ratings, but modified for football. They are "who-beat-who-where-by-how-much" ratings. This is the method our colleague John Swetye uses.[1]

Each team starts the season with 1000 points.

For each game the point differential is compiled using the scale:

1 point differential $= 1$
2 point differential $= 1.5$
3 or more point differential $= (11 + \text{GoalDiff}) / 8$

---

Next is a factor called "difference rating away" and "difference rating home" $=$ dra or drh. The home team gets 66.0979 points which is based on the fact that the home field advantage is worth 2.867 points and there were an average of 43.375 points per game based on 2008-09 data.

So $66.0979 = (2.768 / 43.375) \times 1000 =$ home field adjustment.
dra $=$ (Away Team's Elo Rating) - (Home Team's Elo Rating)
drh $=$ (Home Team's Elo Rating) - (Away Team's Elo Rating) + 66.0979

---

Next, the home and away expected results are calculated:

---

[1]Swetye provided help with the following explanation. See the websites: wikipedia.org/wiki/Elo_rating_system, and wikipedia.org/wiki/World_Football_Elo_Ratings describe the Elo ratings. See also wikipedia.org/wiki/Jeff_Sagarin.

$$AwayE = 1 \ / \ (10 \ \hat{} (-1 \ (dra \ / \ 200)) + 1)$$
$$HomeE = 1 \ / \ (10 \ \hat{} (-1 * (drh \ / \ 200)) + 1)$$

Finally, the ELO ratings for the home and away teams are calculated:

AwayW = 1 if the away team won and 0 if the away team lost
HomeW = 1 if the home team won and 0 if the home team lost

WeightIndex = WgtIndex = 5. In international soccer certain games are given different weights depending on their importance. John gives all NFL games the same weight.

EloAway = previous Elo rating for the away team

EloHome = previous Elo rating for the home team

EloRatingsA = EloAway + WgtIndex * IndexGoalDiff * (AwayW - AwayE)
EloRatingsH = EloHome + WgtIndex * IndexGoalDiff * (HomeW - HomeE)

## The 538 Elo Power Ratings for NFL teams

A good deal of FiveThirtyEight's NFL coverage on their website uses their Elo ratings, a simple system that estimates each team's skill level using only the final scores and locations of each game. As I have done in the past few years, we are using both Swetye's Elo and FiveThirtyEight-type Elo ratings to calculate NFL predictions that include win probabilities and point spreads for every game in this season's NFL schedule, as well as continually updating team rankings.

How do these other Elo ratings work? FiveThirtyEight editor-in-chief Nate Silver discussed their approach which we now summarize. Teams gain and lose ground based on the final score of each game and how unexpected the result was in the eyes of the pregame ratings. Under Elo, teams pick up where they left off: The initial team ratings for 2017 are by definition the same as last season's end-of-year ratings, only more compressed because of regression toward the mean. (Specifically, they regress each team's rating to the mean by one-third, with the league average team clocking in slightly above 1500.)

This is called James-Stein estimation where you blend the individual team performance with the average. It is a version of mean reversion and usually predicts better.

Going into Week 1, the Atlanta Falcons and New England Patriots were again the NFL's highest-rated teams, albeit with lower Elo ratings than when they faced off last season in Houston for Super Bowl LI. Why? Like other well-designed predictive rating systems, including ESPN's Football Power Index, Elo is appropriately cautious early in the season; a team must prove itself to warrant a very high or very low rating. Combine that with the luck inherent in the NFL — the best teams do not always win — and even the Patriots have only an 18 percent chance of winning Super Bowl 52 in February 2018. That forecast is actually quite high by Elo standards; indeed, it's the highest preseason Super Bowl win probability we have had since they began publishing these numbers. But 18% will seem conservative to the NFL fans who assume the Patriots have a 95.5% chance of winning the Super Bowl until Tom Brady retires or Bill Belichick resigns.

The following comments were adapted from the FiveThirtyEight website:

Elo does not reflect injuries or personnel changes, which helps explain why the forecast for the New York Jets, who spent the summer getting rid of all their players with talent, may seem rosy. Before the 2017-18 season, the Jets had a 17% chance of making the playoffs; that was very optimistic compared with the longshot odds that a Las Vegas sportsbook gave the Jets to win the Super Bowl (1,000-to-1!). Jets fans: Their Elo rating will catch up with them if they are as bad as billed.

**FiveThirtyEight: What are some of some of Elo's best qualities?:** Elo is simple, transparent and easy to work with. It can do a lot with a little, such as calculating point spreads and the probability of either team winning a game.

**Can I use Elo to beat Vegas?:** Silver said he would not try that. Vegas lines account for a much wider array of information than Elo's do. The 538 Elo's got about 51% of games against the point spread. That's not nearly enough to cover the house's cut, much less to make a living. In betting, this I argue that you can make gains and a living using mean reversion, risk arbitrage strategies and behavioral biases. We test this for the 2017-18 season in chapter 17. The ratings help you win games but are not enough to win money. To actually win money you have to use a strategy like mean reversion risk arbitrage which we use in the betting chapters.

**The Elo had the Seattle Seahawks favored by 10 points in their Thursday-night game against the Green Bay Packers, while Vegas has the Seahawks as six-point favorites instead.:** That's a perfect example. Has anything strange been going on with the Packers? Well, their star quarterback, Aaron Rodgers, was injured, came back for one game and is again on injured reserve. Elo only keeps track of the final scores, the dates of games and where the games were played not individual players.

**How can the Elo be used?**: The 538 Elos are a benchmark. Elo does a good job of accounting for wins and losses, margin of victory. Elo retains a memory from past seasons, so it knows that the Jacksonville Jaguars normally are not as likely to win the Super Bowl as the Denver Broncos although they were much better in 2017.

The parameter K tells us how much to update the ratings after each game. In a sport like baseball, where there are lots of games, any one additional game doesn't tell you all that much, so K takes on a low value. In the NFL, it's much higher. Specifically, it's 20. If you set K a lot higher than that, the Elo would move too much from game to game. And if you made K much lower, it would be too unresponsive to changes in the quality of team's play.

The Detroit Lions have an Elo rating of 1467. An average team has an Elo rating of 1500 — so the Lions are below average. But it could be worse. In 2009, the Lions got all the way down to a rating of 1223. Most NFL teams wind up in the range of 1300 to 1700.

If you have one team at 1650 and another at 1400, you can translate the Elo ratings into a point spread. Take the difference in the ratings and divide by 25. If one team is rated 250 higher, that means that the spread is 10.

Historically, home field advantage has been worth about 65 Elo ratings points or 2.6 NFL points.

In a game between Team A and Team B, Team A's win probability is

$$Pr(A) = 1/(10(-ELODIFF/400) + 1)$$

where ELODIFF is Team A's Elo rating minus Team B's Elo rating.

A team's Elo rating will always improve after it wins and always decline after it loses. How much it improves will depend on how much of a favorite or an underdog it was.

**An example was the 2008 Super Bowl**

The Elo did not have the New York Giants rated so highly compared to the New England Patriots. But the Giants' Elo rating improved a lot after they won that game — more than the Patriots' would have if they won instead. Elo has its flaws, but they can be fixed. The lower a team is rated, the easier for it to gain ground by winning.

For the NFL, the Elo adds one point to team's margin of victory and then take its natural logarithm. Then it multiplies that by the K value. This means that the Elo moves more with big wins rather than narrow ones, with diminishing returns. So Elo moves little with the fifth TD when a team is ahead 28-0.

Autocorrelation is the tendency of a time series to be related with its past and future values. If the Dallas Cowboys are rated at 1550 before a game against the Philadelphia Eagles, their rating will go up if they win and go down if they lose. But it averages 1550 after the game. If we expected the Cowboys' rating to rise to 1575 on average after the game, we would have had to rate them more highly before.

If the Cowboys were favored against the Eagles, they should win more often than they lose. Elo compensates by subtracting more points for a loss than I give them for a win.

The problem comes when the Elo accounts for margin of victory. Not only do favorites win more often, but when they do win, they tend to win by a larger margin. Since Elo gives more credit for larger wins, its ratings tend to get inflated over time. So you have to discount the margin of victory more when favorites win and increase it when underdogs win [using the formula]:

Margin of Victory Multiplier =
LN(ABS(PD)+1) * (2.2/((ELOW-ELOL)*.001+2.2))

Where PD is the point differential in the game, ELOW is the winning team's Elo Rating before the game, and ELOL is the losing team's Elo Rating before the game.

To begin the season, Elo takes their rating from the end of last season and James Stein adjusts it to revert to the mean by one-third. Since the mean Elo rating is 1500, a team finished last season with a rating of 1800, gets adjusted to 1700 when the new season begins.

A game's results affect Elo forever once it is played, just with a smaller and smaller weight that gradually diminishes over time. Games toward the end of the season count more, especially games during last year's playoffs.

## An educated guess that paid off

Betfair offered a C$1000 prize to the person or persons who correctly predicted the total passing yards in the 2010 Super Bowl for those who bet C$25 plus. So I entered the contest using some good advice from Randy

Robles of Elias Sports by way of my racing colleague John Swetye. The advice was "Brees will throw for 358 and Manning for only 263 (because he will not have to throw for much more)". So I submitted 621. The result was

| Manning | predicted | 263, | actual 333 |
|---------|-----------|------|------------|
| Brees   | predicted | 358, | actual 288 |
| Total   | predicted | 621, | actual 621 |

So I won. Randy and John can take the credit but it was nice to win and collect a prize.

## Elo ratings and the probability of winning

While the Elo rating system is a method for calculating the relative skill levels of teams in competitor-versus-competitor games, it can be used to generate probabilities of winning.

Performance is not measured absolutely; it is inferred from wins and losses for home and away teams. Team ratings depend on the ratings of their opponents, and the results scored against them at home and away.

The difference in rating between two teams determines an estimate for the expected score between them. A team's expected score is their probability of winning. Thus an expected score of 0.75 could represent a 75% chance of winning and a 25% chance of losing.

If team $A$ has a rating of $R_A$ and team $B$ a rating of $R_B$, the formula (using the logistic curve) for the expected score of team $A$ is

$$E_A = \frac{1}{1 + 10^{-(R_A - R_B)/400}}.$$

Similarly the expected score for team $B$ is

$$E_B = \frac{1}{1 + 10^{-(R_B - R_A)/400}},$$

where $E_A + E_B = 1$. In the Elo calculations the logistic curve has a base 10. The exponent is determined from team ratings rather than the performance against all teams.

In practice, since the true strength of each team is unknown, the expected scores are calculated using the teams' current ratings. When a team's actual scores exceed their expected scores, the Elo system takes this as evidence that team's rating is too low, and adjusts upward. Similarly when a game is below its expected score, that team's rating is adjusted downward. Elo's original suggestion, which is still widely used, was a simple linear adjustment proportional to the amount by which a player overperformed or underperformed their expected score. The maximum possible adjustment per game, called the K-factor, was set at $K = 16$ for strongest team and $K = 32$ for weakest team.

Supposing team $A$ has a chance of winning of $E_A$ but actually achieved $S_A$, where $S_A = 1$ for a win and $S_A = 0$ for a loss. The formula for updating their rating is

$$R'_A = R_A + K(S_A - E_A).$$

## Evaluating the Elo Ratings

So the big question is do these ratings add value? We evaluate the 538 Elo ratings in chapter 17 for the 2017-18 season. Here is how they did in the 2007-8 season.

Indianapolis was a 1-2 favorite to win the 2010 Super Bowl and you could get New Orleans +10.5 at the same odds.

Let's go through the playoffs just picking the team with the higher Elo rating and see how we would have done noting the favorite in each case using the end of season ratings unless the teams did not try the last few weeks, in which case I used the 14-week ratings.

| Game | | | Comment |
|---|---|---|---|
| Baltimore at New England | 1004.5 | 1010.8 | Ravens won as underdog |
| NY Jets at Cincinnati | 1020 | 984.2 | Jets won as favorite |
| Green Bay at Arizona | 1024.7 | 1004.1 | Cardinals underdog won |
| Philadelphia at Dallas | 1013 | 1034 | Cowboys won as favorite |

So it's 2-2 so far

| | | | |
|---|---|---|---|
| Baltimore at Indianapolis | 1004.5 | 1056.4 | favored Colts won |
| NY Jets at San Diego | 1020 | 1041.3 | underdog Jets won |
| Arizona at New Orleans | 1004.1 | 1065.2 | favorite Saints won |
| Dallas at Minnesota | 1034 | 1037.7 | favorite Vikings won |

Two easy wins, one upset, one hard to say. I bet Minnesota but they did not look good in the last three games — not so much resting so call the score 2-1 with one pass here. But the Elo is 3-1 as there is a home field advantage of 2.867 points. Then Minnesota would be favored by 6.567 points.

| NY Jets at Indianapolis | 1020 | 1056.4 | favored Colts won |
| Minnesota at New Orleans | 1037.7 | 1065.2 | favored Saints won |

Super Bowl

| Indianapolis vs New Orleans | 1056.4 | 1065.2 | underdog Saints (at Miami) won with the higher Elo |

So 3 of 3 for the Elo ratings in the Conference Championship and Super Bowl. So the Elo ratings did quite well!

# Chapter 6

# Analytical Tools: Arbitrage, mean reversion, risk arbitrage and the favorite-longshot bias

You can hedge bets as the odds change based on the current score and field position. My experience is that the sports betting market is more efficient than the financial markets, so therefore harder to beat. Of course, die hard efficient market types will like to forget that efficient markets has taken a severe beating in the 1987 and 2007-2009 stock market crashes. They simply cannot explain these events, nor the consistent high returns of some superior investors.[1]

Why are the sports betting markets more efficient? The reasons seem to be more sophisticated bettors and a simpler more well defined game. But there are many upsets and hedging when you are ahead is advisable because many leads evaporate quickly.

One thing that's innovative, challenging and fun and helpful in hedging is the wide variety of bets available and at odds determined by long/short players. For example, for the Super Bowl you can bet straight match odds plus the favorite, say Indianapolis, at +1 points and other amounts and the underdog, say New Orleans, at $+3$, $+4\frac{1}{2}$, $+5\frac{1}{2}$, $+6$, $+7$, ... $+10\frac{1}{2}$, etc. Each bet has reasonable tight bid-ask spreads so presumably represents the same stochastic process for the scores. But watch out, as things change fast. My experience is that these non-standard bets have wider bid-ask spreads than the straight match odds bets.

---

[1]See Ziemba's books, *Great investment ideas* and *Investing in the modern age* for analysis. Both are in paperback from World Scientific and Amazon.

On occasion, management needs to adjust the odds to encourage bettors to rebalance their bets to eliminate the imbalances akin to how Dublin book-makers do it. The places where there is too much long or short, the odds are made more favorable by rebalancing these wagers. Since the betting exchanges are not allowed to US bettors there will be a push to deregulate and expand this more sophisticated way of betting. After all, derivatives are very similar and they provide opportunities in the U.S. and the rest of the world.

## Review of arbitrage

Arbitrage in its pure form is to construct a sure bet so that no matter the outcome, you either break even or turn a profit. Most observers say that arbitrage does not exist but actually it does in many instances because there are different financial markets for the same sports betting or financial security situation. This is because different people have different sets of information and beliefs. Let's take the simplest case: either A or B wins. Let $O_{ah}$ be the odds given on the event that A wins from betting source $h$ and $O_{bi}$ that for B winning from betting source $i$. With these UK odds, the odds are the total return per 1 unit bet. In comparison, US odds are UK odds -1 and their payoffs are US odds +1 = UK odds.

Pure arbitrage exist when

$$(O_{ah} - 1)(O_{bi} - 1) \geqslant 1.$$

This is utility free and holds for all utility functions. Risk arbitrage, as discussed in the New Orleans-San Francisco game to follow, is to start with a bet on A and then get a B to satisfy the pure arbitrage condition.

A reference on this topic is Lane and Ziemba (2004) which has papers on many sports betting studies plus soccer and lotteries. This book, like all of mine, is available on Amazon and the World Scientific websites.

## Mean Reversion

The idea in mean reversion is that when prices move in one direction a large amount they often revert back. Poterba and Summers (1983) showed that US stocks tend to mean revert. The application in NFL betting is to use this mean reversion to create risk arbitrages.

In Betfair you have the great advantage of being able to bet continuously. So you can take advantage of the usual mean reversion in these games, that is, points reversals that create risk arbitrages. My usual method in a Thorpian-inspired fashion is to create an A-B trade where $(O_A)(O_B) \geqslant 1$

using British odds, so you cannot lose. So you go long A (your pick, usually the favorite) then you hope that A gets way ahead. Then you bet on B to get the risk arbitrage. See Lane and Ziemba (2004) for the technique. But if A gets behind you double up because A then has better odds. New England often gets behind but wins later in the game. If you double up you need A to rally. If it does not, you lose but most of the time they do rally. Since this is risky, it is risk arbitrage not arbitrage.

What you want for mean reversion is major lead changes that change the odds a lot so you can bet well and then gain when your team comes back. A good example was Seattle at Washington on wildcard weekend in 2016. Seattle had a good run but mostly won at home. It helps that Paul Allen of Microsoft fame, the Seahawks owner, built one of the noisiest stadium in the NFL. On the road, the Seahawks were weak. See chapter 4 on jet lag effects of west coast teams going east over two or more time zones and performing poorly. Thanks to RGIII, Washington grabbed an early 14-0 lead. A bet on Seattle then had very high odds behind a rookie quarterback. But RGIII, the great running and passing Washington quarterback,was known to be injured and probably should not have played. But he insisted that he play so the coach Mike Shanahan let him play. I won't get into the debate as to whether Shanahan should have overruled RGIII, especially as he looked more injured late in the game, but it was clear that this RGIII was still effective passing but not up to par running since he was hurt. A great risk was taken here focusing on short term gain forgetting about long run health of this franchise quarterback. Meanwhile, Russell Wilson, all 5 feet 11 of him, is cool in the clutch and led the comeback. His block helping great running back Marshan Lynch seal the game.

So mean reversion worked well in that game. My all time favorite with four lead changes in the last 3+ minutes is the 2012 San Francisco-New Orleans playoff game.

The analysis of the Green Bay at San Francisco shows Kaepernick won the game with some dynamic running as well as good passing. Fortunately, I was able to win using mean reversion even though I started out betting on Green Bay with San Francisco winning.

If teams get 21 or more points behind they will often come back but rarely win as the other team will score a bit more to win. There however, are tremendous odds here so in some rare instances it can work. But it is like buying a lotto ticket. Lots of hope but usually little return. The Seattle-Atlanta game and the Atlanta-New England Super Bowl 51 were such examples.

In 2012-13, Denver was rejuvenated by Peyton Manning's arrival. The four time league MVP had a neck injury that caused him to miss the entire 2011/12 season. Indianapolis did not want to pay him his $28 million salary given the uncertainty about his playing health for 2012/13 and drafted Andrew Luck. They had to pay Manning's 2011/12 salary and Indianapolis finished 11-5 and made the playoffs. Without Manning, the team went 2-14 and thus they got Luck in the draft as they then had the first pick and took Luck over RGIII who was close as a second pick. Luck was a good pick. Meanwhile, Denver was 8-8 in 2011/12 with Tim Tebow and did win the first round of the playoffs with a spectacular overtime pass from Tebow against Pittsburgh. However, director of football operations John Elway wanted a better passing quarterback and was able to sign Manning. It was not clear if Manning was all right health wise and high level football-wise. But after a 2-3 start, Denver won its next eleven games to finish 13-3. They were a 1.27 favorite on Betfair. but lost the game.

## Review of the favorite-longshot bias

The favorite longshot bias first found in racetrack betting,[2] is one of the most useful results for bettors in sports markets of many types and in the stock market, especially in options markets. The idea is simple: favorites are underbet and longshots are over bet. Daniel Kahneman working with the late Amos Tversky won the Nobel prize in 2002 with this idea plus their approach to the study of real world decisions through experiments and concepts like framing, availability, loss aversion, etc. They formalized the economic theory of this bias and showed how to use it in several contexts outside sports or financial betting. This bias was known to bookmakers for the past 100 years. Indeed, bookmakers regularly change the odds to create this bias and the chalk on their boards is mostly on the favorites. Figure 6.1 from Ziemba and Hausch (1986) *Betting at the Racetrack* shows the bias. This graph is based on about 300,000 horses running in races up to 1986. Other graphs in Ziemba and Hausch (1986) going back to the 1940s, in the UK and elsewhere, are similar. See also Ziemba (2015).

Observe that there actually was a small profit in betting horses to win at US odds of 3-10 (UK odds of 1.30 or less) and that at odds of 100-1, the fair odds are about 700-1 so that such bets were worth about 13.7 cents per dollar bet. The California and New York graphs differ because of different track takes. The advent of betting exchanges particularly the

---

[2]See Hausch, Lo and Ziemba (1994, 2008) for the early studies dating at least to 1947 and Ziemba and Hausch (2008) and Ziemba (2018) for more recent studies of the favorite-longshot bias and other topics.

biggest most user friendly one, Betfair, plus rebate shops for large bettors and other changes in the betting procedures has led to a shifting of this graph. Figures 6.1-6.3 show the bias based on more recent data. Observe the important fact that favorites are no longer underbet enough to turn a profit betting them and the flatness of the curve until you get to fairly long priced horses. You can still short longshots on Betfair and make a profit if you are careful.

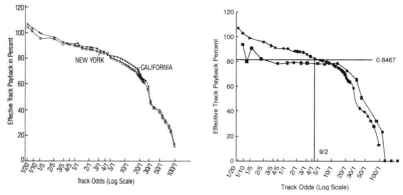

(a) California and New York for 300,000 (b) California Source: Ziemba and Hausch plus races over various years and tracks. (1986) and Ziemba (2008)
Source: Ziemba and Hausch (1986)

Figure 6.1: The effective track payback less breakage for various odds levels

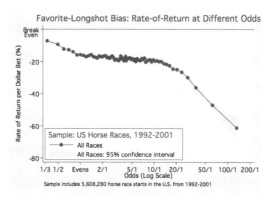

Figure 6.2: The Favorite-Longshot Bias, 1992-2001. Source: Snowberg and Wolfers (2008)

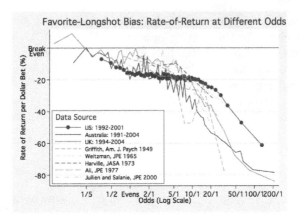

Figure 6.3: Various favorite-longshot bias studies. Source: Snowberg and Wolfers (2008)

# Chapter 7

# How the Playoffs are organized and the 2009-2010 Playoffs and Super Bowl

## How the playoffs work

The rules for assigning future games are in Figure 7.1; basically the higher rated teams get to play the lower rated teams still alive in the playoffs.

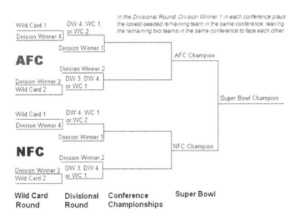

Figure 7.1: The playoffs. Source: Wikipedia

There are 32 teams in eight groups of four teams each. The American conference, the old AFL, has East, South, North and West and so does the National Conference. The preseason has five games, which are tests for teams to get ready. Since the teams do not want to risk injury, these games are hard to predict. The league gives the high draft picks each year to the weakest teams to try to even out their abilities.

During the 17-week season, each team plays 16 games. The winners of each of the eight sections automatically make the playoffs. Four additional teams (two from each conference) are wild cards making up the total of 12 teams. Teams with the best records get home field advantage in one or all games in the playoffs.

> The first round of the playoffs is dubbed the Wild Card Playoffs (the league in recent years has also used the term Wild Card Weekend). In this round, the third-seeded division winner hosts the sixth seed wild card, and the fourth seed hosts the fifth. The first and second seeds from each conference receive a bye in the first round, which entitles these teams to automatic advancement to the second round, the Divisional Playoffs, where they face the Wild Card Weekend survivors. Unlike the NBA, the NFL does not use predetermined brackets. In the second round of the playoffs, the top seed hosts the lowest surviving seed, while the other two teams pair off. The two surviving teams from each conference's Divisional Playoff games meet in the respective AFC and NFC Conference Championship games, with the winners of those contests going on to face one another in the Super Bowl. Only twice since 1990 has neither a number one-seeded team nor a number two-seeded team hosted a conference championship game (the 2006 AFC Championship and the 2008 NFC Championship).

The winner of each conference plays in the Super Bowl. Given this playoff structure and probabilities of winning at home and away for each i,j combination, one can, as we have done in hockey, compute fair odds of advancing in the playoffs. WTZ set the line in hockey for the BC Lottery Commission and made such calculations. The NFL is similar.

## The 2010 NFL Super Bowl

The NFL Super Bowl game in 2010 was in Miami. The event has expanded and expanded. A 30 second commercial costs almost $3 million in 2010 and, in 2018, it rose to $5 million. The pomp lasts all week with the game important but only a part of the activity. Sports betting is simply another financial market. But it's a big one with $50 billion plus bet in Las Vegas and much more in other places. I focus on the betting exchange Betfair in London which allows short as well as long bets. Betfair has British odds so 3-1 means you bet one to collect three if you win and lose one if you lose. That's US 2-1 where you bet 1, win 2, and collect 3.

Table 7.1: Evolution of the Swetye Elo ratings, December 22, 2009 to Post Season 2010

| December 22 | | Up to Week 14 | | End Regular Season | | Final Post Season | |
|---|---|---|---|---|---|---|---|
| Arizona | 1017.8 | Arizona | 1004.8 | Arizona | 1004.1 | Arizona | 997 |
| Atlanta | 986.4 | Atlanta | 977.7 | Atlanta | 996.8 | Atlanta | 996.8 |
| Baltimore | 1005.2 | Baltimore | 1006.1 | Baltimore | 1004.5 | Baltimore | 1006.1 |
| Buffalo | 947.6 | Buffalo | 958.3 | Buffalo | 951.1 | Buffalo | 951.1 |
| Carolina | 978.7 | Carolina | 964.4 | Carolina | 1000.6 | Carolina | 1000.6 |
| Chicago | 956.8 | Chicago | 959.4 | Chicago | 968 | Chicago | 968 |
| Cincinnati | 1012.5 | Cincinnati | 1007.7 | Cincinnati | 984.2 | Cincinnati | 989.5 |
| Cleveland | 924.3 | Cleveland | 918.1 | Cleveland | 934.5 | Cleveland | 934.5 |
| Dallas | 1022.4 | Dallas | 1009.7 | Dallas | 1034 | Dallas | 1024.6 |
| Denver | 991.7 | Denver | 993.7 | Denver | 972.2 | Denver | 972.2 |
| Detroit | 926.8 | Detroit | 920.9 | Detroit | 912 | Detroit | 912 |
| Green Bay | 1006.2 | Green Bay | 1019.2 | Green Bay | 1024.7 | Green Bay | 1018.8 |
| Houston | 986.1 | Houston | 990.3 | Houston | 995.9 | Houston | 995.9 |
| Indianapolis | 1056.3 | Indianapolis | 1056.4 | Indianapolis | 1027.1 | Indianapolis | 1026.2 |
| Jacksonville | 970.8 | Jacksonville | 969 | Jacksonville | 955.1 | Jacksonville | 955.1 |
| Kansas City | 927.3 | Kansas City | 928.7 | Kansas City | 937.3 | Kansas City | 937.3 |
| Miami | 981.6 | Miami | 990.6 | Miami | 967.4 | Miami | 967.4 |
| Minnesota | 1019.7 | Minnesota | 1037.7 | Minnesota | 1019.7 | Minnesota | 1025.4 |
| New England | 1011.7 | New England | 1010.8 | New England | 1010.8 | New England | 997.7 |
| New Orleans | 1053.9 | New Orleans | 1065.2 | New Orleans | 1036.4 | New Orleans | 1052.9 |
| NY Giants | 998.4 | NY Giants | 980.5 | NY Giants | 966.7 | NY Giants | 966.7 |
| NY Jets | 990.2 | NY Jets | 1002.9 | NY Jets | 1020 | NY Jets | 1015.4 |
| Oakland | 949.1 | Oakland | 930.3 | Oakland | 934 | Oakland | 934 |
| Philadelphia | 1021.6 | Philadelphia | 1022.7 | Philadelphia | 1013 | Philadelphia | 1004.5 |
| Pittsburgh | 994.4 | Pittsburgh | 988.3 | Pittsburgh | 1002 | Pittsburgh | 1002 |
| San Diego | 1032.5 | San Diego | 1034 | San Diego | 1041.3 | San Diego | 1034.8 |
| San Francisco | 969.3 | San Francisco | 982.1 | San Francisco | 979.4 | San Francisco | 979.4 |
| Seattle | 958.1 | Seattle | 960.8 | Seattle | 940.9 | Seattle | 940.9 |
| St. Louis | 911.6 | St. Louis | 905.1 | St. Louis | 896.7 | St. Louis | 896.7 |
| Tampa Bay | 934.9 | Tampa Bay | 913.6 | Tampa Bay | 934.7 | Tampa Bay | 934.7 |
| Tennessee | 976.1 | Tennessee | 979.2 | Tennessee | 968.5 | Tennessee | 968.5 |
| Washington | 937.9 | Washington | 963.7 | Washington | 928.2 | Washington | 928.2 |

## Super Bowl Playoff Ratings

Indianapolis and New Orleans rested players after they had clinched home field advantage throughout the playoffs and ended up 14-2 and 13-3, respectively. New Orleans, a dream team, was trying to undo the impact of Hurricane Katrina which destroyed much of New Orleans. So we present here the various estimates of the outcome of the game.

Indianapolis and New Orleans were the highest rated teams if you do not count the last three weeks. San Diego had the highest rating over the 17-week full regular season. They had 11 straight wins and were a major force but were eliminated when their pro-bowl nominated kicker, who was a perfect 16/16 in field goals under 40 yards, actually missed three field goals. These errors and bad scenarios were all over the playoffs. In the New Orleans-Minnesota game, Minnesota greatly outplayed New Orleans but five turnovers gave the game to New Orleans. Drew Brees, the great New Orleans quarterback, was not as sharp as usual. Meanwhile, Brett Farve, the 40-year-old Minnesota quarterback, outplayed him but in the end made an error. He was in position to go out of bounds and leave their kicker with an easy game winning field goal, but the punishment of the New Orleans defense wore him down physically and mentally so he regressed to a cowboy pass, which was intercepted. The New Orleans defensive players continually drove him to the ground so his was visibly tired near the end of the game. He is a very durable player but it seems that he should use the Peyton Manning approach to simply drop to the ground immediately after a pass is thrown or a running play is executed. Then if he is hit, which is less likely, it is a 15-yard roughing the passer penalty. The game went into overtime and New Orleans won the coin toss then won the game on a field goal.

So the big question is do these ratings add value? Well Indianapolis was a 1-2 favorite to win the 2010 Super Bowl and you could get New Orleans +10.5 at the same odds.

Figure 7.2 is the playoff tree for 2010. I bet on all of these games and follow the teams, players, injuries, etc. The betting during the regular season is easier with the favorite-longshot bias being quite helpful. Most of the game outcomes make sense but there are occasional upsets. And the difference between the better teams and the weaker teams is frequently hard to estimate. The playoffs are definitely more challenging and especially so in 2010.

Figure 7.2: The playoff tree, 2010

So let's go through the playoffs just picking the team with the higher Elo rating and see how we would have done noting the favorite in each case. I used the end of season ratings unless the teams did not try the last few weeks, in which case I used the 14-week ratings.

| Game | | | Comment |
|---|---|---|---|
| Baltimore at New England | 1004.5 | 1010.8 | Ravens won as underdog |
| NY Jets at Cinnicinatti | 1020 | 984.2 | Jets won as favorite |
| Green Bay at Arizona | 1024.7 | 1004.1 | Cardinals won as underdog |
| Philadelphia at Dallas | 1013 | 1034 | Cowboys won as favorite |

So it's 2-2 so far

| | | | |
|---|---|---|---|
| Baltimore at Indianapolis | 1004.5 | 1056.4 | favored Colts won |
| NY Jets at San Diego | 1020 | 1041.3 | underdog Jets won |
| Arizona at New Orleans | 1004.1 | 1065.2 | favorite Saints won |
| Dallas at Minnesota | 1034 | 1037.7 | favorite Vikings won |

Two easy wins, one upset, one hard to say. I bet Minnesota but they did not look good in the last three games — not so much resting so call the score 2-1 with one pass here. But the Elo is 3-1 as there is a home field advantage of 2.867 points. Then Minnesota would be favored by 6.567 points.

| | | | |
|---|---|---|---|
| NY Jets at Indianapolis | 1020 | 1056.4 | favored Colts won |
| Minnesota at New Orleans | 1037.7 | 1065.2 | favored Saints won |

Super Bowl

| | | | |
|---|---|---|---|
| Indianapolis vs New Orleans | 1056.4 | 1065.2 | underdog Saints won |
| (at Miami) | | | with the higher Elo |

So 3 of 3 for the Elo ratings in the Conference Championship and Super Bowl. So the Elo ratings did quite well!

# Chapter 8

# The 2010-2011 Playoffs and the Super Bowl

## The playoffs

The Swetye Elo ratings, which are based on actual scores, wins and losses and, adjusting for home field advantage, did quite well in 2009/10. The rankings start the year at 1000 and move up and down as the season progresses. There are 16 games for each team played over 17 weeks, some 256 total games for the 32 teams. Then there are the playoffs of the 12 teams that make the playoffs. Figure 8.1 shows the results for the 12 playoff teams. The results of the playoffs are in Table 8.1 with an analysis of the predictive ability of the ELO ratios.

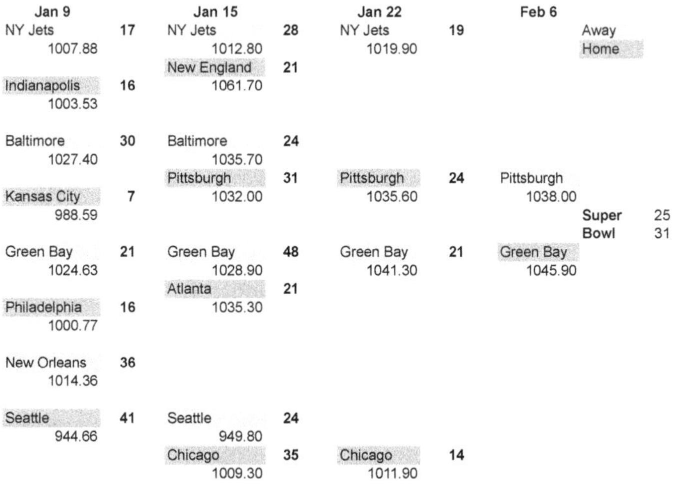

| Jan 9 | | Jan 15 | | Jan 22 | | Feb 6 | | | |
|---|---|---|---|---|---|---|---|---|---|
| NY Jets | 17 | NY Jets | 28 | NY Jets | 19 | | | Away | |
| 1007.88 | | 1012.80 | | 1019.90 | | | | Home | |
| | | New England | 21 | | | | | | |
| Indianapolis | 16 | 1061.70 | | | | | | | |
| 1003.53 | | | | | | | | | |
| Baltimore | 30 | Baltimore | 24 | | | | | | |
| 1027.40 | | 1035.70 | | | | | | | |
| | | Pittsburgh | 31 | Pittsburgh | 24 | Pittsburgh | | | |
| Kansas City | 7 | 1032.00 | | 1035.60 | | 1038.00 | | | |
| 988.59 | | | | | | | | Super | 25 |
| | | | | | | | | Bowl | 31 |
| Green Bay | 21 | Green Bay | 48 | Green Bay | 21 | Green Bay | | | |
| 1024.63 | | 1028.90 | | 1041.30 | | 1045.90 | | | |
| | | Atlanta | 21 | | | | | | |
| Philadelphia | 16 | 1035.30 | | | | | | | |
| 1000.77 | | | | | | | | | |
| New Orleans | 36 | | | | | | | | |
| 1014.36 | | | | | | | | | |
| Seattle | 41 | Seattle | 24 | | | | | | |
| 944.66 | | 949.80 | | | | | | | |
| | | Chicago | 35 | Chicago | 14 | | | | |
| | | 1009.30 | | 1011.90 | | | | | |

Figure 8.1: ELO ratings for the 12 playoff teams and the outcomes

Table 8.1: Analysis of Predictions

January 9

| 1 | NY Jets at Indianapolis | ELO got it right, the ELO scores were close given the about 3 point home home field adjustment |
|---|---|---|
| 2 | Baltimore at Kansas City | ELO got it right |
| 3 | New Orleans at Seattle | ELO failed, big upset |
| 4 | Green Bay at Philadelphia | ELO got it right |

3 right, 1 wrong

January 14, 15

| 1 | NY Jets at New England | ELO failed |
|---|---|---|
| 2 | Baltimore at Pittsburgh | very close ELO with home field adjustment, I bet Pittsburgh but there was no ELO call |
| 3 | Seattle at Chicago | ELO got it right |
| 4 | Green Bay at Atlanta | ELO got it wrong (I bet on Green Bay with points |

1 right, 2 wrong, 1 no call

January 22

| 1 | NY Jets at Pittsburgh | ELO got it rightm Pittsburg won 24-19 |
|---|---|---|
| 2 | Green Bay at Chicago | ELO got it rightk Green Bay won 21-14 |

2 right

February 6, the Super Bowl

Green Bay vs Pittsburgh    ELO got it right, Green Bay won 31-25

So in total it was 7 right and 3 wrong for the ELO rankings.

The ELO ratings with Green Bay at 1045.9 and Pittsburgh at 1038.4 made Green Bay the favorite for the February 6, 2011 Super Bowl. The odds in Betfair and at various odds makers in Las Vegas and elsewhere all agree with Green Bay a 2.5 point favorite and the shorter priced option in the betting. ELO got the Super Bowl right when Green Bay beat Pittsburgh yesterday by 31-25. Three Pittsburgh turnovers and three touchdowns with no interceptions by Green Bay MVP quarterback Aaron Rodgers was the difference. See Figure 8.2 for the top teams and Table 8.2 for the final ELO rankings for all 32 teams.

I was well positioned for the Super Bowl ranking the teams New England first, Pittsburgh second and Green Bay third. I would have a nice gain no

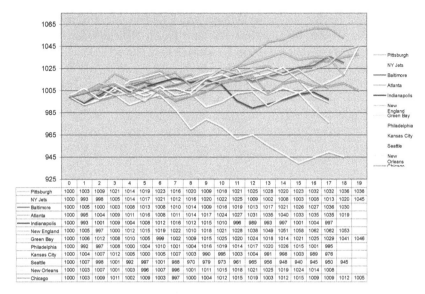

| | 0 | 1 | 2 | 3 | 4 | 5 | 6 | 7 | 8 | 9 | 10 | 11 | 12 | 13 | 14 | 15 | 16 | 17 | 18 | 19 |
|---|---|---|---|---|---|---|---|---|---|---|---|---|---|---|---|---|---|---|---|---|
| Pittsburgh | 1000 | 1003 | 1009 | 1021 | 1014 | 1019 | 1023 | 1016 | 1020 | 1009 | 1018 | 1021 | 1025 | 1028 | 1020 | 1023 | 1032 | 1032 | 1036 | 1038 |
| NY Jets | 1000 | 993 | 998 | 1005 | 1014 | 1017 | 1021 | 1012 | 1016 | 1020 | 1022 | 1025 | 1009 | 1002 | 1008 | 1003 | 1008 | 1013 | 1020 | 1045 |
| Baltimore | 1000 | 1005 | 1000 | 1003 | 1008 | 1013 | 1008 | 1010 | 1014 | 1009 | 1016 | 1019 | 1013 | 1017 | 1021 | 1026 | 1027 | 1036 | 1030 | |
| Atlanta | 1000 | 995 | 1004 | 1009 | 1011 | 1016 | 1008 | 1011 | 1014 | 1017 | 1024 | 1027 | 1031 | 1035 | 1040 | 1033 | 1035 | 1035 | 1019 | |
| Indianapolis | 1000 | 993 | 1001 | 1009 | 1004 | 1008 | 1012 | 1016 | 1012 | 1015 | 1010 | 996 | 989 | 993 | 997 | 1001 | 1004 | 997 | | |
| New England | 1000 | 1005 | 997 | 1000 | 1012 | 1015 | 1019 | 1022 | 1010 | 1018 | 1021 | 1028 | 1038 | 1049 | 1051 | 1058 | 1062 | 1062 | 1053 | |
| Green Bay | 1000 | 1006 | 1012 | 1008 | 1010 | 1005 | 999 | 1002 | 1009 | 1015 | 1025 | 1020 | 1024 | 1018 | 1014 | 1021 | 1025 | 1029 | 1041 | 1046 |
| Philadelphia | 1000 | 992 | 997 | 1008 | 1000 | 1004 | 1010 | 1001 | 1004 | 1016 | 1019 | 1014 | 1017 | 1020 | 1026 | 1015 | 1001 | 995 | | |
| Kansas City | 1000 | 1004 | 1007 | 1012 | 1005 | 1000 | 1005 | 1007 | 1003 | 990 | 995 | 1003 | 1004 | 991 | 998 | 1003 | 989 | 978 | | |
| Seattle | 1000 | 1007 | 998 | 1001 | 992 | 997 | 1001 | 988 | 970 | 979 | 973 | 961 | 965 | 956 | 948 | 940 | 945 | 950 | 945 | |
| New Orleans | 1000 | 1003 | 1007 | 1001 | 1003 | 996 | 1007 | 996 | 1001 | 1011 | 1015 | 1018 | 1021 | 1025 | 1019 | 1024 | 1014 | 1008 | | |
| Chicago | 1000 | 1003 | 1009 | 1011 | 1002 | 1009 | 1003 | 997 | 1000 | 1004 | 1012 | 1015 | 1019 | 1003 | 1012 | 1015 | 1009 | 1009 | 1012 | 1005 |

Figure 8.2: ELO ratings for the 12 playoff teams in 2010-2011

Table 8.2: Final ELO ratings for all teams

| Arizona | 928.0 | Miami | 963.3 |
|---|---|---|---|
| Atlanta | 1018.8 | Minnesota | 953.9 |
| Baltimore | 1029.9 | New England | 1052.8 |
| Buffalo | 933.6 | New Orleans | 1007.5 |
| Carolina | 903.9 | NY Giants | 1000.1 |
| Chicago | 1005.1 | NY Jets | 1015.4 |
| Cincinnati | 948.2 | Oakland | 991.2 |
| Cleveland | 952.1 | Philadelphia | 994.6 |
| Dallas | 965.7 | Pittsburgh | 1038.4 |
| Denver | 923.6 | San Diego | 1006.7 |
| Detroit | 973.3 | San Francisco | 961.3 |
| Green Bay | 1045.9 | Seattle | 945.2 |
| Houston | 957.8 | St Louis | 959.7 |
| Indianapolis | 996.8 | Tampa | 997.2 |
| Jacksonville | 963.6 | Tennessee | 965.8 |
| Kansas City | 976.3 | Washington | 953.0 |

matter who won this tough matchup. These bets were made well before the game with odds at 8-1 to 18-1. New England, my top pick and the favorite was still the top rated team. But they were out, having lost to the NY

Jets. A factor in that loss was the benching for just one set of downs of top receiver Wes Welker by the New England coach Belichick for statements responding to trash talk from the Jets coach and players. Belichick had his players take the high road and not respond. But in that first set of downs there was a Tom Brady interception — a rare event as he had close to 350 passes with no interceptions. This got New England off to a bad start from which they never recovered. So again intangibles affect results!

# Chapter 9

# The 2011-2012 Playoffs and the Super Bowl

## Week 9, 2011–2012 season

Figures 9.1 show the evolution of the Elo ratings for the 2011-2012 NFL season. Table 9.1 has the current standings. Table 9.2 has the picks with two games too close to call. We will see how they perform in week 9.

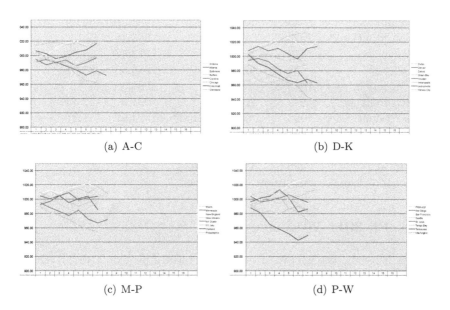

(a) A-C      (b) D-K

(c) M-P      (d) P-W

Figure 9.1: Evolution of Elo ratings 2011-12 NFL season

Table 9.1: Current standing, week 9

(a) AFC                          (b) NFC                          (c) Week 9 games

| AFC | W | L | T | Pct | PF | PA |
|---|---|---|---|---|---|---|
| **East** | **W** | **L** | **T** | **Pct** | **PF** | **PA** |
| Buffalo | 5 | 2 | 0 | .714 | 211 | 147 |
| New England | 5 | 2 | 0 | .714 | 202 | 160 |
| New York | 4 | 3 | 0 | .571 | 172 | 152 |
| Miami | 0 | 7 | 0 | .000 | 107 | 166 |
| **West** | **W** | **L** | **T** | **Pct** | **PF** | **PA** |
| Kansas City | 4 | 3 | 0 | .571 | 128 | 170 |
| San Diego | 4 | 3 | 0 | .571 | 161 | 159 |
| Oakland | 4 | 3 | 0 | .571 | 160 | 178 |
| Denver | 2 | 5 | 0 | .286 | 133 | 200 |
| **North** | **W** | **L** | **T** | **Pct** | **PF** | **PA** |
| Pittsburgh | 6 | 2 | 0 | .750 | 176 | 139 |
| Cincinnati | 5 | 2 | 0 | .714 | 171 | 123 |
| Baltimore | 5 | 2 | 0 | .714 | 185 | 110 |
| Cleveland | 3 | 4 | 0 | .429 | 107 | 140 |
| **South** | **W** | **L** | **T** | **Pct** | **PF** | **PA** |
| Houston | 5 | 3 | 0 | .625 | 206 | 145 |
| Tennessee | 4 | 3 | 0 | .571 | 139 | 145 |
| Jacksonville | 2 | 6 | 0 | .250 | 98 | 163 |
| Indianapolis | 0 | 8 | 0 | .000 | 121 | 252 |

| NFC | W | L | T | Pct | PF | PA |
|---|---|---|---|---|---|---|
| **East** | **W** | **L** | **T** | **Pct** | **PF** | **PA** |
| New York | 5 | 2 | 0 | .714 | 174 | 164 |
| Philadelphia | 3 | 4 | 0 | .429 | 179 | 152 |
| Dallas | 3 | 4 | 0 | .429 | 156 | 162 |
| Washington | 3 | 4 | 0 | .429 | 116 | 139 |
| **West** | **W** | **L** | **T** | **Pct** | **PF** | **PA** |
| San Francisco | 6 | 1 | 0 | .857 | 187 | 107 |
| Seattle | 2 | 5 | 0 | .286 | 109 | 162 |
| Arizona | 1 | 6 | 0 | .143 | 143 | 183 |
| St. Louis | 1 | 6 | 0 | .143 | 87 | 192 |
| **North** | **W** | **L** | **T** | **Pct** | **PF** | **PA** |
| Green Bay | 7 | 0 | 0 | 1.000 | 230 | 141 |
| Detroit | 6 | 2 | 0 | .750 | 239 | 147 |
| Chicago | 4 | 3 | 0 | .571 | 170 | 150 |
| Minnesota | 2 | 6 | 0 | .250 | 172 | 199 |
| **South** | **W** | **L** | **T** | **Pct** | **PF** | **PA** |
| New Orleans | 5 | 3 | 0 | .625 | 260 | 189 |
| Tampa Bay | 4 | 3 | 0 | .571 | 131 | 169 |
| Atlanta | 4 | 3 | 0 | .571 | 158 | 163 |
| Carolina | 2 | 6 | 0 | .250 | 187 | 207 |

**WEEK 9**
**Sunday's Games**
N.Y. Jets at Buffalo, 10 a.m.
Tampa Bay at New Orleans, 10 a.m.
Atlanta at Indianapolis, 10 a.m.
Seattle at Dallas, 10 a.m.
Miami at Kansas City, 10 a.m.
San Francisco at Washington, 10 a.m.
Cleveland at Houston, 10 a.m.
Denver at Oakland, 1:05 p.m.
Cincinnati at Tennessee, 1:05 p.m.
St. Louis at Arizona, 1:15 p.m.
N.Y. Giants at New England, 1:15 p.m.
Green Bay at San Diego, 1:15 p.m.
Baltimore at Pittsburgh, 5:20 p.m.
**Monday's Game**
Chicago at Philadelphia, 5:30 p.m.
**Bye Week:** Carolina, Detroit, Jacksonville, Minnesota.

Table 9.2: ELO ratings and picks, Week 9, Elo Pick *

| Away | | Home | | Difference |
|---|---|---|---|---|
| NY Jets | 998.51 | Buffalo* | 1018.14 | -19.63 |
| Tampa Bay | 982.93 | New Orleans* | 1007.70 | -24.77 |
| Atlanta* | 996.61 | Indianapolis | 936.52 | 60.08 |
| Seattle | 969.43 | Dallas* | 985.50 | -16.07 |
| Miami | 954.22 | Kansas City* | 988.30 | -34.09 |
| San Francisco* | 1028.59 | Washington | 983.45 | 45.14 |
| Cleveland | 979.85 | Houston* | 1013.47 | -33.62 |
| Denver | 962.78 | Oakland* | 985.30 | -22.51 |
| Cincinnati* | 1016.40 | Tennessee | 986.30 | 30.10 |
| St. Louis | 949.55 | Arizona* | 961.99 | -12.44 |
| NY Giants | 1003.55 | New England* | 1014.92 | -11.37 |
| Green Bay* | 1034.16 | San Diego | 995.68 | 38.48 |
| Baltimore | 1016.32 | Pittsburgh | 1013.38 | nc |
| Chicago | 998.62 | Philadelphia | 996.05 | nc |

nc: too close even with home advantage

## Week 12, 2011–2012 season

Figures 9.2 show the evolution of the Elo ratings for the 2011-2012 NFL season through week 12. Table 9.3 has the ratings of all the teams through week 12.

In the NFL the home field advantage is worth about 2.87 football points. That translates to 0.68 Elo points. So 0.68 points ($\approx 0.7$) points should

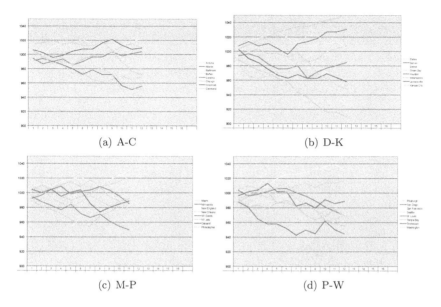

(a) A-C                                        (b) D-K

(c) M-P                                        (d) P-W

Figure 9.2: Evolution of Elo ratings 2011-12 NFL season, Week 12

Table 9.3: Elo ratings through week 12 for games in week 13

| Team | ELO | Team | ELO | Team | ELO |
|------|-----|------|-----|------|-----|
| Arizona | 969 | Green Bay | 1052 | Oakland | 989 |
| Atlanta | 1004 | Houston | 1031 | Philadelphia | 978 |
| Baltimore | 1022 | Indianapolis | 909 | Pittsburgh | 1017 |
| Buffalo | 972 | Jacksonville | 958 | San Diego | 970 |
| Carolina | 956 | Kansas City | 948 | San Francisco | 1032 |
| Chicago | 1009 | Miami | 976 | Seattle | 969 |
| Cincinnati | 1009 | Minnesota | 950 | St. Louis | 945 |
| Cleveland | 950 | New England | 1031 | Tampa Bay | 955 |
| Dallas | 1007 | New Orleans | 1022 | Tennessee | 989 |
| Denver | 985 | NY Giants | 985 | Washington | 970 |
| Detroit | 1005 | NY Jets | 992 | | |

be added to the home team's Elo rating. In the calculations 0.7 is added to the Elo ratings for the home teams. We use this as an approximation and, as we proceed, we will study if certain teams have a larger home field advantage. This, however, is statistically tricky with little data and may not improve on the 0.7. Some candidates are Seattle (loudest stadium), Denver (mile high), New England, and New Orleans.

We begin with a recap of results of week 9 for the Elo picks with John pointing out that even though I felt that the Baltimore/Pittsburgh and Chicago/Philadelphia games were too close to call to bet, the Elo rating did win on both games. Adding 0.7 to Pittsburgh and Philadelphia still gave the advantage to Baltimore and Chicago which won.

There were 8 wins and 4 losses. WTZ's betfair account had a small gain- remember I have to pay a commission when I win so the picks need to be good enough to cover that. Adding these two close games makes it 10 wins to 4 losses.

The winners in week 9 were Tampa Bay 16 losing to pick New Orleans 27. They are really strong and, in addition to having a great quarterback, they are excellent at creating turnovers.

| | |
|---|---|
| Atlanta 31 Indianapolis 7 | Peyton must be sick seeing this |
| San Francisco 19 Washington 11 | Harbaugh going for top coach |
| Houston 30 Cleveland 12 | They are almost a top team |
| Cincinnati 24 Tennessee 17 | ELO pick good<br>Cincinnati the Betfair odds underdog |
| Arizona 19 St Louis 13 | St Louis weak again after fluke<br>New Orleans win |
| Green Bay 45 San Diego 38 | Packers defense did not look good<br>Philip Rivers had a big day passing<br>despite losing. He can be great<br>except for turnovers |
| Seattle 13 to Dallas 23 | Dallas another almost good team<br>where is Tom Landry? |

and the losers:

| | |
|---|---|
| NY Jets 27 Buffalo 11 | Jets have been underachieving<br>Buffalo overachieving |
| Miami 31 Kansas City 3 | Reggie Bush looks strong |
| Denver 38 Oakland 24 | Oakland did not have McFadden<br>Tim Tebow was strong again |
| NY Giants 24 New England | New England defense looked awful<br>Brady was a bit off<br>Manning looked good |

Baltimore-Pittsburgh a good game to watch, but ELO is a tie
Chicago-Philadelphia interesting as well [see above]

Jason Cole who is a good picker got 2 of 3 Texas over Cleveland San Francisco over Washington but lost the Oakland game to Denver

Recall, the Elo does seem to be terrific in the playoffs.

## Week 13: Games and predictions

Table 9.4 has the current Elos for the various games and the inferred Elo probabilities of winning. Table 9.5, for comparison, has spreads and their inferred probabilities. See how the model blows up on the NE/Indianapolis game in the tail. Table 9.6 has the standings.

Table 9.4: Elo for the week 13 games and the probabilities that the away and home teams win. Elo picks *.

| Away | | Home | | ELO Diff | PA | PH |
|------|------|------|------|------|------|------|
| Philadelphia* | 978 | Seattle | 969 | 9.00 | 0.56 | 0.44 |
| Indianapolis | 909 | New England* | 1031 | -122.00 | 0.20 | 0.80 |
| Denver* | 985 | Minnesota | 951 | 34.00 | 0.60 | 0.40 |
| Tennessee* | 988 | Buffalo | 973 | 15.00 | 0.55 | 0.45 |
| Oakland* | 989 | Miami | 976 | 13.00 | 0.54 | 0.46 |
| NY Jets* | 992 | Washington | 971 | 21.00 | 0.56 | 0.44 |
| Atlanta | 1004 | Houston* | 1032 | -28.00 | 0.42 | 0.58 |
| Kansas City | 948 | Chicago* | 1010 | -62.00 | 0.33 | 0.67 |
| Cincinnati | 1009 | Pittsburgh* | 1017 | -8.00 | 0.48 | 0.52 |
| Carolina | 956 | Tampa Bay* | 956 | 0.00 | 0.50 | 0.50 |
| Baltimore* | 1022 | Cleveland | 951 | 71.00 | 0.69 | 0.31 |
| Green Bay* | 1052 | NY Giants | 986 | 66.00 | 0.68 | 0.32 |
| Dallas* | 1008 | Arizona | 970 | 38.00 | 0.61 | 0.39 |
| St. Louis | 945 | San Francisco* | 1032 | -87.00 | 0.27 | 0.73 |
| Detroit | 1005 | New Orleans* | 1022 | -17.00 | 0.45 | 0.55 |
| San Diego* | 970 | Jacksonville | 959 | 11.00 | 0.53 | 0.47 |

**WTZ Favorite-Longshot bias bets at Betfair**

New England at 1.05 Result: New England 31-29 so won bet. New England let them score 21 4th quarter points.

New Orleans at 1.25
Result: na

Green Bay at 1.40
Result: Green Bay won just barely, 38-35; very exciting game, both Rodgers and Manning were excellent; Packers don't look like a 12-0 team

Table 9.5: Elo favorite and probability of win, Spread favorite and spread probability of win compared, week 13

| Elo Favorite | Elo | | | Spread Favorite | Spread | | | Winner | Score |
| | Result | Diff | Prob | | Result | Spread | Prob | | |
|---|---|---|---|---|---|---|---|---|---|
| Philadelphia | L | 9 | 0.56 | Philadelphia | L | 3 | 0.59 | Seattle | 31-14 |
| Tennessee | W | 15 | 0.55 | at Buffalo | L | 1 | 0.53 | Tennessee | 23-17 |
| at Chicago | L | 62 | 0.67 | at Chicago | L | 7 | 0.71 | Kansas City | 10-3 |
| Oakland | L | 13 | 0.54 | at Miami | W | 3 | 0.59 | Miami | 34-14 |
| at Pittsburgh | W | 8 | 0.52 | at Pittsburgh | W | 6 | 0.68 | Pittsburgh | 35-7 |
| Baltimore | W | 71 | 0.69 | Baltimore | W | 6 | 0.68 | Baltimore | 24-10 |
| NY Jets | W | 21 | 0.56 | NY Jets | W | 3 | 0.59 | NY Jets | 34-19 |
| at Houston | W | 28 | 0.58 | Atlanta | L | 3 | 0.59 | Houston | 17-10 |
| at Tampa Bay | L | 0 | 0.50 | at Tampa Bay | L | 3 | 0.59 | Carolina | 38-19 |
| at New Orleans | na | 17 | 0.55 | at New Orleans | na | 9 | 0.77 | | |
| Denver | W | 34 | 0.60 | at Minnesota | L | 1 | 0.53 | Denver | 35-32 |
| at San Francisco | W | 87 | 0.73 | at San Francisco | W | 13 | 0.89 | San Francisco | 26-0 |
| Dallas | L | 38 | 0.61 | Dallas | L | 4 | 0.62 | Arizona | 19-13 |
| Green Bay | W | 66 | 0.68 | Green Bay | W | 7 | 0.71 | Green Bay | 38-35 |
| at New England | W | 122 | 0.80 | at New England | W | 20 | 0.99 | New England | 31-24 |
| San Diego | na | 11 | 0.53 | San Diego | na | 2 | 0.56 | | |

Using Hal Stern's approximation that probability for the favorite winning = $1/2 + .03$(spread) for spread $\leqslant 6$

Table 9.6: Week 13

(a) Stats

(b) Games

**NATIONAL FOOTBALL LEAGUE**

AFC

| East | W | L | T | Pct | PF | PA |
|---|---|---|---|---|---|---|
| New England | 8 | 3 | 0 | .727 | 331 | 223 |
| New York | 6 | 5 | 0 | .545 | 256 | 241 |
| Buffalo | 5 | 6 | 0 | .455 | 261 | 281 |
| Miami | 3 | 8 | 0 | .273 | 212 | 206 |
| **West** | W | L | T | Pct | PF | PA |
| Oakland | 7 | 4 | 0 | .636 | 260 | 274 |
| Denver | 6 | 5 | 0 | .545 | 221 | 260 |
| Kansas City | 4 | 7 | 0 | .364 | 153 | 265 |
| San Diego | 4 | 7 | 0 | .364 | 249 | 275 |
| **North** | W | L | T | Pct | PF | PA |
| Baltimore | 8 | 3 | 0 | .727 | 272 | 182 |
| Pittsburgh | 8 | 3 | 0 | .727 | 233 | 188 |
| Cincinnati | 7 | 4 | 0 | .636 | 259 | 215 |
| Cleveland | 4 | 7 | 0 | .364 | 165 | 216 |
| **South** | W | L | T | Pct | PF | PA |
| Houston | 8 | 3 | 0 | .727 | 293 | 179 |
| Tennessee | 6 | 5 | 0 | .545 | 226 | 212 |
| Jacksonville | 3 | 8 | 0 | .273 | 138 | 200 |
| Indianapolis | 0 | 11 | 0 | .000 | 150 | 327 |

NFC

| East | W | L | T | Pct | PF | PA |
|---|---|---|---|---|---|---|
| Dallas | 7 | 4 | 0 | .636 | 270 | 225 |
| New York | 6 | 5 | 0 | .545 | 252 | 277 |
| Washington | 4 | 7 | 0 | .364 | 183 | 222 |
| Philadelphia | 4 | 8 | 0 | .333 | 271 | 282 |
| **West** | W | L | T | Pct | PF | PA |
| San Francisco | 9 | 2 | 0 | .818 | 262 | 161 |
| Seattle | 5 | 7 | 0 | .417 | 216 | 246 |
| Arizona | 4 | 7 | 0 | .364 | 213 | 256 |
| St. Louis | 2 | 9 | 0 | .182 | 140 | 270 |
| **North** | W | L | T | Pct | PF | PA |
| Green Bay | 11 | 0 | 0 | 1.000 | 382 | 227 |
| Detroit | 7 | 4 | 0 | .636 | 316 | 246 |
| Chicago | 7 | 4 | 0 | .636 | 288 | 232 |
| Minnesota | 2 | 9 | 0 | .182 | 214 | 295 |
| **South** | W | L | T | Pct | PF | PA |
| New Orleans | 8 | 3 | 0 | .727 | 362 | 252 |
| Atlanta | 7 | 4 | 0 | .636 | 259 | 227 |
| Tampa Bay | 4 | 7 | 0 | .364 | 199 | 291 |
| Carolina | 3 | 8 | 0 | .273 | 252 | 305 |

**WEEK 13**

**Sunday's Games**
Cincinnati at Pittsburgh, 10 a.m.
Carolina at Tampa Bay, 10 a.m.
Kansas City at Chicago, 10 a.m.
N.Y. Jets at Washington, 10 a.m.
Atlanta at Houston, 10 a.m.
Oakland at Miami, 10 a.m.
Tennessee at Buffalo, 10 a.m.
Indianapolis at New England, 10 a.m.
Denver at Minnesota, 10 a.m.
Baltimore at Cleveland, 1:05 p.m.
St. Louis at San Francisco, 1:15 p.m.
Dallas at Arizona, 1:15 p.m.
Green Bay at N.Y. Giants, 1:15 p.m.
Detroit at New Orleans, 5:20 p.m.
**Monday's Game**
San Diego at Jacksonville, 5:30 p.m.
**Thursday's Result**
Seattle 31 Philadelphia 14

San Francisco at 1.14
Result: San Francisco won easily 26-0

Baltimore at 1.34
Result: Baltimore won easily 24-10

Elo/Spread/Betfair bets results below
WTZ did not make any Elo bets on Sunday but shows results in Table 9.5.
With two games to go (New Orleans and San Diego), Elo had 9 wins, 5
losses and spread had 7 wins and 7 losses.

## Summary week 12

WTZ and Elo bets had a good week winning most of the games, see Table 9.7. Of the four WTZ did not bet, Elo won 2 and lost 2, WTZ had eleven wins, and 2 losses (both took Elo favored teams with points when spread odds favored Baltimore and Oakland and the odds favorite done by more than the point spread).

We start with the week 17 games and ratings which completed the season. Table 9.8 has the Elo ratings for these games and the recommended selections.

The Elo ratings had 12 correct and 2 wrong, if you do not consider the Jets/Miami and Dallas/Giants games because they are tossups. If you do, it is 1 win and 1 loss more. I made 13 bets at Betfair winning 10 and losing 3.

The wins were:

1. NY Jets $+7\frac{1}{2}$ at 1.53; Miami won 19-17 but spread bet won

2. Green Bay $+6\frac{1}{2}$ at 2.08 QB Rodgers and other key players rested so Lions favored in spread odds but I went for GB + the points; the backup quarterback had 6 TDs so they won, 45-41

3. Chicago at 2.24 won over Minnesota 17-13; Elo chose Chicago the spread underdog

4. Baltimore at 1.77 beat Cincinnati 24-16

5. New England at 1.19 beat Buffalo 49-21, more was bet at 2.04 when Buffalo got a 14-0 lead but more could/should have been bet at 21-0
   This was similar to week 16 when NE got behind 17-0 and odds got to nearly 5.0
   These slow starts does not bode well for the tougher teams in the playoffs
   But home field advantage is worth a lot for NE

6. New Orleans at 1.36 beat Carolina 45-17, they look super!

7. Jacksonville at 1.62 beat Indianapolis 19-13 setting up the #1 pick likely of Andrew Luck
   If they draft him he either gets traded, serves as an understudy to Peyton Manning if he recovers, or starts for a weak team

Table 9.7: Scores, Week 12 — Results of WTZ bets

| | | | | winner | Bet | Result |
|---|---|---|---|---|---|---|
| Green Bay | 27 | Detroit | 15 | Green Bay | Green Bay | won |
| Miami | 19 | Dallas | 20 | Dallas | Miami + 12.5 | won |
| San Francisco | 6 | Baltimore | 16 | Baltimore | San Francisco +3.5 | lost |
| Minnesota | 14 | Atlanta | 24 | Atlanta | Atlanta at 1.22 | won |
| Carolina | 27 | Indianapolis | 19 | Carolina | Carolina at 1.58 | won |
| Tampa Bay | 17 | Tennessee | 23 | Tennessee | Pass | passed, Elo lost |
| Houston | 20 | Jacksonville | 13 | Houston | Houston at 1.41 | won |
| Arizona | 23 | St. Louis | 20 | Arizona | Arizona + 2.5 at 1.98 | won |
| Buffalo | 24 | NY Jets | 28 | NY Jets | Buffalo +9.5 at 1.98 | won |
| Cleveland | 20 | Cincinnati | 23 | Cincinnati | Pass | passed, Elo got it right |
| Washington | 23 | Seattle | 17 | Washington | Pass | passed, Elo lost |
| Chicago | 20 | Oakland | 25 | Oakland | Chicago +3.5 at 1.84 | lost |
| New England | 38 | Philadelphia | 20 | New England | New England | won |
| Denver | 16 | San Diego | 13 | Denver | Denver +6.5 at 1.87 | won |
| Pittsburgh | 13 | Kansas City | 9 | Pittsburgh | Pittsburgh at 1.18 | won |
| | | | | | Kansas City +10.5 at 1.96 | won |
| NY Giants | 24 | New Orleans | 49 | New Orleans | travelling, could not bet | Elo won |

Table 9.8: Week 17 Elo ratings and suggested selections

| Away | ELO Rating | ELO prob | Home | Rating | ELO prob | Stern prob | ELO spread | Elo Pick | Elo W/L |
|---|---|---|---|---|---|---|---|---|---|
| NY Jets | 998 | .50 | Miami | 999 | .50 | .51 | 0.2 | toss up | |
| Detroit | 1032 | .37 | Green Bay | 1080 | .63 | .66 | 5.3 | GB | W |
| Carolina | 994 | .29 | New Orleans | 1071 | .71 | .76 | 8.7 | NO | W |
| Tennessee | 995 | .36 | Houston | 1045 | .64 | .67 | 5.6 | Hou | W |
| Chicago | 994 | .59 | Minnesota | 962 | .41 | .39 | -3.6 | Chic | W |
| Washington | 970 | .36 | Philadelphia | 1021 | .64 | .67 | 5.7 | Phil | W |
| San Francisco | 1057 | .79 | St. Louis | 944 | .21 | .12 | -12.8 | SF | W |
| Buffalo | 974 | .26 | New England | 1066 | .74 | .81 | 10.3 | NE | W |
| Indianapolis | 935 | .42 | Jacksonville | 964 | .58 | .60 | 3.3 | Jack | W |
| San Diego | 1000 | .53 | Oakland | 990 | .47 | .47 | -1.1 | SD | W |
| Kansas City | 963 | .42 | Denver | 991 | .58 | .60 | 3.2 | Den | L |
| Tampa Bay | 930 | .26 | Atlanta | 1022 | .74 | .81 | 10.4 | Atl | W |
| Baltimore | 1034 | .56 | Cincinnati | 1014 | .44 | .43 | -2.3 | Balt | W |
| Seattle | 1003 | .52 | Arizona | 995 | .48 | .47 | -0.9 | Sea | L |
| Pittsburgh | 1039 | .72 | Cleveland | 957 | .28 | .22 | -9.3 | Pitt | L |
| Dallas | 1008 | .51 | NY Giants | 1005 | .49 | .49 | -0.3 | toss up | W |

It leaves Luck with an interesting decision problem — trading to a contender with a weak quarterback possibly but even the best rookie QBs need a couple years to become effective in the NFL

8. Pittsburgh at 1.33 beat Cleveland 13-9

9. San Diego at 2.22 beat Oakland 38-26; Elo picked SD, they are historically very good in December and January

10. San Francisco at 1.14 beat St Louis 34-27

The lost games were:

1. Seattle $+2\frac{1}{2}$ at 2.04 lost to Arizona by 3 points, 23-20; it was exciting to watch Larry Fitzgerald, a superstar receiver!

2. Denver at 1.8 lost to Kansas City 7-3; Tebow mania is waning as teams figure him out

3. Dallas $+3\frac{1}{2}$ at 1.87 lost to Giants 31-14, Elo missed this as did I
   Eli Manning looked sharp and UMass wide receiver Victor Cruz looked like a new Larry Fitzgerald
   The Giants are sleepers and are peaking, so I hedged them in my Super Bowl bets

The twelve teams that made the playoffs have Betfair odds as follows:

| | |
|---|---|
| GBay | 3.05-3.1 |
| NE | 5.3-5.5 |
| NO | 6.6-6.8 |
| Balt | 10.5-11 |
| SF | 13.5-14 |
| Pitt | 13.5-14.5 |
| NYG | 26-27 |
| Atl | 46-50 |
| Hou | 50-60 |
| Det | 65-70 |
| Cinn | 90-100 |
| Den | 100-130 |

The conference odds follow. I have no bets here yet; among other things the bid-ask spreads are very wide. These will be reconsidered closer in when the spreads narrow.

| AFC  |         | NFC |         |
|------|---------|-----|---------|
| NE   | 2.26-3  | GB  | 1.85-2  |
| Balt | 3.55-4.2| NO  | 4-4.3   |
| Pitt | 5.2-9   | SF  | 7.4-8.6 |
| Hou  | 20-26   | NYG | 11-17   |
| Den  | 21-36   | Atl | 17.5-20 |
| Cin  | 34-55   | Det | 30-46   |

| AFC | 2.3-2.9   |
|-----|-----------|
| NFC | 1.53-1.76 |

New Orleans seems strong enough to give Green Bay a battle but that game would be in Green Bay where there is a strong home field advantage.

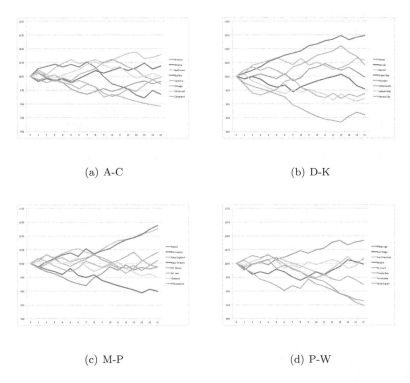

(a) A-C                                    (b) D-K

(c) M-P                                    (d) P-W

Figure 9.3: Evolution of Elo ratings 2011-12 NFL season, Week 16

I previously made approximate Kelly criterion bets, mostly at better odds than now available, so I will win if any of the top seven teams listed above win the Super Bowl and lose if any of the bottom five win. The Kelly strategy means that higher probability outcomes are bet more. See my

Kelly Handbook with Leonard MacLean and Ed Thorp which is on discount and in paper from World Scientific. Also see Ziemba (2016) for more on this including simulations and responses to critiques.

The Giants bet was made after their win over the Cowboys. They are peaking just like the year they beat New England. Cruz is making these same sort of catches as the winner in that Super Bowl game and Eli Manning is hot and has more or less become an elite QB like Brees, Brady and Rodgers and his injured brother. I win the most if Green Bay, New England or New Orleans win and more modest with the other four.

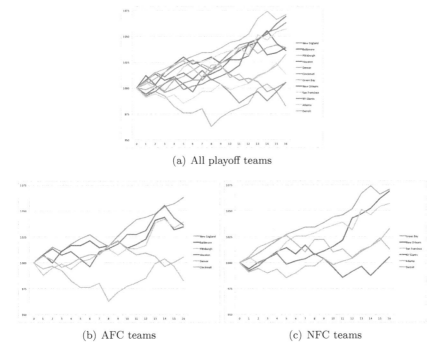

(a) All playoff teams

(b) AFC teams                    (c) NFC teams

Figure 9.4: Evolution of Elo ratings 2011-12 for the teams in the playoffs

## The Playoffs

Figure 9.3 shows the Elo ratings through the 16 game season for all the teams grouped alphabetically and Figure 9.4 has the playoff teams.

They start on Wildcard weekend, Saturday and Sunday January 7 and 8 for the wildcard 1 and 2 and division winners ranked 3rd and 4th in each conference. That's:

in the AFC
Pittsburgh (12-4) at Denver (8.8)
and
Cincinnati (9-7) at Houston (10-6)
in the NFC

Detroit (10-6) at New Orleans (13-3)
and
Atlanta (10-6) at the New York Giants (9-7)

Figure 9.5 shows the progression for the January 14 and 15 divisional playoffs and January 22 Conference championship games and the February 5
Superbowl.

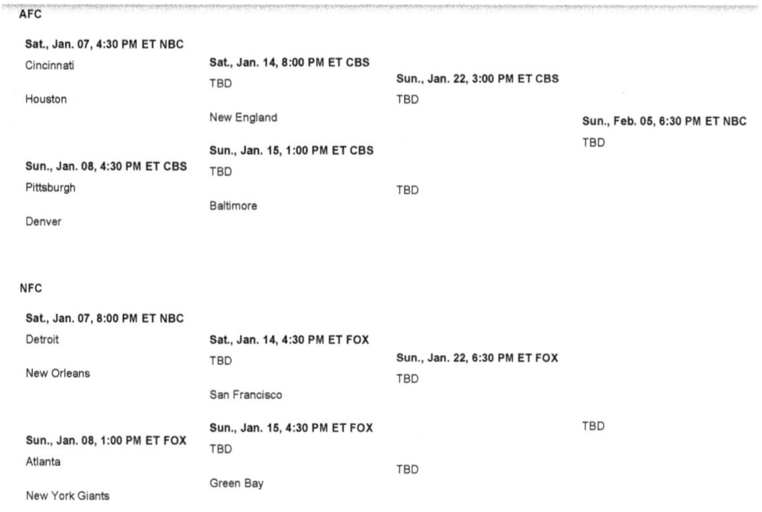

Figure 9.5: NFL Playoffs, 2012

New England, Baltimore, Green Bay and San Francisco have a bye in the
first round then home field advantage. New England and Green Bay are
the top seeds in the AFC and NFC having home field advantage until the
Super Bowl assuming they win their games. There have been lots of upsets
this year so we will see how the playoffs evolve according to the spread and
Elo suggestions.

## Table 9.9: NFL Results, Week 17

Sunday January 1, 2012

| | 1 | 2 | 3 | 4 | Total | |
|---|---|---|---|---|---|---|
| Detroit | 9 | 10 | 15 | 7 | 41 | Final |
| ›Green Bay | 10 | 14 | 7 | 14 | 45 | |

DET: M. Stafford 36-59, 520 yds, 5 TDs, 2 INTs
GB: M. Flynn 31-44, 480 yds, 6 TDs, 1 INT
Box Score - Recap

| | 1 | 2 | 3 | 4 | Total | |
|---|---|---|---|---|---|---|
| Indianapolis | 0 | 3 | 3 | 7 | 13 | Final |
| ›Jacksonville | 7 | 3 | 6 | 3 | 19 | |

IND: A. Collie 9 Rec, 96 yds, 1 TD
JAC: M. Jones-Drew 25 Rush, 169 yds
Box Score - Recap

| | 1 | 2 | 3 | 4 | Total | |
|---|---|---|---|---|---|---|
| NY Jets | 7 | 3 | 0 | 7 | 17 | Final |
| ›Miami | 3 | 3 | 0 | 13 | 19 | |

NYJ: M. Sanchez 21-32, 207 yds, 2 TDs, 3 INTs
MIA: C. Clay 1 Rec, 1 yd, 1 TD
Box Score - Recap

| | 1 | 2 | 3 | 4 | Total | |
|---|---|---|---|---|---|---|
| Carolina | 7 | 10 | 0 | 0 | 17 | Final |
| ›New Orleans | 14 | 10 | 14 | 7 | 45 | |

CAR: J. Stewart 9 Rush, 79 yds, 1 TD
NO: D. Brees 28-35, 389 yds, 5 TDs, 1 INT
Box Score - Recap

| | 1 | 2 | 3 | 4 | Total | |
|---|---|---|---|---|---|---|
| ›Chicago | 0 | 14 | 0 | 3 | 17 | Final |
| Minnesota | 10 | 3 | 0 | 0 | 13 | |

CHI: R. Williams 4 Rec, 60 yds, 1 TD
MIN: P. Harvin 10 Rec, 115 yds
Box Score - Recap

| | 1 | 2 | 3 | 4 | Total | |
|---|---|---|---|---|---|---|
| Buffalo | 21 | 0 | 0 | 0 | 21 | Final |
| ›New England | 0 | 14 | 14 | 21 | 49 | |

BUF: R. Fitzpatrick 29-46, 307 yds, 2 TDs, 4 INTs
NE: T. Brady 23-35, 338 yds, 3 TDs, 1 INT
Box Score - Recap

| | 1 | 2 | 3 | 4 | Total | |
|---|---|---|---|---|---|---|
| ›Tennessee | 0 | 13 | 3 | 7 | 23 | Final |
| Houston | 7 | 3 | 3 | 9 | 22 | |

TEN: M. Hasselbeck 22-35, 297 yds, 2 TDs
HOU: B. Tate 16 Rush, 97 yds, 1 TD
Box Score - Recap

| | 1 | 2 | 3 | 4 | Total | |
|---|---|---|---|---|---|---|
| Washington | 0 | 0 | 7 | 3 | 10 | Final |
| ›Philadelphia | 3 | 7 | 3 | 21 | 34 | |

WAS: R. Grossman 22-45, 256 yds, 1 TD, 1 INT
PHI: M. Vick 24-39, 335 yds, 3 TDs, 1 INT
Box Score - Recap

| | 1 | 2 | 3 | 4 | Total | |
|---|---|---|---|---|---|---|
| ›San Francisco | 7 | 13 | 7 | 7 | 34 | Final |
| St. Louis | 7 | 0 | 3 | 17 | 27 | |

SF: M. Crabtree 9 Rec, 92 yds, 2 TDs
STL: K. Clemens 14-31, 226 yds, 1 TD, 1 INT
Box Score - Recap

| | 1 | 2 | 3 | 4 | Total | |
|---|---|---|---|---|---|---|
| Tampa Bay | 0 | 7 | 11 | 6 | 24 | Final |
| ›Atlanta | 21 | 21 | 0 | 3 | 45 | |

TB: D. Briscoe 8 Rec, 53 yds, 2 TDs
ATL: M. Turner 17 Rush, 172 yds, 2 TDs
Box Score - Recap

| | 1 | 2 | 3 | 4 | OT | Total | |
|---|---|---|---|---|---|---|---|
| Seattle | 0 | 3 | 7 | 10 | 0 | 20 | Final |
| ›Arizona | 7 | 3 | 7 | 3 | 3 | 23 | OT |

SEA: L. Washington 7 Rush, 78 yds, 1 TD
ARI: J. Skelton 22-40, 271 yds, 1 TD, 1 INT
Box Score - Recap

| | 1 | 2 | 3 | 4 | Total | |
|---|---|---|---|---|---|---|
| ›San Diego | 7 | 17 | 7 | 7 | 38 | Final |
| Oakland | 7 | 6 | 6 | 7 | 26 | |

SD: P. Rivers 19-26, 310 yds, 3 TDs, 1 INT
OAK: C. Palmer 28-43, 417 yds, 2 TDs, 1 INT
Box Score - Recap

| | 1 | 2 | 3 | 4 | Total | |
|---|---|---|---|---|---|---|
| ›Kansas City | 7 | 0 | 0 | 0 | 7 | Final |
| Denver | 0 | 0 | 3 | 0 | 3 | |

KC: D. McCluster 12 Rush, 61 yds, 1 TD
DEN: W. McGahee 28 Rush, 145 yds
Box Score - Recap

| | 1 | 2 | 3 | 4 | Total | |
|---|---|---|---|---|---|---|
| ›Pittsburgh | 0 | 3 | 10 | 0 | 13 | Final |
| Cleveland | 0 | 6 | 3 | 0 | 9 | |

PIT: I. Redman 19 Rush, 92 yds, 1 TD
CLE: J. Cribbs 7 Rec, 91 yds
Box Score - Recap

| | 1 | 2 | 3 | 4 | Total | |
|---|---|---|---|---|---|---|
| ›Baltimore | 10 | 7 | 0 | 7 | 24 | Final |
| Cincinnati | 3 | 0 | 7 | 6 | 16 | |

BAL: R. Rice 24 Rush, 191 yds, 2 TDs
CIN: B. Scott 6 Rush, 34 yds, 1 TD
Box Score - Recap

| | 1 | 2 | 3 | 4 | Total | |
|---|---|---|---|---|---|---|
| Dallas | 0 | 0 | 7 | 7 | 14 | Final |
| ›NY Giants | 7 | 14 | 0 | 10 | 31 | |

DAL: L. Robinson 4 Rec, 61 yds, 2 TDs
NYG: E. Manning 24-33, 346 yds, 3 TDs
Box Score - Recap

Table 9.10: The Elo probabilities and selections for Wildcard Weekend

| Away | Rating | ELO prob | Home | Rating | ELO prob | Stern prob | ELO spread | Elo Pick | My Pick |
|------|--------|----------|------|--------|----------|------------|------------|----------|---------|
| Cincinnati | 1000 | .42 | Houston | 1029 | .58 | .60 | 3.3 | Houston | probably Cinn |
| Detroit | 1029 | .36 | New Orleans | 1078 | .64 | .67 | 5.6 | New Orleans | New Orleans |
| Atlanta | 1018 | .51 | NY Giants | 1014 | .49 | .48 | -0.5 | Atlanta (close) | probably NY |
| Pittsburgh | 1042 | .65 | Denver | 986 | .35 | .31 | -6.3 | Pittsburgh | Pitts |

## Table 9.11: NFL Statistics for 2011/12 season

### AMERICAN FOOTBALL CONF.

**OFFENCE (Yards Per Game)**

| Team | Rush | Pass | Yds |
|---|---|---|---|
| New England | 110.3 | 317.8 | 428.0 |
| San Diego | 116.5 | 276.6 | 393.1 |
| Oakland | 131.9 | 247.6 | 379.5 |
| Pittsburgh | 118.9 | 253.4 | 372.3 |
| Houston | 153.0 | 219.1 | 372.1 |
| Buffalo | 120.1 | 231.4 | 351.5 |
| Baltimore | 124.8 | 213.9 | 338.7 |
| Tennessee | 89.9 | 245.2 | 335.1 |
| Cincinnati | 111.1 | 208.8 | 319.9 |
| Miami | 124.2 | 193.2 | 317.4 |
| Denver | 164.5 | 152.1 | 316.6 |
| NY Jets | 105.8 | 206.1 | 311.8 |
| Kansas City | 118.3 | 192.5 | 310.8 |
| Cleveland | 95.7 | 193.1 | 288.8 |
| Indianapolis | 99.6 | 187.2 | 286.8 |
| Jacksonville | 123.1 | 136.2 | 259.3 |

**DEFENCE (Yards Per Game)**

| Team | Rush | Pass | Yds |
|---|---|---|---|
| Pittsburgh | 99.8 | 171.9 | 271.8 |
| Houston | 96.0 | 189.7 | 285.7 |
| Baltimore | 92.6 | 196.3 | 288.9 |
| NY Jets | 111.1 | 201.0 | 312.1 |
| Jacksonville | 104.2 | 208.8 | 313.0 |
| Cincinnati | 104.7 | 211.6 | 316.3 |
| Cleveland | 147.4 | 164.9 | 332.4 |
| Kansas City | 132.0 | 201.3 | 333.3 |
| Miami | 95.6 | 249.5 | 345.1 |
| San Diego | 122.2 | 224.4 | 346.6 |
| Tennessee | 128.3 | 226.8 | 355.1 |
| Denver | 126.3 | 231.5 | 357.8 |
| Indianapolis | 143.9 | 227.0 | 370.9 |
| Buffalo | 139.0 | 232.1 | 371.1 |
| Oakland | 136.1 | 251.4 | 387.6 |
| New England | 117.1 | 293.9 | 411.1 |

**PASSING**

| Player, Team | Yds | TD | Int | Rat. |
|---|---|---|---|---|
| Brady, NE | 5,235 | 39 | 12 | 105.6 |
| Schaub, Hou | 2,479 | 15 | 6 | 96.8 |
| Rthlisbergr, Pit | 4,077 | 21 | 14 | 90.1 |
| Rivers, SD | 4,624 | 27 | 20 | 88.7 |
| Moore, Mia | 2,407 | 16 | 9 | 87.1 |
| Hasselbeck, Ten | 3,571 | 18 | 14 | 82.4 |
| Flacco, Bal | 3,610 | 20 | 12 | 80.5 |
| Palmer, Oak | 2,753 | 13 | 16 | 80.5 |
| Dalton, Cin | 3,398 | 20 | 13 | 80.4 |
| Fitzpatrick, Buf | 3,832 | 24 | 23 | 79.1 |
| Sanchez, NYJ | 3,474 | 26 | 18 | 78.2 |
| Orton, Den/KC | 1,758 | 9 | 9 | 77.8 |
| Cassel, KC | 1,713 | 10 | 9 | 76.6 |
| McCoy, Cle | 2,733 | 14 | 11 | 74.6 |
| Tebow, Den | 1,729 | 12 | 6 | 72.9 |
| Painter, Ind | 1,541 | 6 | 9 | 66.6 |
| Gabbert, Jac | 2,214 | 12 | 11 | 65.4 |

**RUSHING**

| Player, Team | Att. | Yds | Avg |
|---|---|---|---|
| Jones-Drew, Jac | 343 | 1,606 | 4.7 |
| Rice, Bal | 291 | 1,364 | 4.7 |
| Foster, Hou | 278 | 1,224 | 4.4 |
| McGahee, Den | 249 | 1,199 | 4.8 |
| Mathews, SD | 222 | 1,091 | 4.9 |
| Bush, Mia | 216 | 1,086 | 5.0 |
| Benson, Cin | 273 | 1,067 | 3.9 |
| Greene, NYJ | 253 | 1,054 | 4.2 |
| Johnson, Ten | 262 | 1,047 | 4.0 |
| Bush, Oak | 256 | 977 | 3.8 |
| Tate, Hou | 175 | 942 | 5.4 |
| Jackson, Buf | 170 | 934 | 5.5 |
| Mendenhall, Pit | 228 | 928 | 4.1 |
| Green-Ellis, NE | 181 | 667 | 3.7 |
| Tebow, Den | 122 | 660 | 5.4 |

**RECEIVING**

| Player, Team | Rec. | Yds | Avg |
|---|---|---|---|
| Welker, NE | 122 | 1,569 | 12.9 |
| Gronkowski, NE | 90 | 1,327 | 14.7 |
| Marshall, Mia | 81 | 1,214 | 15.0 |
| Wallace, Mia | 72 | 1,193 | 16.6 |
| Bowe, KC | 81 | 1,159 | 14.3 |
| Brown, Pit | 69 | 1,108 | 16.1 |
| Jackson, SD | 60 | 1,106 | 18.4 |
| Green, Cin | 65 | 1,057 | 16.3 |
| Washington, Ten | 74 | 1,023 | 13.8 |
| Johnson, Buf | 76 | 1,004 | 13.2 |
| Heyward-Bey, Oak | 64 | 975 | 15.2 |
| Wayne, Ind | 75 | 960 | 12.8 |
| Garcon, Ind | 70 | 947 | 13.5 |
| Hernandez, NE | 79 | 910 | 11.5 |
| Boldin, Bal | 57 | 887 | 15.6 |

### NATIONAL FOOTBALL CONF.

**OFFENCE (Yards Per Game)**

| Team | Rush | Pass | Yds |
|---|---|---|---|
| New Orleans | 127.9 | 329.2 | 457.1 |
| Philadelphia | 146.7 | 253.0 | 399.7 |
| Carolina | 149.6 | 246.1 | 395.7 |
| Green Bay | 98.5 | 297.0 | 395.5 |
| Detroit | 96.7 | 287.5 | 384.1 |
| NY Giants | 88.1 | 293.5 | 381.6 |
| Dallas | 117.2 | 263.3 | 380.5 |
| Atlanta | 105.5 | 267.7 | 373.2 |
| Washington | 98.9 | 235.1 | 334.0 |
| Minnesota | 149.3 | 182.3 | 331.6 |
| Chicago | 128.2 | 192.9 | 321.1 |
| Tampa Bay | 94.9 | 226.1 | 320.9 |
| Arizona | 99.6 | 220.7 | 320.3 |
| San Francisco | 128.5 | 181.7 | 310.2 |
| Seattle | 105.2 | 194.2 | 299.4 |
| St. Louis | 103.7 | 178.0 | 281.7 |

**DEFENCE (Yards Per Game)**

| Team | Rush | Pass | Yds |
|---|---|---|---|
| San Francisco | 77.3 | 230.9 | 308.1 |
| Philadelphia | 112.6 | 212.3 | 324.9 |
| Seattle | 112.3 | 219.9 | 332.2 |
| Atlanta | 97.0 | 236.6 | 333.6 |
| Washington | 117.8 | 222.1 | 339.8 |
| Dallas | 99.1 | 244.1 | 343.2 |
| Chicago | 96.4 | 254.1 | 350.4 |
| Arizona | 124.1 | 231.0 | 355.1 |
| Minnesota | 107.0 | 251.2 | 358.2 |
| St. Louis | 151.7 | 206.7 | 358.4 |
| Detroit | 128.1 | 239.4 | 367.6 |
| New Orleans | 108.6 | 259.8 | 368.4 |
| NY Giants | 121.3 | 255.1 | 376.4 |
| Carolina | 130.8 | 246.8 | 377.6 |
| Tampa Bay | 156.1 | 238.4 | 394.4 |
| Green Bay | 111.8 | 299.8 | 411.6 |

**PASSING**

| Player, Team | Yds | TD | Int | Rat. |
|---|---|---|---|---|
| Rodgers, GB | 4,643 | 45 | 6 | 122.5 |
| Brees, NO | 5,476 | 46 | 14 | 110.6 |
| Romo, Dal | 4,184 | 31 | 10 | 102.5 |
| Stafford, Det | 5,038 | 41 | 16 | 97.2 |
| Manning, NYG | 4,933 | 29 | 16 | 92.9 |
| Ryan, Atl | 4,177 | 29 | 12 | 92.2 |
| Smith, SF | 3,150 | 17 | 5 | 90.7 |
| Cutler, Chi | 2,319 | 13 | 7 | 85.7 |
| Vick, Phi | 3,303 | 18 | 14 | 84.9 |
| Newton, Car | 4,051 | 21 | 17 | 84.5 |
| Kolb, Ari | 1,955 | 9 | 8 | 81.1 |
| Jackson, Sea | 3,091 | 14 | 13 | 79.2 |
| Freeman, TB | 3,592 | 16 | 22 | 74.6 |
| Grossmn, Wsh | 3,151 | 16 | 20 | 72.4 |
| Bradford, StL | 2,164 | 6 | 6 | 70.5 |
| Ponder, Min | 1,853 | 13 | 13 | 70.1 |
| Skelton, Ari | 1,913 | 11 | 14 | 68.9 |

**RUSHING**

| Player, Team | Att. | Yds | Avg |
|---|---|---|---|
| Turner, Atl | 301 | 1,340 | 4.5 |
| McCoy, Phi | 273 | 1,309 | 4.8 |
| Gore, SF | 282 | 1,211 | 4.3 |
| Lynch, Sea | 285 | 1,204 | 4.2 |
| Jackson, StL | 260 | 1,145 | 4.4 |
| Wells, Ari | 245 | 1,047 | 4.3 |
| Forte, Chi | 203 | 997 | 4.9 |
| Peterson, Min | 208 | 970 | 4.7 |
| Murray, Dal | 164 | 897 | 5.5 |
| Williams, Car | 155 | 836 | 5.4 |
| Blount, TB | 184 | 781 | 4.2 |
| Stewart, Car | 142 | 761 | 5.4 |
| Newton, Car | 126 | 706 | 5.6 |
| Bradshaw, NYG | 171 | 659 | 3.9 |
| Helu, Wsh | 151 | 640 | 4.2 |

**RECEIVING**

| Player, Team | Rec. | Yds | Avg |
|---|---|---|---|
| Johnson, Det | 96 | 158 | 1,681 |
| Cruz, NYG | 82 | 111 | 1,536 |
| Fitzgerald, Ari | 80 | 153 | 1,411 |
| Smith, Car | 79 | 129 | 1,394 |
| Graham, NO | 99 | 149 | 1,310 |
| White, Atl | 100 | 181 | 1,296 |
| Nelson, GB | 68 | 96 | 1,263 |
| Nicks, NYG | 76 | 133 | 1,192 |
| Colston, NO | 80 | 107 | 1,143 |
| Harvin, Min | 87 | 122 | 967 |
| Jackson, Phi | 58 | 104 | 961 |
| Jones, Atl | 54 | 96 | 959 |
| Jennings, GB | 67 | 101 | 949 |
| Gaffney, Wsh | 68 | 115 | 947 |
| Witten, Dal | 79 | 117 | 942 |

Table 9.10 shows the Elo probabilities and selections for wildcard weekend. For my bets I will go with the New Orleans and Pittsburgh but likely take NY over Atlanta and Cincinnati over Houston, especially with points.

Some useful data is presented in Table 9.11.

## Modified thoughts of Jason Cole in yahoosports.com

Jason is a good observer to follow. Some points from his analysis — we, of course, know most of them and they are embedded in the odds to some extent (and our discussions) but less so with the ELO ratings. Cole's is a more fundamental analysis rather than Elo's technical analysis.

1. New England and Green Bay -terrific offenses with great quarterbacks but very weak defenses. They have given up 8.0 and 7.8 yards/play. The other five teams allowing 7.8+ are all out of the playoffs with no winning records. They have been winning shootouts. Both are vulnerable but could meet in the Super Bowl; they and New Orleans are the favorites.

2. Baltimore 6-0 against playoff teams (Pittsburgh twice, Cincinnati twice, San Francisco and a healthy Houston). But they had road losses against weak non-playoff teams Tennessee, Jacksonville and rather good teams Seattle and San Diego. Quarterback marginal and in fight with offensive co-ordinator. At home look tough.

3. Houston — full of injuries and not scoring much. Elo 1029 at home versus Cincinnati 1000 game will be tighter than that. Cincinnati may be the bet with points.

4. Denver — I am a big Tim Tebow fan from U Florida days but he has been figured out. The last 3 games were all losses. He was 30 of 73, 439 yards, 1 touchdown, 4 interceptions and 3 lost fumbles. Pittsburgh is, according to Cole, the best balanced team. They average 1.4 yards/play 5.9-4.5 than opponents. They have a weak offensive line, especially on the road and their top back Mendenhall is out injured. Denver's Betfair odds are 1.31. I am already on Pittsburgh.

5. Cincinnati — their new quarterback Andy Dalton and wide receiver A J Green have been strong but they were 0-7 against playoff teams and 9-0 against non-playoff teams.

6. San Francisco — the great success, is strong on defense with a top running back. But they and Denver were out gamed by their opponents. New England in 2001 won the Super Bowl with such a deficit but no others. Conclusion — their offense does not seem good enough to make up for the weak offense against the high flyers.

7. New Orleans are likely the most dangerous team with the top quarterback Drew Brees. But they average 38 points in 11 games under a roof and 25.8 outdoors. And have two turnovers in five outdoor games and 14 in the 11 indoors. The first round looks ok against Detroit and I bet them but you only get 1.20. But outdoors against San Francisco and especially Green Bay looks a lot tougher.

8. NY Giants — Cole argues that the running game is weak. He does admit that Eli Manning is strong. I think I go with them against Atlanta. They are peaking. Atlanta was 1-4 against playoff teams.

9. Detroit — they are improved but against New Orleans there it does not look likely. They are 1-5 against playoff teams and 0-5 against teams with winning records.

## Conclusion

I feel good about the top seven. Green Bay and New England are the favorites. New Orleans might be the top team but outside is at a big disadvantage. San Francisco I doubt they can win. Pittsburgh is always tough but losing Mendenhall is a big minus and Big Ben is still a bit injured. Baltimore could win but I favor others and the Giants are the sleeper, but if they progress, I might hedge out my bet there. The others are doubtful in my view.

## The February 5, 2012 Super Bowl in Indianapolis

The game is between two teams: New England and the New York Giants with elite quarterbacks. This is Tom Brady's fifth time in the Super Bowl for New England with wins in 2001, 2003, and 2004 and a loss against these same Giants in 2008. His fifth appearance ties John Elway for most Super bowl appearances. John won two Super Bowls for the Denver Broncos. Should New England win, Brady will tie his boyhood hero, Joe Montana as well as Terry Bradshaw who won four for San Francisco in the 1980s and Pittsburgh in the 1970s, respectively. Eli Manning won in 2008 on a miraculous play. While his team only has an 12-7 record, Manning has been brilliant and set the record fourth quarter touchdowns during the regular 16 game season. He also has many long passes.

If the Giants upset them, Eli will have two Super bowl wins versus only one for his more famous older quarterback brother Peyton. Peyton, along with Drew Brees, Tom Brady and Aaron Rodgers are generally considered the elite quarterbacks. Eli declared early this year that he was one too and he was criticized for saying this. While it is up to others to decide about this, he has been playing at that level and that has ignited his team from a 7-7 record to the Super Bowl beating the favored Green Bay and San Francisco. New England is a 3-point odds favorite going into this game or 59% versus 41% probability of winning. The Elos are 1072 versus 1027 implying a 5-point New England advantage and 63% versus 37% probability of winning. The Betfair odds favor New England at 1.74-1.76 versus 2.32-2.34 for the Giants. The Giants $+2\frac{1}{2}$ are 2.08-2.14 with New England at 1.89-1.91. And with $+3\frac{1}{2}$ the Giants are favored, reflecting the 3 point spread, at 1.72-1.73 versus New England's 2.36-2.38. But New England struggled against Baltimore and was lucky to win. Tom Brady had a poor game against the tough Baltimore defense, as he later acknowledged, and actually had four interceptions. Two were real and two more were called back because of defensive penalties against no touchdowns. But he won the game with a leaping quarterback sneak from the one yard line. In the previous week, Brady was exceptionally sharp throwing a record tying six touchdown passes against Denver. An injury to top tight end Rob Gronkowski which could be a factor in the Super Bowl did not help. Meanwhile, Eli has been sharp in all the games and the Giants performances and the team's Elo have been rising sharply as the figure 9.6 going into the Super Bowl shows. And the last New England loss was 24-20 to these very Giants; New England then has won 10 straight games. But New England's Elo is way above the Giants so they must be the pick. The game has a lot of events surrounding it for a whole week including much TV and other analysis. Madonna is doing the half-time show and the TV ads are $3.5 million per 30 seconds! Clint Eastwood narrated a 2-minute Chrysler ad for $14 million!

## Recap of the Super Bowl

It was a very good game and another exercise in risk arbitrage and mean reversion. I favored New England but just barely so I hedged my bet with some long Giants plus $3\frac{1}{2}$. This cost 507 to gain 360 and meant if New England won by 4 or more, a 1107 gain would be reduced to 600. But 125 would be gained if the Giants won versus a loss of 235 before this hedge. Also, if New England won by 1-3 point then the 360 plus the 1107 or 1467 would be won. The game started with New England 1.65-1.66 the favorite with the Giants at 2.5-2.52.

The Giants got a safety for a 2-0 lead when Brady threw from the pocket to nobody down the field from the end zone. The Giants proceeded to then score a touchdown for a 9-0 lead as Manning was 10/10 passing a Super

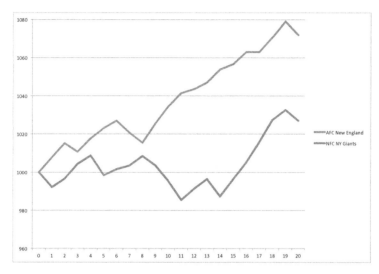

Figure 9.6: Elo ratings for New England versus NY Giants going into the Super Bowl

Bowl opening record. New England could have prevented this TD with a fumble recovery but for a 12 men on the field miscue. Then I went long 75 New England at odds of 2.46 so the Giants were then favored to win the game. Brady then became Brady and had 14 straight completions breaking Joe Montana's 13/13 record. This yielded a field goal and a touchdown for a 10-9 halftime lead. I could then rehedge the A long New England bet with an A′ arbitrage bet at 2.52 on the Giants so this risk arbitrage became an arbitrage with a +0.5 New England win gain versus a +89 NY gain on this part of the bet. New England had won the coin toss and deferred to get the ball at the start of the second half. So they were trending. Another touchdown made it 17-9 for an 8-point lead. The New England odds became 1.39-1.40 so it was time to go long Giants at 3.55-3.6. But the odds moved very fast and I was only able to get 16 of a 75 bet on but I left a limit order at 4.3 for the 59 balance which later got filled. My experience in options markets trading is that keeping stink bids in is often a wise idea in markets that can have fast reversals. Brady was now up to 16 straight completions and even though NE did not score the 4.3 got filled. The Giants had two drives that led field goals and a closer 17-15 New England lead. Had this been the turn-of-the-year effect where you can stop the race when you are ahead I would have cashed out but this was not the futures markets. But the Giants odds were getting more towards favored but not low enough to cover again yet.

At the 4-minute mark, a pass to the usually sure handed Wes Walker, the NFLs leading receiver, was dropped but it was a bit high. An announcer said he catches 100 out of 100 of these so this must be the 101. This led to a 3 and out rather than a first down on the 20. A score then or even running down the clock would have put the game out of reach and not given the Giants another chance.

A major concern for the game was the high ankle sprain to top wide receiver tight end Rob Gronkowski. At 6 feet 6 inches and 280 pounds with a huge wing span and terrific hands, he was a very good receiver and had set the record at 17 touchdowns for a tight end. But was he ok? He was not used much so the other great tight end, Aaron Hernandez got most of the throws. But there was one 20 yard pass to Rob. So Brady took a chance with a long pass to Gronkowski but his agility was compromised and a usual huge gain turned into an interception. The hedge was completed. It was now the fourth quarter and the time that Eli Manning had the most touchdowns. And time was running out. Manning threw another remarkable pass for 38 yards to Manningham at the 3.39 mark and then hit him again twice with 2.32 remaining. A Bradshaw run got the ball to the 12, the Giants were now favored at 1.37-1.38 with NE at 3.65-3.75 so 50 was bet on NE. So the risk arbitrage bets yielded the arbitrage +60 NE +275 NY.

Coach Bill Belichick knew the key was to let the Giants score as fast as possible to give Brady a chance for a game winning touchdown — as a field goal would not be enough. Had NE stopped NY they would have kicked a game winning field goal. Jacob, the big running back, tried to stop on the 1-yard line after the NE defenders let him through, as ordered by Belichik, but fell backwards into the end zone. So the score was 21-17 as the two-point conversion attempt failed. Brady had 57 seconds from his 20 yard line. At 52 seconds, Branch moved the ball. Then Hernandez dropped a pass. Then Brady was sacked back to the 13 of New England. With 4th down and 16, Brady hit Branch for a first and 10 out of bounds to stop the clock at 32 seconds. A pass to Hernandez with 17 seconds got the ball to the NY 44. A Giants 12 men as the field got the ball to the 50.

A final *hail Mary pass* into the end zone with 5 seconds let fell to the ground. Two New England players including Gronkowski tried to get it while being swarmed with Giants. So the Giants won again 21-17. My gain was the original 125 + 275 from the arbitrage or 400. This was lower than if New England won but again, the mean reversion risk arbitrage turned a potential loss by being on the losing team into a gain.

Some observations:

1. The elite quarterbacks certainly include Eli Manning. He was 10 of 14 for 118 yards in the 4th quarter with his seventh game winning drive of the season. Eli now has two Super Bowl wins, one more than his illustrious brother Peyton who has one. Of course Peyton has four MVPs during the regular season and Eli has none of these. Eli's two Super Bowl MVPs are the same as Brady's two. He also is one of only five players in the NFL history with multiple Super Bowl MVP awards. Besides Brady and Eli, Terry Bradshaw and Bart Starr have two with Joe Montana leading with three.

2. It is surprising how many trivial 12 men on penalties there are and how much they hurt their teams.

3. The Giants looked very solid not like a 7-7 team. They have really improved and peaked at the right time. I am glad I saw it coming and bet at 28-1.

4. Brady played well — with a healthy Gronkowski they likely would have won.

5. Elo did not get the game right like it did the last two years. The trending of Elo as well as its level and the serious tail issue for games with a big favorite are things to study in the future. Elos performance this year was so-so with 6 wins and 4 losses. Combining with mean reversion and risk arbitrage makes it easier to win.

6. The Las Vegas future book on next year's Super Bowl favors New England at 5-1 with the Giants at 8-1 so they seem over bet!

## Recap of the Playoffs

Figure 9.7 shows the evolution of the Elo ratings through the 16 game season for the twelve playoff teams. Table 9.12 shows the results of the Elo forecasts.

They started on Wildcard weekend, Saturday and Sunday January 7 and 8 for the wildcard 1 and 2 and division winners ranked 3rd and 4th in each conference. That's:

in the AFC
Pittsburgh (12-4) at Denver (8-8)
and
Cincinnati (9-7) at Houston (10-6)
in the NFC

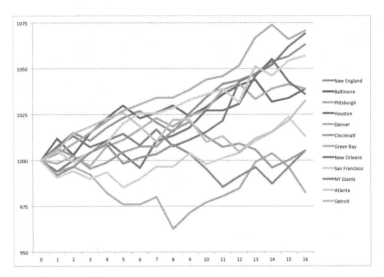

Figure 9.7: Evolution of Elo ratings for the twelve playoff teams

Table 9.12: How did the Elo rating system do in the playoffs in 2012?

Wildcat Weekend

| Cincinnati | 991 | at | Houston | 1029 | Won |
|---|---|---|---|---|---|
| Pittsburgh | 1034 | at | Denver | 984 | Lost |
| Detroit | 1022 | at | New Orleans | 1075 | Won |
| NY Giants | 1016 | at | Atlanta | 1007 | Won |

Conference Games

| Denver | 976 | at | New England | 1071 | Won |
|---|---|---|---|---|---|
| Houston | 1024 | at | Baltimore | 1044 | Won |
| New Orleans | 1070 | at | San Francisco | 1064 | Loss ??Pass??* |
| NY Giants | 1027 | at | Green Bay | 1062 | Loss |

Confrence Championships

| Baltimore | 1035 | at | New England | 1079 | Won |
|---|---|---|---|---|---|
| NY Giants | 1033 | at | San Francisco | 1059 | Loss |

Super Bowl

| New England | 1072 | | NY Giants | 1027 | Loss |
|---|---|---|---|---|---|

*Close but I won the risk arbitrage, see below. So call it a pass.

Detroit (10-6) at New Orleans (13-3)
and
Atlanta (10-6) at the New York Giants (9-7)

By making bets early on the six best teams and later on Houston at 46-1 and the New York Giants at 28-1 (just as they seemed to be peaking). I created a no lose arbitrage to win no matter who would win the Super Bowl. The largest bet was on New England with substantial amounts on New Orleans and Green Bay. The latter two were eliminated but New England remains. To balance my New England Super Bowl bet I have hedged the Giants long at $3\frac{1}{2}$ with the main bet New England but a no lose situation and a possible even bigger gain should New England win by 1-3 points.

Figure 9.8 shows the progression for the January 14 and 15 divisional playoffs and January 22 Conference championship games and the February 5 Super Bowl, including the results going into the Super Bowl of the playoffs, followed by an analysis of some of the games and the record of the Elo ratings.

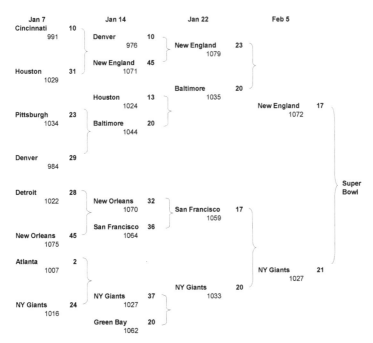

Figure 9.8: Results of the NFL Playoffs, 2012

The analysis of some interesting games follows after a review of arbitrage and risk arbitrage and the favorite long-shot bias which is greatly used in our bets.

## New Orleans at San Francisco: a game for the ages for risk arbitrage bettors

New Orleans (14-3) had an explosive offense plus a defense that caused many turnovers. At home, in a domed stadium, they have been dominant but on the road in outdoor stadiums in the north, they have done well but were not as dominant, scoring two touchdowns less per game.

San Francisco (13-3) had a top defense and a great runner, Frank Gore, and an improving but not quite top notch quarterback, Alex Smith.

The Elo slightly favored New Orleans with 1075 versus 1068 or 52% versus 48% chance of winning or a 1-point spread. The odds spread was +3 for New Orleans meaning a 59% to 41% edge for New Orleans. The Betfair odds favored New Orleans and I bet them 10 at 1.56 and 190 at 1.57.

As we see below, this game was a good example of risk arbitrage — that is, bet an A then later bet on B, in an A versus B game, in such a way that you cannot lose when $O_A O_B > 1$; see the section below on risk arbitrage. It is called risk arbitrage because this match might not occur. The usual situation is that you bet initially on the favorite which will be at short odds on the underdog rise so that a bet can be made to create a real arbitrage where you cannot lose. But the game did not evolve that way. However as shown below it is another typical risk arbitrage situation. That is the case where the favorite gets behind and you bet more on them but now at better odds assuming that the score will eventually mean revert so you can cover the longer odds bets and create the arbitrage. The game was of this type not once but multiple times. New Orleans had some turnovers and San Francisco got to a 14-0 lead, so 100 more was bet at 3.3. Then after a San Francisco field goal and a 17-0 lead 50 more was bet at 4.8. New Orleans rallied to 17-14 at half time. This led to covering bets that is short New Orleans/long San Francisco of 50 at 1.86, 100 at 1.88, 50 at 1.89, 100 at 1.90 and 50 at 1.81. The arbitrage was complete with a gain if either team won +125.40 for New Orleans and +50 for San Francisco.

Early in the second half New Orleans had another turnover their fifth fumble. San Francisco has a top punter and field goal kicker so the score went to 20-14 and later to 23-17. The last playoff team to win with 5 turnovers was the 1982 Jets. With 4 turnovers, the record is 9 wins 121 losses in the playoffs and 10% wins in the regular season. And with a -4 turnover deficit as here at 1-5, the record is 1-71 with the one exception, the 1977 Raiders. Twenty-five more was hedged short SF at 1.61 to yield +135 New Orleans versus +35 for San Francisco for the arbitrage.

Darren Sproles then scored on a 44 yard New Orleans touchdown pass from Drew Brees to give them a 24-23 lead. Now New Orleans is favored at 1.56 so 25 was shorted on New Orleans to give +136.4 New Orleans and +60.25 San Francisco for the arbitrage.

The last 3.53 minutes of this game were terrifically exciting with four lead changes and mean-reversion and risk arbitrage trades every minute or so. Here's more of the recap: With 2.18 remaining Smith hit a 31-yard pass to get San Francisco into field goal range. One option was to then run the clock down, kick the field goal to gain the lead with so little time left for New Orleans that they cannot score so San Francisco would win. But Smith ran 28 yards to get a touchdown for a 29-24 San Francisco lead. The odds were then San Francisco 1.52-1.56 and New Orleans 2.84-2.88.

A two point conversion attempt, that would have yielded a 7-point lead, failed and the Betfair odds widened to 1.33-1.42 San Francisco 3.4-4 New Orleans.

Then with 1.37 left Brees threw a 66 yard touchdown pass to Jimmy Graham to make the score 30-29 and with a two-point conversion 32-39, Brees to Sproles.

So it looked like New Orleans had pulled the game out — but not quite.

The odds then became 1.23-1.25 New Orleans and 5-5.2 San Francisco. A bet of 25 short on New Orleans yielded +128.90 New Orleans +85 San Francisco for the arbitrage.

With 14 seconds left, on the 13-yard line, San Francisco was threatening and the odds were 15-21 New Orleans 1.05-1.05 San Francisco. And, with 9 seconds, the odds were 26-36 New Orleans 1.03-1.04. Then Smith hit another touchdown pass for 14 yards to Vernon Smith and the odds became 100-330 New Orleans no bid-1.01 San Francisco. I bet 3 at 100-1 on New Orleans to yield +425.90 New Orleans +82.25 San Francisco.

San Francisco won 36-32 and I won +82.25 even though my original bet was on New Orleans. It is a good example to the strategy to *work the position until you win* using the mean reversion and arbitrage ideas. I frequently have to work the position in the options markets when trouble arises. And it is important to think through these *corrective actions* in advance.

Figure 9.9 shows the evolution of the Elos as the playoffs progressed.

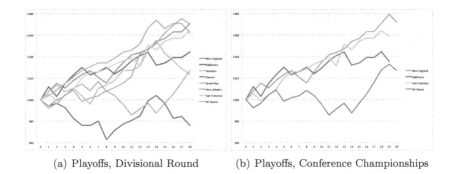

(a) Playoffs, Divisional Round       (b) Playoffs, Conference Championships

Figure 9.9: Evolution of Elo ratings as the playoffs progressed

## New York Giants at Green Bay

The Giants limped into the playoffs with a 9-7 record, but two impressive
wins indicated that they were a threat. In the wild card, they crushed
Atlanta 24-2. Then it was on to Lambeau field and the favored Green Bay
Packers. Green Bay won last year's Super Bowl and had the best record
in this season, 15-1. They were at home and favored with Betfair odds of
1.35-1.36. As the game progressed, it was clear that Green Bay was not
as sharp as usual with many dropped passes, fumbles and other misses.
Meanwhile, the Giant's quarterback Eli Manning was very sharp. In the
end, the Giants won 37-20. They were on a roll and a force to be reckoned
with. The they went on to beat San Francisco 20-17 and were in the Super
Bowl against favored New England.

## Pittsburgh at Denver: which Tebow will show up?

The highly favored veteran Pittsburgh Steelers came into the mile high
stadium in Denver quite banged up. Their top runner Richard Mendenhall
was injured and their two time winning Super Bowl quarterback Big Ben
Roethlisberger had been hobbling around for several weeks.

Denver (8-8) won their division so they had home field advantage in one
of the most home advantage stadiums with thin air at 5200 feet. Denver
started the season poorly then Tim Tebow, a strong runner for a quarterback, started winning games late in the fourth quarter and in overtime.
His kneeling and waving his hands to God created a new dictionary word:
*Tebowing.* The Tebow-mania reached a high pitch and they won seven
straight games before being blown out in Denver by the Patriots.

The game was tight all the way and went into overtime. It ended spectacularly with an 80 yard Tim Tebow pass as the first play in overtime. It was a dramatic and sudden end to the year for Pittsburgh and a great victory for Denver 29-23. Tebow was back.

## Denver at New England: a learning experience for Tebow to watch the great Brady

After the spectular win in Denver against a wounded Pittsburgh, the scene moved to Foxborough and the mighty Patriots. Could Tebow pull off yet another miracle? The odds greatly favored New England and bets of 95 at 1.15 , and 1.05 at 1.16 were made — so the odds were very short.

New England scored first with a pass from Brady to Welker. The odds then became 1.09-1.11. Tebow had a good run but then there was a fumble and the odds fell to 1.07-1.08. So half the position was hedged at 1.09 to make the bet -100 Denver +23 New England. Then Brady threw another touchdown to tight end Rob Gronkowski who set the NFL touchdown record for tight ends. So the score was 14-0 so the last 100 was hedged at 1.06 to give an arbitrage of +0 Denver +18.05 New England. This moved the position from win 31.05 but with loss risk to this no risk arbitrage. Then Brady was intercepted to yield a 14-7 score and odds of 1.09. A Brady to Gronkowski touchdown made it 21-7 with odds at 1.04-1.05. A fourth Brady touchdown, for 61 yards to Deion Branch made it 28-7 with odds of 1.02-1.03. Yet another Brady touchdown, the fifth to Bronkowski made it 35-7 with odds of 100-190 for Denver and no bid-1.01 for New England.

Yet another, the record tying sixth touchdown (Steve Young and Darrell Lamonica did it before) made the score 42-7. Rather than let Brady set the record and throw 7 TDs, coach Bill Belichick went for a final goal and the game ended 45-10. It was a powerful performance and Tim Tebow acknowledged that he learned from this experience. Now Denver is out and New England hosts Baltimore at home.

Tebow had a minor career as a quarterback but his greatest skill was as a runner. Unfortunately, he wanted to be a quarterback not a full back or returned to be used in short yard situations. After this season, he drifted from team to team as a backup quarterback then retired to be an announcer of college football games. Later he tried his hand at baseball at which he continues to be fairly successful in 2018. Our view is that he would have had a better and longer NFL career as a runner because he simply was not effective as a passing quarterback but very effective as a runner.

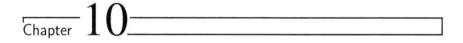

# Chapter 10

# The 2012-2013 Playoffs and the Super Bowl

In this chapter we trace the NFL playoffs leading to the 2013 super bowl on February 3rd in the New Orleans super dome. By tracing bets I made on Betfair, I hope to illustrate some general investment ideas and their use. These US football markets, which trade continuously on Betfair, have considerable mean reversion in scores and field position that gets quickly translated into odds. Hence there is risk arbitrage that helps you win the bets even if the team you start betting on actually loses the game. The goal is to make bets so that no matter which team wins, you make a profit. That means that (US odds on A)(US odds on B)>1 or (UK odds- -1 on A)(UK odds -1 on B)>1.

Lane and Ziemba (2008) discuss the math here in the context of Jai Alai. Usually one makes a sequence of bets with high odds if you win (long) and low odds if you lose (short).

I start the column by reviewing how the playoffs are organized and then discuss the sequence of games week by week leading to the super bowl.

There are a number of bets and some like the eventual super bowl winner are made during the regular season well before the start of the playoffs. Then these bets are altered as new information unfolds. I wrote this as the playoffs proceeded not at the end and kept my analysis going; that helps me think about this.

## The NFL football betting market

There are 32 teams in eight groups of four teams each. The American conference, the old AFC, has East, South, North and West and so does the National Conference. The preseason has five games, which are tests for teams to get ready. Since the teams do not want to risk injury, these games are hard to predict. The league gives the high draft picks each year to the weakest teams to try to even out their abilities.

During the 17-week season, each team plays 16 games. The winners of each of the eight groups automatically make the playoffs. Four additional teams (two from each conference) are wild cards making up the total of 12 teams. Teams with the best records get home field advantage in one or all games in the playoffs. See Figure 7.1.

> The first round of the playoffs is dubbed the Wild Card Playoffs (the league in recent years has also used the term Wild Card Weekend). In this round, the third-seeded division winner hosts the sixth seed wild card, and the fourth seed hosts the fifth. The 1 and 2 seeds from each conference receive a bye in the first round, which entitles these teams to automatic advancement to the second round, the Divisional Playoffs, where they face the Wild Card Weekend survivors. Unlike the NBA, the NFL does not use predetermined brackets. In the second round of the playoffs, the top seed hosts the lowest surviving seed, while the other two teams pair off. The two surviving teams from each conference's Divisional Playoff games meet in the respective AFC and NFC Conference Championship games, with the winners of those contests going on to face one another in the Super Bowl. Only twice since 1990 has neither a number one-seeded team nor a number two-seeded team hosted a conference championship game (the 2006 AFC Championship and the 2008 NFC Championship).

The winner of each conference plays in the Super Bowl. Given this playoff structure and probabilities of winning at home and away for each $ij$ combination, one can, as we have done in hockey, compute fair odds of advancing in the playoffs. I set the line in hockey for the BC Lottery Commission and made such calculations. The NFL is similar.

## The 2013 Super Bowl

Figure 10.1 shows the 12 teams in the playoffs. My analysis led to six longs and six shorts to be the final winner of the Super Bowl. The longs were Denver, New England, San Francisco, Green Bay, Seattle and Atlanta. And I more or less ranked them this way. I am a New England fan and they might win especially if Rob Gronkowski, their huge tight end is healthy.

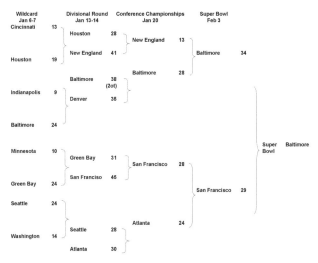

| Wildcard<br>Jan 6-7 | | Divisional Round<br>Jan 13-14 | | Conference Championships<br>Jan 20 | | Super Bowl<br>Feb 3 | |
|---|---|---|---|---|---|---|---|
| Cincinnati | 13 | Houston | 28 | | | | |
| | | | | New England | 13 | | |
| | | New England | 41 | | | Baltimore | 34 |
| Houston | 19 | | | | | | |
| | | | | Baltimore | 28 | | |
| | | Baltimore | 38<br>(2ot) | | | | |
| Indianapolis | 9 | Denver | 35 | | | | |
| Baltimore | 24 | | | | | | |
| | | | | | | Super Baltimore<br>Bowl | |
| Minnesota | 10 | Green Bay | 31 | | | | |
| | | | | San Francisco | 28 | | |
| | | San Francisco | 45 | | | San Francisco | 29 |
| Green Bay | 24 | | | | | | |
| Seattle | 24 | | | | | | |
| | | | | Atlanta | 24 | | |
| | | Seattle | 28 | | | | |
| Washington | 14 | Atlanta | 30 | | | | |

Figure 10.1: The NFL playoff tree, 2013

He has had a bruised forearm and missed many games but is ready for the playoffs although he re-injured it in New England's game against Houston which is discussed below. Together with Aaron Hernandez they form the best tight end duo in the NFL. And with Tom Brady and other very good receivers they are formidable. Rob's absence is a definite negative for New England. But Denver with Peyton Manning at his best is a deserving favourite. All these teams have excellent quarterbacks from Brady and Manning to last years MVP Aaron Rogers of Green Bay who has the best quarterback rating this season and the outstanding Seattle rookie Russell Wilson. Russell showed again why he is a legitimate candidate for rookie of the year in the Washington Redskins wildcard game discussed below.

To my mind all three of the great rookie quarterbacks are deserving so a joint three of them nominating Andrew Luck of Indianapolis and Robert Griffin III, known as RG3, with Wilson would be a nice way to have a rewarding rookie of the year award. In the end they gave the rookie of the year to RG3 who certainly had a great year. Wilson did the best in the playoffs winning on wild card weekend and helping stage a remarkable comeback in the next round leading to an almost certain win ahead by one point with 25 seconds to go. But as racing guru Andy Beyer says about racing handicapping: *it is a supreme intellectual challenge* applies here so see the section below on this exciting game in Atlanta against Atlanta. Atlanta's quarterback, Matt Ryan, is tops too with the NFL's highest completion record and very few off target throws. The San Francisco has two good but not great quarterbacks Colin Kaepernick and Alex Smith. But after Colin's terrific performance in week 2 of the playoffs, I am reassessing this *not great* label; he certainly was great then. The San Francisco coach Jim Harbaugh tutored Andrew Luck at Stanford and Alex Smith who had a 70% completion rate in 2012 before being replaced by Kaepernick. So far this looks like a gutsy, brilliant move by Harbaugh; so Ziemba wrote in 2013. After Kaepernick brilliant early play of San Francisco when he replaced Smith he became a bit erratic in his passing, however his running has always been brilliant so he is a marginal quarterback in a period in which he would normally be able to help some of the teams.

Well, in 2017, Alex Smith is going great guns with top contender Kansas City and Kaepernick, who has a huge Afro hairdo, cannot get signed by any team because he is the symbol of NFL protests against blacks who are harassed and shot by police. He kneels during the national anthem. Others do the some thing but they have not been ostracized. The league has singled him out and shut him out hoping to squash all protests. President Trump joined the situation which has become a bit of a mess, but freedom of speech is protected by the constitution.

I was short Atlanta but with home field advantage throughout the NFC part of the playoffs and a terrific record of and great receivers such as future hall of fame tight end Tony Gonzalez and the best set of wide receivers Julio Jones and Roddy White in the NFL and I could not remain short.

In one winner bet situations, like who will get selected for the Republican nomination or a horse race or the Super Bowl its usually optimal by the Kelly investment criterion as well as other good criteria with most data sets to do mostly or even all shorts. The reason being that with only one winner and you short N entrants you for sure win N-1 of them and if a good long wins you win all N shorts. My Super Bowl bets had 6 longs and 6 shorts, a variant of this. Seattle and Atlanta are the least likely to win followed by Green Bay. With Denver, New England and San Francisco the top picks. I would not be surprised if any of them won. Green Bay has the cool excellent Aaron Rogers so could do it as well.

The Super Bowl odds on Betfair and team records were

| Denver | 4.1-4.2 | 13-3 |
|---|---|---|
| New England | 4.7-4.8 | 12-4 |
| San Francisco | 4.4-7.6 | 11-4-1 |
| Green Bay | 8.2-8.4 | 12-5 |
| Seattle | 9.4-9.6 | 12-5 |
| Atlanta | 9.4-9.6 | 13-3 |

and any one of these could win the Super Bowl. But I think it will be one of the top 3 or 4. In this week's coming games-see the layout in Figure 2 and the results of wild card weekend given there.

In this coming week's divisional round games the bets seem to be Denver over Baltimore in Denver a notorious home field advantage. And New England over Houston in New England a place where the Patriots do not lose much late in the season. Atlanta versus Seattle in Atlanta is a tough one. The Betfair odds for the January 13 and 14 games were:

Baltimore 4.5-4.6 at Denver 1.27-1.28
Green Bay 2.32-2.34 at San Francisco 1.75-1.76
Seattle 2.22-2.24 at Atlanta 1.3.-1.32
Houston 4.8-4.9 at New England 1.25-1.26

Green Bay at San Francisco looked like a great matchup. The Betfair odds were 2.46 for the underdog Green Bay which was my initial bet. This game is discussed below.

My feeling was to go with Aaron Rogers the far superior quarterback. But San Francisco is tough and it's at home. Earlier in the year when San Francisco picked up receivers Randy Moss and Mario Maningham, a star from last year's Super Bowl winner the New York Giants who did not make the playoffs this year. My esteemed options trader colleague Blair Hull who has been an NFL market maker as well, reminded me that shorting the super bowl winner the next year is one of the obvious bets. There have been 47 super bowls counting this year's to be played soon. Of these 47, there have been seven repeat winners or about one seventh losers of this strategy. Also some of these teams have been so strong dynasties that shorting them would not have been wise. The seven repeat winners were:

Green Bay 1967, 1968
Miami 1973, 1974
Pittsburgh 1975, 1976, 1979, 1980
San Francisco 1989, 1990
Dallas 1993, 1994
Denver 1998, 1999
New England 2004, 2005

There has never been a three-peat so shorting these seven after they won the second time in a row produced seven winning shorts. Teams that were 7-7 then had a winning streak to win the super bowl like the New York Giants in 2012 are good candidates to short. But teams that were 14-2, say, and then won the super bowl are less obvious as shorts.

I never understood why Moss and Terrell Owens another great receiver with personal problems did not get picked up by top teams. After all when Tom Brady hit the record of 50 touchdown passes in 2008 fully 23 were to Moss and Owens can't even get a team. I then rushed to the Betfair site to bet more on San Francisco once they got Moss and Manningham knowing they had a great defense and a great running back Frank Gore, assuming they might bid for Peyton Manning — rumour has it they tried but he went to John Elway at Denver who took over as director of football operations with the goal to win the super bowl. Elway did win twice after three appearances on the losing Super Bowl team so had five super bowl appearances.

But I am short the other six teams. Four of these got knocked out during wild card weekend, see Figure 10.1. So I was then long six and short two on Betfair. My two remaining shorts, Houston and Baltimore, I assume will lose to New England (like they did a few weeks prior and with a healthy Gronkowski it looks likely) and to Denver. That's Baltimore. Sorry Ray Lewis, but the defense won't be enough. I figured as Manning would greatly outshine the erratic but pretty good Joe Flacco, Denver will win, especially at home. So if this happens, my two shorts are gone and I have only the four longs remaining. My bets are structured on Betfair so that no matter which of the six wins the super bowl, I win. That's what I wrote and believed. But as you will see below, Baltimore upset Denver. The defense of Baltimore was good but Flacco outplayed Manning. But again, mean reversion led to a profit in the game despite starting to bet on the eventual loser.

## The divisional round

My bets going into the divisional round were:

**Super Bowl bets**

| New England | +1600 | 3-3.1 |
|---|---|---|
| San Francisco | +1684 | 3.65-3.75 |
| Atlanta | +841 | 8-8.4 |
| Baltimore | -478 | 8.6-8.8 |
| Seattle | +882 | 9.2-9.6 |
| Houston | -1603 | 16.5-17 |

**AFC bets**

| New England | +280 |
|---|---|
| Baltimore | -520 |
| Houston | -460 |

**NFC bets**

| | |
|---|---|
| Green Bay | +98 |
| Atlanta | -108 |
| San Francisco | +272 |
| Seattle | -3 |

I now discuss these games.

## Green Bay at San Francisco

This was a tough one but I went with Green Bay and their MVP quarterback Aaron Rogers at 2.46, the underdog. Green Bay had a great 44 yard pass to Jones from Rogers and then on a run, it was 7-0 Green Bay. So I hedged out at 1.75. Later, the score was 14-7, then 14-14. As the score difference went up and down, my bets were

| | | | |
|---|---|---|---|
| Green Bay long at | 2.46 | and short at | 1.75 |
| | 2.32 | | |
| | 2.40 | | |
| | 2.68 | | |
| San Francisco long at | 2.66 | and short at | 1.94   and   1.44 |

So the net result was a gain no matter who won.

So it became 21-14 for San Francisco. The Green Bay got to 21-21. Akers, the San Francisco field goal kicker who has been threatened with death for his poor kicking — you see the US violence! But he got this one to make it 24-21 for San Francisco and odds of 1.61-1.62 San Francisco and Green Bay 2.6-2.62 that ended the half.

Green Bay got the ball at the start of the second half and went three and out. So did San Francisco. Then Green Bay tied the game 24-24 on a Mason Crosby field goal. Then Kaepernick in his first playoff start took over and ran for a 56 year TD. By then he had 163 yards running on 12 carriers and 2 TDs. Green Bay could not score. Kaepernick did it again this time, a 44 yard pass to Vernon Davis which led to a Frank Gore TD and a 38-24 score. Then another TD made it 45-24. A late Jennings TD from Rogers finished the game at 45-31 so San Francisco won.

So the initial long Green Bay bet did not yield a losing game because of the mean reversion risk arbitrage. The great Aaron Rogers had a pretty good game but had one key interception. Meanwhile San Francisco quarterback Colin Kaepernick had a spectacular game with 181 years rushing and 263 years passing and two touchdowns.

## Seattle at Atlanta

I went long Atlanta (1.70 at the start) because of their home field advantage, superior record, rather good team and Seattle being weak on the road. Atlanta jumped out to a 20-0 lead so I made some hedging moves. All the bets were as follows (odds long and short and amounts in ()).

| Atlanta | long | 1.7(200) |
|---------|------|----------|
|         |      | 1.72 (100) |
| Seattle | long | 2.04 (18.5) |
|         |      | 12.5 (28) |
|         |      | 14 (10) |
|         |      | 1.23 (50) |
|         |      | 1.15 (50) |
|         |      | 1.19 (20) |
| Atlanta | short | 1.36 (300) |
|         |      | 1.25 (80) |
|         |      | 1.32 (?) |
| Seattle | short | 7.6 (40 |
|         |      | 7.4 (14) |
|         |      | 5 (75) |

The scores move fast but Betfair is slow and takes 5 seconds to process the bets once you enter them so the prices often change before you can change your overall bet. That causes problems — bad fills like the stock market.

Then the score moved to 20-7 and 27-7. It was all Atlanta. Then in the second half, Russell Wilson and the rest of the team woke up and scored three consecutive touchdowns to take the lead at 28-27 with 25 seconds left and it seemed that Seattle had made yet another spectacular comeback. That seemed like too little time for Atlanta to come back and get a game winning field goal. But that was not to be. Matt Ryan rose to the challenge and with two time outs managed the 25 seconds well. He completed two long passes and that left 8 seconds on the clock. Then Seattle coach Pete Carroll made a crucial decision — try to get the kicker nervous by calling a time out just as he is kicking the supposedly game winning 49 year field goal. Unfortunately, this strategy backfired as the kicker Ryan Langwell of Atlanta missed that kick but hit the second one. So Atlanta won 30-28. Seattle had 6 seconds left and blocked the Atlanta kick so got decent field positions. Atlanta wisely squibbed the kickoff being too afraid to kick to Seattle's great Leon Washington, always a danger to return for a touchdown. Then with 2 seconds left, Wilson's hail Mary pass to the end zone was intercepted by Julio Jones. At 65 yards it was too far to try a Seattle field goal. Wilson ended up 23/34 passing for 378 years and 2 touchdowns and established himself as a great rookie and star already.

## Houston at New England

I bet on New England, my favorite team at 1.23 so a big favorite. Many Patriots games start out with them behind then they roar back. This one started with a 94 yard kickoff return by Manning that yielded a field goal so at 3-0 for Houston the odds moved to 1.38 so I bet more. So I then had 100 at 1.23, 200 at 1.26 and 100 at 1.38.

New England got a TD to make it 7-3, then a field goal to 10-3. But Gronkowski reinjured his bruised forearm — not good for future playoff games and then they still had to win this one. Brady threw a 47 yard pass to Wes Welker then a 34 yard touchdown to Shane Vereen, his second TD, so it was 17-3. Houston then made it 17-10 with a TD. Then another Brady to Ridley TD. So it was 24-13 and the Patriots were rolling. Rob Nikovich of New England intercepted a Matt Schaub pass and Ridley ran it to the 5. Then another TD pass to Lloyd — Brady's 40th career playoff TD. Then Brady to Vereen again for 38-13. Houston scored to 38-20 then 38-26 and a two point conversion made it 38-28. The odds were then 1.02-1.03 and 40-44 for Houston with 5.08 left. Houston tried an on side kick but New England recovered, hit a field goal and the game ended 41-28. So besides winning a little, this knocked out one more of my super bowl shorts. So going into January 20's games, I am long New England, San Francisco plus Atlanta and short Baltimore. New England next plays Baltimore in Foxborough as a 9 point favorite. That's the AFC playoff. The NFC playoff is San Francisco a 3-4 point favorite at Atlanta.

## Baltimore at Denver

Peyton Manning and Tom Brady are fierce competitors and brilliant students of the game and at their best at home. So I expected both New England and Denver to win. But Denver lost. Here's the story. The bet was on Denver at 1.27 and they scored the first TD. Then Flacco responded to make it 7-7. Then a Manning pass was on target but was deflected into an interception for a Baltimore TD to make it 14-7 Baltimore. A pass interference call was not made which would have nullified this. Denver got the ball and the odds were then 1.68 but the slowness to bet on Betfair lowered the odds I could get to 1.48. It takes fully 5 seconds to bet — a big operational risk. Denver scored to make it 14-14 and 1.29 odds. Another Denver TD made it 21-14 and 1.15-1.16 then 1.11-1.12. The usually reliable defender Champ Bailey could not keep up with Baltimore's receiver Tony Smith and the score was tied at 21. Denver scored on a long kick off return to go up 28-21 with odds now 1.17-1.18. A Baltimore TD tied it at 28 with odds 1.47-1.48. Trinda Holiday was the first NFL player to get punt and kickoff returns for TDs in the playoffs. Denver made it 35-28. Time was running out and the odds dropped to 1.03-1.04. Flacco tied it and left Manning at 31 seconds and 2 time outs. But coach John Fox elected to drop a knee and go into overtime. With Manning as the quarterback, I would have let him pass — see how Matt Ryan good but not Mannings's equal, saved Atlanta with less time in the Seattle game (above).

Baltimore won the toss. Again, Champ Bailey was Chump Bailey and botched another Joe Flacco pass by creating a penalty. But Baltimore did not score. Then with 51 seconds to go in the first overtime. Manning threw an interception and that led to in the second overtime. There overtimes in the NFL are simply breaks in the action not like basketball with a new tipoff. So Baltimore retained the ball. Rice ran to the 35, then they moved to the 30 and Justin Tucker won the game for Baltimore with a field goal. My hedging worked — I gained and a big plus is that with Denver out, New England gets to play Baltimore at home instead of Denver away thus upping their chances to win the super bowl or at least get into it.

My bets before this week's game for the Super Bowl were with four longs and two shorts. This was before the Houston/New England game so Houston is out. This leaves three longs (New England, San Francisco and Atlanta) with Baltimore short. Going into January 20, 2013, the NFC and AFC championship games had odds of

| San Francisco (3-4 point favorite) | 1.54-1.55 | at | Atlanta | 2.82-2.86 |
|---|---|---|---|---|
| Baltimore | 4.1-4.3 | at | New England (9 point favorite) | 1.31-1.32 |

My initial bets were

| New England | 200 | 1.31 |
|---|---|---|
| Atlanta | 100 | 2.82 |
| Atlanta+3.5 | 100 | 1.04 |

The other bets were for the super bowl

New England   +1625.99   2.18-2.22
San Francisco  +1709.49   3.05-3.1
Atlanta        +866.68    8-8.2
Baltimore      -1445.88   10-10.5

...and in the AFC

New England   +240   1.3-1.37
Baltimore     -560   4.2-4.5

...and in the NFC

San Francisco  +459.55   1.54-1.56
Atlanta        +79.00    2.78-2.86

## The Conference Championships

### The NFC: San Francisco at Atlanta

San Francisco, the away team, was favored by about 4 points at odds of 1.38. Atlanta had been strong at home and at 2.74-2.76, the bet seemed best there assuming one could hedge out if Atlanta got ahead any time in the game. Besides a straight Atlanta bet (-78.62 vs +143.00), I had 100 on Atlanta +3.5 at 1.04.

Atlanta scored first to make it 7-0 on passes to Julio Jones and Tony Gonzalez. I hedged out 80 at 1.82. My NFL championship bets were +579 San Francisco and +37 Atlanta.

Atlanta got a field goal to make it 10-0. I was then, after hedging/mean reversion, San Francisco +41 versus Atlanta +47 so a winner either way. And the Atlanta +3.5 became San Francisco +25 and Atlanta +31 hedging out the 100 at 1.58.

Atlanta scored again with another TD pass to Jones so it was 17-0 and now Atlanta became 1.30-1.31. San Francisco woke up and Le Michael James ran for a TD to make it 17-7. Then they scored again to close the gap to 17-14.

With 57 seconds left, Atlanta quarterback Matt Ryan made several good passes to Julio Jones, Roddy White and Tony Gonzalez with Gonzalez getting the TD (the 107th of his hall of fame career) with 25 seconds left in the half to make it 24-14 Atlanta.

So by the half, Ryan was 18 for 24 with 3 TDs and no interceptions.

San Francisco got the ball to start the second half. Kaepernik, who won the Seattle game mostly by running, showed his passing ability. A 22 yarder to Moss, Gore 6 to the 45 on the ground then to the Atlanta 45. Then a pass for 21 to Delanie Walker to the 21, then to Moss to the 5. Kaepernik was then 11/12. Gore ran for the TD to make it 24-21.

The tide was turning in San Francisco's favor and more so when Ryan threw an interception by Culliver on the San Francisco 44. A Vernon Davis reception got it to the 25 and James got it to the 20. Then Akers, who has received death threats for missing the most (13) field goals in the NFL, missed another one. After a pro bowl pick last year. This year has been very poor for Akers and this has hurt San Francisco. So San Francisco got no points. Atlanta got the ball but star running back Michael Turner left with an ankle injury. Then Ryan made another mistake by fumbling with Adam Smith getting the recovery.

My NFC Conference bets were then

| San Francisco | +319 | 1.64-1.82 |
| Atlanta | +257 | 2.2-3.15 |

For the Super Bowl I had

| New England | +1646.99 |
| San Francisco | +1730.49 |
| Atlanta | +1142.99 |
| Baltimore | -1424.88 |

and in the Super Bowl contestants

| New England | +320 |
| the rest | -100 |

which I moved to New England +245, the rest 0, so I could not lose on that bet. In Super Bowls, San Francisco was a perfect 5-0.

San Francisco drove to the 5 with a run by Gore. Then Crabtree got to the goal line but fumbled by being stripped and the Falcons recovered it so Atlanta had the ball on their one yard line. Atlanta got to 3rd and 5 then to Gonzales to the 8 but had to punt.

San Francisco returned to the 38 of Atlanta. Gore got to the 30 then with 11.17 left in the 4th quarter. Dixon ran for the first down. Then Jones to the 17, Crabtree to the 9 with a gain of 8. Then Gore scored the TD to make San Francisco ahead for the first time in the game at 28-24. With 6.13 left, Atlanta had the ball. Jones was then 10 catches for 158 years. Douglas got to the San Francisco 30 then to the 19 and with 2 minutes left, second and 9 from the 15. Smelling got to the 10. A field goal would not help as San Francisco was ahead by 4 points. Third and fourth down produced nothing so San Francisco got the ball. Atlanta had two time outs.

Atlanta got the ball with 1.00 left but needed a TD to win the game. At 10 seconds and 6 seconds, passes failed so San Francisco won the game.

Jones ended up 11 catches for 182 yards.

I won the NFC Conference bet +319.55 vs +257 for Atlanta. My bets were then for the Super Bowl:

| | |
|---|---|
| San Francisco | +1576.99 |
| New England | +1758.98 |
| Baltimore | -1494.88 |

and for the Super Bowl combo

+245 New England/San Francisco
+0 Baltimore/San Francisco

So it was looking promising going into the New England/Baltimore game.


## The AFC: Baltimore at New England

The Patriots beat Baltimore handily in New England and this was a re-match in the playoffs. New England was a 9 point favorite and that led to odds of 1.31-1.32 and 4.2-4.3 for Baltimore. Formulas to convert point spread to odds are provided in papers by Professor Hal Stern; see Hausch, Lo and Ziemba (2008).

My bets were as follows:

Conference markets
| | | |
|---|---|---|
| New England | +240 | 1.31-1.32 |
| Baltimore | -560 | 4.2-4.3 |

Super Bowl Combinations
| | | |
|---|---|---|
| New England-San Francicso | +245 | 1.29-1.34 |
| Baltimore-San Francisco | 0 | 4.2.4.4 |

Super Bowl
| | | |
|---|---|---|
| New England | +1775 | 2.24-2.28 |
| San Francisco | +1858.50 | 2.16-2.18 |
| Baltimore | -1296.87 | 9.6-9.8 |

Game
  New England    +62    1.31-1.32
  Baltimore      -200   4.2-4.3

Rob Gronkowski was out — a real negative for New England and, as I will argue below, super important in the final outcome. New England received then, after successive three and outs of both team, got a field goal with Hernandez running 6 to the 12 but they failed to score the TD. So the score was 3-0. Flacco was sharp 5/5 and a 25 yard pass got Baltimore to the 15. Ray Rice ran to the 2 then got the TD so it was 7-3. New England fought back. A 15 yard penalty got the ball to New England's 39.

Lloyd ran for a first down to the 50. Ridley ran to the 43 then a Welker reception from Brady got it to the 15. Then Ridley to the 8 and Hernandez to the 2 and Welker scored. It was then 10-7 New England and they looked sharp. They sacked Flacco and Baltimore three and out made them kick from the goal. Welker made a good return. Then a pass to Hernandez gained 17. Then the first of several key mistakes from the 25. Brady waited too long to call the time out so there was no time for a play before the field goal try. They made the field goal to make it 13-7 but again could not get the TD. That ended the half. New England was ahead but had squandered two TD chances for field goals.

Baltimore got the ball to start the second half. There was a pass to Jones to the 25 and one to Boldin to the 49 but a three and out gave New England the ball. Welker caught the kickoff but only got to the 9. Ridley got a first down to the 20. Then Welker got to the 50. Bernard Pollard, who makes very tough hits — legal but brutal and in my opinion these should be illegal, hit Welker. He had knocked Brady out for a year and injured Welker before. By then Hernandez already had 8 catches. Then the usually reliable Welker dropped a pass (maybe shaken up by Pollard's hit?) and they had to punt. Baltimore got the ball on a return to the 50. Then a pass to Rice got it to the 35 then the 30. Then Baltimore for 12 to the 8 then to 6 and a TD to Pitta so it was 14-13.

I did not like the feel of it so bid at 1.23 to hedge out my New England 200 bet on this game. But the market was 1.23 and I did not go there. A mistake on my part. I felt New England without Gronkowski. was not sharp enough and was making too many mistakes and did not score TDs.

New England got the ball. Welker got to the 25 and Danny Woodhead got it to the 41. A holding penalty hurt and it was a three and out. Torrey Smith gained 23 to the New England 44. New England was offside — another mistake. Pierce got to the 24 then the 18 then Flacco ran to the

9 and Boldin got to the 5. Price got a first down and Baltimore scored to make it 21-13.

My bets were in serious trouble but there was not much I could do so did nothing. In retrospect — some hedging would have been better. I just assumed incorrectly that New England would come back but they simply could not score TDs. The cure would have been a healthy Gronkowski — they lost the 2012 Super Bowl for the same reason.

The statistics bear this out. With Gronkowski, Brady's completion percent is 65.7% versus 58.4% without him. And yards per play drop from 6 to 5.4. Also the TD/interception ratio falls from 23-3 to 11-6. So he is a major factor!

It got worse. Ridley gained 9 then a first down. Then Lloyd got to the 42, then Ridley fumbled the first turnover of the game. The gig was up — New England had likely had it. Baldin scored another Baltimore TD to make it 28-13. On TV they reminded us that New England was 67-0 when leading at halftime. Brady threw an interception with the ball batted into the air to end the game so New England was now 67-1 when leading at half-time. Flacco outplayed Brady just like he outplayed Peyton Manning the week before.

**Results of the Conference Playoffs**

So I lost the AFC bets, the bet on the game, the bets on New England to win the Super Bowl. It was disappointing. My bets for the Super Bowl since San Francisco beat Atlanta were San Francisco +1119.50; Baltimore +13.13.

So I could not lose there. Since San Francisco was favored to win the Super Bowl, I could move at good prices some of the San Francisco gain into a Baltimore gain. Flacco was looking like the elite quarterback he claims he is so maybe he will outplay Kaepernick. Anyway, I decided to have more on Baltimore and less on San Francisco. When the New England bets went off and I shorted San Francisco at about 1.56, my bets were

San Francisco   +1359.53   1.6-1.61
Baltimore        +253.13    2.64-2.66

Shorting 300 at 1.61 gave San Francisco +1176.5, Baltimore +553.13.

The Super Bowl was brother versus brother: Jim (49ers coach) vs John Harbaugh (Baltimore coach) — a historic matchup, the first time ever that head coaches were in the same family.

## Super Bowl 47: San Francisco versus Baltimore

I was in France lecturing to the Reims Management School about financial market bubbles. France blocks Betfair and the Super Bowl was not on French TV and all the free video hookups for the game didn't work, but I was able to buy access for 7.99€ and could watch the game. But there was no changing of my bets — I could not lose as my previous hedging led to +1176.5 if San Francisco won and +553.13 if Baltimore won. San Francisco was favored and seems to be the better team but Baltimore was trending better and better with each new game and quarterback Joe Flacco had no playoff interceptions in wins against Andrew Luck, Peyton Manning and Tom Brady, the latter two in their opponents very favored home turf. There was a lot of mean reversion so I could have gained from that had I been somewhere where Betfair was allowed.

San Francisco got the ball first and went 3 and out. They were 5-0 in previous Super Bowls and their quarterbacks Joe Montana and Steve Young threw 17 TDs with no interceptions. Baltimore won its only previous Super Bowl appearance as the Ravens. The Baltimore Colts became the Indianapolis Colts. This was Colin Kaepernick's ninth start, the third fewest ever to start in the Super Bowl. Ray Lewis, the inspirational leader at the Ravens, was set to retire after this game. In 17 seasons he has not slowed down and his 44 tackles in the 2013 post season was the most ever.

Baltimore got the ball. Rice got a first down and a Torrey Smith got it to the 19. Then Anquan Boldin who would star all day, caught a TD pass from Joe Flacco, his 4th in the playoffs, so it was 7-0.

San Francsico got the ball on the 20 with no return of the kickoff. After a Gore (-2) a pass to Crabtree got to the 40. Then Gore ran to the 48 and Kaepernick ran to the 43 of Baltimore for a first down to the 32 and a Vernon Davis reception got them to the 8. Kaepernick missed an open Crabtree and then got sacked at the 18. Akers got the field goal so it was 7-3.

This was now the 6th time in the playoffs where a team was inside the Baltimore 25 with only one TD allowed. So the Ravens defense has been strong in the red zone. The brothers Jim and John were 7/7 in the post season. So who would lose? Ed Reed, the great defensive back of the Ravens got injured in a collision with Crabtree so was out but did return later in the game.

Lots of competing companies like Coke and Pepsi had numerous $3.8 million 30 second ads. Most were not creative like the famous mean Joe Green Coke ad where a small boy give Joe a coke while he was walking through the tunnel after the game, heading to the locker room, looking exhausted.

Baltimore started moving. Flacco started sharp and got to the 31 with a pass to Dennie Pitta. Then a pass got to Anquan Boldin, who had a great game, got them to the 35. A long pass to Torrey Smith was overthrown and they finally sacked Flacco back to the 42, and were out of field goal range. Ed Reed returned. San Francisco got a good run by Kaepernick to the 29 running away from the dangerous hitter Pollard.

Davis got another 1st down to the Baltimore 40. Le Michael James ran for 9 and 5. Gore got 7 to the 29. Then James fumbled (his 2nd of the post season) and Baltimore got the ball on the 37. Gains by Pitta, Dickson and Rice got to the 22. A 15 yard facemask penalty helped and Rice got it to the 3. Then Flacco got the TD to Pitta so the score was then 14-3. That made Flacco 10 TDs and no interceptions in the post season — he was on his way to elite quarterback status and a lucrative new contract. The irony is that Baltimore might release their top receiver, Boldin, to have money to pay Flacco. Of course, it was Boldin who helped Flacco look good with spectacular catches. In fact what happened was Boldin was released and traded and Flacco was never that good again.

San Francisco got the ball and gave it back to Baltimore on an Ed Reed interception (the 9th of his post season career). Before that San Francisco quarterback Joe Montana (the surgeon) and Steve Young (the scrambler) were 17/17 in Super Bowls.

Baltimore got to the 38 of San Francisco. Then Rice to the 33 and then to the 27 and the 22. Then a pass to Rice to the 15. Boldin missed a pass that was almost intercepted. A pass went over Smith's head in the end zone. And then a Justin Tucker field goal attempt — but it was a fake and Tuker nearly got the 1st down being one yard short. So the 49ers took over on their 6. An almost interception on a pass to Moss plus a gain of 6 by Gore led to a 3 and out.

It was now 2.07 to go in the half with Baltimore getting the second half kickoff and two time outs here. Offensive pass interference was not called. A long Flacco pass to Jacoby Jones and it was 21-3.

San Francisco got to the 45 then with 57 seconds left Davis gained 8. Gore for no gain then a time out. At 3rd and 2 with 21 seconds left Kaepernick did not throw — a serious error — and Lewis sacked him. With 3 seconds to go, Akers hit his second field goal so the first half ended 21-6.

Jacoby Jones opened the second half with a record setting 109 year kickoff return. There have been 108 yard TDs but this was the first 109. So it was 28-6. Flacco was 13/20 for 192 yards and 3 TDs and no interceptions while Kaepernick was 8/13 for 139 with no TDs and an interception. Roger Goodell was in his box with a superstar running back with 35 TDs and 8 yards a carry — an 8 year old girl!

San Francisco returned the kickoff to the 13. A pass to Crabtree gained 29 and Gore got to the 46 after Kaepernick gained 15 to the 40 following a -6 sack. Then suddenly the lights in half the stadium went out and stayed out for 34 minutes. This seemed to energize San Francisco. Moss got a first down gaining 50 then to Davis and a Crabtree TD. So it became 28-13.

There was a sack of Flacco on the 8 then a San Francisco return to the 20. And quickly a pass to Davis to the 6 and a Gore TD so now it was 28-20. San Francisco was on a roll and then Baltimore's Rice fumbled, his 3rd of the post season. San Francisco was on the 24 of Baltimore then. Gore got to the 21. Then a 3rd on 7 produced nothing. Akers 39 yards field goal missed on 4th on 7 but Williams ran into Akers for a roughing the kicker penalty to make it 4th and 2. But now from 34 yards, Akers hit the field goal and it was 28-23. Akers who missed the most field goals this year had the most (44) made last year.

Baltimore got to the 27 and on 2nd and 7 Pierce gained 4. Boldin got the first down. Pitta and Rice had gains and Pierce got the first down on the 18 and the 3rd quarter ended. Pierce left with a strained knee. Rice gained 4 and a Flacco to Boldin pass got to the 5. Rice got to the 1 and that made a 100 yard game for him. From 3rd and goal, Flacco miraculously eluded tacklers so avoided a big loss. But no TD just a field goal to make it 31-23.

San Francisco got to the 21 on the kickoff. Then Gore got to the 29. Moss caught a 32 yard pass to the Baltimore 40 — say New England why did you get rid of Moss? Gore got to the 20 and Kaepernick to the 15 and then for the TD. That 15 yard TD run was the longest by a quarterback in Super Bowl history. So it was 31-29. A two point conversion attempt failed when Baltimore blitzed and Kaepernick's pass sailed away.

Baltimore got to the 22 on the kickoff. Pierce got to the 38 and on 2nd and 8. Boldin apparently got the 1st down to the 45. A San Francisco challenge of the spot succeeded so it was 3rd and 1. Another pass to Boldin got it to the 40. Rice took it to the 28. Then with 5.25 left, Pierce gained 1 and it was 3rd and 7. A San Francisco off side penalty made it 3rd on 2. But the pass failed and Baltimore got a 38 yard field goal to make it 34-29.

The kickoff was not returned so SFO got the ball on the 20. Gore got 7. Then with 3.43 remaining, Kaepernick ran for a 1st down. A long pass to Davis was dropped. Crabtree gained 24 to Baltimore's 40. Gore gained 7 to the 33. James gained 5 and then there was the 2 minute warning. From 2nd and goal on the 5, a pass was missed then another so it was 4th and goal. Yet another pass failed. There was 1.46 left and Rice gained then San Francisco used their final time out. With 0.51 left, a punt was coming. But San Francisco, with a 5 point lead, elected to take a safety and use precious clock time that used 8 seconds from 12 to 4 left. A kick from the 20 following the safety used up the 4 seconds and Baltimore, the underdog in its last 3 games in the playoffs, won 34-31. Flacco was named MVP and is going now for a Brady/Manning type contract of about $18 million per year. He got $20 million! Actually Drew Brees of New Orleans had the highest salary at $20 million per year until 2017 when Derek Carr, the quarterback of the Oakland Raiders got $25 million per year.

It was Ziemba's opinion that Baltimore won the game by stopping opponents from scoring in the red zone and brilliant receiving by Boldin. HIs prediction was that getting rid of Boldin because all the money was spent on Flacco would lead to poorer future team performance and it did.

I won the +553 bet less the commission. Although I won, there were two bad mistakes, namely, not eliminating the Baltimore shorts earlier and getting more neutral on New England once it looked like they had lost it early in the second quarter of the Baltimore game. Without Gronkowski, they are not as good as they need to be to win. Baltimore's defense was terrific, especially in the red zone.

# Chapter 11

# The 2013-2014 Playoffs and the Super Bowl

We take this up after week 16 in late December 2013 and finish on February 2, 2014 after the Super Bowl. There was one more week to play and then each team will have played 16 games with one week off. Some observations:

1. Baltimore won last year's Super Bowl, beating San Francisco. Joe Flacco, the Baltimore quarterback, was excellent in the playoffs with no interceptions and many touchdowns. He was the Super Bowl MVP. This led to a $20 million elite status for him but at the expense of getting rid of his top receiver, Anquan Boldin, who was traded to San Francisco and not surprisingly became their top receiver. In addition, Ray Lewis, the great defensive linebacker and team leader retired. Historically, both the winner (over bet) and the loser (mean reverting back) were poor bets the following year. And Baltimore failed to make the playoffs. Flacco had 23 interceptions this year, returning to his pretty good but not elite quarterback status. But San Francisco is in the playoffs and doing well and almost made it to the Super Bowl.

2. New England coach Bill Belichick, usually a smart manager, got rid of his second best receiver Wes Welker. A monumental mistake based on silly personal revenge — all starting with Belichick punishing Welker for a small amount of trash talk by keeping him out of a key playoff game which in my opinion was lost when Brady threw an interception with Welker not there. And Welker went to Manning adding to the powerful Denver offense. Meanwhile, New England's top receiver, Rob Gronkowski, recovered from injury then got knocked out again. And the third best receiver, Aaron Hernandez, was accused of murder so was dropped from the team. They also let Deion Branch go to Indianapolis and Danny Woodhead go to San Diego. They also lost

149

to injury top defense aces Vince Wilfork and Jerod Mayo. There were players coming and going but somehow with Tom Brady's great passing skill, they go into week 17 having won all their home games and are 11-4 having won their AFC North division again. And they won in week 17 to finish 12-4 and become the #2 seed in the AFC so have a bye during wildcard weekend and home field until possibly the AFC championship in Denver. *Note added later:* I underestimated Belichick. Instead of rebuilding around star quarterback Tom Brady, he got Brady some decent receivers and a group of four very good running backs. So he reinvented the team into rushing not passing. Meanwhile, he has a great quarterback and perhaps the best one in the clutch in the whole NFL. Bravo to Belichick. Brady and Belichick are the best quarterback coaches in playoff history with 18 wins. See January 10's game analysis below.

3. There has been no dominant team with lower ranked teams beating top teams or making the games close to the finish. Seattle is the top ranked team with the best defense, a top quarterback and running back and a strong offensive line and most important the noisiest stadium in the NFL. They call that the 12th man and it works. Opposing teams have a record number of false starts while playing in Seattle. They simply cannot hear instructions. Seattle looked invincible at home with no losses since rookie Russell Wilson became their quarterback last year. But even they got beaten at home by the Arizona Cardinals last week. Arizona was no slouch and is at 10-5 and a possibility of a wild card position after this weekend's games. Unfortunately, they did not make the playoffs losing in overtime to San Francisco.

4. Peyton Manning threw 55 touchdowns breaking Tom Brady's record of 50 and he beat Dan Marino's passing yards record of 5477 by a single yard. Denver became the first NFL team to score over 600 points, averaging 37.9 points per game. Meanwhile, Drew Brees threw for over 5000 yards in 2013 his fourth such accomplishment. No other quarterback has more than one 5000 yards season. Philadelphia is 8-2 with Nick Foles quarterbacking with a 119 QB rating, the 3rd best in league history and higher than even Peyton Manning's 2013 year. Foles had 27 touchdowns and only 2 interceptions. I went with New Orleans because Philadephia's defense is 29th which is poor. Foles became the starting quarterback following a Michael Vick injury. This game will be tough though with Pierre Thomas, New Orleans leading rusher out. But New Orleans has top running and passing games so can pile up a lot of points They are not favored so hedging out might be the plan here.

Table 11.1: The standings after week 17

AFC
East Division

| Team | W | L | T | PCT | PF | PA | Home | Road | DIV | CONF |
|---|---|---|---|---|---|---|---|---|---|---|
| New England - y | 12 | 4 | 0 | .750 | 444 | 338 | 8-0-0 | 4-4-0 | 4-2-0 | 9-3-0 |
| New York | 8 | 8 | 0 | .500 | 290 | 387 | 6-2-0 | 2-6-0 | 3-3-0 | 5-7-0 |
| Miami | 8 | 8 | 0 | .500 | 317 | 335 | 4-4-0 | 4-4-0 | 2-4-0 | 7-5-0 |
| Buffalo | 6 | 10 | 0 | .375 | 339 | 388 | 4-4-0 | 2-6-0 | 3-3-0 | 5-7-0 |

North Division

| Team | W | L | T | PCT | PF | PA | Home | Road | DIV | CONF |
|---|---|---|---|---|---|---|---|---|---|---|
| Cincinnati - y | 11 | 5 | 0 | .688 | 430 | 305 | 8-0-0 | 3-5-0 | 3-3-0 | 8-4-0 |
| Pittsburgh | 8 | 8 | 0 | .500 | 379 | 370 | 5-3-0 | 3-5-0 | 4-2-0 | 6-6-0 |
| Baltimore | 8 | 8 | 0 | .500 | 320 | 352 | 6-2-0 | 2-6-0 | 3-3-0 | 6-6-0 |
| Cleveland | 4 | 12 | 0 | .250 | 308 | 406 | 3-5-0 | 1-7-0 | 2-4-0 | 3-9-0 |

South Division

| Team | W | L | T | PCT | PF | PA | Home | Road | DIV | CONF |
|---|---|---|---|---|---|---|---|---|---|---|
| Indianapolis - y | 11 | 5 | 0 | .688 | 391 | 336 | 6-2-0 | 5-3-0 | 6-0-0 | 9-3-0 |
| Tennessee | 7 | 9 | 0 | .438 | 362 | 381 | 3-5-0 | 4-4-0 | 2-4-0 | 6-6-0 |
| Jacksonville | 4 | 12 | 0 | .250 | 247 | 449 | 1-7-0 | 3-5-0 | 3-3-0 | 4-8-0 |
| Houston | 2 | 14 | 0 | .125 | 276 | 428 | 1-7-0 | 1-7-0 | 1-5-0 | 2-10-0 |

West Division

| Team | W | L | T | PCT | PF | PA | Home | Road | DIV | CONF |
|---|---|---|---|---|---|---|---|---|---|---|
| Denver - y | 13 | 3 | 0 | .813 | 606 | 399 | 7-1-0 | 6-2-0 | 5-1-0 | 9-3-0 |
| Kansas City - z | 11 | 5 | 0 | .688 | 430 | 305 | 5-3-0 | 6-2-0 | 2-4-0 | 7-5-0 |
| San Diego - z | 9 | 7 | 0 | .563 | 396 | 348 | 5-3-0 | 4-4-0 | 4-2-0 | 6-6-0 |
| Oakland | 4 | 12 | 0 | .250 | 322 | 453 | 3-5-0 | 1-7-0 | 1-5-0 | 4-8-0 |

NFC
East Division

| Team | W | L | T | PCT | PF | PA | Home | Road | DIV | CONF |
|---|---|---|---|---|---|---|---|---|---|---|
| Philadelphia - y | 10 | 6 | 0 | .625 | 442 | 382 | 4-4-0 | 6-2-0 | 4-2-0 | 9-3-0 |
| Dallas | 8 | 8 | 0 | .500 | 439 | 432 | 5-3-0 | 3-5-0 | 5-1-0 | 7-5-0 |
| New York | 7 | 9 | 0 | .438 | 294 | 383 | 4-4-0 | 3-5-0 | 3-3-0 | 6-6-0 |
| Washington | 3 | 13 | 0 | .188 | 334 | 478 | 2-6-0 | 1-7-0 | 0-6-0 | 1-11-0 |

North Division

| Team | W | L | T | PCT | PF | PA | Home | Road | DIV | CONF |
|---|---|---|---|---|---|---|---|---|---|---|
| Green Bay - y | 8 | 7 | 1 | .531 | 417 | 428 | 4-3-1 | 4-4-0 | 3-2-1 | 6-5-1 |
| Chicago | 8 | 8 | 0 | .500 | 445 | 478 | 5-3-0 | 3-5-0 | 2-4-0 | 4-8-0 |
| Detroit | 7 | 9 | 0 | .438 | 395 | 376 | 4-4-0 | 3-5-0 | 4-2-0 | 6-6-0 |
| Minnesota | 5 | 10 | 1 | .344 | 391 | 480 | 5-3-0 | 0-7-1 | 2-3-1 | 4-7-1 |

South Division

| Team | W | L | T | PCT | PF | PA | Home | Road | DIV | CONF |
|---|---|---|---|---|---|---|---|---|---|---|
| Carolina - y | 12 | 4 | 0 | .750 | 366 | 241 | 7-1-0 | 5-3-0 | 5-1-0 | 9-3-0 |
| New Orleans - z | 11 | 5 | 0 | .688 | 414 | 304 | 8-0-0 | 3-5-0 | 5-1-0 | 9-3-0 |
| Atlanta | 4 | 12 | 0 | .250 | 353 | 443 | 3-5-0 | 1-7-0 | 1-5-0 | 3-9-0 |
| Tampa Bay | 4 | 12 | 0 | .250 | 288 | 389 | 3-5-0 | 1-7-0 | 1-5-0 | 2-10-0 |

West Division

| Team | W | L | T | PCT | PF | PA | Home | Road | DIV | CONF |
|---|---|---|---|---|---|---|---|---|---|---|
| Seattle - y | 13 | 3 | 0 | .813 | 417 | 231 | 7-1-0 | 6-2-0 | 4-2-0 | 10-2-0 |
| San Francisco - z | 12 | 4 | 0 | .750 | 406 | 272 | 6-2-0 | 6-2-0 | 5-1-0 | 9-3-0 |
| Arizona | 10 | 6 | 0 | .625 | 379 | 324 | 6-2-0 | 4-4-0 | 2-4-0 | 6-6-0 |
| St. Louis | 7 | 9 | 0 | .438 | 348 | 364 | 5-3-0 | 2-6-0 | 1-5-0 | 4-8-0 |

Table 11.2: Elo ratings for week 17

| Team | Elo | Team | Elo |
|------|-----|------|-----|
| Arizona | 1027.7 | Miami | 989.2 |
| Atlanta | 957.5 | Minnesota | 968.3 |
| Baltimore | 989.2 | New England | 1044.8 |
| Buffalo | 976.6 | New Orleans | 1037.3 |
| Carolina | 1046.0 | NY Giants | 978.2 |
| Chicago | 983.2 | NY Jets | 974.9 |
| Cincinnati | 1038.7 | Oakland | 944.0 |
| Cleveland | 948.5 | Philadelphia | 1027.3 |
| Dallas | 997.8 | Pittsburgh | 1010.0 |
| Denver | 1062.7 | San Diego | 1019.6 |
| Detroit | 992.3 | San Francisco | 1052.5 |
| Green Bay | 989.7 | Seattle | 1063.3 |
| Houston | 926.0 | St. Louis | 996.8 |
| Indianapolis | 1021.3 | Tampa Bay | 959.8 |
| Jacksonville | 935.4 | Tennessee | 986.9 |
| Kansas City | 1030.5 | Washington | 938.4 |

5. The standing and ELO ratings after week 17, going into wildcard weekend are in Tables 11.1 and 11.2. These adjust for the home field advantage and give the probability of winning and Hal Stern's probability estimates. The real home field advantage seems to be larger. For example, New Orleans with Drew Brees quarterbacking have never won a road playoff game. And you will see below that that continued in January 2014.

6. Green Bay at home with Aaron Rogers back and freezing weather might be tough but San Francisco seems too tough given that Green Bay just snuck into the playoffs. So I went with them.

7. My Super Bowl bets are shown in Table 11.3: here you can see the bid-ask prices and under each team is my gain or loss showing what I can win or lose on the Super Bowl with no more changes.

So far I am short Carolina, the #2 seed in the NFC who have a bye in the wildcard week end. So I have to watch that. And I am short Philadelphia, another danger. They beat Dallas so Dallas is out. I am long all the others with a gain if any of them wins the Super Bowl. In the end, as you will see below, both Philly and Carolina got beat so I ended up with the four top teams in my view: Seattle, Denver, San Francisco and New England with good gains no matter who wins the Super Bowl.

Table 11.3: My Betfair bets on the Super Bowl, in £

| | | 103.30% | Back | Lay | 98.70% | |
|---|---|---|---|---|---|---|
| Seattle Seahawks | 3.65 | 3.7 | 3.75 | 3.85 | 3.9 | 3.95 |
| £782.70 | £268 | £190 | £862 | £1537 | £447 | £2422 |
| Denver Broncos | 3.9 | 3.95 | 4 | 4.1 | 4.2 | 4.3 |
| £444.90 | £439 | £44 | £1220 | £222 | £958 | £500 |
| Carolina Panthers | 10.5 | 11 | 11.5 | 12.5 | 13 | 13.5 |
| £-1,718.00 | £1019 | £99 | £402 | £100 | £48 | £5 |
| New England Patriots | 9.8 | 10 | 10.5 | 11.5 | 12 | 12.5 |
| £902.88 | £61 | £380 | £673 | £263 | £209 | £226 |
| San Francisco 49ers | 10 | 10.5 | 11 | 11.5 | 12 | 12.5 |
| £702.00 | £392 | £170 | £1311 | £96 | £338 | £352 |
| Cincinnati Bengals | 17.5 | 18 | 18.5 | 19.5 | 20 | 21 |
| £13.42 | £39 | £1026 | £628 | £139 | £106 | £115 |
| Green Bay Packers | 21 | 22 | 23 | 24 | 25 | 26 |
| £10.00 | £160 | £222 | £100 | £33 | £196 | £135 |
| Philadelphia Eagles | 21 | 22 | 23 | 24 | 25 | 26 |
| £-2,668.00 | £16 | £94 | £232 | £114 | £183 | £346 |
| New Orleans Saints | 29 | 30 | 32 | 34 | 36 | 1000 |
| £182.00 | £65 | £257 | £121 | £52 | £23 | £2 |
| Indianapolis Colts | 36 | 38 | 40 | 42 | 44 | 46 |
| £452.89 | £106 | £197 | £143 | £63 | £37 | £16 |
| Kansas City Chiefs | 32 | 34 | 36 | 40 | 42 | 44 |
| £197.00 | £15 | £13 | £161 | £100 | £7 | £7 |
| San Diego Chargers | 48 | 50 | 55 | 60 | 65 | 70 |
| £752.00 | £102 | £285 | £91 | £25 | £38 | £134 |

Here 3.65 is odds with 268£ offered long on Seattle at that price and £1537 is offered short at odds of 3.85. These are British odds so 3-1 means bet 1 to possibly collect 3 and win 2. Should Seattle win the Super Bowl, I would win £782.70 but lose £1718 if Carolina wins. That is if I make no changes as the playoffs progress.

In addition I have the following Super Bowl combo bets:

| Initial combos | After Baltimore lost and did not make the playoffs |
|---|---|
| Denver/Seattle +113 | Denver/Seattle +125 |
| New England/Seattle +248 | New England/Seattle +260 |
| Baltimore/Seattle +253.00 | |
| all others -112 | |

Table 11.4: NFL Team Total Offense Statistics, Net Total Yard Leaders, 2013

| RK | TEAM | YDS | YDS/G | PASS | P YDS/G | RUSH | R YDS/G | PTS | PTS/G |
|----|------|-----|-------|------|---------|------|---------|-----|-------|
| 1 | Denver | 7317 | 457.3 | 5444 | 340.3 | 1873 | 117.1 | 606 | 37.9 |
| 2 | Philadelphia | 6676 | 417.3 | 4110 | 256.9 | 2566 | 160.4 | 442 | 27.6 |
| 3 | Green Bay | 6404 | 400.3 | 4268 | 266.8 | 2136 | 133.5 | 417 | 26.1 |
| 4 | New Orleans | 6391 | 399.4 | 4918 | 307.4 | 1473 | 92.1 | 414 | 25.9 |
| 5 | San Diego | 6293 | 393.3 | 4328 | 270.5 | 1965 | 122.8 | 396 | 24.8 |
| 6 | Detroit | 6274 | 392.1 | 4482 | 280.1 | 1792 | 112.0 | 395 | 24.7 |
| 7 | New England | 6152 | 384.5 | 4087 | 255.4 | 2065 | 129.1 | 444 | 27.8 |
| 8 | Chicago | 6109 | 381.8 | 4281 | 267.6 | 1828 | 114.3 | 445 | 27.8 |
| 9 | Washington | 5915 | 369.7 | 3751 | 234.4 | 2164 | 135.3 | 334 | 20.9 |
| 10 | Cincinnati | 5894 | 368.4 | 4139 | 258.7 | 1755 | 109.7 | 430 | 26.9 |
| 11 | Houston | 5556 | 347.3 | 3813 | 238.3 | 1743 | 108.9 | 276 | 17.3 |
| 12 | Arizona | 5542 | 346.4 | 4002 | 250.1 | 1540 | 96.3 | 379 | 23.7 |
| 13 | Minnesota | 5508 | 344.3 | 3427 | 214.2 | 2081 | 130.1 | 391 | 24.4 |
| 14 | Atlanta | 5490 | 343.1 | 4243 | 265.2 | 1247 | 77.9 | 353 | 22.1 |
| 15 | Indianapolis | 5468 | 341.8 | 3725 | 232.8 | 1743 | 108.9 | 391 | 24.4 |
| 16 | Dallas | 5461 | 341.3 | 3954 | 247.1 | 1507 | 94.2 | 439 | 27.4 |
| 17 | Seattle | 5424 | 339.0 | 3236 | 202.3 | 2188 | 136.8 | 417 | 26.1 |
| 18 | Cleveland | 5423 | 338.9 | 4040 | 252.5 | 1383 | 86.4 | 308 | 19.3 |
| 19 | Buffalo | 5410 | 338.1 | 3103 | 193.9 | 2307 | 144.2 | 339 | 21.2 |
| 20 | Pittsburgh | 5400 | 337.5 | 4017 | 251.1 | 1383 | 86.4 | 379 | 23.7 |
| 21 | Kansas City | 5396 | 337.3 | 3340 | 208.8 | 2056 | 128.5 | 430 | 26.9 |
| 22 | Tennessee | 5390 | 336.9 | 3496 | 218.5 | 1894 | 118.4 | 362 | 22.6 |
| 23 | Oakland | 5340 | 333.8 | 3340 | 208.8 | 2000 | 125.0 | 322 | 20.1 |
| 24 | San Francisco | 5180 | 323.8 | 2979 | 186.2 | 2201 | 137.6 | 406 | 25.4 |
| 25 | NY Jets | 5090 | 318.1 | 2932 | 183.3 | 2158 | 134.9 | 290 | 18.1 |
| 26 | Carolina | 5069 | 316.8 | 3043 | 190.2 | 2026 | 126.6 | 366 | 22.9 |
| 27 | Miami | 5007 | 312.9 | 3567 | 222.9 | 1440 | 90.0 | 317 | 19.8 |
| 28 | NY Giants | 4920 | 307.5 | 3588 | 224.3 | 1332 | 83.3 | 294 | 18.4 |
| 29 | Baltimore | 4918 | 307.4 | 3590 | 224.4 | 1328 | 83.0 | 320 | 20.0 |
| 30 | St. Louis | 4877 | 304.8 | 3125 | 195.3 | 1752 | 109.5 | 348 | 21.8 |
| 31 | Jacksonville | 4701 | 293.8 | 3441 | 215.1 | 1260 | 78.8 | 247 | 15.4 |
| 32 | Tampa Bay | 4432 | 277.0 | 2820 | 176.3 | 1612 | 100.8 | 288 | 18.0 |

Glossary: YDS: Net total yards YDS/G: Net yards per game PASS: Net passing yards P YDS/G: Net passing yards per game RUSH: Rushing yards R YDS/G: Rushing yards per game PTS: Total points PTS/G: Points per game

8. Useful information on the various teams is in Tables 11.4 (total offense statistics), 11.5 (the turnover statistics) and 11.6 (the offensive and defensive ratings). Seattle is #1 on defense and Carolina #2. On offense Denver is first and Detroit which is not in the playoffs is second. These ratings are useful but flawed as they just measure one thing: yards gained. So Detroit and Houston which lost 14 straight games) are examples of how it is misleading. But it is some helpful information. Seattle is the best with takeaways (39) and looks like the top team in the NFL.

Table 11.5: Team Take-Aways, Give-Aways Statistics — 2013

| RK | TEAM | Takeaway | | | Giveaway | | | |
|---|---|---|---|---|---|---|---|---|
| | | INT | FUM | TOTAL | INT | FUM | TOTAL | DIFF |
| NFC | | | | | | | | |
| 1 | Seattle | 28 | 11 | 39 | 9 | 10 | 19 | 20 |
| 2 | San Francisco | 18 | 12 | 30 | 8 | 10 | 18 | 12 |
| | Philadelphia | 19 | 12 | 31 | 9 | 10 | 19 | 12 |
| 4 | Carolina | 20 | 10 | 30 | 13 | 6 | 19 | 11 |
| 5 | Tampa Bay | 21 | 10 | 31 | 12 | 9 | 21 | 10 |
| 6 | Dallas | 15 | 12 | 27 | 12 | 8 | 20 | 7 |
| 7 | Chicago | 19 | 9 | 28 | 13 | 10 | 23 | 5 |
| 8 | St. Louis | 14 | 15 | 29 | 11 | 10 | 29 | 0 |
| | New Orleans | 12 | 7 | 19 | 12 | 7 | 19 | 0 |
| 10 | Arizona | 20 | 10 | 30 | 22 | 9 | 31 | -1 |
| 11 | Green Bay | 11 | 11 | 22 | 16 | 9 | 25 | -3 |
| 12 | Atlanta | 10 | 11 | 21 | 17 | 11 | 28 | -7 |
| 13 | Washington | 16 | 10 | 26 | 19 | 15 | 34 | -8 |
| 14 | Minnesota | 12 | 8 | 20 | 19 | 13 | 32 | -12 |
| | Detroit | 15 | 7 | 22 | 19 | 15 | 34 | -12 |
| 16 | NY Giants | 17 | 12 | 29 | 29 | 15 | 44 | -15 |
| AFC | | | | | | | | |
| 1 | Kansas City | 21 | 15 | 36 | 8 | 10 | 18 | 18 |
| 2 | Indianapolis | 15 | 12 | 27 | 10 | 4 | 14 | 13 |
| 3 | New England | 17 | 12 | 29 | 11 | 9 | 20 | 9 |
| 4 | Buffalo | 23 | 7 | 30 | 15 | 12 | 27 | 3 |
| 5 | Cincinnati | 20 | 11 | 31 | 20 | 10 | 30 | 1 |
| 6 | Denver | 17 | 9 | 26 | 10 | 16 | 26 | 0 |
| | Tennessee | 13 | 12 | 25 | 16 | 9 | 25 | 0 |
| 8 | Miami | 18 | 6 | 24 | 19 | 7 | 26 | -2 |
| 9 | San Diego | 11 | 6 | 17 | 11 | 10 | 21 | -4 |
| | Pittsburgh | 10 | 10 | 20 | 14 | 10 | 24 | -4 |
| 11 | Baltimore | 16 | 8 | 24 | 23 | 6 | 29 | -5 |
| 12 | Jacksonville | 11 | 10 | 21 | 21 | 6 | 27 | -6 |
| 13 | Cleveland | 14 | 7 | 21 | 20 | 9 | 29 | -8 |
| 14 | Oakland | 9 | 13 | 22 | 20 | 11 | 31 | -9 |
| 15 | NY Jets | 13 | 2 | 15 | 22 | 7 | 29 | -14 |
| 16 | Houston | 7 | 4 | 11 | 22 | 9 | 31 | -20 |

Glossary: INT: Take-away interceptions FUM: Take-away fumbles TOTAL: Total take-aways

INT: Give-away interceptions FUM: Give-away fumbles TOTAL: Total give-aways

DIFF: Difference between take-aways and give-aways

## Table 11.6: Offensive/Defensive Statistics

| NAME | SCORE | Y/PL | FD | RA | RY | Y/PR | PA | PY | Y/PP | TY | TIME | TO | PEN |
|---|---|---|---|---|---|---|---|---|---|---|---|---|---|
| Denver | 37.88 | 6.33 | 27.19 | 28.81 | 117.06 | 4.06 | 42.19 | 340.25 | 11.81 | 457.31 | 30:31 | 1.62 | 7.31 |
| Kansas City | 27.88 | 5.33 | 20.76 | 27.88 | 129.76 | 4.65 | 34.82 | 217.82 | 10.20 | 347.59 | 31:28 | 1.12 | 6.06 |
| Chicago | 27.81 | 6.03 | 21.50 | 25.25 | 114.25 | 4.52 | 36.19 | 267.56 | 11.48 | 381.81 | 31:02 | 1.44 | 5.31 |
| New England | 27.75 | 5.41 | 23.62 | 29.38 | 129.06 | 4.39 | 39.25 | 255.44 | 10.76 | 384.50 | 30:21 | 1.12 | 4.31 |
| Dallas | 27.44 | 5.70 | 20.31 | 21.00 | 94.00 | 4.48 | 36.62 | 247.12 | 10.54 | 341.12 | 29:02 | 1.25 | 6.38 |
| Philadelphia | 27.41 | 6.24 | 21.88 | 30.71 | 155.65 | 5.07 | 31.82 | 252.12 | 12.87 | 407.76 | 26:20 | 1.12 | 5.82 |
| Cincinnati | 26.88 | 5.37 | 20.62 | 30.06 | 109.69 | 3.65 | 36.69 | 258.50 | 11.36 | 368.19 | 32:50 | 1.88 | 6.38 |
| Green Bay | 26.06 | 5.96 | 21.94 | 28.69 | 133.50 | 4.65 | 35.62 | 266.75 | 11.66 | 400.25 | 30:53 | 1.56 | 5.38 |
| Seattle | 26.06 | 5.57 | 19.19 | 31.81 | 136.75 | 4.30 | 26.25 | 202.25 | 12.12 | 339.00 | 30:32 | 1.19 | 8.00 |
| New Orleans | 25.88 | 5.95 | 22.65 | 25.12 | 97.53 | 3.88 | 40.06 | 303.94 | 11.09 | 401.47 | 32:48 | 1.24 | 6.00 |
| Indianapolis | 25.65 | 5.52 | 20.35 | 25.18 | 108.41 | 4.31 | 36.88 | 244.76 | 10.98 | 353.18 | 29:16 | 1.06 | 4.12 |
| San Francisco | 25.38 | 5.39 | 17.88 | 31.56 | 137.56 | 4.36 | 26.06 | 186.19 | 12.21 | 323.75 | 30:34 | 1.12 | 6.44 |
| San Diego | 24.75 | 5.94 | 23.31 | 30.38 | 122.81 | 4.04 | 34.00 | 270.50 | 11.45 | 393.31 | 33:35 | 1.31 | 5.94 |
| Detroit | 24.69 | 5.69 | 21.88 | 27.81 | 112.00 | 4.03 | 39.62 | 280.12 | 12.08 | 392.12 | 32:22 | 2.12 | 6.88 |
| Minnesota | 24.44 | 5.44 | 19.31 | 26.44 | 130.06 | 4.92 | 34.12 | 214.19 | 10.54 | 344.25 | 28:28 | 2.00 | 4.38 |
| Arizona | 23.69 | 5.34 | 20.56 | 26.38 | 96.25 | 3.65 | 35.88 | 250.12 | 11.02 | 346.38 | 31:00 | 1.94 | 6.06 |
| Pittsburgh | 23.69 | 5.28 | 19.50 | 24.62 | 86.44 | 3.51 | 36.62 | 251.06 | 10.66 | 337.50 | 30:53 | 1.50 | 5.00 |
| League Average | 23.50 | 5.37 | 19.99 | 27.09 | 113.00 | 4.17 | 35.45 | 236.14 | 10.88 | 349.15 | 30:16 | 1.59 | 6.11 |
| Carolina | 22.88 | 5.07 | 19.94 | 30.19 | 126.62 | 4.19 | 29.56 | 190.19 | 10.42 | 316.81 | 31:54 | 1.19 | 5.00 |
| Tennessee | 22.62 | 5.22 | 19.44 | 28.88 | 118.38 | 4.10 | 33.31 | 218.50 | 10.66 | 336.88 | 30:17 | 1.56 | 6.31 |
| Atlanta | 22.06 | 5.36 | 20.62 | 20.06 | 77.94 | 3.88 | 41.19 | 265.19 | 9.53 | 343.12 | 30:20 | 1.75 | 5.69 |
| St. Louis | 21.75 | 5.04 | 17.62 | 26.62 | 109.50 | 4.11 | 31.62 | 195.31 | 10.38 | 304.81 | 29:05 | 1.31 | 7.69 |
| Buffalo | 21.19 | 4.85 | 18.81 | 34.12 | 144.19 | 4.23 | 32.62 | 193.94 | 10.38 | 338.12 | 28:43 | 1.69 | 6.88 |
| Washington | 20.88 | 5.34 | 20.56 | 28.31 | 135.25 | 4.78 | 38.19 | 234.44 | 10.57 | 369.69 | 30:53 | 2.12 | 6.19 |
| Oakland | 20.12 | 5.34 | 17.19 | 27.31 | 125.00 | 4.58 | 32.44 | 208.75 | 11.21 | 333.75 | 29:54 | 1.94 | 7.25 |
| Baltimore | 20.00 | 4.51 | 18.44 | 26.44 | 83.00 | 3.14 | 38.69 | 224.38 | 9.89 | 307.38 | 30:21 | 1.81 | 7.00 |
| Miami | 19.81 | 5.00 | 17.38 | 21.81 | 90.00 | 4.13 | 37.12 | 222.94 | 9.99 | 312.94 | 28:42 | 1.62 | 4.38 |
| Cleveland | 19.25 | 5.03 | 18.81 | 21.75 | 86.44 | 3.97 | 42.56 | 252.50 | 10.66 | 338.94 | 28:41 | 1.81 | 6.50 |
| NY Giants | 18.38 | 4.98 | 17.50 | 23.81 | 83.25 | 3.50 | 35.44 | 224.25 | 11.04 | 307.50 | 29:16 | 2.75 | 5.69 |
| NY Jets | 18.12 | 4.99 | 17.50 | 30.81 | 134.88 | 4.38 | 30.00 | 183.25 | 11.02 | 318.12 | 30:13 | 1.81 | 6.75 |
| Tampa Bay | 18.00 | 4.52 | 16.81 | 26.25 | 100.75 | 3.84 | 32.12 | 176.25 | 9.69 | 277.00 | 29:36 | 1.31 | 7.56 |
| Houston | 17.25 | 5.10 | 19.19 | 25.88 | 108.94 | 4.21 | 39.56 | 238.31 | 10.28 | 347.25 | 31:31 | 1.94 | 7.00 |
| Jacksonville | 15.44 | 4.61 | 16.94 | 23.62 | 78.75 | 3.33 | 37.00 | 215.06 | 9.86 | 293.81 | 27:22 | 1.69 | 6.00 |

## Wildcard Weekend

For now, going into the wildcard weekend, I will keep the risk and deal with it later if Philadelphia should beat New Orleans. I assume that neither Philadelphia or Carolina can beat Seattle in Seattle.

My week 16 bets are displayed in Table 11.7. So I lost two games and won the other 11 bets with two on Kansas City where I won the bet even thought they lost the game.

Table 11.7: Week 16 bets

| Away | | Home | Odds | My Pick & Bet | Result |
|------|---|------|------|---------------|--------|
| Baltimore+6.5 | at | Cincinnati | 2.00 | Baltimore | lost* |
| Buffalo | at | New England | 1.31 | New England | won |
| Carolina | at | Atlanta | 1.46 | Carolina | won |
| Cleveland | at | Pittsburgh | 1.36 | Pittsburgh | won |
| Denver | at | Oakland | 1.22 | Denver | won |
| Detroit | at | Minnesota | pass | | |
| Green Bay | at | Chicago | 1.74 | Green Bay | won |
| Houston | at | Tennessee | pass | | |
| Jacksonville | at | Indianapolis | 1.72 | Indianapolis | won |
| Kansas City | at | San Diego | 4.30 | Kansas City | won** |
| Kansas City+10.5 | at | San Diego | 1.78 | Kansas City | won |
| NY Jets | at | Miami | 1.44 | Miami | loss |
| Philadelphia | at | Dallas | pass | | |
| San Francisco | at | Arizona | pass | | |
| St Louis | at | Seattle | 1.21 | Seattle | won |
| Tampa Bay | at | New Orleans | 1.21 | New Orleans | won |
| Washington | at | NY Giants | 1.42 | NY Giants | won |

\* Could have exited at a gain when 6-0 but bid-ask spread was too wide to trade. These Betfair bets with points are very illiquid.
*Won on both bets by hedging with mean reversion when Kansas City was ahead. They rested 20 of 22 starters but the subs played well and almost won the game. They are the #5 seed in the AFC, a win would not have changed this hence they rested their top players to avoid injury.

The AFC possibilities to make the playoffs were Baltimore, San Diego, Miami and Pittsburgh and San Diego made the playoffs.

The layout of the playoffs is in Figure 11.1.

Figure 11.1: The 2014 playoff tree

The layout of the 2013 playoffs is as follows:
In the AFC Denver (13-3) has the #1 seed and New England (12-4) #2 so both would get first round byes and Denver would have home field advantage throughout the playoffs.
In the NFC, Seattle (13-3) is #1 and Carolina (12-4) is #2.

Teams that can make the wildcard weekend are:
In the AFC Kansas City (11-4)has one slot and one of Baltimore (8-7), Pittsburgh (7-8), Miami (8-7), San Diego (8-7) will be the other.
In the NFC, San Francisco (11-4), New Orleans, (10-5) and Arizona (10-5).

The AFC possibilities to make the last playoff spot were:
Baltimore in with a win and San Diego and Miami lose
San Diego in with a win and Miami loss
Miami in with a win and Baltimore losses San Diego
Pittsburgh in with a win and the other three lose.

The result was Arizona losing out with the other two becoming wildcard teams, San Diego in the AFC.

The Elo ratings for the Wildcard Weekend games are in Table 11.8 and the Betfair odds are in Table 11.9.

Table 11.8: Elo ratings for Wildcard Weekend games

| Away | Rating | Elo Prob | Home | Rating | Stern Pr Home | Elo Spread |
|------|--------|----------|------|--------|---------------|------------|
| Kansas City | 1030 | 0.50 | Indianapolis | 1030 | 0.50 | 0.00 |
| New Orleans | 1037 | 0.50 | Philadelphia | 1036 | 0.50 | -0.10 |
| San Diego | 1020 | 0.42 | Cincinnati | 1048 | 0.60 | 3.20 |
| San Francisco | 1052 | 0.65 | Green Bay | 999 | 0.32 | -6.10 |

Table 11.9: Wildcard Weekend Betfair odds

| Kansas City Chiefs at Indianapolis Colts | 1.89 | 1.91 | 2.10 | 2.12 |
|---|---|---|---|---|
| New Orleans Saints at Philadelphia Eagles | 2.48 | 2.52 | 1.66 | 1.67 |
| San Diego Chargers at Cincinnati Bengals | 3.40 | 3.50 | 1.40 | 1.41 |
| San Francisco 49ers at Green Bay Packers | 1.83 | 1.84 | 2.20 | 2.22 |

Indianapolis already beat Kansas City at home and look stronger and are slightly favored. I went with them despite the 50-50 Elo ratings. The final game is San Diego at Cincinnati. Philip Rivers is a top QB especially at this time of the year but Cincinnati seems too tough and should win especially if their QB Andy Dalton does not turn the ball over much.

I just made four simple bets on the wildcard games which were
100£ Indianapolis at 1.94
100£ New Orleans at 2.28
100£ San Francisco at 1.81
100£ Cincinnati at 1.39

## Synopsis of the Wildcard games

**Kansas City at Indianapolis:** This was a game for the ages — serious mean reversion. It started as a blowout for Kansas City. They capitalized on three Andrew Luck interceptions plus a fumble. At halftime, the score was 31-10. They got 28 points ahead early in the third quarter. Alex Smith, the Kansas City quarterback, was 30 for 46 with four touchdowns and no interceptions. He continues to complete about 70% of his passes. Then Indianapolis led by Luck scored to close the gap. One touchdown was when Donald Brown who never fumbles and had scored two touchdowns lost one near the goal line but as luck would have it the ball bounced into Andrew Luck's hands and he leapt to score the touchdown. Then Kansas City got a field goal to make it 41-38. Then one more touchdown and an extra point with 4 minutes to go and Indy won 45-44. The odds on Betfair for Indy must have been astronomical because they looked hopelessly beat at 31-10. But I did not check this assuming the bet was lost. I did win my bet in the end with no hedging.

**New Orleans at Philadelphia:** Philly was favored and was on a hot streak with a quarterback Nick Foles with 27 touchdowns versus 2 interceptions. And New Orleans had never won a road game in the playoffs. But I went with Drew Brees and the very strong New Orleans offense and defense and coaching staff. Interestingly Drew Brees and Nick Foles went to the same high school in Texas so have a connection. In the end with no time on the clock New Orleans won 26-24 with a 32 yard field goal. The Philly kicker was 1 for 2 in field goals with the miss deciding the game.

**San Diego at Cincinnati:** San Diego has traditionally been weak early in the season but very strong in December and January. Their quarterback Philip Rivers is a top one and won comeback player of the year award in 2013. San Diego needed six games in the last two weeks to go their way to get into the playoffs and luckily made it. Cincinnati on the other hand was a division winner and was greatly favored but their quarterback Andy Dalton has had interception problems in the playoffs in the past. I erred by taking the big favorite Cincinnati and they did not look good and Dalton had two interceptions plus one fumble. Rivers was clean with 12 of 16 and no interceptions. So the result was a 27-10 San Diego win. So I lost my bet.

**San Francisco at Green Bay:** Green Bay won their division with an 8-8 record and just got star quarterback Aaron Rodgers back for their last game, winning over the Chicago Bears. Without Rodgers they had a losing record. Rodgers played a terrific game. San Francisco was 12-4 and a wildcard and a presumably better team, so I bet on them. San Francisco quarterback Colin Kapernick had 91 yards on the ground and 214 passing. He made the difference and the game was won with no time left with a field goal.

The Betfair odds for the January 11, 12 games were as follows:

| | | | | |
|---|---|---|---|---|
| New Orleans Saints at Seattle Seahawks | 4.40 | 4.50 | 1.28 | 1.29 |
| Indianapolis Colts at New England Patriots | 3.85 | 3.95 | 1.34 | 1.35 |
| San Francisco 49ers at Carolina Panthers | 2.00 | 2.02 | 1.98 | 2.00 |
| San Diego Chargers at Denver Broncos | 4.50 | 4.60 | 1.27 | 1.29 |

**Analysis:** Seattle rested at home looks very tough. New Orleans did win on the road in the Wildcard game with Philadelphia, their first road playoff win. Drew Brees does not seem to be as sharp as usual. So all in all, the pick seems to be Seattle where they have won 22 of 23 home games and have the loudest NFL stadium. The odds do favor Seattle but this is no sure thing so the payoff is not huge for the risk. But Seattle won again just like they did on New Orleans first visit to Seattle.

The Colts looked good in the second half against Kansas City and Andrew Luck is a top quarterback who can do everything well — he's also big — 6' 4", 240 pounds. After a lot of trouble including 3 interceptions he showed his brilliance to pull out the game. New England, my favorite team, is tough at home and Tom Brady revels in these situations. I have been very concerned about the great players leaving the Patriots. Brady has done well given his depleted receiving corps so they are the bet. But like Seattle, the odds are no bargain. So again, a small bet is suggested. I won the bet but missed the point that Coach Belichick showed his brilliance by reinventing the team as a super running machine with four good running backs. So they, with Brady at quarterback, look very tough. As a testimony to Belichick, Peyton Manning has said that Belichick is the best coach in the NFL.

San Francisco beat Green Bay but just barely. Colin Kapernick had another good game running and passing. Carolina is tough and has another great scrambler at quarterback, Cam Newton. So this will be a good matchup. The Betfair odds slightly favor San Francisco and that will be my bet. I am short Carolina for the Super Bowl so should Carolina win, they go likely to Seattle. If they face New Orleans, it would be at home. So I have three chances for some team to knock them out. So rather than an expensive hedge, I prefer to risk it with Carolina short.

The final game pits the charging Chargers which usually are very good in December and January: they just made it to the playoffs and are peaking. Their quarterback Philip Rivers is pro bowl quality. And San Diego has done well playing Denver in Denver. Denver is, justifiably, a big favorite. They have the top offense and the red hot quarterback Peyton Manning. Wes Welker has recovered from his concussion so they are ready to go. Again, it is a tough call, but I, like Seattle and New England, will go with Denver with a small bet.

## Synopsis of the Divisional Playoffs Games, January 10, 11, 2014

My major bets were on the Super Bowl winner and the two entrants in the Super Bowl. I took the risk on Carolina assuming they would be beaten and that happened when San Francisco beat them 23-10. Also I assumed that San Diego, New Orleans and Indianapolis were likely to be knocked out so lowered my long bets on them to win the Super Bowl. So I stressed the big four there: Seattle, Denver, San Francisco and New England. I did not get involved with mean-reversion bets as each game had the team I took leading early. I had three of the favorites (Seattle, Denver and New England) and I took San Francisco in the odds tossup in that race.

So it was 4/4 winners on my small bets and a nice gain with respect to the Super Bowl.

The Super Bowl bets are in Table 11.10:

Table 11.10: Betfair odds and my bets in £

|  | 101.40% | Back | Lay | 94.50% |  |  |
|---|---|---|---|---|---|---|
| **Super Bowl odds** |  |  |  |  |  |  |
| Seattle Seahawks | 2.88 | 2.90 | 2.92 | 2.94 | 2.96 | 2.98 |
| £1,345.70 | £4357 | £4236 | £80 | £558 | £391 | £309 |
| Denver Broncos | 3.10 | 3.15 | 3.20 | 3.25 | 3.30 | 3.35 |
| £1,007.90 | £1597 | £1994 | £1870 | £793 | £493 | £452 |
| San Francisco 49ers | 4.60 | 4.70 | 4.80 | 4.90 | 5.00 | 5.10 |
| £1,265.00 | £489 | £1881 | £702 | £1426 | £3449 | £268 |
| New England Patriots | 6.40 | 6.60 | 6.80 | 7.00 | 7.20 | 7.40 |
| £1,465.88 | £565 | £1636 | £1696 | £471 | £425 | £631 |
| **Super Bowl combo odds** |  |  |  |  |  |  |
| Denver / Seattle | 2.3 | 2.32 | 2.34 | 2.46 | 2.48 | 3 |
| £125.00 | £157 | £40 | £13 | £85 | £892 | £2 |
| Denver / San Francisco | 3.8 | 3.95 | 4 | 4.4 | 4.5 | 4.6 |
| £-100.00 | £523 | £44 | £27 | £15 | £14 | £43 |
| New England / Seattle | 4.5 | 4.7 | 4.8 | 5 | 5.3 | 5.4 |
| £260.00 | £51 | £17 | £15 | £50 | £31 | £25 |
| New England / San Francisco | 7.4 | 7.6 | 7.8 | 9 | 9.2 | 9.4 |
| £-100.00 | £200 | £41 | £22 | £4 | £18 | £25 |

The Betfair odds for the divisional games are:
New England Patriots @ Denver Broncos    2.96    3.05    1.49    1.51
San Francisco 49ers @ Seattle Seahawks    2.78    2.8    1.56    1.57

Table 11.11: Elo ratings for Divisional Games

| Away | Rating | Elo Prob | Home | Rating | Stern Pr Home | Elo Spread |
|---|---|---|---|---|---|---|
| New England | 1053 | 0.43 | Denver | 1076 | 0.58 | 2.6 |
| San Francisco | 1062 | 0.46 | Seattle | 1077 | 0.55 | 1.6 |

*What to do?* I have locked in a nice profit on the Super Bowl no matter who wins so I think I should stick with that. In the Super Bowl combo bets I only lose if San Francisco gets in. I could hedge them out for about 50£ but since I only lose 100£ if they are in and Seattle looks better than they, I think I just let that stay as is. So what bets will I make in the two games: I will go with New England at about 3-1 British odds and Seattle at 1.59-1 with small bets in this exercise.

The Brady vs Manning matchup will be their 15th meeting. Brady is 10-4 and has outplayed Manning even in this, Manning's greatest year. The last four meetings were in Table 11.12. Manning is 6-0 in rematches with teams that beat him earlier in the season and 7-14 versus the Patriots.

Table 11.12: Last four matchups between Brady and Manning

| Date | Passing | Yards | TDs | Int | Rating | Score |
|------|---------|-------|-----|-----|--------|-------|
| Nov 24, 2013 | Brady: 34/50 | 344 | 3 | 0 | 107.4 | NE 34, DEN 31 (ot) |
|  | Manning: 19/36 | 150 | 2 | 1 | 70.4 | rallied from 24 to 0 |
| Oct 7, 2012 | Brady: 23/31 | 223 | 1 | 0 | 104.6 | NE 31, DEN 21 |
|  | Manning: 31/44 | 337 | 3 | 0 | 115.4 |  |
| Nov 21, 2010 | Brady: 19/25 | 186 | 2 | 0 | 123.1 | NE 31, IND 28 |
|  | Manning: 38/52 | 396 | 4 | 3 | 96.1 |  |
| Nov 15, 2009 | Brady: 29/42 | 375 | 3 | 1 | 110.7 | IND 35, NE 34 |
|  | Manning: 28/44 | 327 | 4 | 2 | 97.4 |  |

Given the strong running game of the Patriots plus Brady and generous 3 to 1 British odds, they are the bet. Seattle has beaten San Francisco the past 2 meetings with a combined score of 71 to 16 and is a $3\frac{1}{2}$ point favorite. They were 8 and 0 at home in 2012 and 8 and 1 this year. Their 12th man, the loud crowd, helps a lot. So the bet is Seattle.

My bets so far are: 300£ NE at 3.1 and 150£ Seattle at 1.59.

## The Conference Championship Games

**New England at Denver** It was a well played game with no interceptions and no fumbles. Denver was not known for defense and in fact was 27th rated against the pass. But they were able to shut down the powerful New England running game which gained only 64 yards on 16 carries. La Garett Blount who gained over 200 yards in their last game, gained 6 yards on 5 carries.

So the team had to resort to Tom Brady's passing which was good 24 of 38 for 256 yards. And Brady threw for one touchdown and ran in another.

But it was not enough to hold back the furious Denver onslaught. Manning was sharp with 32 of 43 and two touchdowns. A very key dirty play was Wes Welker acting revenge on Bill Belichick for not keeping him in New England. Welker deliberately injured a knee of pro bowl safety Aqib Talib. With Talib out, Manning saw the blood like a shark and hit wide end receiver Demaryius Thomas with 7 passes for 134 yards and one touchdown. Manning had other receivers including Julius Thomas with 8 for 85, Eric Decker 5 for 73 and Welker 4 for 38 plus four others with at least one catch each.

Denver scored first with a field goal and then a touchdown to make it 10-0. I upped my bet on New England at 4.8-1 and had a chance to mean revert hedge at around 4-1 but waited. I had made an operational error and had double bet New England plus I had them with $5\frac{1}{2}$ and 6 points. New England got behind 20-3 and then they made a charge to close the gap to 23-10 and then 26-16 on a 5 yard Brady run. The 2 point conversion failed and the game ended 26-16.

I lost on all my New England bets:
300@ 3.1
300 @ 3.03
NE+$5\frac{1}{2}$ 100 bet @ 1.98 hedged to -80 loss
NE+6 100 bet @ 1.79 hedged to -96 loss

Plus I lost the money bet on them to reach the Super Bowl with Seattle and win the Super Bowl. So this did not go well. But I still had a good profit more than this loss in the Super Bowl bets and I was hoping that Seattle would beat San Francisco to make some gains there.

**San Francisco at Seattle** This was a battle of two excellent defensive teams. Seattle was the best in the NFL with San Francisco not far behind. San Francisco started out with a field goal and then a touchdown for a 10-0 lead. So I doubled up with some bets at better odds. Wilson, who had a decent day, with one fumble and no interceptions, threw a 51 yard pass to Doug Baldwin and that led to a field goal and a 10-3 score at half time. I bet 100 more on Seattle to win the Super Bowl at 4.7 to 1 and 100 more at 2.72 to win the game. Marshan Lynch who had a good day, 109 yards from 22 carries, ran for a 40 yard touchdown. That was the longest touchdown run in the Jim Harbaugh era. Seattle contained Frank Gore who only gained 14 yards in 11 caries. But Colin Kapernick, the versatile quarterback, had a number of designed runs and gained 130 yards on 11 carries — a lot for a quarterback. He also threw for 14 out of 24 but had one fumble and two interceptions including the game clincher. The score was 23-17 and San Francicso was charging with little time left and looked like they might score and win the game 24-23 as Kapernick was rattling pass after pass. But Seattle which had the most interceptions (28 in the NFL) got one near the buzzer when all pro Richard Sherman tipped a pass into the hands of Smith and the game was over.

Prior to that there was a lot of exciting action. Seattle had the ball on the one yard line and Wilson's handoff to Lynch was a bit high and that led to a fumble. Seattle was then 0/3 in the end zone. They had gotten the ball on a questionable play when the Seattle runner actually fumbled but the referees did not see it. And it was a non-reviewable play. Rather stupid rule — all plays should be reviewable! So Seattle got a break but did not score. San Francisco started charging and then Kapernick threw an interception. Seattle got the ball and got a field goal. San Francisco battled but in the end the game ended with Sherman's big play with 20 seconds to go. Sherman led the NFL with 8 interceptions this year.

I did well on the Seattle game winning all my bets. Along the way I considered mean-reverse hedging but waited instead as I thought Seattle would win in the end. I could see the tide turning in the 3rd quarter. My bets were:
150 to win 88.50
150 to win 87
75 Seattle+3 to win 27.75
100 @ 2.52
100 @ 2.72, and
100 @ 4.7 to win the Super Bowl.
I also won the Denver/Seattle to be in the Super Bowl bet.

So I have the following bets going for the February 2nd Super Bowl:
if Seattle wins, I win +1,849.70
if Denver wins I win +1,819.00
I shifted some Seattle to Denver at 1.9 to make these about equal. Currently:
Seattle 2.16-2.75
Denver 1.84-1.85 and this has not changed much now to almost gametime Denver is favored to win. So assuming I don't have other bets to lose on the gain from the whole exercise is about +1000. Recall Betfair charges a commission on net winning bets. It would have been more if New England had won but they were a bit flat as Denver stronger. Like last week, all home teams won. Betfair just upped their basic commission to 6.5% from 5% and there are discounts for quantity bets.

The weather for the game looked good and mild enough to not detract from the passing so that favors Denver with their five receivers with 10+ touchdowns. But historically the best defensive teams have won well more than half of the Super Bowl games against the best offensive teams. There are many measures of this but this favors Seattle plus they have Percy Harvin back to add to their offense. Russell Wilson has few turnovers, less than Peyton Manning. Peyton won three awards for the 2013-14 season including top offensive player and MVP for a record fifth time. He is because of his neck injury, getting dumped by Indianapolis in favor of the outstanding rookie Andrew Luck and this year's record breaking offensive record, the sentimental favorite. On net, I slightly prefer Seattle so moved about 15% of the Denver bet to Seattle with points. This was 150 for Seattle $+1\frac{1}{2}$ 2 2.06 to win 157, 50 on Seattle $+2\frac{1}{2}$ @ 196 to win 47 and 100 on Seattle $+8\frac{1}{2}$ @ 1.40 to gain 40. So my gain is higher if Seattle wins, then I win the Seattle money line bet plus these three bets.

Should Denver win by 1, I win the Denver bets and these three point bets; if Denver wins by more, I win less. But I assume there will be mean reversion risk aversion bets but not big ones.

The February 2, 2013 48th Super Bowl at Met Life stadium in East Rutherford, New Jersey was played in good weather with the temperature above $49°$ that in Seattle and Denver. This was the first Super Bowl played outdoors in a cold climate. Seattle prides itself on the 12th man — the loudest stadium in the NFL. Their stadium was built by Paul Allen of Microsoft fame just for this purpose.

Seattle won the toss and deferred receiving the ball until the second half. As the game started, the noise was so loud that Peyton Manning's signal could not be heard. So there was a mixup and the center Manny Ramirez sent the ball way high and it landed off Manning into the end zone. Knowshon Marino of Denver recovered but it was a safety and Seattle took an early 2-0 lead and got the ball. The 12 seconds score was the fastest in Super Bowl history, breaking the record of 14 seconds for Chicago's Devin Hester's opening kickoff against Mannings Colts in 2007. Golden Tate returned the kick to the 36. Percy Harvin was finally available to play and as the 7th play of the season his first touch today he ran 30 yards. There was a Wilson pass to Kerse to the 18. Two runs by Wilson produced nothing except a lost challenge on the spot. Coach Pete Carroll went for a field goal. A false start moved it back 5 yards but the 31 yard field goal was successful so the score was 5-0.

Seattle was now favored on Betfair so I shorted 100 @ 1.8 so my money line bet was Seattle +1769.70 Denver +1919. The other point bets had wide bid-asks as usual so I did nothing there.

Seattle's kick was out of the end zone and a late hit resulted in a 15 yard penalty so the ball was on Denver's 35. Manning, who threw for 55 of the 76 touchdowns Denver scored in 2013, missed a couple of short passes and it was 3 and out. In the regular season Denver had the 2nd fewest 3 and outs. Golden Take took the kickoff at the 28. Lynch gained 2 and a pass to Tate got a first down. Robinson gained 6 to the 45. Lynch gained nothing. A pass to Baldwin gained 6 and a first down. Harvin gained 5 on a pass from Wilson. Then a long Wilson pass to Baldwin got to the 5. Lynch again nothing. A 10 yards offensive, holding penalty put the ball on the 15. Again Lynch got nothing.

I shorted 100 more Seattle @ 1.66 to make my bet +1703.70 Seattle +2019 Denver.

Wilson made a good pass on 3rd down to Kerse who lost it. A 32 yard field goal made it 8-0.

Denver got the ball as the 20. Manning hit a pass to Walker for 5 then Marino fumbled but Denver recovered. Seattle led the NFL in 2013 with 39 takeaways and Wilson and the others were pretty clean. Denver's lost fumbles were the worst in the NFL. Not to give the story away, but this game was already looking like a Seattle blowout and it would end with no sacks, no fumbles, no interceptions by Seattle and 1 sack, 4 fumbles, 2 lost and 2 interceptions by Denver.

Manning's pass was intercepted by Kam Chancellor on the 37. Harvin gained 15 to the 22 and a pass got it to the 18 as quarter one ended. Lynch got to the 9, his first decent run; he was 11 yards in 7 carries so far. Lynch lost 1. A pass to Baldwin got to the 5. A pass was incomplete but a defensive penalty on Tony Carter got the ball to the 1 and a first down. Lynch, who came to Seattle in a 2010 trade from the Buffalo Bill's scored the touchdown. So with the extra point, it was 15-0. Denver had a 17 yard return on the kickoff to their 15.

The odds now had Denver @ 4.3 to 1 so I went 100 long Denver hoping to close the mean-reversion risk arbitrage lower a bit later once Denver got moving. They did a bit as shown below and the odds briefly touched the 3.2-3.3 area, but I did not close. A mistake on my part!

Marino got a first down. Thomas gained 7. Marino got to the 40. It was 3rd and 2 inches. Thomas got this first down. Manning hit a pass and another to Welker to the 40, for a first down. They got to the 30. A run was stopped inches short of a first down. Monte Ball got a first down. Denver got a 10 yard pass interception penalty so the ball was on the 42. Marino got to the 35. Then a tipped ball got into Malcolm Smith's hands and he ran for a touchdown. Recall he was the one who got the Richard Sherman tip in the San Francisco game to win that game as well. So the score was 22-0 after the extra point. So my 100 @ 4.3 did not look good anymore. The odds on Denver were now very wide at 1.16 Seattle 7.6 Denver.

Denver fumbled again on the kickoff but the runner was down so it did not count in the 4 fumbles 2 lost. This being sort of a fifth.

Manning had guts to throw to Demaryius Thomas who was guarded by the now famous Richard Sherman. That gained 18 yards. Sherman's outburst at the end of the San Francisco game when he tried to shake hands with San Francisco receiver Michael Crabtree led to a lot of publicity. Since Sherman was very articulate and a top student with high marks at Stanford his fame grew from the incident that the press put a huge magnifying glass on.

Denver got a first down to the 28. We were at the 2 minute warning. Marino got 6 to the 21 and a false start moved it back to the 26. It was 3rd and 9. A Marino run got it within 2 yards of a first down. On 4th down, Denver went for it. A pass from Manning was tipped and almost intercepted. But Seattle took over on downs. The odds now were 1.11-1.0 and it was half time. Throughout there were the famous Super Bowl ads at $4 million per 30 seconds. The half time show was with Bruno Mars and the Red Hot Chilly Peppers with lots of cymbals and noise for the young viewers and noise for me. There was lots of moving around so it was well received by those hundreds on the field.

Pete Carroll instructed Percy Harvin to just run with the ball on kickoffs no matter where it was. That was good advice. The ball was not in the end zone but on Seattle 13. After 87 yards, Percy had it in Denver's end zone and after the extra point the score was 29-0 so the game was essentially over. Seattle had it pretty well clinched. Harvin was having a terrific game (137 yards on 4 touches) as were all the Seahawks and essentially none of the Denver Broncos. But Demaryius Thomas caught 13 passes for 118 yards, breaking the Super Bowl record. And Peyton Manning completed 34 passes another Super Bowl record. Wes Welker caught 8 of these for 84 yards. Eric Decker, shadowed by top defense ace Richard Sherman, caught only one pass for 6 yards. Julius Thomas had 4 for 27 yards.

Denver got the ball on the 21. There was another near pick. I bet 300 on Seattle at 1.05 to salvage 15 on my three 100 Denver bets. Then I bet another 100 on Seattle at 1.03. So my 100 at 4.3 became Seattle -85- then -82 and Denver +3 then -70. In my other account I bet 400 at 1.03 to salvage 12 to make it +1715 Seattle +1619 Denver. Elway in the stands looked stunned. So did Eli Manning. Elway had lost to Joe Montana

55-10 in Super Bowl24 and Eli lost 23-0 (this year in this very stadium) — but they were shocked at Payton being so destroyed. Marino injured his back.

It was 2nd and 9 for the first down. Thomas caught a Manning pass then fumbled. That was the 3rd Denver turnover. Seattle got the ball plus a penalty for unnecessary roughness. Wilson hit a 12 yard pass. That was 16 drop backs for Wilson with no sacks or turnovers. He has sure earned his $619,000 salary. It was small compared to Mannings's $17.5 million. Bravo to general manager John Schneider, coach Peter Carroll and innovative owner Paul Allen of Vulcan Sports Entertainment for assembling a terrific young team averaging 26.4 years — tied for youngest in Super Bowl history. Lynch got nothing. Wilson made a pass for 19 to Lockette. The Jermaine Kerse made a spectacular twisting catch and ran into the end zone. That made it 36-0.

Denver got the ball and got a pass to the 23 but then a holding call for a 10 yard penalty. Announcer Troy Aikman, himself a three time Super Bowl winner with the Dallas Cowboys said "Seattle is winning at every position" or so it seemed. Welker gained 12 on a pass. The bid-ask odds were now 730-990 Denver and -1.01 Seattle.

Welker gained another +22 to the 14. Then finally to Manning hit Demaryius Thomas for a touchdown. A 2 point conversion also to Welker made it 35-8.

Seattle got the ball on the 48 on a good run back but there was a penalty on Seattle for holding which nullified it. Recall Seattle was the most penalized NFL team — they are rough so get many penalties. Miller and Tate caught passes to the 40. It was now 250-280 Denver and -1.01 Seattle.

Wilson scrambling as he is so good at, hit Doug Baldwin for 6. Then again to Baldwin for another touchdown to make the score 43-8. There was 11.28 left and the Betfair odds were 990 Denver and 1.01 Seattle.

Sherman suffered a high ankle injury so was carried off. The injury might take months to heal but he should be ok for next season.

Seattle got the ball back and went three and out. The Broncos took over.

Yet another Denver turnover occurred when Chris Clemens knocked a fumble out of Manning's hands. And the game was over.

Another post season Peyton disaster. He is now 11-12 in the post season and 1-2 in Super Bowls. Denver is 2-5 with Elway 2-3. There will be lots of discussion on his legacy. He did break the completion record but had 2 interceptions plus the fumble. Seattle's defense was so strong that it was hard for Manning. They won the game rather than Denver and Manning losing it. Wilson was excellent but his great offense line helped him a lot — no sacks for example. Wilson at 5'11" versus Mannings 6'5" has shown, like Drew Brees, that short quarterbacks can be successful if on the right team. Wilson set the NFL record of 28 wins plus a Super Bowl in his first two years.

Marcus Allen, MVP of Super Bowl 18, presented the Vince Lombardi trophy to the Seattle owner and coach. Seattle behind top running back Shaun Alexander was in the 2005 Super Bowl but lost to Pittsburgh. The MVP could have gone to Wilson or Harvin and others but they gave it to Malcolm Smith.

Betfair charged me 5% (later raised to 6.5%) but no discount and this amounted to 19.39+1.95+2.34+7.85= 31.53 on winnings on the game of 5964.07-4118.97 = 1845.10.

My analysis is what I did and learned. After the game I got some professional bettor information from Runline, who is a Las Vegas and offshore investor and Bunker, a longtime professional bettor colleague. They wrote as follows:

There was talk all week in Las Vegas about whether the game would get to a 3 point spread advantage for the favorite Denver, at which point "sharps" would take Seattle. This was realistically never going to happen.

Bunker noted that many pros bet Denver early, when Las Vegas opened with Seattle favored, planning to get off it later knowing that Denver would be overbetting their own version of mean-reversion. So there was pend-up Seattle demand just for them to get flat. Bunker said that the Asian and offshore markets were consistently a point lower on Denver than Seattle all week. On gameday, the differences got wider. Pinnacle went as low as Denver -1 -104 and Denver -113 in the hours before kickoff. Asia had Denver at -2.5 +106 to +108. Meanwhile, Las Vegas was at -2.5 -120/+2.5 E. Runline went into the game with legs of Denver -110 and Denver -2 even coupled with Seattle +3 -110 and +2.5 even. Most were not able to access both markets so easily.

This shows how effectively the global market was segmented between sharp, sophisticated players offshore and in Asia, and recreational/noise traders in Las Vegas. Regulation and restrictions on capital flows prevents easy arbitrage trades from being eliminated. This is shown in the fact that most of the bigger Las Vegas bets ($50,000+) were on Denver. About 65% of the money went to Denver so the bookmakers got their Seattle bias. The largest bet was for $300,000 on Seattle. The total Las Vegas bet was $119.4 million.

Las Vegas was still taking Denver bets in good volume there, and wanted to avoid going to -3 because a) they risk getting sided or middled overall' and b) large bets on Seattle would instantly overwhelm any Denver money. 3 is a huge jump from 2.5. The 3 is worth about 20 cents. Southpoint went to 3 for a minute or two, twice, but that was it.

Las Vegas was able to go into the game net long Seattle, as desired, but at much better prices than bookmakers serving professional clients were able to extract. This came out pre-game and was the subject of some laughter among colleagues. Las Vegas bookmakers are insanely insular. It does give a reasonable view of pre-game pricing during the week:

linemakers.sportingnews.com/nfl/2014-02-01/super-bowl-odds-bets-sharps-broncos-seahawks

Here is a breakdown of early returns. Books were on Seattle to the tune of 35% of net handle on point spread bets, apparently. So a big decision in their favor. ("Decision" here is insider jargon for a book's net exposure to an outcome), see:

reviewjournal.com/columns-blogs/matt-youmans/sports-books-ride-seahawks-all-way-bank

Seattle became the sixth underdog in the last seven years to cover the point spread which favored Denver by about 2.5.

# Chapter 12

# The 2014-2015 Season, Playoffs and the Super Bowl

I take this up going into the 15th of the 17 week season. In the past John Swetye has helped me by computing the Elo ratings. We now have another independent source — Nate Silver, a superstar predictor's website www.fivethirtyeight.com and his 2012 book *The Signal and the Noise*. Nate has a terrific record of predicting all sorts of events — political, sports and other areas. His Elo ratings are different from John's using the formulas we discuss in chapter 5 which begin with each teams preseason standing from the previous year. For example, Seattle, last year's Super Bowl winner, started at #1, fell to #3 and now are back at #1 tied with New England. John's was just based on the current season's results so this is possibly an improvement.

The Elo ratings are based on the results of each week's games: outcome, margin of victory, strength of oppo-nent and home field advan-tage effect.[1] Another approach based on betting market data was developed by and is re-ported on Mike Beuoy's web-site, `Inpredictable.com`. The two approaches in 2014 are converging to similar predic-

Tom Brady planning the next play

---

[1]The home field spread = (home team Elo — away Elo)/8.845. The home field advantage spreads can be added to the team spread which can be plus or minus. Then Stern probabilities equal 50% + 3%(spread) for the home team.

Table 12.1: Week 15 NFL Matchups According to the Elo Ratings

Dec. 11, 2014

| HOME TEAM | ELO RATING | ELO WIN% | VISITING TEAM | ELO RATING | ELO WIN% | ELO POINT SPREAD | |
|-----------|-----------|----------|---------------|-----------|----------|------------------|---|
| St. Louis | 1514 | 47% | Arizona | 1602 | 53% | Arizona | -1.0 |
| Buffalo | 1489 | 38% | Green Bay | 1640 | 62% | Green Bay | -3.5 |
| Carolina | 1476 | 77% | Tampa Bay | 1334 | 23% | Carolina | -8.5 |
| Baltimore | 1603 | 91% | Jacksonville | 1268 | 9% | Baltimore | -16.0 |
| Cleveland | 1421 | 43% | Cincinnati | 1537 | 57% | Cincinnati | -2.0 |
| Atlanta | 1452 | 42% | Pittsburgh | 1574 | 58% | Pittsburgh | -2.5 |
| N.Y. Giants | 1441 | 77% | Washington | 1299 | 23% | N.Y. Giants | -8.5 |
| New England | 1717 | 82% | Miami | 1517 | 18% | New England | -10.5 |
| Indianapolis | 1587 | 74% | Houston | 1471 | 26% | Indianapolis | -7.5 |
| Kansas City | 1536 | 83% | Oakland | 1324 | 17% | Kansas City | -11.0 |
| San Diego | 1552 | 42% | Denver | 1674 | 58% | Denver | -2.5 |
| Tennessee | 1300 | 54% | N.Y. Jets | 1339 | 46% | Tennessee | -1.0 |
| Detroit | 1556 | 71% | Minnesota | 1464 | 29% | Detroit | -6.5 |
| Seattle | 1717 | 79% | San Francisco | 1548 | 21% | Seattle | -9.5 |
| Philadelphia | 1593 | 64% | Dallas | 1558 | 36% | Philadelphia | -4.0 |
| Chicago | 1424 | 52% | New Orleans | 1473 | 48% | Chicago | -0.5 |

FAVORED TEAM

FIVETHIRTYEIGHT

tions so it's a good check. I have my own mental model in my thinking that utilizes fundamentals, trending, momentum and mean reversion. And mine might differ from the Elo or Inpredictable ratings, but the best is to consider all the information.

A real drawback though of the Elo ratings is that they do not consider fundamentals. For example, Aaron Rodgers, the top 2014/15 MVP candidate, was injured for a period of time. The Elo ratings for Green Bay did not adjust for that. They are simply not the same team with him out. Another example was the week 17 adjustment of New England. They lost this last game 17-9 to Buffalo but they had already secured home field games throughout the playoffs plus a first week bye when one of Pittsburgh and Baltimore both potentially tough competitors will be eliminated. So downgrading New England in the Elo when they only played their key players sparingly is not correct. Tom Brady is 25-2 at home in December. For trading, one must do more analysis and merge this information with Betfair prices, Las Vegas odds and fundamentals to create good wagers. Then use mean reversion to create good risk arbitrage wagers. It is really an exercise in the merging of expert opinion from several experts, a well studied topic in decision analysis. This is similar to professional racetrack betting with factor markets that maximize the track odds. The successful models have many factors plus the odds and both add value to create better probabilities of success. For now, let's discuss the final weeks and the playoffs and Super Bowl.

Table 12.2: FiveThirtyEight's NFL Elo Ratings, December 11 and 31, 2014

| | TEAM | ELO RATING | ELO CHG | RANK CHG | | TEAM | ELO RATING | ELO CHANGE | RANK CHANGE |
|---|---|---|---|---|---|---|---|---|---|
| 1 | New England | 1717 | +18 | -- | 1 | Seattle | 1760 | +5 | -- |
| 2 | Seattle | 1717 | +23 | -- | 2 | New England | 1687 | -43 | -- |
| 3 | Denver | 1674 | +8 | -- | 3 | Denver | 1672 | +5 | -- |
| 4 | Green Bay | 1640 | +7 | -- | 4 | Green Bay | 1639 | +16 | -- |
| 5 | Baltimore | 1603 | +32 | +5 | 5 | Dallas | 1632 | +12 | -- |
| 6 | Arizona | 1602 | +9 | -- | 6 | Pittsburgh | 1623 | +18 | -- |
| 7 | Philadelphia | 1593 | -23 | -2 | 7 | Baltimore | 1582 | +8 | +3 |
| 8 | Indianapolis | 1587 | +5 | -- | 8 | Indianapolis | 1579 | +10 | +3 |
| 9 | Pittsburgh | 1574 | +43 | +7 | 9 | Arizona | 1577 | -14 | -1 |
| 10 | Dallas | 1558 | +25 | +5 | 10 | Cincinnati | 1576 | -18 | -3 |
| 11 | Detroit | 1556 | +9 | +2 | 11 | Philadelphia | 1559 | +23 | +2 |
| 12 | San Diego | 1552 | -18 | -1 | 12 | Detroit | 1559 | -16 | -3 |
| 13 | San Francisco | 1548 | -45 | -6 | 13 | Kansas City | 1552 | +22 | +1 |
| 14 | Cincinnati | 1537 | -43 | -5 | 14 | Buffalo | 1544 | +43 | +3 |
| 15 | Kansas City | 1536 | -9 | -1 | 15 | San Francisco | 1536 | +14 | -- |
| 16 | Miami | 1517 | -32 | -4 | 16 | Carolina | 1530 | +41 | +3 |
| 17 | St. Louis | 1514 | +21 | +2 | 17 | San Diego | 1526 | -22 | -5 |
| 18 | Buffalo | 1489 | -8 | -- | 18 | Houston | 1500 | +6 | -- |
| 19 | Carolina | 1476 | +55 | +6 | 19 | New Orleans | 1472 | +10 | +4 |
| 20 | New Orleans | 1473 | -55 | -3 | 20 | Miami | 1468 | -46 | -4 |
| 21 | Houston | 1471 | +19 | +1 | 21 | N.Y. Giants | 1462 | -23 | -1 |
| 22 | Minnesota | 1464 | +10 | -1 | 22 | Minnesota | 1461 | +10 | +2 |
| 23 | Atlanta | 1452 | -7 | -3 | 23 | St. Louis | 1458 | -5 | -1 |
| 24 | N.Y. Giants | 1441 | +33 | +2 | 24 | Atlanta | 1435 | -41 | -3 |
| 25 | Chicago | 1424 | -25 | -2 | 25 | N.Y. Jets | 1403 | +46 | +2 |
| 26 | Cleveland | 1421 | -5 | -2 | 26 | Cleveland | 1376 | -8 | -1 |
| 27 | N.Y. Jets | 1339 | -10 | -- | 27 | Chicago | 1371 | -10 | -1 |
| 28 | Tampa Bay | 1334 | -9 | -- | 28 | Oakland | 1325 | -5 | -- |
| 29 | Oakland | 1324 | +45 | +3 | 29 | Tampa Bay | 1308 | -10 | -- |
| 30 | Tennessee | 1300 | -33 | -1 | 30 | Washington | 1300 | -12 | -- |
| 31 | Washington | 1299 | -21 | -1 | 31 | Jacksonville | 1277 | -6 | -- |
| 32 | Jacksonville | 1268 | -19 | -1 | 32 | Tennessee | 1252 | -10 | -- |
| | | | | | | *IN NFL PLAYOFFS* | | | |

FIVETHIRTYEIGHT                                   FIVETHIRTYEIGHT

I mostly agree with the ratings for the top teams in Table 12.2. Week 15, December 11 is on the left and the final week of the regular season is on the right. But one must adjust as follows: for example, St Louis, which has a losing record and will not make the playoffs, is ranked #1 in several defense categories, better even than Seattle. They are favored at home with a 6-7 record versus the 10-3 Arizona Cardinals. Whereas the Elo's are 1602 #6 for Arizona which was +9 in Elo for their last week win, and #17 St Louis 1514, which was +21 in Elo points given their second straight shutout win.

Denver has been in the top four all 15 weeks, see Table 12.3. New England has been in the top four except for 2 weeks. San Francisco has dropped out and Cincinnati and San Diego have dropped a bit. Arizona is a sleeper. Usually to be in the top ten of the 32 teams you need a top notch quarterback. They have a great defense, a fabulous receiver, Larry Fitzgerald, and a group of backup quarterbacks. Still they are #6 despite losing 4 of

Russell Willson, the Seattle Seahawks quarterback had the best three year start ever in the NFL (34-12)

their last 6 games. The top four teams all have super star quarterbacks. New England (Tom Brady), Seattle (Russell Wilson), Denver (Peyton Manning) and Green Bay (Aaron Rodgers). Baltimore has crept up into fifth position as has Pittsburgh, both with very good quarterbacks, Joe Flacco and Ben Roethlisberger, respectively. The others in the top group who most likely will make the playoffs by winning their divisions are Indianapolis (Andrew Luck) and Philadelphia (using backup Mark Sanchez, a good but not great quarterback while top quarterback Nick Foles is injured).

FiveThirtyEight.com compares the Elo rating with Las Vegas odds predictions; the regular season had a 129-108-4 record against the Las Vegas spread. Sunshine's Forecasts website shows that 2014 was Elo's best season against the spread since 1989. Table 12.5 compares Elo and Las Vegas with reality in the number of wins by team for the regular 16 game season.

My Betfair wagers before the playoffs focused on New England and Seattle as my top picks with most of the bet made early in the season when these two teams were 2 and 2 and 3 and 3, respectively. I was also long Denver (which I later turned into a minor short), Green Bay (which is a real contender), Philadelphia, Indianapolis and Arizona (which I want to move into a short with a third string quarterback, I feel they will lose soon). Detroit I am massively short. They have the #2 defense, a great cast of receivers and good runners, the quarterback Matthew Stafford is good but error prone, so they are only a minor threat to actually win the Super Bowl. Baltimore and Pittsburgh I want to be more long. Pittsburgh is always tough and won two Super Bowls with the current coach. Joe Flacco, the Baltimore quarterback has a playoff record of 13 TDs, no interceptions and a 116.6

Table 12.3: The Seahawks have always soared in 2014

Top four teams in FiveThirtyEight's NFL Elo ratings, week by week

| WK. | 1st | 2nd | 3rd | 4th |
|---|---|---|---|---|
| 1 | **Seattle** 1674 | San Francisco 1644 | New England 1620 | Denver 1619 |
| 2 | **Seattle** 1685 | San Francisco 1662 | Denver 1631 | New England 1587 |
| 3 | **Seattle** 1658 | Denver 1639 | San Francisco 1621 | New England 1618 |
| 4 | **Seattle** 1671 | Denver 1624 | New England 1622 | Cincinnati 1607 |
| 5 | **Seattle** 1671 | Denver 1624 | San Francisco 1612 | San Diego 1608 |
| 6 | **Seattle** 1679 | Denver 1646 | San Francisco 1622 | San Diego 1619 |
| 7 | Denver 1659 | **Seattle** 1645 | San Francisco 1640 | New England 1631 |
| 8 | Denver 1683 | New England 1634 | **Seattle** 1620 | San Francisco 1616 |
| 9 | Denver 1698 | New England 1647 | **Seattle** 1643 | San Francisco 1616 |
| 10 | New England 1677 | Denver 1668 | **Seattle** 1645 | Arizona 1631 |
| 11 | New England 1677 | Denver 1676 | **Seattle** 1655 | Arizona 1542 |
| 12 | New England 1707 | Arizona 1654 | **Seattle** 1639 | Denver 1632 |
| 13 | New England 1719 | **Seattle** 1683 | Denver 1640 | Arizona 1630 |
| 14 | New England 1699 | **Seattle** 1694 | Denver 1666 | Green Bay 1633 |
| 15 | New England 1717 | **Seattle** 1717 | Denver 1674 | Green Bay 1640 |

♡ FIVETHIRTYEIGHT

rating in the playoffs and led them to victory against New England twice. In 2012 they beat New England in Foxbourgh and went on to win the Super Bowl from a wild card start. Of course, that was against a New England team with top receiver Rob Gronkowski out with an injury. Dallas I want to move from a short to a long because they are peaking as we enter the playoffs. I am short and want to remain short New Orleans, Cincinnati, San Diego, Kansas City, Atlanta, Buffalo, Houston, Miami and Cleveland. Carolina remains a short. They are on a roll but I doubt they can go far in the playoffs. I do not see them beating Seattle in Seattle.

In the end, after week 17 Indianapolis did win their division but Philadelphia did not make the playoffs. The shorts on Miami, Houston, Kansas

Table 12.4: FiveThirtyEight's NFL Elo Playoff Odds, Week 15

Dec. 11, 2014

| TEAM | ELO RATING | WINS | LOSSES | TIES | POINT DIFF. | WIN DIVISION | MAKE PLAYOFFS | WIN SUPER BOWL |
|---|---|---|---|---|---|---|---|---|
| **AFC East** | | | | | | | | |
| New England | 1717 | 12.5 | 3.5 | 0.0 | +171 | >99% | >99% | 26% |
| Miami | 1517 | 8.6 | 7.4 | 0.0 | +58 | <1% | 12% | <1% |
| Buffalo | 1489 | 8.2 | 7.8 | 0.0 | +29 | <1% | 3% | <1% |
| N.Y. Jets | 1339 | 2.8 | 13.2 | 0.0 | -160 | 0% | 0% | 0% |
| **AFC North** | | | | | | | | |
| Baltimore | 1603 | 10.3 | 5.7 | 0.0 | +131 | 33% | 78% | 3% |
| Pittsburgh | 1574 | 9.9 | 6.1 | 0.0 | +55 | 40% | 70% | 2% |
| Cincinnati | 1537 | 9.3 | 5.7 | 1.0 | -14 | 25% | 62% | 1% |
| Cleveland | 1421 | 7.9 | 8.1 | 0.0 | -13 | 1% | 3% | <1% |
| **AFC South** | | | | | | | | |
| Indianapolis | 1587 | 11.0 | 5.0 | 0.0 | +116 | 91% | 96% | 4% |
| Houston | 1471 | 8.5 | 7.5 | 0.0 | +54 | 9% | 22% | <1% |
| Jacksonville | 1268 | 2.8 | 13.2 | 0.0 | -182 | 0% | 0% | 0% |
| Tennessee | 1300 | 3.2 | 12.8 | 0.0 | -164 | 0% | 0% | 0% |
| **AFC West** | | | | | | | | |
| Denver | 1674 | 12.1 | 3.9 | 0.0 | +114 | >99% | >99% | 14% |
| San Diego | 1552 | 9.3 | 6.7 | 0.0 | +13 | <1% | 33% | <1% |
| Kansas City | 1536 | 8.8 | 7.2 | 0.0 | +59 | 0% | 22% | <1% |
| Oakland | 1324 | 2.6 | 13.4 | 0.0 | -182 | 0% | 0% | 0% |
| **NFC East** | | | | | | | | |
| Philadelphia | 1593 | 11.1 | 4.9 | 0.0 | +99 | 71% | 78% | 5% |
| Dallas | 1558 | 10.7 | 5.3 | 0.0 | +48 | 29% | 56% | 2% |
| Washington | 1299 | 3.7 | 12.3 | 0.0 | -130 | 0% | 0% | 0% |
| N.Y. Giants | 1441 | 5.4 | 10.6 | 0.0 | -35 | 0% | 0% | 0% |
| **NFC North** | | | | | | | | |
| Green Bay | 1640 | 12.1 | 3.9 | 0.0 | +141 | 76% | 99% | 13% |
| Detroit | 1556 | 10.6 | 5.4 | 0.0 | +45 | 24% | 80% | 3% |
| Minnesota | 1464 | 7.2 | 8.7 | 0.0 | -26 | 0% | <1% | <1% |
| Chicago | 1424 | 6.3 | 9.7 | 0.0 | -104 | 0% | 0% | 0% |
| **NFC South** | | | | | | | | |
| New Orleans | 1473 | 6.7 | 9.3 | 0.0 | -19 | 36% | 38% | <1% |
| Atlanta | 1452 | 6.3 | 9.6 | 0.0 | -19 | 37% | 37% | <1% |
| Carolina | 1476 | 5.9 | 9.1 | 1.0 | -58 | 27% | 27% | <1% |
| Tampa Bay | 1334 | 2.8 | 13.2 | 0.0 | -135 | 0% | 0% | 0% |
| **NFC West** | | | | | | | | |
| Seattle | 1717 | 11.2 | 4.8 | 0.0 | +111 | 58% | 94% | 18% |
| Arizona | 1602 | 11.5 | 4.5 | 0.0 | +35 | 42% | 89% | 7% |
| San Francisco | 1548 | 8.3 | 7.7 | 0.0 | -31 | 0% | 3% | <1% |
| St. Louis | 1514 | 7.3 | 8.7 | 0.0 | -6 | 0% | <1% | <1% |

❤ FIVETHIRTYEIGHT

Table 12.5: Elo vs Vegas vs Reality

Preseason projections for teams' regular-season wins vs. actual total

| TEAM | ELO | VEGAS | ACTUAL |
|---|---|---|---|
| Arizona | 8.3 | 7.5 | 11 |
| Atlanta | 6.8 | 8.5 | 6 |
| Baltimore | 8.9 | 8.5 | 10 |
| Buffalo | 7.2 | 6.5 | 9 |
| Carolina | 9.4 | 8.0 | 7 |
| Chicago | 7.7 | 8.5 | 5 |
| Cincinnati | 9.3 | 9.0 | 10 |
| Cleveland | 5.9 | 6.5 | 7 |
| Dallas | 8.0 | 8.0 | 12 |
| Denver | 10.0 | 11.5 | 12 |
| Detroit | 7.5 | 8.5 | 11 |
| Green Bay | 7.8 | 10.5 | 12 |
| Houston | 6.2 | 7.5 | 9 |
| Indianapolis | 9.3 | 9.5 | 11 |
| Jacksonville | 5.4 | 5.0 | 3 |
| Kansas City | 7.3 | 8.0 | 9 |
| Miami | 7.7 | 8.0 | 8 |
| Minnesota | 7.5 | 6.0 | 7 |
| N.Y. Giants | 8.0 | 8.0 | 6 |
| N.Y. Jets | 7.2 | 7.0 | 4 |
| New England | 10.6 | 10.5 | 12 |
| New Orleans | 9.5 | 9.5 | 7 |
| Oakland | 4.7 | 5.0 | 3 |
| Philadelphia | 8.6 | 9.0 | 10 |
| Pittsburgh | 9.1 | 8.5 | 11 |
| San Diego | 8.8 | 8.0 | 9 |
| San Francisco | 10.3 | 10.5 | 8 |
| Seattle | 10.9 | 11.0 | 12 |
| St. Louis | 7.4 | 7.5 | 6 |
| Tampa Bay | 6.5 | 7.0 | 2 |
| Tennessee | 7.9 | 7.0 | 2 |
| Washington | 5.9 | 7.5 | 4 |

FIVETHIRTYEIGHT                                      SOURCE: LOGICAL APPROACH

City, Philadelphia, Atlanta, San Diego, Buffalo, Cleveland and New Orleans were all won as these teams did not make the playoff.

So with these adjustments and long bets on the above dangerous teams, my Betfair wagers going into the playoffs are in Table 12.6. I downgraded Denver to a slight short despite their high Elo. Perennial MVP Peyton Manning is not in this year's running. In the later 2014 games he seems injured or off his usual brilliant self. Three TDs, six ints and a 76.8 quarterback rating in December reflects this. We will see if Manning is effective in the playoffs, but at low odds, Denver is a minor short. Seattle, New England, Green Bay, Dallas and possibly others look better relative to their odds.

Table 12.6: Betfair wagers before playoffs

| Super Bowl Winner - Matched: GBP 1,582,305 | | | | Going In-Play | Rules | |
|---|---|---|---|---|---|---|
| Liability: £2,680.00 | Cash Out £2,572.03 | Profit £-107.97 | [?] | | | |

| Bet view: £2 | Back | Lay |
|---|---|---|
| New England Patriots £824.00 | 4.6 £362 | 4.8 £289 |
| Seattle Seahawks £2,847.00 | 5.2 £189 | 5.4 £145 |
| Denver Broncos £275.50 | 5.9 £74 | 7.4 £79 |
| Green Bay Packers £361.76 | 7.2 £235 | 8.2 £79 |
| Philadelphia Eagles £93.00 | 18.5 £35 | 19 £17 |
| Indianapolis Colts £128.99 | 24 £331 | 27 £88 |
| Arizona Cardinals £950.00 | 26 £25 | 28 £3 |
| Detroit Lions £-2,185.00 | 28 £158 | 32 £125 |
| Baltimore Ravens £200.00 | 38 £19 | 44 £3 |
| Dallas Cowboys £-2,510.00 | 42 £63 | 46 £34 |
| Pittsburgh Steelers £488.40 | 46 £55 | 48 £27 |
| New Orleans Saints £-2,470.00 | 55 £14 | 70 £7 |
| Cincinnati Bengals £-2,680.00 | 50 £28 | 55 £27 |
| San Diego Chargers £-1,810.00 | 85 £10 | 90 £43 |
| Kansas City Chiefs £-389.84 | 120 £2 | 170 £10 |
| Carolina Panthers £-1,210.00 | 170 £2 | 190 £2 |
| Atlanta Falcons £-1,210.00 | 180 £5 | 240 £18 |
| Buffalo Bills £-409.60 | 230 £2 | 630 £2 |
| Houston Texans £-2,610.00 | 310 £3 | 1000 £10 |
| Miami Dolphins £-2,560.00 | 450 £4 | 1000 £4 |
| Cleveland Browns £-1,210.00 | 500 £2 | |

I also had side bets such as who wins divisions and what pair of teams makes the playoffs — Seattle-New England is the largest bet with some on Green Bay and Denver. For the Super Bowl, my pairs of entrants biggest bet is Seattle/New England (+895.36). I was also long Seattle/Denver (+65.00), Seattle/Pittsburgh (+536.00) and Green Bay/New England (+465.05). This cost me 229 if one of the shorts occurs.

For the AFC winner, I have +176.45 on New England at 1.95-2.05 now. If they lose to Denver, Pittsburgh, Cincinnati,or Indianapolis I lose 33.65 or 85.14 if Baltimore wins. Adding to this I am bidding 20 short Denver at 3.5 as I think they are not this good. Others have too wide spreads to consider

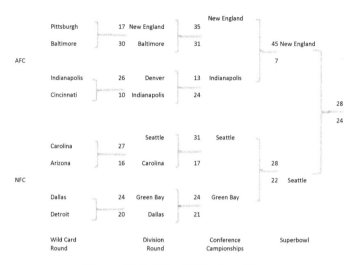

Figure 12.1: The 2015 playoff tree.

betting. For the NFC I just have Seattle +220 at 1.81-1.9 and would lose -68 if Green Bay, Dallas, Arizona, Detroit or Carolina wins. Green Bay is 3.6-3.8 and Dallas is 8.2-8.6 which are fairly priced. So no more bets there.

Figure 12.1 displays the 2015 teams and scores of the games.

## Does the highest rated Elo team predict the winner of the Super Bowl?

The highest rated Elo going into the playoffs has not been a good predictor of the eventual Super Bowl winner as Table 12.7 shows. One reason is that 12 teams are in the playoffs and only one is rated highest, namely, 8.25% of the teams, so this is how statistics can lie or be misleading. Since 1997, Elo's top team has won 3 Super Bowls, 18%. Seattle won last year. Six of the last 9 Super Bowl winners played on wild card week so were not #1 or #2 in the AFC or NFC. Contrary to the notion proliferated by the New York Giants last Super Bowl runs, getting hot at the end of the regular season is not necessarily a good recipe for playoff success. The Seahawks lost 2 of their last 4 games heading into the post season in 2013 and the Ravens were 1 to 4 into the 2012 playoffs. Both of these teams won the Super Bowl.

## Table 12.7: Top-Rated Elo Teams' Performance in the Playoffs

Teams listed led in NFL Elo rating at end of regular season

| YEAR | TEAM | ELO RATING | PERFORMANCE IN PLAYOFFS |
|------|------|-----------|-------------------------|
| 1970 | Minnesota | 1676 | Lost in divisional playoffs |
| 1971 | Dallas | 1679 | **Won Super Bowl** |
| 1972 | Miami | 1740 | **Won Super Bowl** |
| 1973 | Miami | 1725 | **Won Super Bowl** |
| 1974 | Oakland | 1711 | Lost AFC Championship |
| 1975 | Pittsburgh | 1736 | **Won Super Bowl** |
| 1976 | Pittsburgh | 1735 | Lost AFC Championship |
| 1977 | Denver | 1702 | Lost Super Bowl |
| 1978 | Dallas | 1729 | Lost Super Bowl |
| 1979 | Pittsburgh | 1695 | **Won Super Bowl** |
| 1980 | Dallas | 1648 | Lost NFC Championship |
| 1981 | Dallas | 1650 | Lost NFC Championship |
| 1982 | Cincinnati | 1636 | Lost in first round |
| 1983 | Washington | 1782 | Lost Super Bowl |
| 1984 | San Francisco | 1735 | **Won Super Bowl** |
| 1985 | Chicago | 1736 | **Won Super Bowl** |
| 1986 | Chicago | 1726 | Lost in divisional playoffs |
| 1987 | San Francisco | 1735 | Lost in divisional playoffs |
| 1988 | San Francisco | 1607 | **Won Super Bowl** |
| 1989 | San Francisco | 1736 | **Won Super Bowl** |
| 1990 | San Francisco | 1721 | Lost NFC Championship |
| 1991 | Washington | 1718 | **Won Super Bowl** |
| 1992 | San Francisco | 1737 | Lost NFC Championship |
| 1993 | Dallas | 1737 | **Won Super Bowl** |
| 1994 | San Francisco | 1706 | **Won Super Bowl** |
| 1995 | San Francisco | 1729 | Lost in divisional playoffs |
| 1996 | Green Bay | 1730 | **Won Super Bowl** |
| 1997 | Green Bay | 1761 | Lost Super Bowl |
| 1998 | Minnesota | 1749 | Lost NFC Championship |
| 1999 | Jacksonville | 1682 | Lost AFC Championship |
| 2000 | Tennessee | 1697 | Lost in divisional playoffs |
| 2001 | St. Louis | 1713 | Lost Super Bowl |
| 2002 | Philadelphia | 1682 | Lost NFC Championship |
| 2003 | New England | 1717 | **Won Super Bowl** |
| 2004 | New England | 1764 | **Won Super Bowl** |
| 2005 | Indianapolis | 1719 | Lost in divisional playoffs |
| 2006 | San Diego | 1733 | Lost in divisional playoffs |
| 2007 | New England | 1828 | Lost Super Bowl |
| 2008 | Indianapolis | 1687 | Lost in wild card playoffs |
| 2009 | San Diego | 1684 | Lost in divisional playoffs |
| 2010 | New England | 1740 | Lost in divisional playoffs |
| 2011 | Green Bay | 1757 | Lost in divisional playoffs |
| 2012 | New England | 1728 | Lost AFC Championship |
| 2013 | Seattle | 1698 | **Won Super Bowl** |
| 2014 | Seattle | 1760 | *TBD* |

# Wild card week end

My wild card weekend bets are discussed below. The Elo's are in Table 12.8.

Table 12.8: NFL wild card matchups according to Elo

**Straight-up record:** 176-79-1 on season (11-5 in Week 17)
**Against point spread record:** 129-108-4 on season (9-7 in Week 17)

| HOME TEAM | ELO RATING | ELO WIN% | VISITING TEAM | ELO RATING | ELO WIN% | ELO POINT SPREAD |
|---|---|---|---|---|---|---|
| Carolina | 1530 | 53% | Arizona | 1577 | 47% | -0.5 |
| Pittsburgh | 1623 | 65 | Baltimore | 1582 | 35 | -4.0 |
| Indianapolis | 1579 | 60 | Cincinnati | 1578 | 40 | -2.5 |
| Dallas | 1632 | 69 | Detroit | 1559 | 31 | -5.5 |

*FAVORED TEAM*

FIVETHIRTYEIGHT

**Analysis**: **Game 1:** Carolina has been trending stronger despite their losing record of 7-8-1 which won their division. They are at home as a division winner but have a lower Elo (1530) than Arizona (1577) but Arizona's value is based mostly on early season results with first string quarterback Carson Palmer and backup Drew Stanton but both of these are injured and using third string quarterback Ryan Lindley and fourth string quarterback Logan Thomas they have lost 4 of their last 6 games. The Elo analysis in Table 12.8 has Carolina -0.5 but this yields a 53% chance of Carolina winning versus 47% for Arizona. The odds makers observing all this have Carolina a 6-7 point favorite. I feel that Carolina might be better but at 1.39-1.40 on Betfair they are not worth betting. They are very turnover risky and Arizona is very good at creating turnovers. Arizona at 3.5-3.6 is a logical mean reversion bet to get these long odds and then cover should they get ahead to create a risk arbitrage. That's a reasonable approach but I took a related route. Arizona's defense is top notch so a low scoring game is likely so I am taking the points with small bets of 50 on Arizona +6.5 and 50 on Arizona +13 at the 1.48 area or lower. These point bets are much less liquid than the money line bets but risk arbitrage mean reversion is possible here.

Arizona's defense was excellent and forced Carolina turnovers that led to two early touchdowns for a 14-6 lead. Unfortunately the spread was too wide to get out of my bets. The Arizona offense was truly awful and had the fewest yards (78) gained of any NFL playoff game ever, plus they had numerous fumbles, miscues and never used their best receiver, Larry Fitzgerald. Third string quarterback Ryan Lindley could simply not run the team. They were 0-3 with him as the quarterback. But as bad as Arizona was, I did luck out and win one of my two bets. The Panthers caught an interception near the end of the game with a score 27-14. My +13 bet was then a wash but Carolina, being on the one yard line, elected to take a safety rather than risk an Arizona touchdown plus an onside kick and a second touchdown, so the score ended 27-16. I won that bet and lost the Arizona +6.5 bet, so the net was a very small loss. Long Arizona then mean-reversion would have led to a net gain because that market is liquid. Bruce Ahrens, who got coach of the year award, has a big problem at quarterback — he should have traded for a decent one. Carolina now goes to Seattle or Green Bay depending on the results of the Green Bay-Detroit game on Sunday.

**Game 2:** The Pittsburgh-Baltimore game is more straightforward. Pittsburgh has a higher Elo (1623) than Baltimore (1582) which amounts to 4 points advantage plus they are at home. Hence the suggested bet is Pittsburgh 200 at 1.66. The game was an excellent one to watch. Baltimore quarterback Joe Flacco, who has an excellent post season record, out dueled Ben Roethlisberger, who had two interceptions near the end of the game which ended 23-15. Baltimore defensive star Terrell Suggs got one of the interceptions and was all over the field the whole game. It was possible to mean-revert to lower the loss on the 200 bet to 175 and to get more long Baltimore for a possible Super Bowl win. They are now down to 24-25 and my longs were at 30, 32, 25, 26 and 50. Baltimore now goes to New England with Betfair odds of 3.75-4.3 versus the home favorite at 1.31-1.36. While Baltimore is a heavy underdog, and I favor New England, I have a large win bet on them at low cost because of their long odds to win 2091 should they be Super Bowl champs. Since they have beaten New England twice in New England recently, this bet is warranted.

**Game 3:** Cincinnati at Indianapolis. The Elo of Indianapolis (1579) is slightly above Cincinnati (1570) with a home field advantage, the Colts are Elo favored by 2.5 points with a 60% chance of winning. I went 200 long at 1.56 Indianapolis with the better money quarterback Andrew Luck who led the NFL with 40 TD passes this year. AJ Green and Germaine Gresham who are a big part of the Bengals offense are both out which will make Cincinnati quarterback Andy Dalton's job hard. They likely will need a big day from star runner Jeremy Hill to be competitive. Since week 9, Hill gained 929 yards, more than Marshawn Lynch (824), DeSean Jackson (814), and De Marco Murray (791). Indianapolis was simply better and dominated the game. Mr Reliable, Adam Vinitari, the 42 year old field goal kicker was 4 out of 4 including a 53 yarder. Adam had two game winning field goals in New England Super Bowl wins and continues great performance. Andrew Luck played well and had one spectacular TD to get the game to 20-10. The punter, McAffe, is also top notch. Andrew is the fifth quarterback in NFL history with three 300 yard playoff games in a row. Cincinnati simply did not get enough running yards given the key players out in this passing game. Quarterback Andy Dalton was ok but he did fumble with 2.49 left to seal the loss. Now the Colts go to Denver for a Luck-Manning match next weekend. Right now Luck is outplaying Manning but Denver will be favored.

**Game 4:** Detroit at Dallas. Football is a rough sport but deliberate dirty play should be punished hard. Detroit's Ndamukong Suh is constantly making dirty plays and basically get away with them because he is a great defensive player and is "good for business". Some 90,000 paying fans were at this game in Arlington, Texas. The latest incident involved stepping on the injured leg of Green Bay quarterback Aaron Rodgers. He had a one game suspension but pleas by the Detroit management that essentially amounted to "with Suh we have a better chance against Dallas" so he got off with a fine. Dallas seems better with their three stars running back De Marco Murray — the NFL's leading rusher, Tony Romo — the NFL's leading percent completion passer with 34 TDs against 9 interceptions and Dez Bryant — the NFL's leading TD pass receiver. This is reminiscent of their Super Bowl winning team's with the trio of runner Emitt Smith, quarterback Troy Aikman, and receiver Michael Irvin. So "America's team" is back with a competitive chance. The Elo's were Dallas 1632 and Detroit 1559, so at home this is a 5.5 point advantage estimate and a 69% chance of winning. I bet 200 at 1.4 on Dallas. For the Super Bowl I am long Dallas +849.39 at 17-17.5 and short Detroit -2271 at 75-80. Suh is a free agent after this season and apparently up to 10 teams, including Detroit, want to bid for his services in the $100 million area. So the good defensive play vastly outweighs the once in a while questionable play.

Detroit struck first getting out to a 14-0 lead. Golden Tate was a big factor both as a receiver (51 yard gain on the first TD), runner after catches (he leads the NFL) and as a blocker (for the Reggie Bush TD). Both Tate and Bush have Super Bowl experience and rings with Seattle and New Orleans, respectively. It is time to get out of my large short on Detroit for the Super Bowl. At 40-1 this was not expensive. So now Detroit is +758.36. I am still short Denver -572.50 at 6.2-6.6, Carolina -2474.40 at 38-40 and Indianapolis -569.01 at 27-28. Since the Colts could easily beat Denver, I need to get them down to at least zero. I doubt they can beat New England and Seattle but 25 is not much to get them positive, so they are now +80.99. So my only shorts now are Denver at -597.50 and Carolina -2432.40. Detroit has gained 175 yards versus only 44 for Dallas. My bet of -200 Detroit +80

Dallas is in trouble and Detroit is now 1.38-1.39 so neutralizing or hedging is difficult.

Dallas finally scored on a Romo to Terrance Williams TD to make it 14-7. With 7 seconds left before half time, Prater kicked the field goal to make the score 17-7, the Lions getting the second half kick off. Dallas got an interception but Dan Baily missed a field goal so it is still 17-7. Detroit got a 37 yard field goal to make it 20-7. Dez Bryant took a Romo pass 43 yards after the catch. Murray scores a Dallas TD but there is a hold against Jason Witten to nullify it. A pass to Cole Beasley gained 14 to the 3. A pitch to Witten got the ball to the 1. Finally, on 4th end goal, Murray got the TD at 2.54 to make the score 20-14. The odds are now 1.6-1.61 Detroit, 2.62-2.64 Dallas. Dallas got the ball after a 3 and out with offensive pass interference on the 3rd down. From the 30, there is a pass to the 50 and Murray gains to the 46. Then Beasley caught a pass to the 33 and a roughing penalty added 15 more yards to get to the 18. Suh got a sack and then got another sack for a loss of 10 to the 35. But Dallas got a 51 yard field goal to tighten the score to 20-17 with 12.16 to go. The kickoff pinned Detroit to the 4 and a loss of 1 put the ball on the 3. On 2rd and 11 there was a pass to the 21. On 3rd and 8 there was a pass to Calvin Johnson with a flag for pass interference. Finally there is a Detroit 3 and out and Dallas gets the ball. Murray, who led the NFL in rushing, had a good run of 18 yards. A Romo to Witten pass got to the 50. A 3rd and 15 had a pass that was too low. There was a roughing the kicker but no flag. Detroit fumbled the kickoff but recovered the ball and went 3 and out. Dallas goes for it on a 4th and 1 and get a delay of game penalty, so they have to punt. But the punt is only good for 10 yards to the 41.

With Dallas charging, I can now adjust my bet slightly from -200, +80. So at least I lower my potential loss should Dallas lose the game.

On 3rd and 8, a pass to Murray is tipped. So they go for it on 4th and 6 — a risky move. But a pass to Witten gets them to the 25. A second and 10 to Beasley is incomplete but there is defensive holding yielding a first down. Bryant gains 3 then an incomplete pass leads to 3rd down and 7. A short pass to Dunbar led to yet another penalty, defensive holding and a first down on the 9. Romo has a perfect pass for a TD but Williams cannot catch it. Murray gets to the 3. Then a false start moves them back to the 8. Finally a Romo to Williams TD gave Dallas the lead 24-20 with 2.32 left. So Dallas has turned the tide with a TD, a field goal and a TD on the last 3 drives. Jerry Jones, the Dallas owner, has a jubilant group of guests including New Jersey governor Chris Christie, a Cowboys fan who comes to all their games. That has caused some political discussion and in recent games Christie had to pay his own expenses. Romo plays a flawless game, passes for two TDs with no interceptions and it 19 for 31. Stafford has 17 out of 43 late game wins from behind. Can he do it again? Tate gets a 6 yard pass for a 1st down with 1.43 left. Stafford fumbles and the Cowboys have it but fumble it back to the Lions. There is an offside on 2nd and 15. Stafford hits passes to Johnson, Ebron and Ridick. It is now 4th and 3. Stafford is sacked and fumbles or did DeMarcus Lawrence? The crowd in Jerry Jones' box goes wild and Jones goes to the field to hug Tony Romo. So Dallas goes to Green Bay and Carolina goes to Seattle in the NFC matchups.

### Divisional Playoffs: Saturday/ Sunday January 10, 11, 2015

I start with a key behavioral finance analysis made by Benjamin Morris on FiveThirtyEight.com, January 8, 2015. We know that teams in the wildcard weekend were rated below the #1 or #2 teams in each division which got byes in wildcard weekend so are in fact weaker than the four elite teams. Indeed four of the eight got eliminated during wildcard weekend.

Now, let's consider the four who won against tough or weak competition: They are called *trial by fire* teams. They face better teams rested with fewer injuries and wear and tear which play at home. The results[2] show that these teams:

- won 52.9% of the games against the bye teams in the Conference Championship game

- were 8-3 in the Super Bowl 1994-2013

- were 11-0-1 against the spread in the Super Bowl

- were 11-6 in conference championship games since 1997

- were 21-6-1 against the spread in the playoffs, that's a one in 500 chance if they were 50-50 as the spread is supposed to create; so it is very statistically significant that these teams beat the spread

- won 6 of the last 7 and 7 of the last 14 Super Bowls

- this compares with a 30% win percentage in the divisional round (24-56) and 32.5% (21-43) since 1997 and 45% in conference championship games (9-11)

So we conclude that these teams improve greatly, and a playoff game win is really worth 2-3 or even 5 regular season games according to Morris's calculations. So who does this favor in 2015?

---

[2]Morris goes back to 1994 when the salary cap was instituted. Prior to the Broncos win in 1997 few of these teams went far in the playoffs and none made the Super Bowl.

Dallas and Indianapolis are two division champions who won their wild-card games against strong teams, namely 11-5 Detroit and 10-5-1 Cincinnati. Dallas at 13-4 now has the best record of the eight teams left in the playoffs.

Table 12.10 has the estimates of the 12 teams in the playoffs to win the Super Bowl. New England is really higher than 22% because of the week 17 Elo not counting fundamentals flaw. For me, I rate Denver lower and Dallas and Baltimore higher in my betting which follows. I am short all but Seattle, New England, Green Bay, Dallas, Pittsburgh and Baltimore. Shorting Denver is a risk but I don't see them beating the Patriots in Foxborough and Seattle in the Super Bowl assuming these games materialize and they could lose next week against the winner of the Cincinnati-Indianapolis game 3. But I am not short Denver much and the odds to me are too low for Denver to be long. Seattle is 22-2 at home in the last 24 games there. On the other hand, the hot Dallas and dangerous Pittsburgh and Baltimore have high odds, so substantial long positions are cheap. One gets knocked off next week. Pittsburgh is favored. Arizona is also a minor short to me. Without a top quarterback, I don't see much risk there. Indianapolis has a top quarterback but the team seems a cut below the top ones. Carolina, I am still short, I doubt they can beat Seattle in Seattle. Cam Newton, their talented but mistake prone quarterback, has a poor record in two previous games in Seattle.

***Elo probabilities of winning the Super Bowl.*** Elo via Nate Silver's calculation as of end of week 14 the record against the spread was 105-86-3 and straight up 144-63.1. The picks have been right 55% of the closing Vegas line which he thinks is luck assuming that the Elo are basically Las Vegas market odds winning 51% of the time and losing after the casino take. I have not done a similar Betfair study as I combine the Elo's with my own analysis. There I face a 6.5% commission on net winning bets. The full score will be revealed after the Super Bowl and is discussed at the end of this column.

After week 15:

| New England | Seattle | Denver | Arizona | Green Bay | Dallas |
|-------------|---------|--------|---------|-----------|--------|
| 26%         | 19%     | 17%    | 11%     | 6%        | 5%     |

The MVP candidates as of week 16 according to Mike Cole, December 23, 2014:

1. Aaron Rodgers, Green Bay Packers quarterback. ***He won for the second time.***
   11-4 record, 36 TD, 5 ints, 8.3 yds/attempt, 65.1% completions

2. JJ Watt, Houston Texans defensive end. ***He won defensive player of the year by a unanimous vote.***
   17-5 sacks, one ints (for a TD), 5 fumble recoveries (one for a TD), 3 receiving TDs
   The last defensive player to win was Lawrence Taylor in 1986 and the last player on a non-playoff team to win was OJ Simpson in 1973, but JJ was sure deserving. He is the most dominant player in the NFL with a record two more than 20 sack seasons plus all his other contributions. Justin Houston of Kansas had 22 sacks.

3. Tom Brady, New England Patriots quarterback
   12-3 record, 33 TDs, 9 ints, 7.6 yds/attempt, 64.5%

4. De Marco Murray, Dallas Cowboys running back. ***He won offensive player of the year.***
   373 carries, 1745 yds, 12 TDs, end of year 1840 yards on 392 carries

5. Tony Romo, Dallas Cowboys quarterback
   11-3 record, 32 TDs, 8 ints, 8.5 yds/attempt, 70.3%

6. Rob Gronkowski, New England Patriots tight end. ***He won comeback player of the year.***
   82 receptions, 1124 yds, 12 TDs

I would add other worthy candidates: Russell Wilson, QB Seattle, 34-12, the most wins in the first 3 years in NFL history, more 2014 yards gained than 18 of the 32 NFL teams, Ben Rothlesberger, QB Pittsburgh, Marshawn Lynch, running back Seattle, 17 TDs, Dez Bryant running back Dallas 14 TDs, and Odell Beckham, Jr receiver of the NY Giants who made the catch of the year and many other great plays. ***Beckham won offensive rookie of the year and offensive play of the year.***

**Game 5:** Baltimore at New England

Swetye's Elo analysis is:

| Team | Elo | Pr(Win) | Elo Spread | Stern Pr(Win)* |
|------|-----|---------|------------|----------------|
| New England | 1068 | 59% | +3.4 | 60% |
| Baltimore | 1037 | 41% | | 40% |

*calculated as 50%+0.03(spread)

The Betfair odds were 3.3-3.75 Baltimore and 1.37-1.43 New England.

My bets were 200 on New England at 1.36 so win 72 or lose 200 and bets on Baltimore +7.5 and +13.5.

Analysis: It was a duel of two very good quarterbacks. Tom Brady is in the discussion as best quarterback ever with many records. He is 18 and 8 post season, 3-2 in Super Bowls, and Conference Champion 5 of his 12 seasons. At home, he has a superior record: 22 and 2 in December. Joe Flacco is 13 TDs with no interceptions in the post season and twice in the last five years he has beaten New England in New England. In 2012 this was en route to winning the Super Bowl. New England was unable to use star receiver Rob Gronkowski who was injured. Baltimore lost runner Ray Rice to domestic abuse but Justin Forsett, at 5.6 yards per carry, which is tops in the NFL, has filled in admirably.

Baltimore scored first on a 5 play 71 yard series with Flacco connecting with 4 different receivers, getting the TD on the 19 yard pass to Aiken. Brady had a few passes completed to Boldin and Gronkowski but could not score and then got intercepted. Steve Smith, the great pickup from Carolina got a second TD from Flacco from 9 yards out. That made it 14-0. So it was time to get out of my Baltimore +13.5 bet. New England got two passes to Gronkowski and Julian Edelman, which got it to the 1 on a 78 yard drive. Then Brady got the TD on a 4 yard run to make it 14-7. Amendola scored on a 15 yard pass to Brady to even the score at 14-14. Daniels got an 11 yard Flacco TD to make it 21-14. Baltimore got a second 14 point lead with a 16 yard Forsett pass from Flacco. New England retaliated with a 5 yard pass to Gronkowski and a 51 yard TD pass from Edelman (who was a college quarterback at Kent State) to Amendola. So the game was tied again at 28 each. Flacco had his first interception by McCordy but that did not lead to anything. Flacco fumbled and New England would have had the ball on the Baltimore 1 but Darrell Revis, usually reliable, had a rare penalty. So that negated an almost sure New England TD and the lead. Forsett got Baltimore to the 40 then got 8 more on 3rd in 1 at the 36. The ball was fumbled out of bounds with a near interception. Forsett got to the 18 then to the 9 and Tonsett got to the 6. Flacco's pass was too high on 3rd and goal so Baltimore kicked a field goal by Tucker to make it 31-28 with 10.17 to go in the fourth quarter. Amendola got the kickoff to the 26. Vereen fumbled but the call was reversed as his knee was down Brady got a first down to the 48 throwing to Gronkowski. Gronkowski and JJ Watt are the only unanimous pro bowl selections. Amendola got to the 38. Brady passed to Edelman to the 23 then a 23 yard TD pass to Brandon LaFell which got the Patriots ahead for the first time in the game 35-31. Brady is now the leader at 46 in post season TDs versus 4.5 for the former leader, Brady's boyhood idol, Joe Montana. So New England has come back twice from 14 point deficits, that's with essentially zero running by New England — it's been essentially all passing, mostly by Brady with one TD from

Edelman. The Ravens got the ball and Flacco had his second interception. After a New England 3 and out that almost used up the clock, Baltimore had 14 seconds to go. On 4th and 15, with 4 seconds to go, Flacco threw a "Hail Mary pass" into the end zone. Rather than trying to catch it, New England players pushed the ball out of the end zone and onto the field so even if a Raven caught it, the time would be up. So the Patriots won 35-31. It was 20 playoff wins for Belichick, the most ever by a coach. Brady was 33/50 with 3 TDs and one interception. I won the Baltimore +13.5 bet for +26 and the Baltimore +7.5 for +34.20 and the straight bet for +72.

**Game 6:** Carolina at Seattle

Swetye's Elo analysis is:

| Team | Elo | Pr(Win) | Elo Spread | Stern Pr(Win) |
|------|-----|---------|------------|---------------|
| Seattle | 1068 | 68% | 7.6 | 73% |
| Carolina | 1000 | 32% | | 27% |

Early on there were some 3 and outs. Then Cam Newton threw an interception to Richard Sherman. The legion of boom as it is called for the Seattle secondary defensive core has three pro-bowl selections. Besides Sherman, there is Earl Thomas and Bobby Wagner. And the fourth member, Kam Chancellor, showed in the game that he is at the top too. So passing against Seattle is really tough.[3] Wilson ran for 34 yards and passed to Jermaine Kearse for 30 more. Wilson had a rare miscue and fumbled but got the ball back. Unger, the center, may have caused the problem — he is just back after 11 weeks off. An offensive penalty against Lockett for 15 yards ruined the chance of a field goal, so Seattle punted.

Newton passed to Tolbert for 31. The Seattle's Michael Bennett forced a fumble on the 28. A Willson to Baldwin pass gained 19. Cooper cannot catch a pass, then as 3rd and long, Willson hit Baldwin for a 16 yard TD. So it was then 7-0. Willson, who has a marvelous record as well as a superior Derek Jeter type attitude, is breaking all sorts of records. So far in his three years he has 52 TDs and 2 interceptions in the Red Zone (with 20 yards to go).

Carolina got to the 21 on the kickoff and Newton passed to the 50. With 3rd and short, Newton who's 6'5" and 250 got the first down. Then Sherman almost got a second interception on an incomplete pass. A pass to Billy Brown got a first down. Williams got an 8.5 yard run and the full back, Tolbert got another first down. Carolina got to the 11. Bobby Wagner has

---

[3]Bill Belichick better get his running game going to help Tom Brady who, as you will see in the New England-Baltmore game, basically single handedly (with a little help from Julian Edelman and Rob Gronkowski) beat a tough Baltimore with a non-existent New England running game.

a tackle to prevent a gain. Stewart got to the 7. Then Newton passed to Calvin Benjamin for a TD to make it 7-7.

Seattle's Lynch gets it to the 31. Then Wilson connected to Kearse for a one handed 63 yard TD to make it 14-7. Kam Chancellor got moving with a stop. Newton passed to Jerico Cotcheray for a gain. A 15 yard face mask penalty just before the 2 minute warning moved the ball. Then Benjamin almost got a TD but Newton's pass took him outside the end zone. Newton ran, then fumbled — out of bounds. On 4th and 1 they could go for it with 1.05 left or try a field goal. Newton went into shotgun formation then ran for the 1 yard first down showing how powerful he is. A blitz allowed a pass to the 25. With 23 seconds left, Carolina took a time out. Earl Thomas intercepted a Newton pass. So no field goal. But the play was under review and the on field decision was reversed as the ball hit the ground. So Carolina was 3rd and 8 with 18 seconds left. Tolbert had a small gain. Then on the 40 yard field goal try, Ken Chancellor jumped over the Carolina line and blocked the field goal but Seattle had a false start for a 5 yard penalty and another field goal try. Again, Chancellor jumped the Carolina line but this time ran into the kicker for a second penalty. On the third try, Chancellor did not try to block the kick which was made to make it 14-10. A flag on defense was not accepted. This is the first time I ever saw such a move — it is perfectly legal as long as the jumper touches nobody. It is an additional powerful defensive weapon for Seattle's #1 defense.

Seattle got the ball to start the second half. They got the ball on the 20. Lynch gained to the 25 then fumbled by Wilson recovered. On 3rd and 3, Wilson, who was 8/8 on third downs during the game, passed to Richardson to the 50. On second and 10, Lynch, who was yet to get going, had a short gain. Wilson was sacked to the 40 so they had to punt.

The kickoff was returned to the 40. Then Dixon got to Seattle's 41. That gave Carolina 14 first downs of 7 for Seattle. A sack pushed the ball back to the 50 — that was Seattle first sack of the game. But they had to punt to Seattle's 12. Wilson ran to the 31. A Turbin run and a pass to Wilson plus, finally, a long Lynch run got the ball to the 18, a 25 yard gain, as he hit the out of bounds line. Wilson got it to the 14, Turbin to the 11 and Lynch to the 7. A sack of Wilson ended the third quarter. A Seattle field goal made it 17-10. Seattle has won its last six games allowing zero points in the fourth quarter.

Carolina was three and out when a Newton pass to Tolbert was dropped. Seattle got the ball on the 42 and a 29 yard pass to Wilson led to a pass to the end zone to try for a TD but not quite. Wilson was up to 7/7 on a third down TD to Willson to make it 24-10. Wilson made another great pass to Kearse. Wilson was then 14 for 21 with 3 TDs and again no interceptions. Seattle then had held the lead at some time during the last 53 games.

Newton was sacked by Bruce Irvin then passed to Greg Olson to the 18. Newton ran to the 14 the Kam Chancellor got a 90 yard pick 6 interception to make it 31-10 and was named player of the game. Carolina got a TD to make it 31-17. Their on side kick failed and was recovered by Seattle. It is known that Super Bowl winning teams have a poor record the next year. With this win, Seattle became the first Super Bowl winning team to win any playoff game since 2005. This was now 8/8 in playoff wins for Seattle. I won my straight bet on Seattle, lost the Carolina +2.5 bet and won my shorts on Carolina. Carolina which was 3-8-1 then 7-7-1 the 8-8-1 lost to a superior team. Getting rid of top receiver Steve Smith to Baltimore sure did not help.

**Game 7:** Dallas and Green Bay

Swetye's Elo analysis is:

| Team | Elo | Pr(Win) | Elo Spread | Stern Pr(Win) |
|------|-----|---------|------------|---------------|
| Green Bay | 1062 | 53% | +1.3 | 54% |
| Dallas | 1051 | 47% | | 46% |

My bets were:
50 Dallas +6.5 at 1.84 so -50 or +42
100 Dallas +12.5 at 1.38 so -100 or +38
50 Green Bay at 1.47 so -50 or +22

Analysis: Green Bay is favored as they should be at home. It was a repeat of the famous 1967 Icebowl 47 years ago between these two teams which were meeting again in a very cold environment.

Both Tony Romo and Aaron Rodgers have had excellent seasons. Romo is 8-0 on the road with 20 TDs to only 2 interceptions and 14 and 1 in December. Rodgers, the likely MVP, is also 8-0 at home and is 25-0 in TDs to interceptions. He is 38-0 since the last interception at home. He is a Joe Montana like surgeon!

Green Bay scored first to make it 7-0. Runs by Lacey and Rodgers passes to Jordy Nelson got the job done. Dallas drove for a tying 7-7 TD on runs by Murray, Beasley, Romo and a pass to Witten. Dallas got another TD to make it 14-7. Williams ran for a second Dallas TD to make it 14-7. After a Green Bay 3 and out, Dallas tried a field goal from 50 yards which missed. Green Bay got two passes to Randall Cobb, one for 31 which led to a field goal to make it 14-10. Murray fumbled, his first since week 8 of the regular season. He, despite being the NFL's leading rusher, fumbles a lot, having had five in the regular season. Green Bay got the ball and had a big run by Lacey to the 12. Rodgers got it to the 8. A big fight between the teams erupted. As the third quarter ended, Mason Crosby kicked a field goal to make it 14-13. Dallas got runs from Murray and Randall and a Romo pass to Witten and then Murray ran to the 2 and then scored the TD to make it 21-13. Romo was 7 for 7 on the drive. Green Bay scored on a third and 15 from the 45 on a Rodgesr to Davante Adams pass. That put them 2 points down at 21 to 19. They chose the safe 1 point kick to make it 21-20 assuming that a 2 point conversion could be tried later in the game if necessary. Green Bay was able to sack Tony Romo twice for losses of 8 and 5 and a Murray run was short for the first down. Then Green Bay scored again to make it 26-21. This time, being 5 points behind, they tried a 2 point conversion to attempt to get a 7 point lead but that failed. Romo passed to Bryant to the 40 then was sacked again. A fourth at 2 on the 33, Romo hit. Bryant for a spectacular, possibly game winning, TD. Bryant twisted and made a great catch in the end zone and appeared to have full control even though, as allowed, the ball touched the ground. The referees ruled it an incomplete pass. It was and remains a controversial call as Green Bay got the ball with 2.24 remaining and was able to run out the clock. With a 5 point Green Bay win I won the straight bet on Green Bay and the two bets on Dallas plus points. Green Bay now goes to Seattle for the NFC Championship game which is a rematch of their first game of the season in Seattle which they lost.

**Game 8:** Indianapolis at Denver

Swetye's Elo analysis is:

| Team | Elo | Pr(Win) | Elo Spread | Stern Pr(Win) |
|------|-----|---------|------------|---------------|
| Denver | 1053 | 56% | +2.2 | 57% |
| Indianapolis | 1033 | 44% | | 43% |

The Betfair odds were 3.6-3.65 and 1.38-1.39 for Denver

My bets were:
100 Indianapolis +13.5 at 1.61 so win +61 or -100
50 Indianapolis +8 at 2.1 so +55 or -50 (but I made an operational error, I guess I did not press all buttons so only got a small amount of it)
75 Indianapolis +10 at 1.86 and 1.81
50 Indianapolis at 4.5 so +175 or -50 26th of 32 team quarterbacks)

Analysis: Indianapolis is improving and won in the wildcard round so has that advantage. Denver's defense is #3 behind Seattle and Detroit. They are also #5 on offense. So they look tough. Denver, which has been rated high (in the top four) on Nate Silver's site all year, seems to be slipping. Peyton Manning's 3 TD and 6 interceptions and a 76.8 rating ( 26th of the 32 NFL quarterbacks) in December do not look good. Is he injured? I am short them for the Super Bowl and in this game, I went long Indianapolis at long odds and them long with points. The real issue is whether the real Peyton Manning is piloting Denver.

So I took a fairly big risk by shorting Denver for the Super Bowl and in this game. Also, I simply do not see them beating New England in New England and Seattle. Regarding the game, the idea is their odds are off. The bets on Indianapolis at high odds seem a better risk — all I need to neutralize with a winning risk arbitrage is for Indianapolis to get ahead any time in the game. I know hedging out the bets with points is difficult as those bets are very illiquid with big bid-ask spreads. So hedging them is best in the no points market.

Manning started out 3 for 3. That included a pass to Julian Thomas for 32 and a roughing the passer penalty. A hold against the Colts by Mike Adams helped and DeMarcus Thomas let for a 7-0 Denver lead. The Colts came back. They started backed up to the 3 on the kickoff. A running into the kicker penalty was declined. Anderson ran for 22 yards and Hilton caught two more than twenty yard gains including one to the 15. Then Herron ran for the tying 7-7 TD. The Broncos started on the 20. Sanders got to the 36. Manning fumbled caused by Newsome with Jonathan Freeman recovering. After going 3 for 3, Manning was then 2 of 6. The Colts got a first down to the 28. Luck handled the drive well and ended up with a TD to Allen to make it 14-7. A key play was a pass to Hilton with defensive holding charged to Talib. I could now exit my straight bet. So 50 long Indianapolis at 45, namely lose 50 or gain 175 became the risk arbitrage +39 Indianapolis +50 Denver. But the spreads on 100 Indianapolis +13.5, 75 Indianapolis +10 and 50 Indianapolis +8. I could not trade easily. Wes Welker finally entered the game. Wes has had concussions so has had limited service with fewer receptions. A pass to Welker was incomplete and Denver had to punt. Denver had a Manning pass out of bounds and almost intercepted with 41 seconds to halftime but they were able to get a field goal to make it 14-10 at half time.

In the second half, the Colts scored on a 15 yard pass from Luck to Nicks to make it 21-10. Denver was able to close the gap to 21-13 with a field goal by Barth following a Luck interception. But Adam Vinitari again hit a Colts field goal to seal the game at 24-10. So I won my Super Bowl shorts on Denver plus the +39 straight bet and the +62.97 Colts +10 and the Colts +13.5 for +56. The Colts +8 bet was basically not filled on the operational error.

After the game, John Fox, the Denver coach, and John Elway, the Broncos director of football operations, decided to part ways. For Elway, who retired after winning two straight Super Bowls and receiving death threats because of 3 previous Super Bowl losses, it was winning the Super Bowl or nothing, so Fox and some of his staff had to go. Fox had a very good record and landed a coaching position with the Chicago Bears. Gary Kubiak, the defensive co-ordinator for the Baltimore Ravens and backup to Peyton Manning at Indianapolis, is the new coach. Peyton Manning is pondering his future. Despite a poor game, he had very few more than 5 yard passes. Elway wants him back. Going into 39 he may be slowing but the five time MVP won't want to go out this way.

Bets after the Division Round going into the Conference Championships are:

a) the odds for the Conference Championships right after the Division Round:

b) For the AFC Conference winner:

c) For the NFL Conference winner:

d) Super Bowl combos:

e) Super Bowl winner:

These odds are constantly changing depending on the supply and demand of the bettors, what remains the same are how much I would win or lose on particular outcomes.

Summary of my bets:
For the Conference Championship games I win 203 if the Patriots win and lose 472 if they lose. I win 220 if Seattle wins and 60 if they lose. The bets on this game can be used to adjust the Super Bowl possibilities and the Super Bowl monetary outcomes can be adjusted using the odds available. The Super Bowl odds and my bets seem to closely reflect the real chances with Seattle the best, New England second, Green Bay third and Indianapolis last. Any of the four could win. So the bets that are listed below are more or less ok. Injuries and player availability might adjust my betting. The bets for the Super Bowl look good and are as follow:

If the Patriots win, I will be ahead 1107 + 915.86 if against Seattle or 1107 + 485.50 if against Green Bay.
If the Seahawks win, I will be ahead 3130 + 915.86 if against New England or 3130 − 153 if against Indianapolis.
If the Packers win, I will be ahead 956.59 + 485.50 if against New England or 956.59 − 209 if against Indianapolis.
If the Colts win, I will be ahead 602.99 − 153 if against Seattle or 602.99 − 209 if against Green Bay.

## Table 12.9: Team standings as of week 17

**American Football Conference**

| AFC East | W | L | T | PCT | PF | PA | STRK |
|---|---|---|---|---|---|---|---|
| Patriots | 12 | 4 | 0 | .750 | 466 | 313 | L1 |
| Bills | 9 | 7 | 0 | .563 | 343 | 289 | W1 |
| Dolphins | 8 | 8 | 0 | .500 | 388 | 373 | L1 |
| Jets | 4 | 12 | 0 | .250 | 283 | 401 | W1 |

| AFC North | W | L | T | PCT | PF | PA | STRK |
|---|---|---|---|---|---|---|---|
| Steelers | 11 | 5 | 0 | .688 | 436 | 368 | W4 |
| Bengals | 10 | 5 | 1 | .656 | 365 | 344 | L1 |
| Ravens | 10 | 6 | 0 | .625 | 409 | 302 | W1 |
| Browns | 7 | 9 | 0 | .438 | 299 | 337 | L5 |

| AFC West | W | L | T | PCT | PF | PA | STRK |
|---|---|---|---|---|---|---|---|
| Broncos | 12 | 4 | 0 | .750 | 482 | 354 | W1 |
| Chiefs | 9 | 7 | 0 | .563 | 353 | 261 | W1 |
| Chargers | 9 | 7 | 0 | .563 | 348 | 348 | L1 |
| Raiders | 3 | 13 | 0 | .188 | 253 | 452 | L1 |

| AFC South | W | L | T | PCT | PF | PA | STRK |
|---|---|---|---|---|---|---|---|
| Colts | 11 | 5 | 0 | .688 | 458 | 369 | W1 |
| Texans | 9 | 7 | 0 | .563 | 372 | 307 | W2 |
| Jaguars | 3 | 13 | 0 | .188 | 249 | 412 | L1 |
| Titans | 2 | 14 | 0 | .125 | 254 | 438 | L10 |

**National Football Conference**

| NFC South | W | L | T | PCT | PF | PA | STRK |
|---|---|---|---|---|---|---|---|
| Panthers | 7 | 8 | 1 | .469 | 339 | 374 | W4 |
| Saints | 7 | 9 | 0 | .438 | 401 | 424 | W1 |
| Falcons | 6 | 10 | 0 | .375 | 381 | 417 | L1 |
| Buccaneers | 2 | 14 | 0 | .125 | 277 | 410 | L6 |

| NFC North | W | L | T | PCT | PF | PA | STRK |
|---|---|---|---|---|---|---|---|
| Packers | 12 | 4 | 0 | .750 | 486 | 348 | W2 |
| Lions | 11 | 5 | 0 | .688 | 321 | 282 | L1 |
| Vikings | 7 | 9 | 0 | .438 | 325 | 343 | W1 |
| Bears | 5 | 11 | 0 | .313 | 319 | 442 | L5 |

| NFC East | W | L | T | PCT | PF | PA | STRK |
|---|---|---|---|---|---|---|---|
| Cowboys | 12 | 4 | 0 | .750 | 467 | 352 | W4 |
| Eagles | 10 | 6 | 0 | .625 | 474 | 400 | W1 |
| Giants | 6 | 10 | 0 | .375 | 380 | 400 | L1 |
| Redskins | 4 | 12 | 0 | .250 | 301 | 438 | L1 |

| NFC West | W | L | T | PCT | PF | PA | STRK |
|---|---|---|---|---|---|---|---|
| Seahawks | 12 | 4 | 0 | .750 | 394 | 254 | W6 |
| Cardinals | 11 | 5 | 0 | .688 | 310 | 299 | L2 |
| 49ers | 8 | 8 | 0 | .500 | 306 | 340 | W1 |
| Rams | 6 | 10 | 0 | .375 | 324 | 354 | L3 |

Table 12.10: FiveThirtyEight's NFL Elo playoff odds

Dec. 31, 2014

| TEAM | ELO RATING | REACH DIVISIONAL PLAYOFF | REACH CONFERENCE TITLE GAME | REACH SUPER BOWL | WIN SUPER BOWL |
|---|---|---|---|---|---|
| Seattle | 1760 | 100% | 80% | 59% | 35% |
| New England | 1687 | 100 | 70 | 45 | 22 |
| Denver | 1672 | 100 | 65 | 30 | 14 |
| Green Bay | 1639 | 100 | 62 | 21 | 10 |
| Dallas | 1632 | 69 | 28 | 10 | 5 |
| Pittsburgh | 1623 | 64 | 23 | 10 | 4 |
| Indianapolis | 1579 | 59 | 17 | 6 | 2 |
| Arizona | 1577 | 48 | 12 | 4 | 2 |
| Cincinnati | 1576 | 41 | 13 | 5 | 2 |
| Baltimore | 1582 | 36 | 11 | 4 | 2 |
| Carolina | 1530 | 52 | 11 | 3 | 1 |
| Detroit | 1559 | 31 | 6 | 2 | 1 |

🦔 FIVETHIRTYEIGHT

Table 12.11: Bets on the pairs of teams in the Super Bowl

Table 12.12: Bets on the Super Bowl after Wild Card weekend

Table 12.13: Bets on the NFL Conference Games

Bets on the NFC Conference winner

Bets on the AFC Conference winner

## Conference Championships

**Game 9:** Green Bay at Seattle Swetye's Elo analysis is:

| Team | Elo | Pr(Win) | Elo Spread | Stern Pr(Win) |
|------|-----|---------|------------|---------------|
| Seattle | 1064 | 54% | +0.66 | 52% |
| Green Bay | 1058 | 46% | | 48% |

The Betfair odds were Seattle to win is 1.31-1.32 and Green Bay is 4.2-4.3.

My bets were: I have lots of Super Bowl bets so do not need to bet much on the straight game Seattle +1 is 1.26-1.30, Since I think Seattle will win I bet 200 on Seattle which gives me the bet win 62 or lose 200.

Analysis: It was raining like crazy all day. Paul Allen, the owner of the Seahawks, raised the 12 man flag to the thunderous ovation of the crowd. Seattle won the toss and deferred to the second half. Rodgers is 22 TDs and 5 interceptions in the post season with a 6 and 4 record. His injured calf is the main topic of the talking heads on TV as to whether he can move out of the pocket. As we see in this commentary, he was at his best. Green Bay got the ball on the 20. Jordy Nelson is guarded by Sherman. In the first game of the year when these two teams met, Rodgers threw no passes to whomever Sherman was guarding out of fear of an interception. Bennett had a false start. On 3rd down and 1, Lacey had a 13 yard gain first down to the 43. Seattle is the most penalized team in the NFL and they got one for having 12 men on the field. Adams got a first down to the 43 of Seattle. Cobb got a first down with a declined penalty, yet another Seattle mis-cue. Rodgers' pass was intercepted by Sherman, his 24th in his first 4 years. Lynch gained 3. Wilson's pass to Kearse was intercepted, that's the first pick of Wilson in the last 5 games. Green Bay got to the 4 but a 15 yard unsportsmanlike penalty moved it back to the 19. Rodgers got 12 to the 7. Lacey got to the 1. Kuhn, the full back, got the TD but, under review, his knee hit the ground before the ball crossed the plane of the end zone, so the TD was reversed. Lacey did not get the TD on 3rd down and fourth down and 1 they made the decision to go for a field goal, making it 3-0. Baldwin took the kickoff but Brad Jones created a fumble. It is now 7 minutes into the game, and Seattle, which had only 14 turnovers all year, already had two. Lacey got 8 and then got to the 7. A pass to Jordy Nelson went off his hands and did not get the TD. Cobb got to the 2 but they could not score and had to go for another field goal to make it 6-0. Wilson was sacked and missed a pass so it was another 3 and out. Lacey got to the 31. Aaron Rodgers pass to Richard Rodgers got to the 19, giving Green Bay 8 first downs versus none for Seattle. Lacey got to the 15 the Cobb caught the TD pass. A flag against Seattle was declined so it was 13-0 for Green Bay. Seattle got the ball but had yet another penalty, a false start, which put them on the 15. Lynch got to the 18 then got 4 more. On 3rd down, Wilson's pass to Baldwin was incomplete. Wilson was now 0 for 3 in 3rd downs versus 8 for 8 against Carolina. I bet 100 more on Seattle at 2.76 and 2.78.

Another Seattle penalty. Rodgers missed an open receiver. Lacey got to the 28, Cobb to the 22, and Lacey close to a first down. This led to another field goal attempt from the 40, so it was now 16-0 Green Bay. I bet 100 more on Seattle at 3.1. My bet was now lose 400 or win 446.80.

Wilson had a second interception. Matthews hit Wilson for a roughing the passer and it looked like Wilson was dazed. Green Bay's Nelson got a 23 yard pass to the 23. Then there was an interception of Rodgers by Maxwell, that being the fifth turnover of the game. Lynch ran for 3, then for 14 to get the first Seattle first down.

Aaron Rodgers has had 17 home games without an interception. Brett Favre has rated Rodgers as the best quarterback in football and Tom Brady the most valuable. Turbin got 5, Lockett got 4 more, and Lynch got a first down. Wilson was 0 for 6, finally he got a 21 yard pass to Lockett. A Lynch run gave nothing. It was the 2 minute warning. Wilson threw a pass to Kerse but Sam Shields caught a 3rd Wilson interception. That gave Wilson, who previously had a high quarterback rating n the playoffs, a rating of 0 for this game so far. It is 4 turnovers for Seattle versus 13 all season. Green Bay was at the 20 then the 5th Seattle defense penalty was called on Maxwell. The Packers had a false start. Rodgers got 5 to the 32. It was 3rd and 10 and Rodgers' pass was incomplete to Cobb. In the first game between these teams, Rodgers throw no passes to receivers covered by Sherman. In this game, he has thrown 4 times for 1 completion, 1 interception and 2 incomplete. Green Bay is 40-1 with a 16 point lead at halftime. Wilson was 2 for 9 for 12 yards and 3 ints. Seattle got the ball on the 20 and went 3 and out. Green Bay got the ball on the 39. On 3rd and long, a pass to Cobb was short of the first down. Seattle got the ball, Wilson passed for 8 and Lynch got it to the 41. Clay Matthews got a sack of Wilson back to the 40. Lynch got it back to the 50. Baldwin got to the 18 for a 29 yard gain on 3rd and 19. Lynch almost caught a pass at the end zone but it was broken up. Then Seattle set up for a 38 yard field goal try. They faked the field goal and the place holder, John Ryan, threw a TD pass to Gilliam so it was 16-7. This was the first time a punter has thrown a TD pass in the playoffs. Seattle was back in the game. The Packers got the ball on the 20 and went 3 and out. It was 2.22 to go in the third quarter. Wilson had gone 82 games in a row when his teams (Seattle, Wisconsin in college and NC State) was ahead sometime in the game. Seattle got the ball. A third down pass was dropped so Seattle punted. The Packers got a first down to the 25 on a 32 yard James Starks run. Sherman hurt his arm on a pass but returned with a limp arm. After a false start, Lacey gained 5 and Starks got to the 41. A pass to the 33 gave a first down and Starks got it to the 30. Rodgers is moving fine and his calf injury, which was so much in the discussion, did not seem to bother him. On third and 7 he threw the ball away. Mason Crosby hit a 48 yard field goal to make it 19-7. He is now 15 for 15 in the post season. I bet 50 more on Seattle so I was risking -450 versus +726 should Seattle get 2 TDs and win the game. There was 10.41 left to go. Seattle got a pass to Lockett for a first down. Wilson gained a little on a run. He was yet to have one of his breakout runs. Lynch got 13 to the 39. Baldwin dropped a pass. Lynch had a big gain of 11 carrying several Packers a number of yards for a first down. He was now over 100 yards rushing. A sack of Wilson lost 4. On second and 14, a Wilson throw was almost intercepted by Clinton Dye who just missed it. That would have given Dye, who was guarding Kearse, 3 ints in this game. Seattle punted to the 13 with 6.53 left. Starks gained 1 and then 4. On third and 5, Rodgers' pass was broken up so Green Bay had to punt. Walters got it to the 45. Wilson threw yet another pass to Kease that was intercepted for his 4th int and Seattle's 5th turnover versus 2 for Green Bay. Green Bay could not move the ball and punted with 3.52 left. The odds on Seattle winning were now 50:1, 60:1, 70:1, etc, fluctuating wildly like the January S&P500 which I was also trading, but I did not bet more, wanting to not lose more than 450 on this game. However, a 50 bet here would have been a good idea. Lynch got to the 45 of Seattle and Baldwin gained 35 to Green Bay's 20. Lynch caught a TD pass from Wilson but was out of bounds at the 9 with 257 to go. Lynch ran to the 5, Wilson ran to the 1. On third down, Wilson ran for the TD to make it 19-14. Seattle had the 2 minute warning plus one time out. Kicking off was risky as Green Bay could possibly run off the clock. An on-side kick might work but these often fail. They tried the on-side kick anyway and Seattle's Matthews got the ball. The odds were now 5.5-5.8.

Wilson went out of bounds on the 45. Lynch got it to the 32. I covered 200 of my bet at 2.44. So I was now -250 Green Bay +438 Seattle. I then covered 100 at 2.18 and 150 more to make it Green Bay 0, Seattle +171.80. So I had the mean reversion risk arbitrage in place. Not knowing who would win, I bet 75 more to make it +75 Green Bay, +99.80 Seattle.

Luke Willson got a pass to the 25 and Lynch got the TD to make it 20-19, Seattle ahead. The Wilson did a good scramble and hit Willson for the 2 point conversion to make it 23-20. What a come back! Seattle fans who left, assuming they had lost the game, missed a lot and Green Bay fans were in shock. Green Bay had 3 time outs and the ball. Rodgers was 12 of 37 in similar come backs. He hit Nelson for a 35 yard gain and Cobb to the 48 of Seattle. Rodgers ran to the 40, the edge of field goal range. It was first and 10 with 35 seconds left. Lacey was not looking so missed the pass. On 3rd and 10, Seattle blitzed and Nelson got to 31. Crosby then hit a 48 yard field goal, his 5th in 5 tries in the game with very windy conditions. So with 19 seconds to go it was 22-22 tie. Seattle got the ball with 14 seconds left on the 21 and decided to a knee and go into overtime.

The playoffs have the rather strange rules for overtime as the regular season. They play up to 15 minutes like a regular quarter. If it is still tied, they play another quarter. If the team who wins the coin toss gets a field goal, then the other team gets the ball and either wins the game with a TD, ties it with a field goal or losses by not scoring. If the team that gets the ball, scores a TD the game is over and the other team does not get a chance to score. Seattle won the toss. Baldwin got to the 12 on the kickoff, Wilson is 9-1 against Super Bowl winning quarterbacks. Lynch had a loss. Baldwin got a pass for a first down. Lynch got to the 30 and then had 156 yards rushing and 26 receiving. A Wilson run got nowhere. On 3rd and 6, Wilson hit Baldwin for 38 to the 35, the longest play of the game. Wilson hit Kearse for the game winning TD so Seattle won 28-22. All four Wilson interceptions were Kearse and this time he beat Williams. I won +99.80 on the game, +210 with Seattle the NFC champion and my Super Bowl bets were in place with Seattle and New England.

**Game 10:** Indianapolis at New England

Swetye's Elo analysis is:

| Team          | Elo  | Pr(Win) | Elo Spread | Stern Pr(Win) |
| ------------- | ---- | ------- | ---------- | ------------- |
| New England   | 1071 | 59%     | +2.5       | 57%           |
| Indianapolis  | 1041 | 41%     |            | 43%           |

The Betfair odds were 1.38-1.39 and 3.55-3.6 for Indianapolis.

My bets were:
200 New England at 1.38 so win 76 or lose 200

Analysis: Indianapolis has never beaten New England after the Peyton Manning era. Andrew Luck leads the NFL with 40 TDs and is a terrific quarterback but is error prone. He has 0 and 3 versus New England. New England beat Indianapolis handily in their earlier meeting in Indianapolis and at home I expect the same. Brady at home is almost unbeatable. I did not need to bet much, having the Super Bowl conference winner and Super Bowl pairing bets. It was raining but not snowing at the game. New

England won the toss and deferred to the second half. On the second set of downs, Cribs fumbled the New England punt. Brady passes moved the ball and Blount started the running game which was working well, unlike the Baltimore game where they got only 14 yards rushing, the fewest ever by a winning NFL playoff team. Blount ended up with the TD to make it 7-0. Indianapolis got a 12 yard pass to Herron on the 32 and Luck ran to the 39. Then Herron dropped 2 Luck passes and they got a 51 yard field goal try. Adam Venitari is very reliable but has never hit from so long. He is a legend in New England for his clutch Super Bowl winning kicks. He missed this one. The odds were not 7.4-7.6 and 1.15-1.16.

New England used a trick formation play that they first used in the Baltimore game that moved them from their 41 to the Indianapolis 49 with Edelman making the gain. Shane Vereen gained 30 on a Brady pass to the 15. Indianapolis (Indy) has been weak in the red zone with 80% TDs by opponents — the worst in the NFL. There were many good Blount runs. On 3rd in 9, Edelman got to the 5 and Blount to the 1. Janus Devlin scored the TD to make it 14-0. The odds were then 11-11.5 and 1.09-1.1.

After a set of Indy downs, Brady was intercepted by Jackson near the Indy goal line. But a 15 yard rushing the passer penalty pushed the ball back. Luck hit TY Hilton on a 36 yard pass to the 30. There was a penalty on Collins and the Colts got a first down to the 24. Luck passed to the 9, he was 6 for 18 so far, a weak performance. They got to the 1 and lost the ball. But New England had 12 men on the field that allowed Tipton to get a TD to make it 14-7. The 10 play 93 yard drive was the longest New England allowed all season. New England got the kickoff after a 5 yard penalty, Vereen got 4, Amendola could not catch a pass, Edelman got to the 49, that's the third time New England got a first down on their 3rd down. Blount ran for 5, then for 8 more and another first down. Blount already had 59 yards rushing. He got 9 more to the 40. Brady did a sneak for 3, his pass was tipped an almost intercepted. A late hit on Brady by Gerald Freeman yielded a 15 yard penalty which moved the ball half the distance to the goal line at the 13. Gronkowski caught an out of bounds pass. Brady ran close to a first down, short by inches, with 31 seconds left. Then New England went for it on 4th down with Brady sneaking but not quite making it but Devlin pushed him in a second effort to get the first down. New England tried 3 different plays and Indy stopped all 3 so they got a 21 yard field goal to make it 17-7. The Colts got the ball on the 42 on a skibbler. Then the half ended. The Colts had 1 reception in total from their 3 top receiver: Wayne (0), Hicks (0), Hilton (1).

New England gets the ball at the start of the 2nd half. They are 80-1 at home when leading at the half. After the kickoff, Edelman got a pass to the 45. Several Blount runs got the ball to the 15, he then had 108 yards on 20 carries. Then New England declared their left tackle Nate Solder as a designated receiver that fooled Indy which covered the other receivers, but Brady hit Solder for the TD so the 9 play 87 yard drive ended up with the score at 24-7. The Colts were 3 and out. Gronkowski gained 16 on a Brady pass. Cory Reading sacked Brady. LaFell caught a pass. Gronkowski caught a pass and was pushed back by several Colts but his forward progress got the first down. Brady, who was 7 for 7, hit Edelman to the 14. Blount ran to the 5 and Brady got to the 1. Solder caused a 5 yard penalty because he did not report, so it was second and 6 on the 10. Brady threw his third TD to Gronkowski to make it 31-7. Brady now had 49 post season TDs. The Colts had 2 nice receptions, then Revis, guarding Hilton, got an interception and Blount ran it in for another TD so it was 38-7.

The Colts were 3rd and out again, Blount kept running. Brady passed to Edelman for a first down. Blount got to the 15 and another first down. LaFell caught a pass in the end zone but was out of bounds. Brady passed to Edelman to the 4 then Blount went for his third TD and 139 yards gained. So it was 45-7. Herron ran for 17 and Luck had his second interception. Jonas Gray, who ran for 4 TDs and 200+ yards in an earlier game, came in for a cameo appearance. New England is deep in running backs. So the game ended and Brady goes to the Super Bowl for a record sixth time.

After the game, some sources tried to damage the New England reputation by claiming they used improperly inflated footballs. One could argue that at 45-7, this is simply an excuse, but the episode has caused a lot of attention away from the Super Bowl. Indeed, in the first half, the balls were tested and were under inflated. It seems that an attendant adjusted the pressure in the balls but it is not clear yet what went on.

**Game 11—The Super Bowl:** Seattle versus New England in Phoenix

Swetye's Elo analysis is:

| Team | Elo | Pr(Win) | Elo Spread | Stern Pr(Win) |
|------|-----|---------|-----------|---------------|
| New England | 1075 | 52% | +0.74 | 52% |
| Seattle | 1069 | 48% | | 48% |

The Betfair odds and my bets were:
I won +1048.86 on my bet that Seattle and New England would be the two teams in the Super Bowl. I also won +76 on the New England game 10 and +203.13 when New England won the AFC championship. At Betfair

odds, that left +3453 if Seattle wins at 1.93-1.95 and 1.99-2.00 and +1430 if New England wins at 2.06-2.08 and later 2-2.02. So I moved these bets to +2529 Seattle and +2401.21 New England.

Analysis: My intuition looking at the facts is that this Super Bowl is close to a toss-up. Seattle, the supposedly better team, was extremely lucky to win the game against Green Bay; they played terrible until the end of the game. After 4 interceptions, Russell Wilson was sharp in getting the lead and a tie in the last few minutes and then a victory in the overtime. Marshawn Lynch was superb and showed once again that he is one of the best, if not the best, running back in the NFL. He has 1281 yards after the first hit during the last two years, more than any other runner in the NFL. That talk about getting rid of him next year sure seems very ill advised. Indeed as we went into the Super Bowl, it seems the Seahawks are offering Lynch a contract in the $10 million a year range to finish his career there. A testament to Seattle's strength is winning with 4 ints and 5 turnovers. In the New England game, they simply outclassed Indianapolis in a rout. So I neutralized the Super Bowl bets so I win about the same no matter which team wins. It is a great event worldwide with hundreds of millions bet. For the game itself seats are in the $4,000 range. If you are going and do not have a free seat, buying late is cheaper ($2,572 last year and $3750 average price the week before). And for those watching on TV, the 40 second ads are going for $4.5 million. Oops, this is a game for the ages so tickets got to $8800 and $20,000 for choice ones.

Apparently the Las Vegas odds makers did not judge their line properly. The idea is to get the same amount of money bet on each team by creating odds that are fair for the bettors then by taking 10% on the losers meaning $110 is bet to win 100. They are guaranteed to make millions. Of course, the Betfair system is safer since person x bets with person y one winning and one losing and then the house takes a cut of the winner's net gain. The Vegas line initially was 2.5-3 points in favor of Seattle but most bettors preferred New England, but within 24 hours, they moved the line to 0, that is equal chances. The so-called smart money (and I am pleased to have done the same) bet on New England at these superior odds. So the net result is much more bet on New England than 50%. So if they win, the Vegas sports books will take a big loss, unless they are able to hedge. Even if they hedge they will have to give back some of their 10% as the odds prices have changed. But if Seattle wins, they will make a large gain. For me, being about equal seems best as I view the game as a toss-up that could go either way. Richard Sherman with a lame arm, and a pregnant girl friend who may give birth on Super Bowl Sunday; Earl Thomas with a separated shoulder, and Cam Chancellor with a bruised knee all have injuries that might affect the game but they all played Sunday. Swetye's Elo analysis actually favors New England.They gained 13 Elo points with their big win to 1075, while Seattle only gained 5 points in their narrow win to 1069 yielding an Elo spread of 0.74 points.[4] So the probability that New England wins is 52% and the Stern probability is also 52%. For me, it's a toss-up with my two favorite teams. New England has more experience and a superior coach while Seattle is very talented.

My first move was to shift 300 from Seattle to New England. Seattle on the Saturday before the game is favored at 1.97-1.98 versus New England at 2.02-2.04. So 300 at 2.02 gives +2787.21 New England and +2149 Seattle and New England +6.5 at 1.47 to either win +94 or lose −200. The odds on Sunday have moved more towards Seattle so I bet 149 more on New England at 2.06 to make it +2945.15 New England and +2000 for Seattle. Now going into the game, the odds closed up to New England 2-2.02 and Seattle at 1.98-1.99. Seattle won the coin toss and deferred. After one first down New England went 3 and out. Seattle, the most penalized team in the NFL, got its first penalty running into the kicker. Seattle was 3 and out. Vereen got a short gain to the 35. Edelman got a first down. Blount ran to the 48. On 3rd and 3, a pass to Gronkowski got the first down. A pass to Vereen got to the 40. Blount ran to the 34 and then to the 25 for a first down. Brady pass to Amendola to the 18. Brady was now 8 of 9. Brady passed to the 10. Blount got no gain. Then Brady threw an interception caught by Jeremy Lane which killed the drive. Lane was injured on the play and did not return to the game giving Brady a chance to work on his replacement. The quarter ended 0 to 0.

Seattle was 3 and out. Edelman got a kick to the 35. Amendola got a pass to the 48. A pass to LaFell got to the 41. Vereen got a first down. Brady passed to Gronkowski in the end zone but did not connect but he hit Vereen to the 35 and Edelman for 23 yards to the 12. Then Brady threw a TD pass to LaFell. I now bet 300 on Seattle at 2.68. The odds now were 1.57-1.58 New England and 2.72-2.74 Seattle. So now my bet was New England 2645.15 and Seattle 2505.10. I got 505.15 on Seattle for my 300 bet. I now want to try to get out of my New England +6.5 bet at 1.25.

There was a second sack of Wilson at the 18. Lynch got to the 21 and on 3rd and 8 a long pass to Kearse was broken up. Wilson now had no complete passes. It looked like this was a repeat of the Green Bay game. The Seattle punt went to the 27 of New England but they did nothing.

---

[4]A big win is tempered in the Elo system. One point in the final score difference is one Elo point; 2 points is 1.5 and more than 2 points is (11+score difference)/8.

Lynch ran to the 35 and then to the 39. On 3rd and short there was a false start by Luke Willson. It is now the second longest game with no completions, but Wilson got a first down to the 40. Lynch ran to the 45. A long pass to Chris Matthews got to the 10. Lynch ran to the 7 and then to the 3 and got the TD. So it was 7-7. Lynch led the NFL in TDs with 17. I now reversed my 300 bet long on Seattle by shorting at 2.12.

A pass to Amendola got to the 2 minute warning. New England leads the NFL in points scored in the last 2 minutes of the first half. They got to the 41 and then Edelman got to the 49. Seattle Cliff Averiel was offside so they got a first down. Two passes to Vereen who was mismatched being guarded by KJ Wright. Then Gronkowski got the TD pass to make it 14-7. Brady was now 20 of 27. He is always motivated because he was picked in the 6th round as the 199th pick. Turbin gained 19 with 24 seconds left. Wilson ran to the 49 with 11 seconds left. There was a face mask call and the question was should Seattle go for a field goal for go for it? Wilson responded with a TD pass to Matthews. It was now 14-14. Lynch was now up to 45 yards gained and the half ended. I was out of my New England +6.5 bet with +44.15 if New England won the bet and Seattle 0. I now bet 200 more on New England at 2.04. My extra bets during the game gained by 12 if New England won and 514.15 if Seattle won.

Lynch got to the 38, he was now 14 for 63. Lynch got to the 10 and Seattle kicked a field goal to lead 17-14. I bet 250 more on New England at 2.16.

It was 3rd and 6 and a pass went to Gronkowski for a first down and Brady threw his 2nd interception this one caught by Bobby Wagner. Wilson got to the 18 and there was a penalty on New England. Lynch ran to the 4 and then to the 3. A pass to Doug Baldwin scored the TD to make the score 24-14. The usually reliable Revis was beat on the pass. This is the largest deficit Brady has faced in 6 Super Bowls. I now bet 200 on New England at 5-1 and another 100 at 5.2-1.

Brady passed to Edelman to the 48. There was a penalty on the center. Another pass to Edelman got to the 36. On 3rd and 9 Amendola cannot make the catch. It is now the 4th quarter. New England got the ball back with 10 minutes to go. Edelman got a 21 yard pass to the 39 on 3rd and 14. Earl Thomas was called for unnecessary roughness. Vereen got to the 25. Averiel was out of the game with a concussion. A Brady pass to Edelman got to the 3 with 8.20 to go. That's now 24 passes Edelman has caught in the last 3 games. A Brady pass to Amendola got the TD to make it 24-21. I now bet 300 more on New England at 3.1. That gave my game bets New England 2152 and Seattle −335.85.

Seattle went 3 and out. Vereen gained 8 and then got to the 48 of Seattle. Gronkowski got to the 42. The Patriots were now favored in the odds. Vereen caught a pass from Brady. Edelman was called for offensive pass interference. On 2nd and 11 with 4.47 to go, Brady passed to Gronkowski to the 32. Gronkowski had 59 TDs in 72 games before this TD. I now bet 200 on Seattle at 2.4.

A first down to Gronkowski got to the 20. Vereen got to the 12 with 3.19 to go. LaFell got a first down on the 6. It was now 2.52 to go. Blount got to the 3 and Edelman got Brady's 4th TD pass to make it 28-24. My extra bets were now +1952 New England, −55.85 Seattle.

Seattle charged back. A pass to Lynch got to mid field. Wilson threw a pass that Kearse could not handle. They took a time out on 2nd and 10. A long pass to the end zone was knocked away. A Wilson pass got a first down on the 40 with 1.28 to go. Kearse made a spectacular catch on his back on the ground juggling the ball but the ball did not hit the ground and therefore was a legal catch for a 33 yard gain. The ball was at the 5. Lynch got to the 2. It was 2nd down and then the coach made a complicated decision. On down 2 he decided to throw the ball because they only had one time out and wanted to waste that down, possibly score the winning touch down and stop the clock. Then they would have two chances to run with one time out in between and score leaving New England no time to come back. This execution failed as there was an interception by Butler. This was a controversial decision that shocked the Seattle fans and players but that was the analysis of the Seattle coach. Wilson took blame for the loss. Brady was named MVP for the third time and set the record for completions in a game (37 of 50 for 338 yards). He was sharp except for the two interceptions, on the final drive that led to the winning TD he was 8 for 8. We know from prospect theory, horse racing favorite-longhot bias and common sense that losing hurts more than winning benefits and Brady is sure in this camp. He is now 4 for 6 in Super Bowl appearances tied with Terry Bradshaw and Joe Montana for the 4 wins. Wilson is now 6 and 2 in playoff games and 1 to 1 in Super Bowls. In the previous 7 games, he had a 96.3 rating. Some 112.8 million watched the game, the most watched US TV show ever.

My bets were good. I won 2644.15 on my Super Bowl bets on New England plus 2152 on New England in this game (the 200 and 100 at 5-1 and 5.2-1 provided 800 plus 420 of this) plus 44.15 for the New England +6.5 bet. The mean reversion risk arbitrage bets again worked well. I am doing the same thing — with good success, but less fun — in my futures fund on the S&P500, which, since December, is up, down, up, down day and night.

# Chapter 13

# The 2015-2016 Season, Playoffs and the Super Bowl

I took this up after eleven weeks play of the 17 weeks with 10 or 11 games played by each of the 32 teams. There have been many interesting developments.

1. The Carolina Panthers are the only undefeated team at 11-0. They are the number one seed in the NFC followed by the Arizona Cardinals at 9-2. Minnesota Vikings at 8-3 in the North lead the Washington Redskins at 5-ckman 6 lead the East. The wildcards are the Green Bay Packers at 7-4 and the Seattle Seahawks at 6-5.

2. The New England Patriots have been the top team all year and lead the AFC at 10-1. The Cincinnati Bengals lead the North at 9-2 followed by the West leader the Denver Broncos at 9-2 and the Indianapolis Colts leading the South at 6-5. The wildcards are the Kansas City Chiefs and the Houston Oilers both at 6-5.

3. Denver seems to have the best defense designed by John Elway and, despite very poor play by star quarterback Peyton Manning, they are still a force to be reckoned with. In his last game, Manning had four interceptions, was 5 of 20 with a zero quarterback rating. He is injured and probably should retire, having been ably replaced by 6 foot 8 inch Brock Osweiler, who has done well.

Seattle had a bad start with star defensive player Kam Chancellor holding out for monies from next year's salary to be moved to this year's salary. This was all very strange and led to a 0-2 start then 2-4. They are not the powerhouse they were the last few years. Other problems are that powerful running back Marshan Lynch is injured but has been ably replaced by Thomas Rawls until he got sidelined with a broken ankle. Top receiver

Jimmy Graham, who they obtained in a trade giving up their all pro center Max Unger, also is injured and out for the season. The loss of Unger seemed to affect Wilson who was not as sharp in the early part of the season. Meanwhile, Russell Wilson is getting better line protection and in the last game had 5 TDs and no interceptions. He looked really sharp with a 157 rating. Going back to 1960, Wilson is the first quarterback with a 138.5+ rating for four consecutive games. During this period, he had a 75.4% completion on record with 16 TDs and no interceptions, winning all four games.

Cincinnati had been strong but I am still short them — see my Betfair bets so far. I assume that New England will beat them in Foxborough if they get that far in the playoffs.

The Texans are led by JJ Watt, who is again setting defensive records and was again voted defensive player of the year. Patriot's coach Bill Belichick compares Watt to the great New York Giants linebacker Lawrence Taylor, both in a class by themselves. He, along with Tom Brady, Cam Newton, Russell Wilson and Adrian Peterson, are MVP candidates. Brady was voted into the Probowl over Newton but declined to play.

Minnesota has a good quarterback Teddy Bridgewater and Adrian Peterson is running tremendously. Still I don't think they will be in the Super Bowl.

Green Bay had a 6-0 start then has lost 4 of its last 5 games and pulled a miraculous victory over Detroit week 11. The game was over with the Packers on their 35 yard line with zero time when a face mask call gave them one more chance. Rodgers threw a *hail mary pass* 65+ yards, arching high and they won. This was a good, but lucky come back win after a 20-0 start by Detroit. Later he threw one more of these spectular long passes.

**Updating after week 13** My current Super Bowl bets are in Table 13.1. Cincinnati has now lost three games and franchise quarterback Andy Dalton injured his thumb and is out at least for some games. He was replaced by A J McCarron who has promise but little experience. So my large short on them looks ok. They are 10-3, two games ahead of Pittsburgh for the AFC north league. Pittsburgh is a threat but I am short them. They are in the hunt for a wildcard spot in competition with the NY Jets, 8-5, and the Kansas City Chiefs, also 8-5. I am short these three teams assuming that two of them will not make the playoffs and the other will get defeated by one of the top teams.

Table 13.1: Betfair bets to week 11

## Super Bowl Winner

Going In-Play    Cash Out    Rules                    Matched: GBP 1,587,205    Refresh

| 26 selections | Back all | Lay all |
|---|---|---|
| **New England Patriots** £787.83 | 4.6 £552 | 4.7 £614 |
| **Carolina Panthers** £581.16 | 5.4 £951 | 5.5 £421 |
| **Arizona Cardinals** £421.02 | 8.6 £929 | 8.8 £340 |
| **Seattle Seahawks** £5,153.96 | 8.8 £118 | 9 £72 |
| **Green Bay Packers** £778.36 | 13.5 £488 | 14 £327 |
| **Denver Broncos** £13.62 | 14 £285 | 14.5 £210 |
| **Pittsburgh Steelers** -£4,371.84 | 13 £125 | 13.5 £4 |
| **Cincinnati Bengals** -£4,599.84 | 22 £36 | 23 £59 |
| **Kansas City Chiefs** -£3,271.84 | 23 £36 | 24 £43 |
| **New York Giants** -£4,261.84 | 75 £13 | 85 £8 |
| **Minnesota Vikings** -£2,244.15 | 70 £113 | 80 £62 |
| **Indianapolis Colts** -£4,081.84 | 75 £85 | 80 £2 |
| **Philadelphia Eagles** -£3,294.84 | 75 £25 | 85 £5 |
| **New York Jets** -£3,271.84 | 95 £83 | 100 £2 |
| **Houston Texans** -£3,271.84 | 170 £11 | 200 £40 |
| **Washington Redskins** -£3,271.84 | 150 £18 | 170 £6 |
| **Dallas Cowboys** -£4,771.84 | 360 £19 | 880 £9 |
| **Jacksonville Jaguars** -£3,271.84 | 500 £2 | 880 £5 |
| **Buffalo Bills** -£1,592.22 | 420 £4 | 780 £4 |
| **Tampa Bay Buccaneers** -£3,271.84 | 540 £5 | 990 £5 |
| **Oakland Raiders** -£3,271.84 | 1000 £8 | |
| **Chicago Bears** -£3,844.64 | 1000 £18 | |
| **New Orleans Saints** -£3,271.84 | 1000 £26 | |
| **Atlanta Falcons** £6,196.89 | 1000 £47 | |
| **St Louis Rams** -£3,400.96 | 1000 £29 | |
| **Miami Dolphins** -£4,271.84 | 1000 £41 | |

Seattle is on a roll. Russell Wilson had 3 and 5 TD games with no interceptions. After a 0-2 and 2-4 start, they now look in sharp form. Wilson has evolved into less running and more excellent passing in the pocket. They pretty well have the wildcard locked up against Washington, 6-7, but have to get the Super Bowl route out of Seattle with one additional game. Kam Chancellor has a minor tail bone injury but can play. Hence their defense looks complete. My bets on them at 21-1 to win the Super Bowl look terrific now.

Denver is fading and I lowered my long bet to basically neutralize them. Peyton Manning is probably finished. Six foot eight Brock Osweiler is filling in ok. He had three wins and then a loss to Oakland. The rest of the team does not look as sharp as they were before when the defense carried them undefeated. They are 10-3 and 2 games ahead of Kansas City at 8-5 to win the AFC-west.

New England at 11-2 also has lots of injuries. Lagarette Blount is out for the season but Rob Gronkowski is back and when he is playing they score about 10+ points more per game. They lost two games and home field advantage but now have it back basically throughout the playoffs. They have a 19% chance of winning the Super Bowl according to the Nate Silver website www.546.com but they are still the favorite on Betfair.

At 23%, Nate Silver's estimate, to win the Super Bowl is undefeated Carolina (13-0). Cam Newton is having an MVP year and their offense and defense both look sharp. They are the deserving favorites and have home field advantage throughout the playoffs pretty well locked in. One of their coaches is Mike Shula, son of Don Shula, the 85 year old coach of the 1972 undefeated Dolphins.

Arizona at 11-2 is three games ahead of Seattle with 3 games to go, so is most likely the #2 NFC seed and thus have the NFC-west locked up. With Carson Palmer having a great year and a terrifically coached defense and offense, they are a major contender.

Green Bay at 9-4 has been shaky but looks to win over Minnesota (8-5) the NFC-north. Aaron Rodgers has been inconsistent but is a star quarterback. They have fewer injuries than other teams. They are in the top group but seem less powerful than the big 4: New England, Carolina, Arizona and Seattle.

Indianapolis, 6-7, is winning the AFC south section but does not seem to be a threat. Their attempt to buy players to beat New England such as Frank Gore, has not really worked. Star quarterback Andrew Luck has been injured, has not been playing many gains and is inconsistent. He has been ably replaced by 41 year old Matt Hasselback.

The current playoff lineup is

AFC first round byes: #1 Patriots, #2 Bengals;

AFC wildcard: #6 Jets at #3 Broncos; #5 Chiefs at #4 Colts

In the hunt: Steelers 8-5, Chiefs 8-5, Jets 8-5


NFC first round byes: #1 Panthers, #2 Cardinals;

NFC wildcard: #6 Vikings at #3 Packers; #5 Seahawks at #4 Redskins

In the hunt: Buccaneers 6-7, Eagles 6-7, Giants 6-7, Falcons 6-7.

## Notes from Week 15 games

Near the end of the season, a lot gets settled every week. There are two weeks to go. MVP candidates Tom Brady, Cam Newton, Russell Wilson, and Carson Palmer, all quarterbacks and all had good days with exceptional performances and their teams all won. Antonio Brown, Pittsburgh's top receiver is also a worthy MVP candidate. New England (12-2) beat Tennessee (3 and 9) 33 to 16. Tom Brady had 3 TDs and no interceptions with New England looking sharp. Carolina, going for 14-0 was ahead of the NY Giants by 28 points. Then the Giants tied it at 35 — wow what amazing mean reversion! But they still lost with a late field goal set up with a Cam Newton run. Newton had 5 TDs, over 100 yards running and no interceptions. There was a huge fight all game long between top defensive back Josh Norman of Carolina and the Giant's great receiver Odell Beckham who was penalized 3 times and suspended for 1 game.

Seattle (9-5) won again with Russell Wilson setting more records. He was 21-30 with 3 TDs and no interceptions. In the last 5 games he has 19 TDs and no interceptions. A new record is that he is the first NFL quarterback in 50 years with 3+ TDs in 5 consecutive games. Two TDs went to Doug Baldwin who tied the 1987 NFL record of Jerry Rice of 10 TDs in 4 games. Previously Baldwin tied Brett Favre's 9 TDs to Sterling Sharp in 1994 in 4 games. The 2+ TDs in each of 4 consecutive games is also a new Baldwin record, tying Calvin Johnson in 2011 and Cris Carter in 1995. Wilson is now 15-2 in December in his career. Seattle is also the top running NFL team with Wilson leading with 456 yards among the still active non injured players. The team has 25 straight games with at least 100+ yards on the ground. With Tyler Lockett, Jermaine Kearse, Baldwin Willson and, possibly, Marshan Lynch, Wilson has many targets. Seattle is also the leading team in giving up yards gained for the fourth year in a row.

San Diego (4-10) avoided another loss with Philip Rivers throwing 3 TDs and ex Patriot Danny Woodhead scoring 3 receiving and 1 running TD. Three teams, San Diego, St Louis and Oakland, wanted to move to Los

Angeles. All the owners need to determine who gets to move where. For the time being St Louis has won the approval to move to LA, while the fate of the other teams is still uncertain. Kansas City (9-5) which started out 1-5 has now won 8 straight games including defeating Baltimore 34-13 this week. Quarterback Alex Smith was consistent again — not flashy but steady. San Francisco sure botched it by replacing him with flash in the pan Colin Kapernick with an ill advised lucrative long term contract based on a few good games. Green Bay (10-4) beat Oakland 30-20 and has moved into the lead in the NFC-North, above Minnesota (9-5). Kansas City still has a chance to beat Denver for the AFC-West lead. AJ McCarron started in place of injured Andy Dalton and had an error free game piloting Cincinnati (11-3) to a 24-14 win over San Francisco (4-10). Carson Palmer had one TD pass to give him 32 for the season in the Arizona 40-17 win over Philadelphia. Arizona (12-2) clinched the NFC-West title and will earn a first round bye if they beat Green Bay in week 17. Philadelphia (6-8) can actually win the NFC-East title if they beat Washington (7-7) at home and the New York Giants (6-8) on the road. Pittsburgh (9-5) beat Denver (10-4) with a strong comeback from 21 points behind. Big Ben Roethlishberger passed for 380 yards and 3 TDs. Pittsburgh is a real threat and I am short them for the Super Bowl so I may have to hedge out this risk later if they make the playoffs and do not get beat early.

After playoff line after week 15 is:
AFC first round byes: #1 Patriots, #2 Bengals;
AFC wildcard: #6 Steelers at #3 Broncos; #5 Chiefs at #4 Texans
In the hunt: # Jets, #8 Colts, # Jaguars

NFC first round byes: #1 Panthers, #2 Cardinals;
NFC wildcard: #6 Vikings at #3 Packers; #5 Seahawks at #4 Redskins
In the hunt: #7 Falcons, #8 Eagles, #9 Giants

## Wild card week end, January 9,10 2016

The twelve teams that made the playoffs have odds along with my bets on them are in Table 13.2.

My wild card weekend initial bets were:
Pittsburgh +106 vs Cincinnati -150
Kansas City +175 vs Houston -300
Green Bay +97 vs Washington -100
Seattle +98 vs Minnesota -200

Table 13.2: Playoff odds and bets end of Week 16

| 12 selections | | Back all | Lay all |
|---|---|---|---|
| **Arizona Cardinals** £1,856.97 | | **5.6** £360 | **5.7** £549 |
| **New England Patriots** £1,418.30 | | **5.4** £708 | **5.5** £690 |
| **Carolina Panthers** £705.51 | | **5.8** £55 | **5.9** £594 |
| **Seattle Seahawks** £2,198.12 | | **8** £275 | **8.2** £825 |
| **Denver Broncos** -£3,233.58 | | **7.6** £22 | **7.8** £774 |
| **Pittsburgh Steelers** £516.34 | | **15** £1117 | **15.5** £1270 |
| **Kansas City Chiefs** £1,036.48 | | **20** £144 | **21** £220 |
| **Green Bay Packers** -£3,233.71 | | **32** £22 | **34** £1144 |
| **Cincinnati Bengals** -£3,233.72 | | **32** £305 | **34** £390 |
| **Minnesota Vikings** -£3,233.63 | | **48** £16 | **50** £134 |
| **Washington Redskins** -£3,233.72 | | **75** £54 | **80** £172 |
| **Houston Texans** -£3,233.72 | | **85** £46 | **90** £51 |

I won all four of the bets on wild card weekend on January 9-10 plus a few small bets on my favorite team with points. Also I gained because I was short the four losing home teams. It was quite rare for all four home teams to lose.

**Analysis**: **Game 1:** Kansas City 30 at Houston 0
Kansas City, after a 1-5 start, won 10 straight games even with their star running back Jamaal Charles injured all year. Quarterback Alex Smith had a great year (with two weeks to go in the regular season he had 16 TDs and 4 interceptions) and was steady guiding the team. Coach Andy Reid was having an outstanding year. Their game was a rout with Kansas City running all over Houston winning 30-0. Houston's quarterback Brian Hoyer had 3 interceptions and 1 fumble.

**Game 2:** Pittsburgh 18 at Cincinnati 16
This was yet another game where a minor miscue changed a win into a loss. Cincinnati has been strong all year being undefeated for much of the season. But they seem to always self destruct in the playoffs where they have never won a game since 1991. Regular quarterback Andy Dalton was out with a minor injury. His replacement, untested rookie AJ McCarron, had a decent performance but late in the game, 2 unnecessary penalties let Pittsburgh eke out a close victory.

Figure 13.1: The 2016 playoff tree.

**Game 3:** Seattle 10 at Minnesota 9

Seattle has a great team but they had a weak season. They started out 0-2 with Kam Chancellor, the key defensive player in the legion of boom, boycotting these games asking for some future pay to be paid now. Then they were 2-4. Finally, thanks mostly to great play by Russell Wilson, they won most of their games but did not look sharp in some of them. They made the playoff as a wild card team. In all six of their losses they had the lead in the 4th quarter and lost it. Wilson had 4024 yards, 34 TDs and 8 interceptions. In the last 8 games he had 25 TDs and 2 interceptions.

Minnesota, on the other hand, excelled all year and won their division. Star running back Adrian Peterson is back and won the rushing title like he did in 2008 and 2012 (his MVP year). Their quarterback Teddy Bridgewater also had a good year with 32 TDs and 11 interceptions.

The weather was severe and was the third coldest NFL game ever. This favored running, namely Minnesota. I bet on Seattle and the game was a defensive struggle. Again, Wilson kept Seattle in the game. Their key play was a snap by the center that went way past Wilson, some 16 yards behind the line of scrimmage. But he scrambled and finally hit a 35 yard pass to Tyler Lockett who took the ball to the four and that led to their lone TD, a pass to Doug Baldwin, making the score 9-7 Minnesota who had 3 field goals. Chancellor striped Peterson of the ball and Seattle was on the Minnesota 40. Wilson passed to Kerse to the 29 and this led to a 47 yard field goal to make it 10-9 Seattle. But Minnesota had the game won with a relatively easy 27 yard field goal in the final seconds. Minnesota had the ball the 13th so it was an easy field goal on 4th and 1 with 26 seconds to go, but the kicker Blain Walsh missed, resulting in a 10-9 Seattle win. So Seattle squeaked by and I won 212 on my bet.

**Game 4:** Green Bay 35 at Washington 18
Green Bay quarterback Aaron Rodgers had a slow start, completing only one of 8 passes for 11 yards in the first quarter. But by the half, he had completed more than half of his 28 passes for 159 yards. Green Bay was down 11-0 but gradually pulled ahead. Rodgers had 210 yards passing and 2 TDs. Kurt Cousins, who had a very good year, passed for 329 yards and 1 TD in a losing effort.

**Divisional Playoffs: Saturday/ Sunday January 16-17**

I am long seven of the teams with a large short bet on Green Bay that got created with no long bets on Green Bay. These games were played on January 16-17. I was scheduled to give two talks related to stock market crashes at the Campus for Finance meeting in Germany. That was a terrific trip going on the 11th and returning on the 15th. I knew that Betfair, with their flawed betting model only taking commissions on the net winnings rather than the total bet, would eventually close down minor markets. I had written some columns for their website in 2013 so knew that they were going to shut down betting in Canada. Now they have been bought out by Paddy Power. The way it works is that I could no longer make changes in bets post January 14. Then, depending on the results of the Super Bowl and other events I have bet on, they will cash out the account.

The Super Bowl and combo bets are now as follows with the four shorts eliminated in the wild card week:

| 8 selections | Back all | Lay all |
|---|---|---|
| **New England Patriots** £870.81 | **5.4** £426 | **5.5** £855 |
| **Carolina Panthers** £468.02 | **5.6** £110 | **5.7** £937 |
| **Arizona Cardinals** £1,039.48 | **5.9** £385 | **6** £269 |
| **Seattle Seahawks** £1,380.63 | **7.2** £338 | **7.4** £216 |
| **Denver Broncos** £189.74 | **6.6** £188 | **6.8** £1478 |
| **Kansas City Chiefs** £218.99 | **14.5** £170 | **15** £100 |
| **Pittsburgh Steelers** £178.85 | **19.5** £543 | **20** £52 |
| **Green Bay Packers** -£4,051.20 | **15.5** £143 | **16** £25 |

| 16 selections | Back all | Lay all |
|---|---|---|
| New England/Carolina £407.81 | 6.8 £24 | 14.5 £2 |
| New England/Arizona £253.36 | 5.8 £22 | 14.5 £2 |
| New England/Seattle £1,921.01 | 8.2 £30 | 17.5 £2 |
| New England/Green Bay £344.94 | 16.5 £26 | 48 £2 |
| Denver/Carolina -£724.64 | 8 £30 | 11 £36 |
| Denver/Arizona -£278.64 | 10 £18 | 17 £2 |
| Denver/Seattle -£202.64 | 11 £30 | 27 £2 |
| Denver/Green Bay -£349.64 | 28 £8 | 80 £3 |
| Kansas/Carolina £775.36 | 15 £59 | 21 £6 |
| Kansas/Arizona £508.95 | 13.5 £24 | 27 £2 |
| Kansas/Seattle £655.36 | 13 £25 | 38 £2 |
| Kansas/Green Bay -£724.64 | 42 £18 | 60 £20 |
| Pittsburgh/Carolina -£1,354.64 | 15.5 £2 | 48 £2 |
| Pittsburgh/Arizona -£2,269.64 | 10 £37 | 75 £2 |
| Pittsburgh/Seattle -£2,679.24 | 13.5 £30 | 120 £2 |
| Pittsburgh/Green Bay -£826.64 | 20 £31 | 160 £2 |

**Game 5:** Kansas City 20 at New England 27

It was Tom Brady's 30th playoff game in his 16 years. He holds the record of 53 TDs in the post season. This year he had the lowest number of interceptions in his career, 7. New England had a lot of injuries and after starting 10-0 lost 4 of the next 6 games with injuries to Dion Lewis, Lagarette Blount, Rob Gronkowski, and Julian Adelmann who missed 7 games with a broken foot. But they were basically in good shape for this playoff game. Kansas City started 1-5 and then won its next 11 games. The game started out with an 8 yard pass from Brady to Gronkowski, they went 80 yards in 11 plays. Then Cairo Santos kicked a 34 yard field goal for Kansas City. Brady scored on a 1 yard run on an 11 play 98 yard drive. Santos kicked another 32 yard field goal to make it 14-6 New England. Gronkowski scored on a 16 yard pass from Brady to culminate a 5 play 69 yard TD making the score 21-6. Albert Wilson completed a 10 yard TD from Alex Smith. Gostkowski had 42 and 32 yard field goals to make the score 27-13. Char Candorick West had a 1 yard run to score for Kansas City but it was too little too late.

**Game 6:** Green Bay 20 at Arizona 26

Palmer had some completions including some to Larry Fitzgerald. Larry had 3 drops all year and remains a top receiver. Arizona scored to make it 7-0. Rodgers countered but was intercepted on the 1, however he was saved by a penalty. This led to a field goal to make it 7-3 Arizona. Late in the game Arizona got a field goal to make it 20-13. A Green Bay TD with 5 seconds left tied the game 20-20 on a long high arched Rodgers hail mary pass. Arizona won the coin toss in overtime. A pass to Fitzgerald after Palmer's scrambling gained 75 yards. That made Larry 171 yards on 7 catches. Then Arizona scored from the 5 to win 26-20.

**Game 7:** Seattle 24 at Carolina 31

The game was a classic example of mean reversion. Seattle had the top defense for the fourth year in a row giving up 17.3 points on average. Meanwhile Carolina had the top offense at 31.3. The first half was all Carolina and ended 31-0. Seattle did not seem sharp at all, Wilson had 2 interceptions and Carolina was on a roll. The the second half was all Seattle with Wilson back to his previous sharpness. Kerse and Lockett scored TDs on passes from Wilson but it was too much to make up and the game ended 31-24.

**Game 8:** Pittsburgh 16 at Denver 23

Denver started with 2 field goals to make it 6-0. Pittsburgh countered with a TD to make it 7-6. Pittsburgh had a 58 yard pass to the 22. A field goal made it 10-6. The teams traded field goals to make it 10-9, 13-9 and 13-12. Pittsburgh quarterback Ben Roethlisberger threw for over 300 yards. He did that twice against Denver and was the only quarterback to do this. CJ Anderson of Denver scored a TD with a 2 point conversion. That plus a field goal made it 23-13. Denver had 5 field goals plus this TD and won 23-16.

*Conference Championships, January 24*

My bets for the Super Bowl are now:

New England +863
Carolina +486
Arizona +1051
Denver +202


To be in the Super Bowl:
New England and Carolina +408
New England and Arizona +253
Denver and Carolina -725
Denver and Arizona -278

So I effectively have a New England bet in their game against Denver.

The Las Vegas odds for winning the Super Bowl are: New England 19-10
Carolina 39-20
Arizona 18-5
Denver 22-5

**Game 9, AFC Championship**: New England 20 at Denver 22

It was the 17th Brady-Manning confrontation. In Denver Brady is 2-6 but they are 5 and 5 in the last 10 meetings and 2 and 2 in the playoffs, Manning is 12-13 in the playoffs. Both have had long brilliant careers, but at 38 for Brady and 39 for Manning, they are late in the game.[1] Brady is having a top year and looks sharp. He has 38 TDs and 7 interceptions. Meanwhile, Manning has looked like someone who should retire and has 9 TDs and 17 interceptions. New England is a 2.5 favorite. They have been in the AFC Championship game for the fifth straight year. In week 12, a depleted New England without Julian Edelman and Danny Amendola got beaten in Denver 30-24, which ended their undefeated season. In that game, Denver had 179 rushing yards, many by CJ Anderson and Ronnie Hillman, who together had nearly 1600 yards on the season. New England lost four of their last six games. Injuries explain most of this. For this championship game, they are at full strength.

New England won the coin toss and elected to receive the football. This gives Brady one more possession and Manning one less and shows the respect that Belichick has for Manning. The key to the game turned out to be Wade Phillips, the defensive coordinator of Denver, who created a defense that throttled the defense of New England even though Brady had all his weapons. Secondly, the supposedly over the hill Manning played very well with no interceptions and some TDs.

Denver scored first so the score was 7-0. New England then scored a TD on a Steven Jackson one yard run. In a rare miss, Stephen Gostkowski missed the extra point so the score was 7-6. That miss proved crucial later when, with the score 22-20, New England had to go for 2 points extra and missed it, ending the game. But there were other decisions that share the blame for the close loss, including not going for a field goal in the 4th quarter and going for it and not making it with 6 minutes to go. Von Miller got an interception and he would be making great defensive plays all game long and in the trash talk tormenting the Patriots. There were very few passes that Brady was able to complete to the big three of Gronkowski, Edelman

---

[1]Maybe for Manning who shortly retired, but Brady was MVP in 2018 at 40 and wants to play till he is 45 and his team is competitive.

and Amendola. However he did get some passes to Gronkowski and that led to a field goal so the score was 14-9. The mile high altitude in Denver was a problem with some players including Gronkowski needing oxygen. There was another Denver field goal making the score 17-9. There were other Belichick decisions that are questionable expost. Three times there were inside the Broncos 20 in the 4th quarter and got only 6 points. Brady had 2 interceptions and Brady none. Manning ran for 1 TD. Finally Brady hit Gronkowski for a long gain and they scored to make it 22-20. But Taleb tipped the Brady pass for a 2 point extra point which failed. An onside kick failed and the game ended.

**Game 10, NFC Championship**: Arizona 15 at Carolina 49

Carolina has the best record (15-1). Cam Newton is a clear favorite for MVP which he won almost unanimously. He, like Russell Wilson, is a double running and passing threat. Jonathan Stewart and Mike Tolbert add to the Panthers running attack, which gained 2282 yards, second behind the Bills' 2432. In each of the past 31 games they rushed for at least 100 yards. Seattle was the NFL's number one defense, allowing only 82 yards per game, yet Stewart gained 59 yards on the first play against them. During the season, Stewart had 985 yards with 6 TDs and Newton had 636 rushing and 10 TDs. Arizona had the sixth best defense against running, 191 yards per game. Their defense was fifth best at 322. It again was the Cam Newton show. He threw for 335 yards, ran for 80, passed for two TDs and ran for two more. The 49-15 score was the highest point total in NFL history. Carolina started out 17-0 and never looked back.

The Arizona Cardinals at 14-0 in the series were no match defensively or offensively for the 15-1 Panthers. Arizona's star quarterback Carson Palmer had 4 interceptions and there were 3 other Arizona turnovers.

*Super Bowl, February 7*
**Game 11 — The Super Bowl:** The Super Bowl was held in Santa Clara at the Levi Stadium. It was Carolina's first trip to the Super Bowl in more than a decade. Denver is a regular there. John Elway who orchestrated this year's return was in five Super Bowls. He lost the first three but retired in 1999 having won the 1998 and 1999 Super Bowls. At 37 and 38, he was the oldest quarterback to play in the Super Bowl and he won those two games. Peyton Manning is older at 39. Denver had a drought for a number of years and was not very competitive. Then they hired Elway to rebuild the club as director of football operations. He designed each position including quarterback Manning. Manning is a 5 time MVP and was cut by Indianapolis to hire Andrew Luck. Manning had serious health problems but recovered and Elway had confidence in him and that has

paid off. Elway had Manning take a 4 million pay cut to 15 million with 2 million bonuses for appearing in the Super Bowl which he will now get and another 2 million for winning. Most likely Manning will retire after this season and go out on top. Both Brady and Manning have good outcomes in their matchups. Brady was 11 and 6 in the 17 meetings and Manning was 7-2 in Denver and 3-2 in the post season.

The Panthers are 4-4.5 favorites in the early Super Bowl betting.

The game was a rather dull defensive struggle with Denver winning 24-10. Denver linebacker Von Miller was the star and given the MVP by forcing two Cam Newton fumbles. Malik Jackson recovered one of them. The defense orchestrated by Denver defensive co-ordinator Wade Phillips was strong all day and flustered Newton and the high powered Carolina offense which had gained 100+ yards rushing in each of the past 31 games. Newton was criticized for not trying to recover the second fumble as he avoided De Marcus Ware and seemed to let Denver get the ball. Newton was sacked seven times. He was 18 for 41 for 265 yards with 1 interception and 2 fumbles for a mediocre 55.4 quarterback rating.

Peyton Manning managed the game well except for 1 interception, 1 fumble and no TDs. He was 13 for 23 for 141 yards and a similar mediocre 56.6 quarterback rating. He now is 2-2 in Super Bowls with the two wins equally that of his brother Eli who twice beat New England with miraculous throws. Denver's Brandon McManus had 34, 33 and 30 yard field goals. The other Denver scoring was a CJ Anderson's 1 yard TD which had a 2 point conversion, Manning passing to Bernie Fowler. Anderson ran for 90 yards on 23 carries. Carolina's Jonathan Stewart had a 1 yard TD.

Peyton won back the 4 million — 19 million to 15 million pay cut with a 2 million bonus for appearing in the Super Bowl and a further 2 million for winning it. He can now retire at the top but he has not yet announced his intentions. Officially, he is on the Denver payroll for 19 million for next year. So if he does not retire, Elway has a problem of what to do. He can continue with Manning or go with Brock Osweiler or go with someone else. The best solution is Manning going out on top and moving to a management role.

Betfair has moved out of Canada so I could not adjust my bets but I had a small gain from Denver's win.

# Chapter 14

# The 2016-2017 Season, Playoffs and the Super Bowl

The year started off with the NFL commissioner Roger Goodell (who is paid a reputed $35 million/year by the owners) enforcing the four game suspension of New England Patriots quarterback Tom Brady. The claim, called deflategate was cheating by using slightly underinflated footballs. Since other top quarterbacks like Aaron Rodgers and Drew Brees pointed out that different quarterbacks preferred different types of footballs, all this plus the fact that New England won the disputed game against Indianapolis by a huge margin, to me was nonsense and a great distraction from the game. It was likely Goodell in a power play.

Let's look at the playoff teams in the NFC and AFC. Neither of last year's Super Bowl teams Carolina and Denver made the playoffs.

**The NFC:**
In the pre season polls, New England, despite the absence of their top player, was a favorite to win the Super Bowl. The backup quarterback, Jimmy Garoppolo, played well in Brady's absence. He won two games then got injured. The third string quarterback Jacoby Brissett took over and New England won one of the next two games but lost to Buffalo. When Brady returned, he was on fire and by the 17th and last week of the season had 25 TDs and only 2 interceptions. After the Miami game, which New England won in Miami where they have often had trouble, Brady was 28/2. Comparing to the best TD/interception ratios, this is the best ever. Nick Foles had a 27/2 record. The difference is Brady does this every year. Brady also has 254 passes with no interceptions, another NFL record and 17 TDs with no interceptions on the road.

Going into the final week, New England and Dallas had the best records at 13 wins- 2 losses. New England lost star receiver Rob Gronkowski, who adds ten point per game to the team. However New England has many other receivers with the favorite being Julian Edelman. Patriots coach Bill Belichick is a master at replacing injured star players with unknowns who perform well. La Garette Blount, a Pittsburgh reject, has become a star with 17 running TDs, a new Patriot record. Michael Floyd was cut from Arizona after a DUI charge. Then after the Patriots picked him up he has played brilliantly. Brady was in the Most Valuable Player MVP running with quarterbacks Aaron Rodgers of Green Bay, Derek Carr of Oakland, and Matt Ryan of Atlanta as well as Dallas rookie running back Ezekiel Elliott and Pittsburgh runner and receiver LéVeon Bell who had 1884 total yards in 12 games.

Atlanta was the most high powered offense in terms of total offense with star receiver Julio Jones. They are 10-5 and have won the NFC-South.

Rodgers, after a slow start with the Green Bay packers at 4-6 in danger of not making the playoffs, led his team to 5 straight victories with some spectacular TD passes. So they sit at 9-6 with one game to go against divisional rival Detroit, which is also 9-6. Rodgers held a team meeting and argued that they could run the table and win all six of their final games to finish 10-6 and make the playoffs. They did that and Rodgers had 14 TDs and no interceptions with 215 passes with no interceptions and a 118.8 quarterback rating in these six games. In the first ten games, Rodgers had 22 TDs and 7 interceptions with a 93.9 rating. Getting back top receiver Gordy Nelson who had 14 TDs and star defensive linebacker Clay Matthews was another plus.

Detroit is a strong team that usually fizzles late in the year. They have a very good quarterback Matthew Stafford who had a good run until a bruised finger led to only one TD against 5 interceptions in the last 3 games. They have had a good year and might make the playoffs despite the retirement of star receiver Megatron (Calvin Johnson).

The script seems to predict Green Bay beating Detroit to win the division NFC-North.

Minnesota started out 5-0 but fizzled later and at 7-8 is out of the play-offs.

I tend to enjoy watching all the games, especially the best teams and root for New England especially and Seattle.

Seattle has been up and down all year, but their division had teams with poor records, so at 9-5-1 they have won the NFC-West. An early series of injuries to star quarterback Russell Wilson slowed his running style. With the retirement of superstar running back Marshan Lynch, their running game was not strong. Thomas Rawls has sort of replaced Lynch but is not in the same league. They seem to win easily at home but lose badly in some away games. An exception was beating New England in Foxboro where the Patriots are almost invincible. So for the playoffs, Seattle could bomb out or go all the way. They do start with a home game against Detroit. Seattle has won their last nine home games, an NFL record. A last minute pickup, top kickoff returner Darren Hester, who replaces Tyler Lockett, might help.

Dallas, like New England, are favored to reach the Super Bowl. Their top quarterback Tony Romo was injured so rookie Dak Prescott took over. Prescott and fellow rookie Ezekiel Elliott led the team to 12 straight wins. Elliot is the rushing leader of the NFL with 1631 yards gained and 16 TDs. Their only losses were to the New York Giants in the season opener and again at the end of the season. The Giants have been on a roll reminiscent of their Super Bowl winning 2007 and 2011 runs where, as underdogs, they beat the Patriots. They spent a lot of money to buy a tremendous set of defensive players. They are a dark horse but lightening could strike three times. Eli Manning in his 13th year is hot and cold but has those two Super Bowl victories, the same as his more famous brother Peyton. The Giants have clinched a wild card berth behind Dallas in the NFC-East.

The NFC playoff teams are: Seattle, Dallas, NY Giants, Atlanta, and Green Bay or Detroit (whoever wins their week 17 game), with Tampa Bay a possibility.

**The AFC**:
In the AFC, the playoff teams are finalized as:
New England, Miami, Houston, Pittsburgh, Oakland and Kansas City.

Oakland at 12-3 is leading the AFC-West ahead of 11-4 Kansas City. Both are in the playoffs with one a wild card depending on the week 17 results. Oakland had a great season led by coach Jack Del Rio, who likes to gamble on risky plays, and top young quarterback Derek Carr. Unfortunately they lost Carr to a broken leg but their great defense led by possible defensive player of the year Khalil Mack might prevail. But the real threat to the Patriots seems to be Kansas City with a strong balanced team and especially Pittsburgh who had a good run led by two time Super Bowl winning quarterback "Big Ben" Roethlisberger and great versatile running and receiving back LéVeon Bell and top receiver Antonio Brown.

**The NFL:**
Going into week 17 the NFL power ratings were: (1) Dallas, (2) New England, (3) Kansas City, (4) Atlanta, (5) Pittsburgh, (6) Green Bay, (7) Seattle, (8) NY Giants, (9) Miami, (10) Oakland, (11) Baltimore (out of playoffs), (12) Detroit, (13) Denver (out of playoffs), (14) Washington, (15) Houston

The website www.fivethirtyeight.com predicts the games.

**Playoff Games**  ①②③④⑤⑥⑦⑧⑨⑩⑪⑫⑬⑭⑮⑯⑰ ⑱

| | WILD CARD | | | | DIVISION | | CONFERENCE | SUPER BOWL |
| | SAT. | | SUN. | | SAT. | SUN. | SUN. | SUN. |
|---|---|---|---|---|---|---|---|---|
| Away team | OAK | DET | MIA | NYG | | | | |
| Pre-game win probabilities | 54% | 29% | 27% | 34% | | | | |
| | 46% | 71% | 73% | 66% | | | | |
| Home team | HOU | SEA | PIT | GB | ATL  NE | KC  DAL | | |

Fivethirtyeight predicts the game outcomes using simulations, based on the ELO ratings which use head to head and home/away bias results discussed in previous *Wilmott columns*. Their rankings are as follows:

| | | | | PLAYOFF CHANCES | | | |
|---|---|---|---|---|---|---|---|
| ELO RATING | 1-WEEK CHANGE | TEAM | DIVISION | MAKE DIV. ROUND | MAKE CONF. CHAMP | MAKE SUPER BOWL | WIN SUPER BOWL |
| 1739 | +21 | New England 14-2 | AFC East | ✓ | 81% | 55% | 35% |
| 1682 | +11 | Kansas City 12-4 | AFC West | ✓ | 67% | 28% | 15% |
| 1643 | +9 | Atlanta 11-5 | NFC South | ✓ | 62% | 32% | 14% |
| 1618 | -38 | Dallas 13-3 | NFC East | ✓ | 62% | 35% | 14% |
| 1633 | +2 | Pittsburgh 11-5 | AFC North | 73% | 28% | 10% | 5% |
| 1608 | +4 | Seattle 10-5-1 | NFC West | 71% | 27% | 13% | 5% |
| 1614 | +21 | Green Bay 10-6 | NFC North | 66% | 27% | 12% | 5% |
| 1571 | -28 | Oakland 12-4 | AFC West | 54% | 13% | 4% | 2% |
| 1564 | +28 | N.Y. Giants 11-5 | NFC East | 34% | 12% | 5% | 2% |
| 1515 | -21 | Detroit 9-7 | NFC North | 28% | 9% | 3% | <1% |
| 1480 | -22 | Houston 9-7 | AFC South | 46% | 8% | 2% | <1% |
| 1525 | -21 | Miami 10-6 | AFC East | 27% | 5% | 2% | <1% |

**Week 17**
The week 17 games that matter for the playoffs were as follows:

1. Atlanta beat New Orleans 38-19 to secure the #2 seed in the NFC.

2. Seattle beat San Francisco 25-23 and they are the #3 seed in the NFC.

3. Washington lost to the NY Giants 10-19 so are out of the playoffs and that means that both Detroit and Green Bay are in the playoffs as are the NY Giants.

4. Tampa Bay won 17-16 over Carolina but did not make the playoffs.

5. New England beat Miami 34-14 so the Dolphins will play at Pittsburgh and the Patriots have the #1 seed in the AFC with a 14-2 record have home field advantage throughout the playoffs.

6. Cleveland (who was 1-14) went into overtime with Pittsburgh (10-5) when the score was 21-21 and ended the game at 24-27. Since Pittsburgh was already in the playoffs they rested their best players.

7. Dallas (13-2) with the #1 seed in the NFC locked up, lost to Philadelphia (7-9) at 27-13 in a meaningless game where Dallas rested their stars and Tony Romo made a cameo appearance.

8. Denver beat Oakland 24-6.

The teams that did poorly were tough on their coaches. Los Angeles, San Diego,[1] San Francisco all fired their coaches. The coach of Denver retired citing health reasons.

In the race for the most TDs:

- Rodgers had 40 and 7 interceptions,

- Ryan 38 with the highest quarterback rating 117.1 and 9.26 yards per pass, an NFL record,

- Brees 37, with over 5000 yards passing for the fourth time,

- Rivers 33,

- Brady 28 in 12 games and only 2 interceptions,

- Carr 28 with six interceptions.

Hall of fame quarterback Kurt Warner rated the QBs as follows:

1. Ryan

2. Brady

3. Carr

4. Rodgers

5. Prescott who has a rookie record 104.9 QB rating

---

[1]San Diego is moving to Los Angeles and will share a $2.5 billion new stadium with the Los Angeles Rams who moved there from St Louis. Oakland would like to move to Las Vegas but that is not settled yet.

The fans rated them as follows:

1. Prescott

2. Brady

3. Stafford

4. Carr

5. Ryan

The fans left Rodgers out, they obviously don't look at the facts.

Backup quarterbacks are in the Houston, Miami, and Oakland games. Connor Cook of Oakland is starting his first playoff game replacing injured Derek Carr. Matt of Miami is replacing injured Ryan Tannehill. Brock Ostweiller signed for $72 million over four years with Houston then they benched him for poor play. Backups can win the Super Bowl, indeed, examples are Tom Brady (4 wins), Terry Bradshaw (4 wins) and Roger Stauback (3 wins).

Houston lost three time defensive player of the year JJ Watt to injury, still they have the best rated defense.

Last year in the wildcard weekend, all four games were won by the away team. This year, all four home teams won. This year the Wildcard round was on January 7-8; the Divisional Championships on Jan 14-15; the Conference Championships on January 22 and the Super Bowl on February 5 in Houston.

Table 14.1: The 2017 Super Bowl Tree

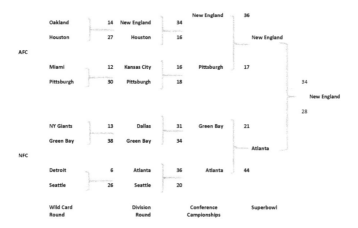

| | Wild Card Round | | Division Round | | Conference Campionships | | Superbowl |
|---|---|---|---|---|---|---|---|

## AFC Wildcard Games

### Oakland Raiders (5) at Houston Texans (4)

Both teams were weak at quarterback. Houston had benched Brock for poor play with more interceptions than touchdowns. The fans must really resent the general manager for spending $72 million for his services over four years with $37 million guaranteed. In 2016, Ostweiller had played a few games for Denver and then Peyton Manning took over and they actually won the Super Bowl but the real credit goes to the defense. In this game, backup Tom Savage was injured and they had to play the 6'8" Ostweiller. Oakland had backup quarterback Connor Cook replacing star Derek Carr who was injured. Cook was making his first snap as a starter.

Oakland is explosive on offense. Houston relies on a strong defense. Oakland was a four point favorite. Brock was not outstanding but he was decent and had no turnovers. He was 14 of 25 for 168 yards passing. That's not much but he had one TD passing and another running with no sacks and a decent 85.5 rating. Cook was 18 for 45 for 161 yards with one TD but had 3 interceptions and 3 sacks and a minuscule 5.5 rating. So not surprising, Houston won 27 to 14.

Houston now goes to New England where they are 16 point underdogs. Ostweiller will have to play another flawless game and create many points. Can he do it? I doubt it. New England has way too much firepower and a very good defense. I expect a rout. The real threat to New England is Pittsburgh.

## Miami Dolphins (6) at Pittsburgh Steelers (3)

Miami was 1-4 then 9-2 to finish 10-6. Quarterback Matt Moore was making his first playoff start having just replaced the injured Ryan Tannehill. Moore was inexperienced in the NFL but was MVP in the Rose Bowl and other top college games. He performed well with 29 completions in 36 throws for 289 yards and one TD, on interception, but two fumbles with one lost, 5 sacks and a 97.8 rating.

Pittsburgh, who was 11-5, had the big three, all now back from injuries. LéVeon Bell was in the MVP race. During the regular season he was the first player to average 100+ rushing and 50+ receiving yards in all his games. Bell had a spectacular game running for 158 yards and two TDs on 29 carries, which was a new Pittsburgh playoff record. Antonio Brown caught five passes for 124 yards and two more TDs. Quarterback Ben Roethinsberger was 13 of 18 with two TD passes, two interceptions, only one sack and a 105.3 rating.

Miami beat Pittsburgh in Miami in the regular season in a game where runner Jay Ajayi ran for 204 yards in 25 carries, one of his three games with 200+ yards rushing. Well not in this game. The tough Pittsburgh defense held him to 33 yards in 16 carries. So with essentially no running game and a good QB performance, Miami was no match for Pittsburgh who won 30-12. The one error was keeping quarterback Roethinsberger once the game was almost for sure won. He got an ankle injury on a pass that was intercepted. He ended the game on the sidelines wearing a boot. Too bad but we will see his condition for the next game. It is easy to make these errors. I am sympathetic. When I had some short calls recently that I sold for 4-5 dollars got to the $1 area, I failed to buy them back assuming they would go to zero. I had to hedge in various ways when they got to $20+. Fortunately the hedging worked and I gained but it was extra work and risk. These almost sure wins in option trading and getting out in the NFL and the S&P500 are a close call. Getting out seems best.

Pittsburgh now goes to face Kansas City, the number 2 seed in the AFC. To me a toss up.

## NFC Wildcard Games

### Detroit Lions (6) at Seattle Seahawks (3)

Detroit had a good year and made the playoffs for the first time in many years. They had no playoff wins since 1992 and on the road since 1957. Quarterback Matthew Stafford had his best year but got a bruised middle finger on his throwing hand. He got a special glove and said he was ok but he had one TD and 5 interceptions in the last three games which they lost. So they limped into the playoffs at 9 and 7 as the second seed in the NFC-North.

Seattle at 10-5-1 was the top seed in the NFC-West and were nearly invincible at home in the extremely loud Century Link Field but weak on the road. They did beat New England in Foxboro. Otherwise on the road they were just so so.

The game was in Seattle where they have won their last nine playoff games. When Seattle was winning the Super Bowl and appearing in it, they relied mainly on three things: great running by Marshan Lynch, good passing and scrambling by quarterback Russell Wilson and a terrific defense with the so-called legion of doom defenders against the opponents passing game. A few good receivers like Doug Baldwin, Jerome Kearse and Jimmy Graham add to the offense. This year, Lynch has retired and top safety Earl Thomas had an injury.

Seattle was able to bring the pieces together to win 26-6. Thomas Rawls ran for a Seattle playoff record 161 yards. Wilson was sharp with 22 of 30 passing for 224 yards with two TDs and the defense held Detroit to two field goals. Paul Richards on defense held Detroit to two field goals. Paul Richardson had some Odell Beckham Jr-like circus catches except in one TD he fouled the defender but the referees missed his hand on the face mask. Baldwin, Wilson's favorite receiver, had 11 catches for 104 yards. The closest they came was to the Seattle 33. Stafford was sacked 3 times and was 18 of 32 for 205 yards with no TDs and no interceptions or fumbles.

Seattle goes next to Atlanta, the second NFC seed. Seattle beat Atlanta 26-22 in the regular season. But that was in Seattle. So Atlanta will be favored but Seattle has more Super Bowl experience and many weapons so they might prevail.

### New York Giants (5) at Green Bay Packers (4)
Green Bay went into the game after six straight wins and a nearly flawless performance by quarterback Aaron Rodgers. Rodgers had 18 TDs and no interceptions. At Green Bay, the Giants quarterback Eli Manning was 2-0 in the playoffs. This led to two Super Bowl wins beating the Patriots in 2007 and 2011 and he won his last five games on the road. It was his first playoff game in five years. The Giants defense was extremely strong and made up for a weak offense. That offense, in addition to Manning, was led by top receiver Odell Beckham Jr who is known for his one handed circus catches and sure hands.

The Giants were not able to score as many as 20 points in their last group of games but they were able to win and finished with a 10-6 record, the same as Green Bay. As the game progressed, Beckham kept dropping passes. Perhaps some were slightly off passes but he usually catches all these and with Anquan Boldin of Detroit, Julio Jones of Atlanta, Rob Gronkowski of New England,Larry Fitzgerald of Arizona and Tyreek Hill and Travis Kelce of Kansas City, Beckham is one of the NFL's top receivers. Beckham and a bunch of his key Giant's players went to Florida on their day off and partied on a boat off Miami with Justin Beiber. Whether or not this affected their play is debatable. In a column, Tom Brady made suggestions along with the fans who pay for these multimillion dollar salaries. It just seemed unwise not to prepare better. The New York press was very hard on Beckham and he went ballistic punching a hole in the wall. Beckham claims that he caught all his passes in practice and the trip to Florida six days prior to the game did not affect him. Out of eleven passes to Beckham, he caught only four in 28 yards. Travarres King, Will Tye, Sherling Sharpe, Victor Cruz and Paul Perkins had 3 or 4 catches to make up some of the slack.

Manning had a decent game but suffered from many drops on good passes he made. He was 23 of 44 for 299 yards with one TD and one interception. He was sacked twice and had a 72.1 QB rating.

After a slow start, when the Giants had good drives but only got field goals it was 6-0. The Giants were 6-1 when they score first and Green Bay is 0-5 when their opponent scores first. Then late in the first quarter, Rodgers got one TD to Davante Adams and then with no time remaining had a hail Mary pass for 42 yards to Randall Cobbs who he favors greatly, especially after their top receiver Jordy Nelson got injured.

Rodgers had two more TDs to Cobb and Aaron Ripkowski ran for the fifth TD. Rodgers was 25 of 40 for 302 yards and 4 TDs with no interceptions again and a 125.2 QB rating. Rodgers is a master at all phases of the QB position including great scrambling ability that frequently results eventually in an open receiver which he hits with a perfect pass. So with his scrambling, he was sacked five times. Both Adams and Cobb had over 100 yards receiving and Jared Cook and Ty Montgomery had 8 more catches for 89 yards.

Green Bay won the game 38-13. Green Bay now moves onto the Divisional round facing number one seed Dallas. Dallas likely will be favored but Green Bay, with Rodgers, will be a formidable opponent and would be my bet.

## Predictions for the rest of the playoffs

Prediction Machine Service forecasts along with 538's update for the division games and my comments:

| Region | Seed | Team | Conf. | Super Bowl | | 538 | WTZ | Len |
| | | | | To be in | To win | | | |
| --- | --- | --- | --- | --- | --- | --- | --- | --- |
| AFC | 1 | NE | 85.0% | 61.0% | 34.5% | 35% | 35% | 35% |
| AFC | 2 | KC | 54.9% | 18.5% | 7.9% | 17% | 12% | 12% |
| AFC | 3 | PIT | 45. 1% | 16.2% | 6.8% | 7% | 14% | 14% |
| AFC | 4 | HOU | 15.0% | 4.3% | 1.2% | 2% | 0.5% | 0.5% |
| NFC | 1 | DAL | 67.0% | 40.3% | 21.9% | 12% | 12% | 18% |
| NFC | 2 | ATL | 61.0% | 29.9% | 15.0% | 13% | 13% | 13% |
| NFC | 3 | SEA | 39.0% | 17.0% | 7.5% | 8% | 10% | 8% |
| NFC | 4 | GB | 33.0% | 12.8% | 5.1% | 8% | 15% | 10% |

We have already seen fivethirtyeight's earlier predictions for the Super Bowl. Here are the predictions from the Prediction Machine Service based on current rosters, strength of schedule, and pace-adjusted team and player statistics simulated 50,000 times with their model Predictalater to generate their results. These are in the table along with the updated 538 model forecast and my thoughts. It is clear that both of these seeding rankings uses home field advantage as a big part of their analysis. The results are consistent with other services and close to my analysis. I would rate Green Bay higher and Houston and Dallas lower. I fear Pittsburgh more than Kansas City to beat New England in the AFC. I have added the opinions of my research colleague Leonard MacLean with whom I am working on a sports statistics book as well as other portfolio theory books for World Scientific. Also, wonderful sports writer Mark Maske's picks are here. Mark writes for the *Washington Post* and his column on this weekend's games are reprinted in the *Vancouver Sun*. His picks the for winners are New England, Pittsburgh, Dallas and Atlanta.

Fivethirtyeight's updated division game forecasts plus my thoughts are:

| Away | SEA | HOU | PIT | GB |
| --- | --- | --- | --- | --- |
| | 38% | 15% | 36% | 43% |
| | 62% | 85% | 64% | 57% |
| Home | ATL | NE | KC | DAL |
| WTZ | 50-50 | NE 99% | 50-50 | GB 60% |
| Len | AT 60% | NE 90% | 50-50 | DAL 55% |
| Maskie | AT | NE | PIT | DAL |

## Divisional Championships

### AFC
### Houston (10-7) at New England(14-2)

New England at home with Brady hot as a pistol versus Houston, a team on the road with weak quarterbacks. Everyone expected a rout. Betfair was shut down in Canada even though I was writing for their website and had a pound account from London, but my colleague Bunker set me up at Pinnacle, a betting site in Curcao. So I was able to wager there. I bet $500 at 1-10 odds their 1.10 on New England to win. I passed on New England -16 as it seemed too risky. I also bet $200 at 1.585, (that is risk 388 to win 200) on New England win the AFC.and for the Super Bowl risked $254.78 to win 400 and later 101.35 to win 150.

Houston has a top defense rated number 1 in some categories despite three time defensive player of the year JJ Watt being out with a back injury. The defense was led by Jadeveon Clowney, Whitney Mercilus and eleven year former Patriot player Vince Wilfork. The game started out with Houston flawless and New England having a few good plays including long Brady passes but looking sloppy. At half time, the score was 17-13 New England. Brock was playing well again and Brady was good but not at his fully sharp best which is much better than all but the best QBs. Dion Lewis had a big gain including a 98 yard TD return to start the third quarter. He also scored one TD running and received one of Brady's two TDs. The other Brady TD went to James White. Lewis fumbled one kickoff that led to a Houston TD. Julian Edelman, Brady's favorite receiver now that Rob Gronkowski is injured, had eight receptions from 13 throws for 137 yards. Chris Hogan had four receptions for 95 yards.

Brady had 28 TDs and 2 interceptions in the regular season and is in the MVP running. He is 22-9 in playoff games and holds essentially all the playoff records for TDs, yards gained, etc. In this game he was 18 of 38 which is less than 50% for 287 yards, most of which were in the second half. He had 2 interceptions but both were tips by receivers on passes that could have been caught but perhaps were slightly off target. In the second half, New England pulled further away and Brock had 3 interceptions. Brock was 23 of 40 for 198 yards. He can make short passes but not long ones like Brady.

The final score was 34-16. So New England did win the -16 bet. I won the $500 1.1 bet and my conference and Super Bowl New England bets were slightly improved and are still alive. But it was a shaky performance. New England will have to play better to play the winner of the

Pittsburgh-Kansas City game. They will be at home where they have a huge advantage.

Coach Belichick is a master at focusing on key players who can play well that day. In this game it was Lewis and Julian Edelman. Top runner La Garette Blount had only 8 runs for 31 yards, maybe he will be used more in future games. Gronkowski is greatly missed. He had added more than 10 points per game. Houston held up quite well and have a fabulous defense, they can only improve. Their coaches Bill O'Brien, Mike Varabel, Larry Izzo, and Romeo Crennel are all ex-Patriots so will guide them well.

I made some Super Bowl bets to create a winning hedge. The idea is to bet a lot on the best team, namely New England, then bet smaller amounts on the good teams so that if the top team does not win but one of these other good teams does win, I am at least even or slightly ahead. I lose if one of the teams not bet on wins. I assumed that Houston, Kansas City and Atlanta would not win the Super Bowl. Well, as you see above, Houston won't win but as you will see below, keeping Atlanta out might be trouble and Kansas City plays tomorrow. The Super Bowl bets were:

- New England risk $356.13 to win 550

- Pittsburgh was supposed to be bet 85 at 9-1; but the betting site was closed so I made a bigger bet on Pittsburgh in the Kansas City game

- Dallas 140 at 5.52-1

- Seattle 60 at 13.89-1

- Green Bay 80 at 11.15-1

**Pittsburgh (12-5) at Kansas City (12-4)**
Andy Reed, the coach of Kansas City, brought his teams to a 19-2 record after they had a two week layoff. Although Kansas City was at home and a slight favorite, I went with Pittsburgh with my bets. They were the money team, with lots of playoff and Super Bowl appearances (winning six times). My bets were $185 Pittsburgh +1.5 and $50 Pittsburgh at 2.08:1.

It was a battle of two great defenses with good offenses as well. Kansas City's defense is led by linebacker Justin Houston and safety Eric Berry. On offense, they have the explosive Tyreek Hill, top tight end Travis Kelce, and a good quarterback Alex Smith.

Pittsburgh had the killer B's quarterback Ben Roethinsberger, receiver Antonio Brown and the runner/receiver LéVeon Bell. Bell has a unique running style. Instead of running through a potential a hole, he pauses and pauses until he finds an open lane. Then he darts through and is very effective in his running game. They say he runs like Marcus Allen. His receiving game is also topnotch. Brown is in the running for top 10 NFL receiver and Ben is solid with two Super Bowl victories. Pittsburgh's defense is led by 38 year old James Harrison, the oldest player on the team and the oldest in the NFL except for Brady. He spends $350,000 per year on various health issues and it shows.

It was a defensive struggle throughout. Pittsburgh dominated and got into the red zone repeatedly. But they could not score. Chris Boswell, their kicker, hit field goal after field goal and ended up setting an NFL record of six field goals. His last one with 5 minutes to go won the game. Ben was 20/31 for 224 yards with no TDs and one interception. Bell was terrific, gaining 170 yards on 30 carries. He's really fun to watch. Brown caught six passes for 108 yards and Jessie James had 83 yards on five receptions and one field goal.

Kansas City had two TDs and one field goal. One was by Smith who was 20 for 34 with one interception. Spencer Ware scored the other TD. An extra two point attempt after Kansas City scored with 7 minutes left failed.

So the score ended Pittsburgh 18 Kansas City 16 and I won by bets. They now face New England in Foxboro where the Patriots seldom lose. But Pittsburgh is a tough opponent so it should be a great game for the AFC championship.

**NFC**
### Seattle (11-5-1) at Atlanta (11-5)
Seattle has been nearly invincible in Seattle (7-1) but they have been weak on the road (3-4-1). Atlanta is the NFL's top offensive team lead by NVP candidate Matt Ryan whose 118 rating is the best, even higher than Tom Brady's 113. Ryan has a good core of receivers led by Julio Jones who was guarded by star cornerback Richard Sherman. After the game, the coach announced a non disclosed knee injury to Sherman which will be penalized by having to give up a draft pick. Atlanta was favored but Seattle had more players with playoff and Super Bowl experience. Quarterback Russell Wilson was 8-3 in playoff games and has 64 wins in his 5 years, the most in the NFL. Thomas Rawls came off a top running performance against Detroit. Atlanta has the NFC sack leader Vic Beasley. I had a Super Bowl bet on Seattle in my hedge and $50 on Seattle at 3.35-1 and $100 on Seattle +6.5 at 1.961:1.

Seattle started out with the first TD. But as the game progressed Atlanta's powerful offense took over and Atlanta won 36-20 so I lost my game and SuerBowl bts. Rawls had a good first quarter but for the game only had 34 yards on 11 carries. The loss of star safety Earl Thomas, the leader of the legion of boom hurt Seattle. Wilson was 17 of 30 for 225 yards on two TDs and played well. He also rushed for 49 yards on 6 carries. Richardson gained 85 yards and Baldwin 80 and a TD. Ryan was sharp with 26 of 37 for 338 yards with 3 TDs and one fumble Atlanta had a balanced attack with eight receivers catching passes. Freeman and Gabriel were the leading receivers. Jones had one TD and 67 yards from 6 receptions. Freeman had 80 yards and Gabriel 71.

Again Graham disappointed with only 33 yards but he got a TD.

### Green Bay (11-6) at Dallas (13-3) A game for the ages!

Green Bay was hot having "run the table", as quarterback Aaron Rodgers said they could, going from a mediocre 4-6 record to 10-6 entering the playoffs and was 11-6. Rodgers was the leader and played brilliantly. He has made many spectacular passes, some of the hail Mary variety. He is at his best in the clutch. He had 319 passes without an interception. Dallas was favored and the #1 seed in the NFC. These two rookies quarterback Dak Prescott and running back Ezekiel Elliot along with star receiver Dez Bryant led them to twelve straight wins. The only losses were to the New York Giants twice plus a meaningless week 17 game.

Prescott played a very good game. He ws 24 of 38 for 302 yards and three TDs, two of which were passed to Bryant who had 9 receptions for 132 yards. Elliot was his usual brilliant self gaining 125 on 22 carries.

Rodgers was equally brilliant except for one interception until the end and then he rose to another level. With little time left, he drove the Packers close enough for a 53 yard field goal to make the score 31-28. Then Prescott did the same leading his team to an over 50 yard tying field goal, 31-31. There were 28 seconds left and instead of running the clock down to just a few seconds, Coach Jason Garrett ordered Prescott to stop the clock by spiking the football. That saw Rodgers only 28 seconds to go most of the field. On one play he was blindsided, a play that usually leads to a fumble but Rodgers did not fumble although they lost some yards. Rodgers responded with a long pass to Cook and the kicker made another over 50 yard field goal but Dallas called a time out just before so he had to do it again and he did. So the game ended Green Bay 34-31. It was a wonderful, exciting game to watch. I won my bets on this game and my Super Bowl bet odds improved and are still alive.

## Conference Championships

### NFC
### Green Bay (12-6) at Atlanta (12-5)

Green Bay had won its final six games of the regular season then beat the New York Giants and then the #1 NFC seed Dallas on the road. Quarterback Aaron Rodgers had many TDs, no interceptions and many crucial passes completed during this.

Atlanta had the top rated offense with Matt Ryan the league's highest rated quarterback at 118. Their offense had a decent running attack and a superior passing game with a number of good receivers led by Julio Jones. Atlanta had beaten Seattle at home. I had lost that game, the only loss in the Division round the previous weekend. In the betting, I went with Green Bay who were the underdogs. I thought Rodgers would out duel Ryan.

Atlanta had scored on its first possession in its last seven games. They did it again, scoring first.Green Bay then ran down the field and failed to get a TD but had a field goal attempt. Their kicker Mason Crosby, who was 28/28, missed this field goal (and later missed an extra point). That was a signal of how the game was to go. Atlanta scored again. When Green Bay was close to scoring a TD, Aaron Ripowski got close to the goal then made his first fumble of the season so Green Bay got nothing again. Although Atlanta piled it on and by halftime it was 24-0. Then in the second half another TD made it 31-0 and the games result was sealed.

Rodgers played well with 27 of 45 passes completed despite some drops for three TDs with one interception. The three TDs went to Davante Adams, Gordy Nelson and Randall Cobb. Cobb had 82 yards and 6 receptions, Cook 7 for 78 and the injured Nelson, wearing a military vest to protect his broken ribs, 6 for 67. Green Bay came back a bit in the second half but onside kicking failed and the deficit was too much to make up.

Neither team had an outstanding ground game but Green Bay gained 99 and Atlanta 101. The big difference in the game was the great play of Ryan who threw for four TDs completing 27 of 38 that gained 392 yards and he ran for a 5th TD. Atlanta won 44-21. Atlanta now goes to the Super Bowl in Houston on February 5 to face New England. It will be a tough battle for them as New England is much more experienced, has a much better defense than Green Bay, and the Brady-Belichick led team will be primed to shut down Atlanta's best receivers, especially Jones and win the Super Bowl.

## AFC
### Pittsburgh (13-5) at New England (15-2)

I thought that Pittsburgh had the best chance of beating New England in the AFC. But with Brady so hot (28 TDs with 2 interceptions) and determined, New England's strong defense in addition to their powerful offense and their great record at home, they were my bet. A big plus was coach Bill Belichick's ability to find new players to star each week and to shutdown the opponent's top player.

Pittsburgh had the killer B's: Ben Roethinsberger, a two time Super Bowl winning quarterback, LéVeon Bell, the league's top runner/receiver and Antonio Brown, one of the very best receivers. They were unable to score any TDs in their last game against Kansas City but got 6/6 field goals from Chris Boswell to win 18-16. Roethinsberger in nine road games in the play-offs had 9 TD and 9 interceptions and was 1-4 versus Brady. Meanwhile, New England crushed Houston as expected in a lack luster performance when the tough Houston defense hassled Brady all day and he had two interceptions — both tips. Rob Gronkowski, New England's top receiver who is worth 10+ points per game, was still injured. But New England still had plenty of good receivers including Julian Edelman, Chris Hogan, Martellis Bennett, Danny Amendola, La Garette Blount, who receives out of the back field, and Dion Lewis, who scored three TDs against Houston.

My bets on New England were:

- risk $388 to win $200

- risk $271 to win $150

- New England -6, risk $100 to win $99

New England got a 10-0 lead on a Gostkowski field goal and a Hogan pass from Brady. Pittsburgh scored on a Williams run but the extra point was missed. Then Brady hit Hogan for another TD. The half ended 17-9 when Boswell hit a 23 yard field goal.

In the second half, New England pulled away with Brady sharp. Blount got one of the TDs and the other went to Edelman. Gostkowski added two field goals. The score ended 36-17. Brady was 32 of 42 for 384 yards, three TDs and no interceptions. Belichick figured a way to stop Bell who had set the NFL record in his last two games, gaining over 150 in each on the ground. In this game, he gained only 20 yards on 6 carries and left the game with a groin injury. Top defender, Malcolm Butler, recall his game-saving goal line catch against Seattle to win their last Super Bowl, was on Bell. Roethinsberger had 31 of 47 for 314 yards, one TD and one interception. Brown had seven receptions for 77 and Rodgers and Williams had seven each as well for 66 and 51 and Jessie James had five receptions for 48 yards. But New England had Hogan for 180 yards on 9 receptions and Edelman for 118 on eight receptions. They had the three Brady TD passes as well.

I won all my bets so the gain of $69 more than paid back the Seattle losses. It was not much of a gain but not a loss. In the Wild Card round, despite missing on Seattle, I made $233. I misjudged Atlanta's powerful offense. For the Super Bowl, I am long New England with a little on Atlanta at a good price. It will be important that Belichick figure out how to stop Julio Jones. Statistics show that Matt Ryan has a higher quarterback rating when Jones is not in the lineup. Ryan threw passes to 13 different receivers this year. Historically, a common strategy is to use the best defender to stop the second best receiver. Then they can double team the best receiver. In any event, Jones must be double covered as no one single defensive back can cover him. He averages an impressive 100.6 yards gained per game. He is second best in the NFL and Edelman is fourth. This will be the first time New England faced a top ten quarterback all season except for Pittsburgh's Big Ben.

New England's better defense will be crucial. I expect Brady to have a strong game and win his fifth Super Bowl and to set the record in his seventh appearance in the Super Bowl in the Brady-Belichick era. Head coaches facing Belichick the first time are 3 and 22. The Patriots are 16-0 when Dion Lewis.

It's the #1 offense (Atlanta with 33+ points per game) against the #2 offense (New England, with 31+ points per game) with New England the top defensive team in takeaways. Both teams had only 11 turnovers all year, tied for best in the NFL It will be a gem of a Super Bowl.

The Super Bowl bets

1. bets made before the Wild Card round on New England:

   - risk $101.35 to win $150

   - risk $254.78 to win $400

2. bets made after the Conference Championships on New England

   - New England -3.5, risk $300 to win $360 at odds of 2.21 to 1

   - New England -3.5, risk $400 to win $480

   - risk $600 to win $399 at odds of 1.666

3. bets made after the Conference Championships on Atlanta

- risk $400 to win $516 at odds of 2.48 to 1

The Hall of Fame Class of 2017 was named and includes: running back La Danian Tomlinson (San Diego Charger), kicker Morton Anderson (Atlanta Falcons and New Orleans Saints), defensive end Jason Taylor (Miami Dolphins), safety Kenny Easley (Seattle Seahawks), owner Jerry Jones (Dallas Cowboys), and quarterback Kurt Warner (Arizona Cardinals and St Louis Rams). The awards were: offensive rookie of the year Zak Prescott (Dallas Cowboys), defensive player of the year Kalik Mack (Oakland Raiders), Walter Payton Players of the Year Larry Fitzgerald (Arizona Cardinals) and Eli Manning (New York Giants) who both entered the NFL in 2004, MVP and offensive player of the year Matt Ryan (Atlanta Falcons), Excessive Celebration Odell Beckham Jr (New York Giants), Art Rooney Sportsmanship running bak Frank Gore (Indianapolis Colts), defensive rookie of the year Joey Bosa (San Diego), coach of the year Jason Garrett (Dallas), clutch player of the year Derek Carr (Oakland), on road performance LéVeon Bell, and play of the year Mike Evans (Tampa Bay).[2]

**The Super Bowl: New England 16-2 vs Atlanta 14-5**

New England was favored by 3 points. Former President George H W Bush who is 91 and in a wheelchair tossed the game coin. Bush's wife, Barbara, also in a wheelchair, looked on. Atlanta won and deferred to the second half. The weather in Houston was good but just in case, the roof was closed.

The game started out slowly with many 3 and outs. Despite predictions of a shoot out, quarter one ended scoreless. Davonte Freeman had some good runs including one 37 yarder. Brady was passing fine but possibly a little off. There were several drops which to me looked perfectly thrown and catchable. Even reliable receiver Julian Edelman had drops.

In the second quarter, Atlanta looked sharp. The usually reliable La Garrett Blount fumbled. Coach Belichick had warned his players that Atlanta was the best at stripping the football. Freeman got one TD. Ryan passed to Austin Hooper for a 19 yard second TD. The score was then 14-0. One of the Patriots leaped over the line to try to stop the extra point attempt.

---

[2]The MVP final five were four quarterbacks: Ryan, Brady, Carr, and Rodgers; and running back Elliot. The coach of the year contenders were Garrett, Belichick, Reid, Delrio, and Case.

He failed and got a 5 yard penalty. Bets with New England plus 7.5 were offered but I passed on them as I felt I had enough.

Finally New England was charging and it looked like a typical carefully designed Brady TD. Then the unthinkable happened. Brady threw a pick6. Robert Alford intercepted the pass and ran 82 yards for the third Atlanta TD. It was now 21-0. I passed on bets of New England plus 14.5 and straight New England win the game at the 7-1 area. This is where I usually make mean reversion bets which with a deficit of 2 scores often works. However with a three score deficit it is usually too much to make up. The largest deficit made up in a Super Bowl game in the previous 50 games was 10. In addition, Atlanta was to get the ball in the second half kickoff. So the game looked hopelessly lost for New England. The 21 point deficit was also the largest one ever in the 17 years of the Brady-Belichick era to overtake and win the game.

Stephen Gostkowski kicked a 41 yard field goal to make it 21-3 with 5 seconds to go and the half ended.

Ever since 1993 when Michael Jackson had higher ratings for the Super Bowl half time show than the game itself, the half time show has been a major part of the event. Lady Gaga, the entertainment this year, came down through the roof. It was so dangerous that it had been pre taped. She put on a dazzling show with music, dancing and flashy costumes. In some sense the new Madonna, she is very popular receiving 41,000 tweets per minute. The fifteen minute halftime show cost $10 million and averaged 117 million Americans watching, more than the 111.3 million who watched the game. The latter might be deceiving as the first half Atlanta rout may have greatly lowered the audience during that period as the game looked hopeless for New England.

Atlanta got the ball in the third quarter. After some stops and punts, Atlanta got a TD pass from Ryan to Tevin Coleman to make it 28-3. I still took no New England mean reversion bets which were now at New England plus 21.5 with the straight odds around 11-1. Brady was sharp and responded with a 5 yard TD pass to James White with 2.06 left in the quarter. Belichick is the master at taking a player who others on weaker teams cannot use well and turning him into a valuable piece of the Patriots better team. White had been cut from the 1-15 Cleveland Browns and became a star on New England. Belichick stresses "do you job" and an unselfish approach to team play. It starts with Belichick and Brady and the other players follow.

The score was then 28-9 because the extra point attempt hit the goal post and was no good. New England tried an onside kick but before it went the required 10 yards, it hit kicker Gostkowski. New England was looking better and Atlanta was helping them with many holding penalties. At 9:44 in the fourth quarter, Gostkowski kicked a 33 yard field goal to make it 28-12. New England needed two TDs plus two extra point conversions to tie the game. Ryan tried to pass but was sacked by Grady Garrett, his third sack of the game. With 8:24 to go, Hightower hit Ryan as he was trying to pass and he fumbled. It was the first Atlanta turnover in the post season. New England got the ball on the 25, Brady then led the team down the field with passes to White and Mitchell. Then at 5:56 New England got the first TD on a 6 yard TD pass to Danny Amendola. James White ran for the 2 point conversion to make the score 28-20.

I know that Belichick makes plays that are optimal when you actually do the analysis. Many coaches make decisions based on gut feel. Dan Quinn, the Atlanta coach, was in his third Super Bowl in four year, having been the defensive coordinator for the Seattle Seahawks. Seattle won the 2014 SuperBowl then lost in 2015 to New England. Seattle was on the 1 yard line with three downs to go. Instead of running Marshan Lynch who almost for sure would have gotten the winning TD in one of the 3 tries, they instead had quarterback Russell Wilson pass. Malcolm Butler intercepted the pass. It was a play that Seattle had never used before but Belichick had his team practice it. Seattle's play was chosen by the offensive coordinator and the coach.

In this game, Quinn and offensive coordinator Kyle Shanahan[3] were about to make a huge error in strategy. With 4:48 left, Julio Jones made a spectacular catch and somehow landed both feet in bounds. Atlanta was then on the New England 22 yard line with a first and 10. They were 8 points ahead. Matt Bryant, the Atlanta kicker, was 27 of 28 in field goals under 49 yards. A field goal would make it an 11 point advantage or a 2 score deficit with 3:50 to go, an almost sure winner of the game. Freeman ran for a one yard loss so the ball was on the 23 and a 40 yard field goal was possible.

Instead of running the clock down and going for the field goal, they decided to pass but Ryan was sacked by Trey Flowers. Now the ball was on the 35 yard line and a 52 yard field goal was still possible. Then the unthinkable happened. Ryan completed a pass but a 10 yard holding call took the ball back to the 45 yard line, out of field goal range. New England got the ball

---

[3]Shanahan will be the new San Francisco 49ers coach and will be replaced by Steve Sarkasian from the Alabama Crimson Tide.

after a punt. Brady then drove the team to the 9 yard line along the way Edelman made a spectacular catch while guarded by 3 defense men. He actually fell and the ball was kept off the ground by having it touch one of the defender's back. Brady was sharp and it was vintage comeback. He led the team down the field and with 57 seconds left, White rushed for a 1 yard TD, his third of the game. Brady passed to Amendola for the 2 point conversion that tied the game a 28-28. The momentum had shifted to New England.

The rules for overtime are that if a team gets a TD they win the game but if they get a field goal, then the other team gets a chance to score a field goal or a winning TD. By luck New England won the toss and it was clear that Brady was destined to drive the team to the winning TD. He did exactly that with White scoring the winning TD on a 2 yard run. So the game ended with the score 34-28.

White had 3 TDs plus 14 receptions, a Super Bowl record. Brady is generous giving much of his salary to help the team hire other good players. He had given the 2015 truck to Butler who got the game winning reception. This year he game White the truck he had won for his fourth Super Bowl MVP.

I won all my New England bets and lost the one Atlanta bet. The gain was +233 (week of January 15 games), +69 (January 22 games), +1389 on the Super Bowl totaling $1691. This was a fine result considering I got Atlanta wrong twice and almost a third time. The other games were winners.

It is easy to be a Monday morning quarterback, but I do believe that Atlanta's management made some errors in their strategy as discussed above. My colleague Professor Leonard MacLean, with whom I have written many research papers and several books including one in progress on sports statistics, independently wrote me about this error. Some Super Bowl statistics:

- Brady was 43 of 62 for 466 yards with 2 TDs, 1 interception and a 95.2 rating

- Ryan was 17 of 23 for 284 yards with 2 TDs, no interceptions, 5 sacks and 1 fumble for a 144.1 rating

- Ryan's average gain per pass was much higher than Brady's

- there was not much rushing

    - Blount gained 31 yards on 11 carries and had 1 fumble

    - White gained 29 on 6 carries

- Dion Lewis 2 on 6 carries

- Brady was 1 for 15 yards

- Atlanta as expected relied on Freeman who had 75 yards in 11 carries and Coleman who had 29 on 7

**An aside on quarterback ratings**

The reason Ryan's rating was so much more than Brady's can be seen from the rating formula which is from the late Tom Cover's problems for his Stanford course on statistics in sports and is on Wikipedia. The passer rating goes from 0-158.3, where this is a perfect rating which is sometimes achieved.

$$Q = \frac{100}{6}\{C + Y + T + I\}$$

where

$$C = \max\left\{\min\left[\frac{100c - 30}{20}, 2.375\right], 0\right\}$$

$$Y = \max\left\{\min\left[\frac{y - 3}{4}, 2.375\right], 0\right\}$$

$$T = \max\left\{\min\left[20t, 2.375\right], 0\right\}$$

$$I = \max\left\{\min\left[\frac{9.5 - 100i}{4}, 2.375\right], 0\right\}$$

and $c, y, t, i$ are completions, yards, touchdowns, interceptions (all per passing attempt), respectively.

So here is why the discrepancy:

- Fumbles do not count but they should

- Interceptions count and Brady had one and Ryan none

- Yards gained per pass count and Ryan is much higher than Brady

Of course, statistics can lie. Brady is pleased and Ryan is not with the outcome of the game. Cover's problems show further that a quarterback who is doing will with 9 of 10 or doing poorly with 3 of 10 can actually increase his rating by throwing an incomplete pass. This and the non counting of fumbles ought to be corrected with a better formula and we will try to come up with one. In general, the formula gives reasonable results apart from these imperfections.

*Comments from Wikipedia*

The rating is from the pro football hall of fame official site. The formula does not include rushing statistics or fumbles nor does it put added weight on performance in situations like third downs or fourth quarter scoring tries. The rating does not account for the quality of receivers or protection from the offensive line. The rating does not measure a quarterback's contributions to team wins. The highest career passing rating is 104.0 by Aaron Rodgers, 2005-2016. He also holds the one season highest rating of 122.5 in 2011. Peyton Manning holds the record for the most games (4) with a perfect passer rating. Phil Simms holds the record for the highest passer rating in a Super Bowl of 150.92 in Super Bowl 21. Ben Roethinsberger holds the record for the lowest passer rating to win a Super Bowl at 22.6 in Super Bowl 40. Wikipedia lists a number of attempts at alternative formulas, but none of them seem to capture the full essence of the quarterback concept which is very complex.

**There were 51 records made or matched in Super Bowl 51. Tom Brady set 8 of them.**

**Records broken:**

1. Most games: 7, Tom Brady

2. Most games, head coach: 7, Bill Belichick

3. Most games won, head coach: 5, Bill Belichick

4. Most points, game: 20, James White

5. Most passes, career: 309, Tom Brady

6. Most passes, game: 62, Tom Brady

7. Most completions, career: 207, Tom Brady

8. Most completions, game: 43, Tom Brady

9. Most passing yards, career: 2,071, Tom Brady

10. Most passing yards, game: 466, Tom Brady

11. Most touchdown passes, career: 15, Tom Brady

12. Most receptions, game: 14, James White

13. Most games, team: 9, New England

14. Largest deficit overcome, winning team: 25 points, New England

15. Most points, overtime period, team: 6, New England

16. Most first downs, game, team: 37, New England

17. Most first downs, game, both teams: 54

18. Most first downs passing, game, team: 26, New England

19. Most first downs passing, game, both teams: 39

20. Most offensive plays, game, team: 93, New England

21. Most passes, game, team: 63, New England

22. Most completions, game, team: 43, New England

23. Most passing yards, game, team: 442, New England

24. Most passing yards, game, both teams: 682

**Records tied:**

1. Most games won: 5, Tom Brady

2. Most touchdowns, game: 3, James White

3. Most two-point conversions, game: 1, James White, Danny Amendola

4. Most sacks, game (since 1982): 3, Grady Jarrett

5. Most two-point conversions, game, team: 2, New England

6. Most two-point conversions, game, both teams: 2

7. Most first downs by penalty, game, team: 4, New England

# Chapter 15

# Analysis, predictions, results and betting 2017-2018

There are many forecasters including ourselves. The assumption is widespread that the New England Patriots will be dominant again and the Super Bowl 51 loser, the Atlanta Falcons, will not be as good this coming season and possibly not even make the playoffs. It is hard to repeat as Super Bowl but there have been two-peats but no three-peats. The Super Bowl loser usually does much worse. The following are *Sports Illustrated* forecasts made before the regular season by Andy Benoit for the season records, wild cards, divisional rounds, championship games in the AFC and NFC and Super Bowl 52 on February 4, 2018 at the US Bank Stadium in Minneapolis, Minnesota. In the post season, it lists the six teams in each conference he expects to be in the playoffs along with their seeds from 1 to 6, This comes from the four divisions of each conference with the teams ranked by their regular season record.

Danny Sheridan, a well known Las Vegas line maker the past 35 years, had the following S&P prediction published in *Cigar Aficionado*, October 2017, titled "Who will win the Super Bowl?".

Sheridan's Super Bowl 52 pick is the New England Patriots 31-NY Giants 29.

Sheridan's odds look like a list that you would find in a Las Vegas casino. He is a very experienced line-maker and these are set in such a way to create a market like one would have at the racetrack for a single winner. We know from the favorite-longshot bias that the favorites have a larger chance than quoted odds and longshots have less chance than their quoted

Table 15.1: Andy Benoit's predictions Super Bowl 52

**AFC POSTSEASON**

1. New England Patriots (14–2)
2. Pittsburgh Steelers (11–5)
3. Oakland Raiders (10–6)
4. Tennessee Titans (10–6)
5. Kansas City Chiefs (10–6)
6. Baltimore Ravens (9–7)

**Wild Card:** Ravens over Raiders, Chiefs over Titans

**Divisional Round:** Patriots over Ravens, Steelers over Chiefs

**Championship Game:** Patriots over Steeleers

**NFC POSTSEASON**

1. Atlanta Falcons (12–4)
2. Minnesota Vikings (11–5)
3. Seattle Seahawks (11–5)
4. New York Giants (10–6)
5. Green Bay Packers (11–5)
6. Tampa Bay Buccaneers (10–6)

**Wild Card:** Seahawks over Bucs, Packers over Giants

**Divisional Round:** Vikings over Seahawks, Packers over Falcons

**Championship Game:** Packers over Vikings

**SUPER BOWL LII**

*Feb. 4, 2018, U.S. Bank Stadium in Minneapolis*

**PATRIOTS 31, PACKERS 27**

odds. An alternative way to look at odds is to get the original line from Las Vegas casinos and that's reported below.

## Las Vegas original line

We can compute our own odds using some model like the Elo modified by player and coaching changes.

Following this are the Elo ratings done in two ways. First, John Swetye collaborating with the Radcliff Rebel and us rates the teams starting from 1000 each year. These values are shown week by week for the 17-week season with 16 games and the 2017-18 playoffs and Super Bowl. These ratings are contrasted with the Elo's from www.fivethirtyeight.com which blend the previous years standings with current performance. Chapter 5 has the Elo rating formulas and ideas.

Table 15.2: Danny Sheridan's prediction for the 2018 Super Bowl 52

| Favorites | Strong Possibilities | Have a chance | Longshots | Complete Bombs |
|---|---|---|---|---|
| New England 4-1 | Pittsburgh 12-1 | Carolina 25-1 | Houston 100-1 | LA Chargers 1 million-1 |
| Dallas 8-1 | Seattle 12-1 | Kansas City 25-1 | Indianapolis 100-1 | Jacksonville 5 million-1 |
| Green Bay 10-1 | Oakland 12-1 | Arizona 30-1 | Miami 200-1 | LA Rams 1 billion-1 |
| | Atlanta 15-1 | Denver 30-1 | Philadelphia 250-1 | Buffalo 1 trillion-1 |
| | NY Giant 15-1 | Tampa Bay 50-1 | New Orleans 250-1 | Chicago 1 quadrillion-1 |
| | | Minnesota 75-1 | Tennessee 300-1 | San Francisco 1 quintillion-1 |
| | | Baltimore 75-1 | Detroit 1000-1 | NY Jets 1 sextillion-1 |
| | | | Cinncinnati 5000-1 | Cleveland 1 googolplex-1 |
| | | | Washington 10000-1 | |

## The picks of the Radcliffe Rebels

The picks from a Montreal sports enthusiast group called the Radcliffe Rebels Office Football Pool each week are in bold boxes and on the left are the away teams with their season record up to that week and Las Vagas spread odds; on the right are the home teams with their season records and the spread and on far final right are the final scores of the games.

### Week 1

| Away | Home | | | Score |
|---|---|---|---|---|
| | | | **Thursday, September 07** | |
| Kansas City (4-0) +8.0 | **NEW ENGLAND (2-2) -8.0** | 12 | L | 42-27 |
| | | | **Sunday, September 10** | |
| Arizona (2-2) -2.5 | **DETROIT (3-1) +2.5** | 2 | W | 23-35 |
| **Philadelphia (3-1) -2.0** | WASHINGTON (2-2) +2.0 | 7 | W | 30-17 |
| **Atlanta (3-1) -6.5** | CHICAGO (1-3) +6.5 | 18 | W | 23-17 |
| NY Jets (2-2) +7.0 | **BUFFALO (3-1) -7.0** | 14 | W | 12-21 |
| Baltimore (2-2) +2.5 | **CINCINNATI (1-3) -2.5** | 13 | L | 20-0 |
| **Pittsburgh (3-1) -10.0** | CLEVELAND (0-4) +10.0 | 16 | W | 21-18 |
| **Jacksonville (2-2) +6.0** | HOUSTON (2-2) -6.0 | 3 | W | 29-7 |
| **Oakland (2-2) +2.5** | TENNESSEE (2-2) -2.5 | 6 | W | 26-16 |
| **Indianapolis (1-3) +3.5** | LA RAMS (3-1) -3.5 | 11 | L | 9-46 |
| Seattle (2-2) +2.5 | **GREEN BAY (3-1) -2.5** | 10 | W | 9-17 |
| **Carolina (3-1) -4.5** | SAN FRANCISCO (0-4) +4.5 | 8 | W | 23-3 |
| NY Giants (0-4) +6.0 | **DALLAS (2-2) -6.0** | 5 | W | 3-19 |
| | | | **Monday, September 11** | |
| **New Orleans (2-2) +3.0** | MINNESOTA (2-2) -3.0 | 9 | L | 19-29 |
| **LA Chargers (0-4) +3.0** | DENVER (3-1) -3.0 | 4 | L | 21-24 |

Win-Loss: 10-5, Points: 86.0

## Week 2

| | | | | |
|---|---|---|---|---|
| | | | Thursday, September 14 | |
| Houston (2-2) +5.5 | **CINCINNATI (1-3) -5.5** | 1 | L | 13-9 |
| | | | Sunday, September 17 | |
| **Arizona (2-2) -7.0** | INDIANAPOLIS (1-3) +7.0 | 2 | W | 16-13 |
| Philadelphia (3-1) +4.0 | **KANSAS CITY (4-0) -4.0** | 8 | W | 20-27 |
| Chicago (1-3) +7.0 | **TAMPA BAY (2-1) -7.0** | 10 | W | 7-29 |
| Minnesota (2-2) +8.5 | **PITTSBURGH (3-1) -8.5** | 6 | W | 9-26 |
| Buffalo (3-1) +6.5 | **CAROLINA (3-1) -6.5** | 14 | W | 3-9 |
| **New England (2-2) -5.5** | NEW ORLEANS (2-2) +5.5 | 4 | W | 36-20 |
| Cleveland (0-4) +7.5 | **BALTIMORE (2-2) -7.5** | 11 | W | 10-24 |
| **Tennessee (2-2) -1.0** | JACKSONVILLE (2-2) +1.0 | 7 | W | 37-16 |
| Miami (1-2) +3.5 | **LA CHARGERS (0-4) -3.5** | 12 | L | 19-17 |
| NY Jets (2-2) +14.0 | **OAKLAND (2-2) -14.0** | 16 | L | 20-45 |
| **Dallas (2-2) -2.5** | DENVER (3-1) +2.5 | 13 | L | 17-42 |
| San Francisco (0-4) +13.5 | **SEATTLE (2-2) -13.5** | 15 | W | 9-12 |
| **Washington (2-2) +3.0** | LA RAMS (3-1) -3.0 | 5 | W | 27-20 |
| Green Bay (3-1) +3.5 | **ATLANTA (3-1) -3.5** | 9 | W | 23-34 |
| | | | Monday, September 18 | |
| Detroit (3-1) +3.0 | **NY GIANTS (0-4) -3.0** | 3 | L | 24-10 |
| | | | Win-Loss: 12-4, Points: 107.0 | |

## Week 3

| | | | | |
|---|---|---|---|---|
| | | | Thursday, September 21 | |
| **LA Rams (3-1) -3.0** | SAN FRANCISCO (0-4) +3.0 | 2 | W | 41-39 |
| | | | Sunday, September 24 | |
| **Baltimore (2-2) -3.0** | Jacksonville (2-2) +3.0 | 11 | L | 7-44 |
| NY Giants (0-4) +5.0 | **PHILADELPHIA (3-1) -5.0** | 4 | W | 24-27 |
| **Pittsburgh (3-1) -7.0** | CHICAGO (1-3) +7.0 | 12 | L | 17-23 |
| Atlanta (3-1) -3.0 | **DETROIT (3-1) +3.0** | 5 | L | 30-26 |
| **Tampa Bay (2-1) +1.0** | MINNESOTA (2-2) -1.0 | 14 | L | 17-34 |
| New Orleans (2-2) +5.5 | **CAROLINA (3-1) -5.5** | 13 | L | 34-13 |
| **Denver (3-1) -3.5** | BUFFALO (3-1) +3.5 | 3 | L | 16-26 |
| Cleveland (0-4) +1.0 | **INDIANAPOLIS (1-3) -1.0** | 1 | W | 28-31 |
| **Miami (1-2) -5.5** | NY JETS (2-2) +5.5 | 8 | L | 6-20 |
| Houston (2-2) +13.5 | **NEW ENGLAND (2-2) -13.5** | 15 | W | 33-36 |
| Seattle (2-2) +2.0 | **TENNESSEE (2-2) -2.0** | 7 | W | 27-33 |
| Cincinnati (1-3) +7.0 | **GREEN BAY (3-1) -7.0** | 16 | W | 24-27 |
| **Kansas City (4-0) -3.0** | LA CHARGERS (0-4) +3.0 | 10 | W | 24-10 |
| **Oakland (2-2) -3.5** | WASHINGTON (2-2) +3.5 | 9 | L | 10-27 |
| | | | Monday, September 25 | |
| Dallas (2-2) -3.0 | **ARIZONA (2-2) +3.0** | 6 | L | 28-17 |
| | | | Win-Loss: 7-9, Points: 55.0 | |

Table 15.3: John Swetye's Week 4 Elos

| Team | Elo | Team | Elo |
|------|-----|------|-----|
| Arizona Cardinals | 993.7 | Los Angeles Chargers | 981.1 |
| Atlanta Falcons | 1010.7 | Los Angeles Rams | 1015.7 |
| Baltimore Ravens | 991.1 | Miami Dolphins | 984.8 |
| Buffalo Bills | 1013.1 | Minnesota Vikings | 1000.5 |
| Carolina Panthers | 1006.8 | New England Patriots | 999.4 |
| Chicago Bears | 981 | New Orleans Saints | 1005.8 |
| Cincinnati Bengals | 992 | New York Giants | 976.8 |
| Cleveland Browns | 972 | New York Jets | 996.4 |
| Dallas Cowboys | 998.4 | Oakland Raiders | 1001.5 |
| Denver Broncos | 1013 | Philadelphia Eagles | 1008.9 |
| Detroit Lions | 1014.5 | Pittsburgh Steelers | 1015 |
| Green Bay Packers | 1011.3 | San Francisco 49ers | 977.9 |
| Houston Texans | 1007.5 | Seattle Seahawks | 1004 |
| Indianapolis Colts | 973.3 | Tampa Bay Buccaneers | 1003.2 |
| Jacksonville Jaguars | 1009.6 | Tennessee Titans | 990.2 |
| Kansas City Chiefs | 1020.3 | Washington Redskins | 1007.7 |

## Week 4

Thursday, September 28

| Chicago (1-3) +7.5 | **GREEN BAY (3-1) -7.5** | 2 | W | 14-35 |

Sunday, October 01

| **New Orleans (2-2) -4.0** | Miami (1-2) +4.0 | 3 | W | 20-0 |
| LA Rams (3-1) +5.0 | **DALLAS (2-2) -5.0** | 12 | L | 35-30 |
| Detroit (3-1) +2.5 | **MINNESOTA (2-2) -2.5** | 4 | L | 14-7 |
| Buffalo (3-1) +8.0 | **ATLANTA (3-1) -8.0** | 14 | L | 23-17 |
| Carolina (3-1) +9.0 | **NEW ENGLAND (2-2) -9.0** | 16 | L | 33-30 |
| Jacksonville (2-2) -4.0 | **NY JETS (2-2) +4.0** | 8 | W | 20-23 |
| **Cincinnati (1-3) -3.0** | CLEVELAND (0-4) +3.0 | 1 | W | 31-7 |
| **Pittsburgh (3-1) -3.5** | BALTIMORE (2-2) +3.5 | 5 | W | 26-9 |
| Tennessee (2-2) -2.5 | **HOUSTON (2-2) +2.5** | 7 | W | 14-57 |
| San Francisco (0-4) +6.5 | **ARIZONA (2-2) -6.5** | 13 | W | 15-18 |
| NY Giants (0-4) +2.5 | **TAMPA BAY (2-1) -2.5** | 9 | W | 23-25 |
| **Philadelphia (3-1) +1.5** | LA CHARGERS (0-4) -1.5 | 11 | W | 26-24 |
| Oakland (2-2) +3.5 | **DENVER (3-1) -3.5** | 10 | W | 10-16 |
| Indianapolis (1-3) +12.5 | **SEATTLE (2-2) -12.5** | 6 | W | 18-46 |

Monday, October 02

| Washington (2-2) +6.5 | **KANSAS CITY (4-0) -6.5** | 15 | W | 20-29 |

Win-Loss: 12-4, Points: 90.0

# Week 5

| Road Home Favs Dogs Random Do Ranks | | Thursday, October 05 |
|---|---|---|

| New England (2-2) -4.5 | TAMPA BAY (2-1) +4.5 | 15 | 5:25 PM CBS |
|---|---|---|---|

Sunday, October 08

| Arizona (2-2) +6.5 | **PHILADELPHIA (3-1) -6.5** | 8 | 10:00 AM FOX |
|---|---|---|---|
| LA Chargers (0-4) +3.0 | **NY GIANTS (0-4) -3.0** | 8 | 10:00 AM CBS |
| Carolina (3-1) +2.5 | **DETROIT (3-1) -2.5** | 5 | 10:00 AM FOX |
| San Francisco (0-4) +1.5 | **INDIANAPOLIS (1-3) -1.5** | 10 | 10:00 AM FOX |
| **Buffalo (3-1) +3.0** | CINCINNATI (1-3) -3.0 | 7 | 10:00 AM CBS |
| Tennessee (2-2) -2.5 | **MIAMI (1-2) +2.5** | 6 | 10:00 AM CBS |
| **NY Jets (2-2) +0.0** | CLEVELAND (0-4) -0.0 | 11 | 10:00 AM FOX |
| Jacksonville (2-2) +8.5 | **PITTSBURGH (3-1) -8.5** | 13 | 10:00 AM CBS |
| **Seattle (2-2) +0.0** | LA RAMS (3-1) -0.0 | 4 | 1:05 PM CBS |
| Baltimore (2-2) +2.5 | **OAKLAND (2-2) -2.5** | 16 | 1:05 PM CBS |
| Green Bay (3-1) +2.5 | **DALLAS (2-2) -2.5** | 14 | 1:25 PM FOX |
| **Kansas City (4-0) -1.0** | HOUSTON (2-2) +1.0 | 12 | 5:30 PM NBC |

Monday, October 09

| **Minnesota (2-2) -2.5** | CHICAGO (1-3) +2.5 | 3 | 5:30 PM ESPN |
|---|---|---|---|

# Week 6

| Road Home Favs Dogs Random Do Ranks | | Thursday, October 12 |
|---|---|---|

| Philadelphia (4-1) +3.0 | **CAROLINA (4-1) -3.0** | 13 | 5:25 PM CBS |
|---|---|---|---|

Sunday, October 15

| Chicago (1-4) +6.5 | **BALTIMORE (3-2) -6.5** | 11 | 10:00 AM FOX |
|---|---|---|---|
| Detroit (3-2) +4.5 | **NEW ORLEANS (2-2) -4.5** | 9 | 10:00 AM FOX |
| **Green Bay (4-1) -3.0** | MINNESOTA (3-2) +3.0 | 6 | 10:00 AM FOX |
| Miami (2-2) +13.0 | **ATLANTA (3-1) -13.0** | 14 | 10:00 AM CBS |
| San Francisco (0-5) +11.0 | **WASHINGTON (2-2) -11.0** | 16 | 10:00 AM FOX |
| **New England (3-2) -9.5** | NY JETS (3-2) +9.5 | 10 | 10:00 AM CBS |
| Cleveland (0-5) +10.0 | **HOUSTON (2-3) -10.0** | 15 | 10:00 AM CBS |
| **Tampa Bay (2-2) -1.0** | ARIZONA (2-3) +1.0 | 4 | 1:05 PM FOX |
| LA Rams (3-2) +2.5 | **JACKSONVILLE (3-2) -2.5** | 5 | 1:05 PM FOX |
| Pittsburgh (3-2) +4.0 | **KANSAS CITY (5-0) -4.0** | 8 | 1:25 PM CBS |
| LA Chargers (1-4) +4.5 | **OAKLAND (2-3) -4.5** | 7 | 1:25 PM CBS |
| NY Giants (0-5) +11.5 | **DENVER (3-1) -11.5** | 12 | 5:30 PM NBC |

Monday, October 16

| Indianapolis (2-3) +6.5 | **TENNESSEE (2-3) -6.5** | 3 | 5:30 PM ESPN |
|---|---|---|---|

# Week 7

Road  Home  Favs  Dogs  Random  Do Ranks                          Thursday, October 19

| Kansas City (5-1) -3.0 | OAKLAND (2-4) +3.0 | 13 | 5:25 PM CBS |

                                                                  Sunday, October 22

| Arizona (3-3) +3.5 | LA Rams (4-2) -3.5 | 6 | 10:00 AM FOX London, England |
| Carolina (4-2) -3.0 | CHICAGO (2-4) +3.0 | 2 | 10:00 AM FOX |
| New Orleans (3-2) -4.0 | GREEN BAY (4-2) +4.0 | 14 | 10:00 AM FOX |
| Baltimore (3-3) +5.5 | MINNESOTA (4-2) -5.5 | 7 | 10:00 AM CBS |
| Tampa Bay (2-3) +2.5 | BUFFALO (3-2) -2.5 | 10 | 10:00 AM FOX |
| Jacksonville (3-3) -3.0 | INDIANAPOLIS (2-4) +3.0 | 5 | 10:00 AM CBS |
| NY Jets (3-3) +3.0 | MIAMI (3-2) -3.0 | 9 | 10:00 AM FOX |
| Tennessee (3-3) -5.5 | CLEVELAND (0-6) +5.5 | 16 | 10:00 AM CBS |
| Dallas (2-3) -6.0 | SAN FRANCISCO (0-6) +6.0 | 15 | 1:05 PM FOX |
| Seattle (3-2) -4.5 | NY GIANTS (1-5) +4.5 | 3 | 1:25 PM CBS |
| Cincinnati (2-3) +5.0 | PITTSBURGH (4-2) -5.0 | 4 | 1:25 PM CBS |
| Denver (3-2) +0.0 | LA CHARGERS (2-4) -0.0 | 8 | 1:25 PM CBS |
| Atlanta (3-2) +3.5 | NEW ENGLAND (4-2) -3.5 | 12 | 5:30 PM NBC |

                                                                  Monday, October 23

| Washington (3-2) +4.5 | PHILADELPHIA (6-1) -4.5 | 11 | 5:30 PM ESPN |

# Week 8

Road  Home  Favs  Dogs  Random  Do Ranks                          Thursday, October 26

| Miami (4-2) +3.0 | BALTIMORE (3-4) -3.0 | 4 | 5:25 PM CBS |

                                                                  Sunday, October 29

| Minnesota (5-2) -9.5 | Cleveland (0-7) +9.5 | 15 | 8:30 AM NFL London |
| San Francisco (0-7) +13.0 | PHILADELPHIA (6-1) -13.0 | 16 | 10:00 AM FOX |
| Chicago (3-4) +9.0 | NEW ORLEANS (4-2) -9.0 | 6 | 10:00 AM FOX |
| Carolina (4-3) +2.0 | TAMPA BAY (2-4) -2.0 | 7 | 10:00 AM FOX |
| Atlanta (3-3) -4.5 | NY JETS (3-4) +4.5 | 10 | 10:00 AM FOX |
| Oakland (3-4) +2.5 | BUFFALO (4-2) -2.5 | 5 | 10:00 AM CBS |
| Indianapolis (2-5) +11.0 | CINCINNATI (2-4) -11.0 | 11 | 10:00 AM CBS |
| LA Chargers (3-4) +7.5 | NEW ENGLAND (5-2) -7.5 | 14 | 10:00 AM CBS |
| Houston (3-3) +5.5 | SEATTLE (4-2) -5.5 | 9 | 1:05 PM CBS |
| Dallas (3-3) -1.5 | WASHINGTON (3-3) +1.5 | 8 | 1:25 PM FOX |
| Pittsburgh (5-2) -2.5 | DETROIT (3-3) +2.5 | 12 | 5:30 PM NBC |

                                                                  Monday, October 30

| Denver (3-3) +7.5 | KANSAS CITY (5-2) -7.5 | 13 | 8:30 PM ESPN |

## Week 9

| | | | | |
|---|---|---|---|---|
| League Picks For: | RADCLIFFE REBELS ▼ | | | |

| | | Thursday, November 02 | | |
|---|---|---|---|---|
| **Buffalo (5-3) -3.0** | NY JETS (4-5) +3.0 | | | 21-34 |

| | | Sunday, November 05 | |
|---|---|---|---|
| LA Rams (5-2) -7.0 | NY GIANTS (1-6) +6.0 | | |
| Denver (3-4) +7.0 | PHILADELPHIA (7-1) -7.0 | | |
| Tampa Bay (2-5) +7.0 | NEW ORLEANS (5-2) -7.0 | | |
| Atlanta (4-3) -3.0 | CAROLINA (5-3) +3.0 | | |
| Indianapolis (2-6) +6.0 | HOUSTON (3-4) -6.0 | | |
| Cincinnati (3-4) +6.0 | JACKSONVILLE (4-3) -6.0 | | |
| Baltimore (4-4) +3.0 | TENNESSEE (4-3) -3.0 | | |
| Arizona (3-4) -2.5 | SAN FRANCISCO (0-8) +2.5 | | |
| Washington (3-4) +8.5 | SEATTLE (5-2) -8.5 | | |
| Kansas City (6-2) +2.5 | DALLAS (4-3) -2.5 | | |
| Oakland (3-5) -3.0 | MIAMI (4-3) +3.0 | | |

| | | Monday, November 06 | |
|---|---|---|---|
| Detroit (3-4) +2.0 | GREEN BAY (4-3) +2.0 | | |
| | | | Win-Loss: 0-1, Points: 0.0 |

## Week 10

| | | Thursday, November 09 | | |
|---|---|---|---|---|
| **Seattle (5-3) -6.0** | ARIZONA (4-4) +6.0 | 15 | 8:25 PM NBC |

| | | Sunday, November 12 | | |
|---|---|---|---|---|
| Green Bay (4-4) +6.0 | **CHICAGO (3-5) -6.0** | 14 | 10:00 AM FOX |
| Cleveland (0-8) +10.5 | **DETROIT (4-4) -10.5** | 16 | 10:00 AM CBS |
| Minnesota (6-2) -1.5 | **WASHINGTON (4-4) +1.5** | 9 | 10:00 AM FOX |
| **NY Jets (4-5) -2.5** | TAMPA BAY (2-6) +2.5 | 7 | 10:00 AM CBS |
| **New Orleans (6-2) -2.5** | BUFFALO (5-3) +2.5 | 12 | 10:00 AM FOX |
| **Pittsburgh (6-2) -10.0** | INDIANAPOLIS (3-6) +10.0 | 6 | 10:00 AM CBS |
| Cincinnati (3-5) +4.5 | **TENNESSEE (5-3) -4.5** | 10 | 10:00 AM FOX |
| **LA Chargers (3-5) +3.5** | JACKSONVILLE (5-3) -3.5 | 8 | 10:00 AM CBS |
| Houston (3-5) +11.0 | **LA RAMS (6-2) -11.0** | 5 | 1:05 PM CBS |
| **Dallas (5-3) +3.0** | ATLANTA (4-4) -3.0 | 3 | 1:25 PM FOX |
| **NY Giants (1-7) -2.5** | SAN FRANCISCO (0-9) +2.5 | 4 | 1:25 PM FOX |
| **New England (6-2) -7.0** | DENVER (3-5) +7.0 | 13 | 5:30 PM NBC |

| | | Monday, November 13 | | |
|---|---|---|---|---|
| Miami (4-4) +9.0 | **CAROLINA (6-3) -9.0** | 11 | 5:30 PM ESPN |

## The standings going into week 10 were:

### NFL
#### Standings

| American Football Conference | | | | National Football Conference | | | | | | |
|---|---|---|---|---|---|---|---|---|---|---|
| **AFC East** | W | L | T | Pct | PF | PA | Home | Away | Strk |
| Patriots | 7 | 2 | 0 | .778 | 257 | 195 | 3-2-0 | 4-0-0 | W5 |
| Bills | 5 | 4 | 0 | .556 | 184 | 196 | 4-1-0 | 1-3-0 | L2 |
| Dolphins | 4 | 4 | 0 | .500 | 116 | 179 | 2-2-0 | 2-2-0 | L2 |
| Jets | 4 | 6 | 0 | .400 | 201 | 222 | 3-2-0 | 1-4-0 | L1 |
| **AFC West** | W | L | T | Pct | PF | PA | Home | Away | Strk |
| Chiefs | 6 | 3 | 0 | .667 | 253 | 208 | 3-1-0 | 3-2-0 | L1 |
| Raiders | 4 | 5 | 0 | .444 | 196 | 214 | 2-2-0 | 2-3-0 | W1 |
| Chargers | 3 | 6 | 0 | .333 | 167 | 172 | 1-3-0 | 2-3-0 | L2 |
| Broncos | 3 | 6 | 0 | .333 | 166 | 239 | 3-2-0 | 0-4-0 | L5 |
| **AFC North** | W | L | T | Pct | PF | PA | Home | Away | Strk |
| Steelers | 7 | 2 | 0 | .778 | 187 | 148 | 2-1-0 | 5-1-0 | W4 |
| Ravens | 4 | 5 | 0 | .444 | 190 | 171 | 2-2-0 | 2-3-0 | L1 |
| Bengals | 3 | 6 | 0 | .333 | 149 | 182 | 2-2-0 | 1-4-0 | L2 |
| Browns | 0 | 9 | 0 | .000 | 143 | 240 | 0-5-0 | 0-4-0 | L9 |
| **AFC South** | W | L | T | Pct | PF | PA | Home | Away | Strk |
| Titans | 6 | 3 | 0 | .667 | 205 | 213 | 4-1-0 | 2-2-0 | W4 |
| Jaguars | 6 | 3 | 0 | .667 | 226 | 134 | 3-2-0 | 3-1-0 | W3 |
| Texans | 3 | 6 | 0 | .333 | 236 | 241 | 2-3-0 | 1-3-0 | L3 |
| Colts | 3 | 7 | 0 | .300 | 179 | 280 | 2-3-0 | 1-4-0 | L1 |

The season is getting into full gear with many injuries, replacements and teams getting it together. The Thursday night game was a thriller, pitting the 5-1 Kansas City Chiefs against the 2-4 Oakland Raiders in Oakland. The Chiefs were a 3 point favorite and our Montreal picker favored Kansas City straight up with no points. Both quarterbacks Alex Smith of the Chiefs and Derek Carr of the Raiders were very sharp. Near the end of the game, Kansas City had a 30-24 lead with both teams making spectacular passing plays. Oakland had the ball and Carr drove them close to TD range but on the final play of the game, his pass was missed and time ran out. But there was a penalty by the defense and the NFL rules say that Oakland would then be allowed one more play. That failed too and again there was a defensive penalty so Oakland was given a third chance. This time Carr completed a TD pass and with a successful extra point they won 31-30. Kansas City is now 5-2 and Oakland 3-4. The Montreal picker lost the game but could have gained betting throughout the game because of much mean reversion.

The Sunday night game was a rematch of Super Bowl 51. Recall Atlanta got 25 points ahead but a Tom Brady led offense reared back and won the game. The evidence is that Super Bowl losing teams have poor following years and often do not even make the playoffs. The game was in Foxborough where the Patriots have a huge home field advantage. Last year's Atlanta team was a tremendous powerhouse especially on offense. Despite Tom Brady's record setting 28 TD to 2 interceptions, Matt Ryan was the league MVP.

New England was 4-2 and a 3.5 point favorite over the 3-2 Atlanta team. This year, despite predictions of a perfect season and at least a large dominance, the Patriots have survived some close battles and lost 2 games. Their defense was shaky. The master coach, Bill Belichick, is very good at regrouping and fixing problems. This supposedly tough matchup turned into a rout. New England had 2 Brady TDs plus 3 Stephen Gostkowski field goals to lead the entire game. Finally a Ryan pass to star receiver Julio Jones gave a TD to make the final score 23-7. The Patriots were sharp on offense as usual, with Brady having no interceptions but this time the defense was topnotch as well. So one is left with the feeling that the Patriots look destined for another Super Bowl appearance and Atlanta was not looking like the strong team of last year. We will see if they make the playoffs, their 3-3 record is not a good start. The Montreal picker got this game correct.

The 3-2 Denver Broncos and the 2-4 Los Angeles Chargers met in Los Angeles. Given a weak QB and Denver on the road, the Las Vegas line was even despite Denver's superior defense. The game was one-sided with Trevor Simian having fumbles and tip passes into interceptions. Travis Benjamin ran for one 46 yard punt for a TD and 42 yard pass from the very sharp Philip Rivers. Joey Boza continued to shine on defense with two sacks. The game ended 21-0 so the Chargers are now 3-4 and the Broncos 3-3. Denver's QB woes continue for expect John Elway to do something. The Montreal picker got this game right as well.

The 3-2 Seattle Seahawks were on the road to meet the 1-5 New York Giants and were favored by 4.5 points despite the jet lag effect of west coast teams going east crossing two or more time zones. Seattle looked good and had a relatively clean game except for a Rawl's fumble that lead to a Manning TD. Russell Wilson had 3 TD passes to Doug Baldwin, Jimmie Graham and Paul Richardson. Richardson's TD was on a spectacular long pass that he and the NY Giant defender fought for, but he ultimately came up with the ball. Seattle won 24-7 to become 4-2 while the Giants now 1-6 seem out of the playoffs already. The Montreal picker got the game right.

With Aaron Rogers injured on a dubious play that seemed illegal to us, the 4-2 Green Bay Packers were a 4 point underdog at home against the 3-2 New Orleans Saints who historically do not play well in cold stadiums.

After Week 9, the AFC leaders were as expected: New England in the east; Tennessee and Jacksonville in the south; Pittsburgh in the north and Kansas City in the west. Denver looks hopeless without a better quarterback. Oakland has been disappointing at 4-5. Cleveland is completely hopeless having lost all its games. Houston and Indianapolis are doing poorly due to injuries to JJ Watt and Andrew Luck among others. Tom Brady is having his usual brilliant year.

In the NFC, the leaders are more surprising. The top team is Philadelphia (8-1). The NY Giants are a woeful 1-7 and their coach might be fired soon. Last year's Super Bowl loser Atlanta (5-4) trails Carolina (6-3) and the Drew Brees led New Orleans was (7-2). An early injury to Aaron Rogers has derailed Green Bay (5-4) who were trailing Minnesota (7-2). The biggest surprise is the LA Rams who have turned a terrific defense and young quarterback Jared Goff into a 7-2 team leading the west above Seattle (6-3).

**The NFL standings going into week 11 were:**

NFL

**American Conference**

| East | W | L | T | Pct | PF | PA |
|------|---|---|---|-----|----|----|
| New England | 8 | 2 | 0 | .800 | 290 | 203 |
| Buffalo | 5 | 5 | 0 | .500 | 208 | 250 |
| Miami | 4 | 6 | 0 | .400 | 157 | 254 |
| N.Y. Jets | 4 | 6 | 0 | .400 | 201 | 222 |

| South | W | L | T | Pct | PF | PA |
|-------|---|---|---|-----|----|----|
| Jacksonville | 7 | 3 | 0 | .700 | 245 | 141 |
| Tennessee | 6 | 4 | 0 | .600 | 222 | 253 |
| Houston | 4 | 6 | 0 | .400 | 267 | 262 |
| Indianapolis | 3 | 7 | 0 | .300 | 179 | 280 |

| North | W | L | T | Pct | PF | PA |
|-------|---|---|---|-----|----|----|
| Pittsburgh | 8 | 2 | 0 | .800 | 227 | 165 |
| Baltimore | 5 | 5 | 0 | .500 | 213 | 171 |
| Cincinnati | 4 | 6 | 0 | .400 | 169 | 199 |
| Cleveland | 0 | 10 | 0 | .000 | 150 | 259 |

| West | W | L | T | Pct | PF | PA |
|------|---|---|---|-----|----|----|
| Kansas City | 6 | 4 | 0 | .600 | 262 | 220 |
| L.A. Chargers | 4 | 6 | 0 | .400 | 221 | 196 |
| Oakland | 4 | 6 | 0 | .400 | 204 | 247 |
| Denver | 3 | 7 | 0 | .300 | 183 | 259 |

**National Conference**

| East | W | L | T | Pct | PF | PA |
|------|---|---|---|-----|----|----|
| Philadelphia | 9 | 1 | 0 | .900 | 320 | 188 |
| Dallas | 5 | 5 | 0 | .500 | 242 | 242 |
| Washington | 4 | 6 | 0 | .400 | 238 | 266 |
| N.Y. Giants | 2 | 8 | 0 | .200 | 162 | 247 |

| South | W | L | T | Pct | PF | PA |
|-------|---|---|---|-----|----|----|
| New Orleans | 8 | 2 | 0 | .800 | 302 | 196 |
| Carolina | 7 | 3 | 0 | .700 | 213 | 180 |
| Atlanta | 6 | 4 | 0 | .600 | 231 | 210 |
| Tampa Bay | 4 | 6 | 0 | .400 | 203 | 228 |

| North | W | L | T | Pct | PF | PA |
|-------|---|---|---|-----|----|----|
| Minnesota | 8 | 2 | 0 | .800 | 241 | 172 |
| Detroit | 6 | 4 | 0 | .600 | 271 | 234 |
| Green Bay | 5 | 5 | 0 | .500 | 204 | 230 |
| Chicago | 3 | 7 | 0 | .300 | 174 | 221 |

| West | W | L | T | Pct | PF | PA |
|------|---|---|---|-----|----|----|
| L.A. Rams | 7 | 3 | 0 | .700 | 303 | 186 |
| Seattle | 6 | 4 | 0 | .600 | 242 | 199 |
| Arizona | 4 | 6 | 0 | .400 | 176 | 254 |
| San Francisco | 1 | 9 | 0 | .100 | 174 | 260 |

| | | | |
|---|---|---|---|
| | | | **Thursday, November 16** |
| Tennessee (6-3) +7.0 | PITTSBURGH (7-2) -7.0 | 3 | 5:25 PM NBC |
| | | | **Sunday, November 19** |
| **Arizona (4-5) +2.0** | HOUSTON (3-6) -2.0 | 10 | 10:00 AM FOX |
| **Kansas City (6-3) -10.0** | NY GIANTS (1-8) +10.0 | 16 | 10:00 AM CBS |
| **Detroit (5-4) -3.0** | CHICAGO (3-6) +3.0 | 9 | 10:00 AM FOX |
| **Baltimore (4-5) -2.0** | GREEN BAY (5-4) +2.0 | 6 | 10:00 AM CBS |
| LA Rams (7-2) +2.5 | **MINNESOTA (7-2) -2.5** | 12 | 10:00 AM FOX |
| Washington (4-5) +7.5 | **NEW ORLEANS (7-2) -7.5** | 11 | 10:00 AM FOX |
| **Jacksonville (6-3) -8.0** | CLEVELAND (0-9) +8.0 | 13 | 10:00 AM CBS |
| **Tampa Bay (3-6) +0.0** | MIAMI (4-5) -0.0 | 8 | 10:00 AM FOX |
| Buffalo (5-4) +4.5 | **LA CHARGERS (3-6) -4.5** | 7 | 1:05 PM FOX |
| **New England (7-2) -7.0** | Oakland (4-5) +7.0 | 14 | 1:25 PM CBS Mexico City |
| Cincinnati (3-6) +2.5 | **DENVER (3-6) -2.5** | 5 | 1:25 PM CBS |
| **Philadelphia (8-1) -4.0** | DALLAS (5-4) +4.0 | 15 | 5:30 PM NBC |
| | | | **Monday, November 20** |
| **Atlanta (5-4) +2.5** | SEATTLE (6-3) -2.5 | 4 | 5:30 PM ESPN |

The Radcliffe Rebels won 11 of the 14 games picked. The losers were
Houston beating Arizona, Cincinnati beating Denver and the NY Giants
beating Kansas City.

Table 15.4: John Swetye's Week 11 Elos

| Team | Elo | Team | Elo |
|---|---|---|---|
| Arizona Cardinals | 977.6 | Los Angeles Chargers | 990.1 |
| Atlanta Falcons | 1008.3 | Los Angeles Rams | 1045.7 |
| Baltimore Ravens | 1000 | Miami Dolphins | 977.6 |
| Buffalo Bills | 996.8 | Minnesota Vikings | 1027.9 |
| Carolina Panthers | 1008.9 | New England Patriots | 1031.2 |
| Chicago Bears | 979.8 | New Orleans Saints | 1044.2 |
| Cincinnati Bengals | 980.2 | New York Giants | 955.5 |
| Cleveland Browns | 945.6 | New York Jets | 988 |
| Dallas Cowboys | 1008.6 | Oakland Raiders | 988.9 |
| Denver Broncos | 969.2 | Philadelphia Eagles | 1043.8 |
| Detroit Lions | 1009.7 | Pittsburgh Steelers | 1025 |
| Green Bay Packers | 998.6 | San Francisco 49ers | 952.9 |
| Houston Texans | 988.3 | Seattle Seahawks | 1019.9 |
| Indianapolis Colts | 961.9 | Tampa Bay Buccaneers | 978.7 |
| Jacksonville Jaguars | 1031.6 | Tennessee Titans | 1003.9 |
| Kansas City Chiefs | 1019.4 | Washington Redskins | 990.8 |

I bet on five Sunday games, all favorites. The bets were as follows:

1. $205.76 at 1.243 odds on the Kansas City Chiefs (6-3) whose Elo was 1010.94 against the NY Giants (1-8) (Elo 955.5). Kansas City was a 10 point favorite. The game was close all the way till the end with both teams' defenses superb. Late in the 4th quarter the Giants led 9-6 and had moved ahead on field goal from the 6-6 tie. Then KC scored a field goal with little time remaining to send the game into overtime. KC got the ball first but could not score. NYG then got another of those spectacular Eli Manning passes that he is famous for. This time, on a 34 yard 4th down pass that Roger Lewis Jr caught while falling down on the ground. Then Aldrick Rosas kicked a 23 yard field goal to win the game 12-9. So the Giants are now 2-8 and the Chief 6-4 and I lost the wager.

2. $200 on New England Patriots (7-2) (Elo 1031.2) at 1,388 odds was against the Oakland Raiders (4-5) (Elo 988.9). New England was a 7 point favorite. The game was played in the historic 7200 foot high Estadio Aztica in Mexico City, the site of the 1970 and 1986 World Cups. This famous stadium, built in 1966, was filled to capacity with ecstatic fans. I recall two trips to Mexico in 1967 and 1994. The first was to speak at a Management Conference when I was still a graduate student. On the second occasion I gave a 4 day course at the Mexican Bolza (stock exchange) joint with Doug Stone, a Frank Russell colleague. Close by are the pyramids including the famous pyramid of the Sun which were in the countryside then and now are all city with Mexico City's population of 30 million reaching all the way here.

Tom Brady has been playing at an MVP level with 47 TDs and just 4 interceptions the past two seasons. Last year, he missed four games because of the dubious deflategate suspensions but has played in all 10 games this year so far. The Patriots stayed in 5200 foot high Denver following last week's game against the Denver Broncos to acclimate to the Mexico City altitude. Brady and the Patriots started out strong and were sharp all the game. Brady was 9-9 in the first TD drive which included a 52 yard pass to Brandon Cooks. Then a pass to Rob Gronkowski, the NFL's second leading receiver, got them to the 3 yard line and Danny Amendola scored the second TD to make it 14-0. Oakland used "Beastmode" Marshan Lynch for an effective 50 yards rushing on 7 carries and finished game 67 yards in 11 carries. One run for 25 yards was his longest since 2014. Brady kept going to Cooks who had 6 catches for 149 yards. The onslaught continued and Brady became the first quarterback with over 300 yards passing in three different countries with 339 in this game. The New England field goal kicker Stephen Gostkowski made 3 from 62, 51 and 40 yards. The rout became 30-0 and the game ended 33-8. Brady had 3 TDs and no interceptions. The Patriots look sharp and ready for another Super Bowl run. The Raiders, badly outclassed did not look good and are now 4-8 versus the Patriots (8-2). The fans were excited and the NFL is planning to have a game in Mexico City for at least the next 3 years.

I won the bet and gained $77.60.

3. $200 at 1.628 on the Detroit Lions (5-4) (Elo 1009.7) and a 3 point favorite against the Chicago Bears (3-6) (Elo 979.8). Detroit was led by quarterback Mathew Stafford who threw for 2 TDs and no interceptions, completing 21 of 31 for 299 yards. The Bears' field goal kicker Connor Barth missed a 46 yarder near the end of the game which would have sent it into overtime. Detroit has gone ahead with 1:35 to go on a 52 yard field goal by Mat Prater. The Lions won 27-24 so I won my bet and gained $125.60.

4. $200 at 1.277 on the New Orleans Saints (7-2) (Elo 1044.2) at home against the Washington Redskins (4-5) (Elo 990.8). The Saints have had for many years one of the top quarterbacks, Drew Brees. This year they have had a more balanced attack, focusing much on runs from Mark Ingram who gained 131 yards in this game. The Saints rallied from 15 down to tie the game. But it took a stop of Samaje Perine on 3rd and 1 at the 2 minute warning to send it into overtime otherwise Washington would have gotten the first down and been able to run out the clock and win the game. Brees passed for 2 TDs and 385 yards but it was Ingram's 20 and 31 back to back carries in overtime to set up Will Lutz's winning 28 yard field goal that won the game at 34-31. I won my bet and gained $55.40.

5. $200 at 1.318 on the Jacksonville Jaguars (6-3) (Elo 1031.6) against the hapless 8 point underdog Cleveland Browns (0-9) (Elo 945.6). Jacksonville won the game 19-7. I won my bet gaining $63.60.

In total I gained $116.44. I did not use mean reversion. New Orleans looked beaten but came back from the 15 point deficit. I should have bet more on the two most likely winning teams, namely New England with the Brady machine and Jacksonville playing a much weaker team. But it was a gain on the week.

Other games I did not bet on were:

1. The Sunday night game was between the Philadelphia Eagles (8-1) (Elo 1008.6) and the Dallas Cowboys (5-4) (Elo 1043.8). Dallas was missing star running Ezekiel Elliott who was suspended for six games for alleged spousal abuse. The running game replacement Alfred Morris gained 91 yards. Their defense was weakened by the absence of left tackle Tyron Smith. Quarterback Zak Prescott had a poor game with 3 interceptions and only 143 passing yards.

   I knew that the addition of LaGarett Blount would help the Eagles and be a huge loss for the Patriots. In my view, this was a real dumb move by Belichick. Besides Blount, the Eagles have Corey Clement, Kenjon Barner and Jay Ajayi. Blount had 18 Patriots TD last year and Ajayi had three 200+ yard gains. Blount, much like Marshan Lynch, is terrific at those 1 yard TD runs. Together the four runners gained 215 yards. Meanwhile, quarterback Carson Wentz has had 25 TD passes already including 2 in this game. After a slow first half, the well balanced Eagles won the game 37-9.

2. The Monday night game in Seattle had the Seahawks (6-3) (Elo 1019.9) hosting the Atlanta Hawks (5-4) (Elo 1008.3). Seattle's famed legion of doom defensive secondary was depleted because of injuries Richard Sherman and Cam Chancellor. Shaquill Griffin, Oday Oboushi and Mike David were injured during the game. The Seahawks have never recovered their ground game once Marshan Lynch retired and then unretired to join the Oakland Raiders. Their offense relies mostly on the passing and scrambling of Russell Wilson. Also they seem to make many strategic errors. The famous 2015 Super Bowl interception, with 26 seconds left in the game when they were on the one yard line and decided not to run Lynch three times but rather to pass. This interception cost them the Super Bowl. We discuss the impact of this decision in the final chapter.

   The game with Atlanta, had a number of strategic errors.

I made the following bets on Week 12 games:

1. Philadelphia a 13.5 favorite over Chicago. I bet $420.17 at 1.119:1 and won $50 when they won 31-3

2. Atlanta a 9.5 favorite over Tampa Bay. I bet $225.23 at 1.222:1 and won $50 when they won 34-20

3. Carolina a 5.0 favorite over NY Jets. I bet $200 at 1.1434 and won $86.80 when they won 35-27

4. Kansas City a 9.5 favorite over Buffalo. I bet $215.52 at 1.232:1 and lost the bet when they lost 10-16

5. New England a 16.5 favorite over Miami. I bet $657.89 at 1.076:1 and won $50 when they won 35-17

6. Cincinnati a 8.5 favorite over Cleveland. I bet $200 at 1.27:1 and won $54 when they won 30-16

7. Seattle a 6.5 favorite over San Francisco. I bet $200 at 1.363:1 and won $72.60 when they won 24-13

8. Pittsburgh a 15.0 favorite over Green Bay. I bet $450.45 at 1.11:1 and won $50 when they won 31-28

I won 7 of the eight bets and $192.

## Week 12 Highlights

| | | | | |
|---|---|---|---|---|
| | | | | **Thursday, November 23** |
| Minnesota (9-2) -2.5 | **DETROIT (6-5) +2.5** | | L | 30-23 |
| **LA Chargers (5-6) -1.0** | DALLAS (5-6) +1.0 | | W | 28-6 |
| NY Giants (2-9) +7.0 | **WASHINGTON (5-6) -7.0** | | W | 10-20 |
| | | | | **Sunday, November 26** |
| Chicago (3-7) +13.5 | **PHILADELPHIA (9-1) -13.5** | 16 | | 10:00 AM FOX |
| Tampa Bay (4-6) +10.0 | **ATLANTA (6-4) -10.0** | 15 | | 10:00 AM FOX |
| **Carolina (7-3) -5.5** | NY JETS (4-6) +5.5 | 14 | | 10:00 AM FOX |
| Buffalo (5-5) +8.0 | **KANSAS CITY (6-4) -8.0** | 13 | | 10:00 AM CBS |
| Tennessee (6-4) -3.5 | **INDIANAPOLIS (3-7) +3.5** | 4 | | 10:00 AM CBS |
| Miami (4-6) +16.5 | **NEW ENGLAND (8-2) -16.5** | 12 | | 10:00 AM CBS |
| Cleveland (0-10) +7.5 | **CINCINNATI (4-6) -7.5** | 11 | | 10:00 AM CBS |
| **Seattle (6-4) -6.5** | SAN FRANCISCO (1-9) +6.5 | 10 | | 1:05 PM FOX |
| **Jacksonville (7-3) -6.0** | ARIZONA (4-6) +6.0 | 9 | | 1:25 PM CBS |
| **New Orleans (8-2) +2.5** | LA RAMS (7-3) -2.5 | 5 | | 1:25 PM FOX |
| Denver (3-7) +3.5 | **OAKLAND (4-6) -3.5** | 3 | | 1:25 PM CBS |
| Green Bay (5-5) +13.5 | **PITTSBURGH (8-2) -13.5** | 7 | | 5:30 PM NBC |
| | | | | **Monday, November 27** |
| Houston (4-6) +7.5 | **BALTIMORE (5-5) -7.5** | 3 | | 5:30 PM ESPN |

## The Power Ratings are now:

1. Patriots 10-2

2. Eagles 10-2

3. Vikings 10-2

4. Steelers 10-2

5. Rams 9-3

6. Saints 9-3

7. Jaguars 8-4

8. Seahawks 8-4

9. Panthers 8-4

10. Chargers 6-6

11. Falcons 7-5

## Week 13 Highlights

| | | | Thursday, November 30 |
|---|---|---|---|
| **Washington (5-6) -1.5** | DALLAS (5-6) +1.5 | 9 | 5:25 PM NBC |

| | | | Sunday, December 03 |
|---|---|---|---|
| San Francisco (1-10) +3.5 | CHICAGO (3-8) -3.5 | 8 | 10:00 AM CBS |
| Detroit (6-5) +3.0 | BALTIMORE (6-5) -3.0 | 10 | 10:00 AM FOX |
| Tampa Bay (4-7) +2.0 | GREEN BAY (5-6) -2.0 | 6 | 10:00 AM FOX |
| Minnesota (9-2) +3.0 | ATLANTA (7-4) -3.0 | 1 | 10:00 AM FOX |
| New England (9-2) -8.5 | BUFFALO (6-5) +8.5 | 16 | 10:00 AM CBS |
| Indianapolis (3-8) +9.5 | JACKSONVILLE (7-4) -9.5 | 15 | 10:00 AM CBS |
| Denver (3-8) -1.5 | MIAMI (4-7) +1.5 | 3 | 10:00 AM CBS |
| **Kansas City (6-5) -3.0** | NY JETS (4-7) +3.0 | 5 | 10:00 AM CBS |
| Houston (4-7) +6.5 | TENNESSEE (7-4) -6.5 | 14 | 10:00 AM CBS |
| Cleveland (0-11) +13.5 | LA CHARGERS (5-6) -13.5 | 13 | 1:05 PM CBS |
| **LA Rams (8-3) -7.0** | ARIZONA (5-6) +7.0 | 11 | 1:25 PM FOX |
| NY Giants (2-9) +9.0 | OAKLAND (5-6) -9.0 | 12 | 1:25 PM FOX |
| Carolina (8-3) +4.5 | NEW ORLEANS (8-3) -4.5 | 4 | 1:25 PM FOX |
| **Philadelphia (10-1) -5.5** | SEATTLE (7-4) +5.5 | 7 | 5:30 PM NBC |

| | | | Monday, December 04 |
|---|---|---|---|
| **Pittsburgh (9-2) -4.5** | CINCINNATI (5-6) +4.5 | 2 | 5:30 PM ESPN |

The big event was the benching of NY Giants quarterback Eli Manning and the firing of coach Ben McAdoo and the general manager Jerry Reese. The Giants were 2-10. Who was to blame? They spent over $200 million on the defensive line who were outstanding last year but not this year. Well, Manning, who had a record of 210 straight starts in 14 years, second only to Brett Favres' record 290, was not really playing poorly. He had, in 2017, 14 TDs and 7 INTs and a 84.1 QB rating, similar to his historical record. He lost five of eight fumbles versus 46 in the previous 13 years, about 3.5 per year. So that was not unusual. He was Walter Payton Man of the Year in 2016 and a two time Super Bowl MVP. He held the record for the most fourth quarter TDs passed in a season until it was broken by Seattle quarterback Russell Wilson. Manning had an 84 quarterback career rating with 334 TDs and 221 INTs and 4287 completions in 7158 attempts (59.9%). So he has historically been one of the best NFL quarterbacks.

McAdoo decided to bench Manning, offering him the option of starting the game to keep the streak going. That would involve Gino Smith replacing Manning, possibly in the second half. Manning refused. Then McAdoo, with the agreement of NY Giants president and CEO John Mora, just benched Manning. Defensive coach Steve Magnola is taking over as interim coach.

The fans did not like that. Of course, it is not clear that Gino Smith would be better as Eli was performing ok but not spectacular. So the mess ended with McAdoo and Reese going and Mora explaining the action. Mora was very professional and stated that both McAdoo and Reese were also professional but he admitted that they had messed up and wholesale changes were needed. McAdoo and Reese have a long history with the team. Many of the fans are wearing NY Giants quarterback jerseys and are behind Manning. Look for a big game on his return against the Dallas Cowboys.

**The top games were:**

- Philadelphia (10-1) at Seattle. Seattle was a 5.5 underdog despite home field advantage against the NFL's highest rated team in terms of record. All year the Seattle offense has relied on Russell Wilson who has put on an MVP type performance. In this game, he had 3 TDs and was 20 of 31 passing for 2227 yards. His 15 fourth quarter TDs tied Eli Manning's record. Wilson has generated over 80% of the Seattle offense and was involved with 29 of their 30 TDs this year; 3 were running and 26 were passes. Behind Wilson and Doug Baldwin who had 5 catches for 84 yards, Seattle won the game 23-10.

## The meeting of the top two 2015 quarterback picks

It is rare that the top two picks in the NFL draft meet. We have had Andrew Luck and RG3 and now we have Jared Goff versus Carson Wentz.

In 2017 Philadelphia was 10-2 after their loss to Seattle and Wentz had 28 TDs against 5 INTs with a 104 quarterback rating, with 2 fumbles lost in the 12 games played in the year so far. In his rookie year in 2016, Philadelphia was 7-9 and Wentz had 16 TD against 14 INTs with a 79.3 quarterback rating. He set the NFL record of 379 completions by a rookie quarterback.

Jared Goff, the # 1 pick in 2015 above Wentz, played at my PhD alma mater, the University of California, Berkeley. He was a junior and dropped out of his senior year to enter the NFL. In 2017, in the 12 games so far, he has 25 TDs to 13 INTs with an 85.6 quarterback rating. Cal was 8-5 in his last year but was 0-9 against division rivals Stanford, UCLA and USC and a 0-3 against division rival Oregon. Still he was thought to be the top US quarterback. He was the first true freshman to start a Cal season opener. He set 26 Cal records and was second only to Aaron Rodgers in passing efficiency with a very high 144. In his junior year he had 43 TDs, 13 INTs and was the number 1 pick of the St Louis Rams who have become the LA Rams. The Rams, under Goff's leadership, are 9-3. He had a 62.2 completion record with 20 TDs and 6 INTs. In his rookie year they were 0-7. This year he has blossomed into top QB.

Russell Wilson is being touted as an MVP in competition with Tom Brady and Carson Wentz, which we discuss later. Wentz and Jared Goff, the second and first picks in the 2015 draft, were playing like the number 1 and 2 picks. They are facing off in week 14. Wentz, the second pick, was at North Dakota State, where he had an 88.2 quarterback rating, rushing for 2 TDs with 45 passing TDs to 20 INTs with a 61.7% completion record on 67.87 yards gained.

## Marshan Lynch

Marshan Lynch is back having gained over 100 yards last week for the Oakland Raiders. After helping Seattle win Super Bowl 48 against the Denver Broncos and not being used in the controversial play that led to New England winning Super Bowl 49, he retired and then unretired and then was traded to the Raiders in April 2017. This was a huge loss for Seattle and is part of the reason why Russell Wilson is over 80% of the Seattle offense.

In high school, Lynch was spectacular in football, baseball, track and wrestling. In football running he was ranked #2 only behind Adrian Peterson. He excelled in the 100 meter dash, high jump and in football, where he played quarterback, wide receiver and line backer in addition to his running, which was outstanding, including 1722 rushing yards and 23 TDs in 8 games and 375 yards and 10 TDs in two post season games. His college record at Cal was also outstanding, averaging 6.6 yards per carry with 29 TDs in 55 games. In the 2005 Las Vegas Bowl, he ran for 194 yards and 3 TDs in 24 carries and was named MVP. He set many records and was on the 2006 all pack 10 first team and was the pack 10 offensive player of 2006. He dropped out of his senior year and was drafted by the Buffalo Bills as the 12th pick in round 1. He started out with a six year $18.925 million contract with $10 million guaranteed and a $3 million signing bonus. In his rookie year, he had 7 TDs and 1115 yards. Then in 2008 he had 8 TDs and 1036 yards and over 300 yards receiving.

In the 2009 off season, he had a misdemeanor weapons charge because he had a gun in a back pack which is illegal in California. He was suspended for 3 games. He played in 2009 but was replaced by Fred Jackson, who gained over 1000 yards. Meanwhile, Lynch only gained 450 yards on 120 carries and had no 100 yard gains. In 2010, he had an ankle sprain and was then traded to Seattle. In his first career playoff game on January 8, 2011 against the New Orleans Saints, he had a spectacular 67 yard run, breaking 9 tackles and with one arm, through Saint's cornerback Tracy Porter to the ground. The play was called "beastmode" by the jubilant fans. That year Lynch had TDs in 10 straight games, a Seattle record.

In 2012 he had 1590 yards on 315 carries with 11 TDs, averaging 99.4 yards per game.

In 2013 he ran for 1257 yards with 12 TDs and was in the pro bowl for the third consecutive year. He was a standout in the Super Bowl which Seattle won 43-6 over Denver.

In 2014 Lynch had his contract restructured. In week 16 he was fined for making an obscene gesture. In the NFC championship game he had 157 rushing yards plus a 26 yard pass to set up one TD and another one with a 24 yard run. In that game, Russell Wilson guided a comeback from a 19-7 deficit with 4 minutes remaining to win in overtime 28-24. In Super Bowl 49, he had 102 yards on 24 carries but Seattle lost to New England as the Russell Wilson pass was intercepted when they could have run Lynch three times for the win. The play had never been used before but Bill Belichick the Patriots coach practiced it with the intercepting cornerback Malcolm Butler.

In 2015, Lynch got a two year $25 million extension. He had sports hernia surgery and undrafted rookie Thomas Rawls had a 209 yard gain against the San Francisco 49ers in week 11. In a wild card game, Lynch, who was scheduled to return, said that he could not play but Seattle still won 10-9. He then returned against Carolina, carrying only six times for 20 yards and 2 passes for 15 yards in a 31-24 loss. Then on Super Bowl 50 day, Lynch announced his retirement via Twitter, posting a picture of his football cleats hanging from a telephone pole. He then mentored Cal players and sat out the 2016 season. Then he joined the Raiders saying I want to let Oakland children see a home grown football star before the Las Vegas move. He signed a two year $9 million contract with bonuses up the $16.5 million. He played well, but was again fined for an obscene gesture. Later he shoved an official and was suspended for one game.

In 2017 he has 588 yards on 140 carries with 6 TDs. But in week 12 he gained over 100 yards in Oakland. He has had no fumbles in 2016 and 2017 with the Raiders and has been effective as a receiver as well. It looks like "Beastmode" is back.

## Week 14 Highlights

YOUR NFL WEEK 14 PICKS FOR CIT'S FOLLIES

Your Pick Confirmation # is: 977972217487

RADCLIFFE REBELS -

ATLANTA over New Orleans, Value: 10
NY GIANTS over Dallas, Value: 2
CINCINNATI over Chicago, Value: 15
Detroit over TAMPA BAY, Value: 9
Green Bay over CLEVELAND, Value: 12
Minnesota over CAROLINA, Value: 8
HOUSTON over San Francisco, Value: 7
BUFFALO over Indianapolis, Value: 11
Oakland over KANSAS CITY, Value: 6
Tennessee over ARIZONA, Value: 5
NY Jets over DENVER, Value: 4
LA CHARGERS over Washington, Value: 13
Philadelphia over LA RAMS, Value: 1
Seattle over JACKSONVILLE, Value: 14
Baltimore over PITTSBURGH, Value: 3
New England over MIAMI, Value: 16

Notes:
Home teams are shown in CAPs
Depending on your pool deadline, you may still have time to change these picks now.

In week 14 I made the following four bets and I lost all of them for a loss of $855.10.

$200 on Seattle at 2.20:1
$200 on Pittsburgh at 1.487:1
$255.10 on New England at Miami where they have a losing record
$200 on Houston at 1.699:1

## Week 15 Highlights

| | | | | |
|---|---|---|---|---|
| | | | | **Thursday, December 14** |
| Denver (4-9) -3.0 | INDIANAPOLIS (3-10) +3.0 | 1 | | 5.25 PM NBC |
| | | | | **Saturday, December 16** |
| Chicago (4-9) +5.0 | **DETROIT (7-6) -5.0** | 9 | | 1.30 PM NFL |
| LA Chargers (7-6) -1.0 | **KANSAS CITY (7-6) +1.0** | 3 | | 5.25 PM NFL |
| | | | | **Sunday, December 17** |
| **Arizona (6-7) +4.5** | WASHINGTON (5-8) -4.5 | 8 | | 10.00 AM FOX |
| **Philadelphia (11-2) -7.5** | NY GIANTS (2-11) +7.5 | 10 | | 10.00 AM FOX |
| Green Bay (7-6) +3.0 | **CAROLINA (9-4) -3.0** | 5 | | 10.00 AM FOX |
| Cincinnati (5-8) +10.5 | **MINNESOTA (10-3) -10.5** | 16 | | 10.00 AM CBS |
| NY Jets (5-8) +15.5 | **NEW ORLEANS (9-4) -15.5** | 15 | | 10.00 AM CBS |
| Miami (6-7) +3.0 | **BUFFALO (7-6) -3.0** | 7 | | 10.00 AM CBS |
| **Baltimore (7-6) -7.0** | CLEVELAND (0-13) +7.0 | 14 | | 10.00 AM CBS |
| Houston (4-9) +12.0 | **JACKSONVILLE (9-4) -12.0** | 13 | | 10.00 AM CBS |
| **LA Rams (9-4) +2.5** | SEATTLE (8-5) -2.5 | 6 | | 1.05 PM FOX |
| Tennessee (8-5) +0.0 | **SAN FRANCISCO (3-10) -0.0** | 4 | | 1.25 PM CBS |
| New England (10-3) -3.0 | **PITTSBURGH (11-2) +3.0** | 2 | | 1.25 PM CBS |
| Dallas (7-6) -3.0 | **OAKLAND (6-7) +3.0** | 12 | | 5.30 PM NBC |
| | | | | **Monday, December 18** |
| **Atlanta (8-5) -6.0** | TAMPA BAY (4-9) +6.0 | 11 | | 5.30 PM ESPN |

Week 15 led off with a Thursday game where the Denver Broncos beat the Indianapolis Colts 25-13 led by QB Brock Ostweiller's 2 passing and 1 rushing TD.

There was a double header on Saturday. In the first game, the Chicago Bears (4-9, Elo 965.9) played the Detroit Lions (7-6, Elo 997.7) at the Ford Field in Detroit. I bet $200 at 1.438 on Detroit who were a 5 point favorite. Detroit has had a history of slow starts and then 4th quarter comebacks to win the game led by QB Matthew Stafford. This was a must win for Detroit who has a slim but not zero chance to make the playoffs. They need to win out to have a good chance to make the playoffs. In this game they took the lead on 2 Matt Prater field goals and never looked back, winning 20-10. I won $87.60 on my bet. Stafford was 25 of 33 with 2 TDs passed to TJ Jones and Eric Ebron, 237 yards gained and a 115.3 rating. It was their 66th game in a row without a 100 yard rusher. The Lions relied on Stafford and his receivers, Marvin Jones Jr, Golden Tate and Eric Ebron, among the eight receivers who caught Staffords passes. Chicago's young QB, Mitchell Trubisky, was 31 of 46 for 1 TD and 314 yards gained, but he had 3 interceptions and a 66.8 rating. Darius Slay had 2 of the 3 interceptions and now leads the league with 8.

The second game was a toss up between the visiting LA Chargers (7-6, Elo 1016.2) and the Kansas City Chiefs (7-6, Elo 1000.6). I bet $100 at 2.00 on Kansas City who had the home field advantage. Kansas City got ahead 10-0 so I hedged betting on LA $50 at 3.88:1 and later $50 at 3.58:1. So I had a risk arbitrage with a sure win no matter who won and a profit should LA win. In the end, I broke even as Kansas City won the game at 30-13.

The Sunday games were as follows: The Philadelphia Eagles (11-2, Elo 1050.5) who were a 7.5 favorite, played the NY Giants (2-11, Elo 951) at the Meadowlands. I bet $200 at 1.322 on Philadelphia. Nick Foles was replacing the injured Carson Wentz. Fotes last start was in 2014 when he had 27 TDs and only 2 interceptions. Foles was then injured and is now returning for his first start. NY received the ball as Philadelphia deferred to the second half, and Eli Manning drove them towards the end zone. On 3rd down, Manning was stopped and it looked like a field goal was coming, but a penalty in the end one gave them the first down. They got the TD but missed the extra point when it was blocked, so NY was ahead 6-0. Philadelphia came back with 4 completions by Foles, with a long pass penalty taking them to the 1, so they moved ahead 7-6. NY came back and took the lead on a Manning pass to lead 13-7. I tried to up my bet on Philadelphia with $50 additional at better odds of 1.66:1, but before I could get filled the bet was gone. NY got a 3rd TD pass from Manning for 67 yards to then make the score 20-7. Philadelphia then came back with one TD to make it 20-14 and later another TD to make it 20-20. Late in the 2nd quarter, NY drove and got a field goal to make the score 23-21 as the first half ended. In the second half, the Eagles drove the ball, but settled for a field goal and a 24-23 lead. Foles then got a 4th TD after 2 long Jay Ajaji runs to make it 31-23 in the 3rd quarter. The Giants got yet another TD but when they tried to make the 2 point extra point attempt, they missed it. Manning was sacked. The Giants also had one field goal blocked. Philadelphia won the game 31-29.

The big game of week 15 was New England (10-3, Elo 1051.4) against Pittsburgh (11-2, Elo 1040) in Heinz Field. These teams each lead their AFC divisions. New England has won the last 4 meetings and was never behind in any of these games so were a 1 point favorite despite being on the road. New England started with a Brady pass to lead 7-0. Then Pittsburgh got it to 7-7. Chris Boswell kicked a 51 yard field goal to give Pittsburgh a 10-7 lead. Star wide receiver Antonio Brown, a leading MVP candidate and the third member of the *killer Bs* (Brown, Ben and Bell) collided with 2 New England defenders and one of his own team mates in the end zone and was out for the rest of the game with a bruised calf. Brady had a 31 yard pass to Gronkowski and was 8 for 8 for 131 yards. They then drove to a 32 yard field goal by Stephen Gostkowski to make the game tied at 10. Helpful in the drive was Kenny Britt just obtained from Cleveland. LéVeon Bell had a spectacular game with . . . running and . . . passing yards. After a few passes, Pittsburgh led 17-10 at half time. New England got the ball to start the 2nd half and one pass got them to the 50. Lewis ran to the 44, a pass to Gronkowski got them to the 25. Burkhead gained 4 to the 21. There was a false start and then a pass to James White. Then, in a gutsy move at 4th and 1, they got a first down with a pass to Gronkowski.

The final minutes of the game were a viewer's delight. Brady went to Gronkowski three times in a row to drive the team close to the end zone. With 70 seconds to go, New England had gone 77 yards quickly and Dion Lewis scored the TD to make the score 25-24. They then went for a 2 point conversion and they got it with a pass to Gronkowski to make it 27-24. Pittsburgh now had 56 seconds to try to tie or win the game in regulation. A run took them to their 21, then another impossible play, a 69 yard run by Smith, took Pittsburgh to the New England 10. With 34 seconds left, Big Ben threw a pass to Jesse James right at the goal line, so it looked like Pittsburgh had won the game, but it was ruled that James did not have full possession as the ball hit the turf as he crossed the goal line. The incomplete pass meant that Pittsburgh, with 28 seconds left, could spike the ball and tie the game and send it into over time. Big Ben wanted to do this, but as we see in other weeks, Pittsburgh's strategy form the coaches has a lot of dubious plays. Instead they pass again and this time it was intercepted by Hamon after Rowe batted it. So New England won 27-24. Both teams were now 11-3 but New England will be the #1 seed and Pittsburgh #2 if they both win out in their last 2 games. Gronkowski had 9 receptions for 168 yards. I won my two bets on New England, $200 at 1.769 and $50 at 2.99 for a gain of $250.80.

In week 15 I concentrated on the favorites. Thirteen of the 14 favorites won and I lost two bets: Oakland who were beat by Dallas and Seattle who were blown away by the LA Rams. I made the following bets:

1. Detroit a 5.0 point favorite. I bet $200 at 1.628:1 and won $87.60 when they won over Chicago.

2. Philadelphia a 7.5 favorite. I bet $200 at 1.322:1 and won $64.40 when they won over NY Giants at 34-29.

3. Carolina a 3.0 favorite. I bet $200 at 1.699:1 and won $139.80 when they won over Green Bay at 31-24.

4. Minnesota a 10.5 favorite. I bet $263.16 at . . . and won $50 when they won over Cincinnati at 34-7.

5. Oakland a 3.0 underdog. I bet $200 at 2.31:1 and lost when they lost to Dallas at Dallas.

6. New England a 3 point favorite. I bet $200 at 1.769:1 and won $153.80 and $50 at 2.98:1 and won $99.0 when they won over Pittsburgh at 27-24.

7. Atlanta a 6 point favorite. I bet $200 at 1.384:1 and won $76.80 when they won over Tampa Bay at Tampa Bay.

8. Seattle a 2.5 favorite. I bet $50 and lost when they were beaten by the LA Rams 54-7 in Los Angeles.

**Other games I didn't bet on**: The Baltimore Ravens (7-6, Elo 1025.3) beat the Cleveland Browns (0-13, Elo 931.9) 27-10. It was the fifth game the Baltimore defense held its opponent to 10 points or less.

The resurgent SF 49ers (3-10, Elo 950.9) beat the Tennessee Titans (8-5, Elo 1004.5) 25-23, behind QB Jimmy Garappolo who was 31 of 43 for 381 yards and 1 TD. He learned a lot as Tom Brady's backup at the Patriots. The 49ers won on a 45 yard field goal by Robbie Gould as time expired. Tennessee relies on QB Marcus Mariota who makes up for a weak running game but was not effect today.

## Week 16 Highlights

Saturday, December 23

| | | | |
|---|---|---|---|
| Indianapolis (3-11) +13.5 | BALTIMORE (8-6) -13.5 | 16 | 1:30 PM NFL |
| Minnesota (11-3) -8.5 | GREEN BAY (7-7) +8.5 | 15 | 5:30 PM NBC |

Sunday, December 24

| | | | |
|---|---|---|---|
| Cleveland (0-14) +6.5 | CHICAGO (4-10) -6.5 | 3 | 10:00 AM CBS |
| Detroit (8-6) -3.0 | CINCINNATI (5-9) +3.0 | 4 | 10:00 AM FOX |
| Tampa Bay (4-10) +10.5 | CAROLINA (10-4) -10.5 | 14 | 10:00 AM FOX |
| Atlanta (9-5) +6.0 | NEW ORLEANS (10-4) -6.0 | 8 | 10:00 AM FOX |
| LA Rams (10-4) -6.5 | TENNESSEE (8-6) +6.5 | 5 | 10:00 AM FOX |
| Buffalo (8-6) +11.5 | NEW ENGLAND (11-3) -11.5 | 13 | 10:00 AM CBS |
| Miami (6-8) +10.5 | KANSAS CITY (8-6) -10.5 | 12 | 10:00 AM CBS |
| LA Chargers (7-7) -6.5 | NY JETS (5-9) +6.5 | 1 | 10:00 AM CBS |
| Denver (5-9) +3.5 | WASHINGTON (6-8) -3.5 | 9 | 10:00 AM CBS |
| Jacksonville (10-4) -4.0 | SAN FRANCISCO (4-10) +4.0 | 7 | 1:05 PM CBS |
| NY Giants (2-12) +3.0 | ARIZONA (6-8) -3.0 | 6 | 1:25 PM FOX |
| Seattle (8-6) +4.5 | DALLAS (8-6) -4.5 | 2 | 1:25 PM FOX |

Monday, December 25

| | | | |
|---|---|---|---|
| Pittsburgh (11-3) -8.5 | HOUSTON (4-10) +8.5 | 10 | 1:30 PM NBC |
| Oakland (6-8) +9.5 | PHILADELPHIA (12-2) -9.5 | 11 | 5:30 PM ESPN |

The Minnesota Vikings (10-3, Elo 1046.3) beat Cincinnati Bengals (5-8, Elo 986.4) 34-7. Minnesota is now the NFC North champs. They are strong on defense and offense and may become the first NFL team to play in the Super Bowl in their home stadium. Jerick McKinnon had 114 yards receiving. The loss led to Marvin Lewis ending his 15 year coaching stint with the Bengals.

Going into week 16. with two games to play for most of the teams, the playoff picture looks like:

| AFC | NFC |
| --- | --- |
| New England 11-3 | Philadelphia 12-2 |
| Jacksonville 10-4 | Minnesota 11-3 |
| Pittsburgh 11-3 | |

The following teams have a chance to make the playoffs if certain outcomes occur such as them winning both games or other teams losing or some combination.

| AFC | NFC |
| --- | --- |
| Buffalo 8-6 | Dallas 8-6 |
| Tennessee 8-6 | New Orleans 8-4 |
| Kansas City 8-6 | Carolina 8-4 |
| Baltimore 8-6 | LA Rams (10-4) |
| LA Chargers 7-7 | Seattle 8-6 |
| | Atlanta 9-5 |
| | Detroit 8-6 |

The playoff rules give the #1 seed home advantage during the playoffs which at the moment are New England in the AFC and Philadelphia in the NFC. The #2 seed gets a bye in the first playoff game and could be at home throughout the playoffs if the #1 seed loses their first games. The current #2 seeds are Pittsburgh in the AFC and Minnesota in the NFC.

The playoff possibilities include the following:

New England (11-3) at home versus Buffalo (8-6) has won the AFC championship for nine years. Buffalo who started out the season with five straight wins have a chance to make the playoffs but to do that they will need to upset New England in December in Foxboro and then beat Miami in Miami. This is unlikely but they could get some help if Baltimore were to lose their last game which is at home against the much weaker Cincinnati, again unlikely. Tennessee (8-6) are in this mix as well. They host the LA Rams (10-4) and host the Jacksonville (10-4) the next week. Though Tennessee is at home for both games, the other teams are stronger.

*more here*

Buffalo got a field goal to start the second half to make it 16-13 in favor of Buffalo. They are holding up well against New England. Another controversial call at the Buffalo 24 yard line on a Dion Lewis 1 yard run. It was overturned and New England got a field goal to make it 16-16. There was double coverage on Gronkowski on a long pass where there was a penalty, so the Patriots got the ball on the 1. Gillispe scored the TD, his fifth of the year to make the score 23-16 with 55 seconds left in the third quarter. Buffalo had a field goal try that failed. New England started on the 40, a 22 yard pass got them into Buffalo territory. Lewis ran to the 22. They scored the TD to make it 30-16. Buffalo had the ball and Tyrod Taylor fumbled the ball but Buffalo recovered. New England charged again with Lewis scoring to make the score 37-16. Buffalo is still in the playoff picture at 8-7. Brady was 21 of 28 for 224 yards with 2 TDs and 1 interception. Lewis was 129 yards on 24 carries. I won my bet .... New England is now 12-3.

Kansas City (8-6) is leading the AFC West and are the third team in the wild card running. They face Miami at home this week and go to Denver the final week. In this division, the LA Chargers are still contenders. They are on the road agains the NY Jets this week and host Oakland the final week. Baltimore (8-6) needs to win out against Indianapolis which they did on Saturday and beat Cincinnati next week at home which seems likely. So Baltimore and Kansas City seem likely to make the playoffs. Tennessee and the LA Chargers have a decent chance.

Seattle is in a must win situation against Dallas in an away game where they are weak. After a 42-7 blasting by the LA Rams, their second loss in a row, they are 8-6. A win in Arlington is needed for Seattle to have a chance to reach the playoffs as a wild card. Their offense is centered around QB Russell Wilson, who generates over 80% of their point running or passing. After two consecutive losses, Wilson is 23-4 in the next game, so they may bounce back. Seattle's offense has no effective running game after Marshan Lynch's departure except for Wilson's scrambling. Also, their defense has been decimated with star corner back/safeties Richard Sherman and Cam Chancellor injured as well as others. The feared *Legion of Doom* Seattle defense, which used to be at the top in the NFL, has given up 156 running yards to Jacksonville and 244 to the LA Rams in these two losses. Dallas (8-6) is also in the wild card running. They lost their first three games without star running back Ezekiel Elliot, who had a six game alleged domestic violence suspension. He is now returning for the final two games. Seattle was a 4.5 point favorite.

Seattle played a sloppy game but got 3 TDs on 3 Dallas turnovers to win 21-12. Dallas had 4 field goals, but could not score a TD despite being inside the 5 yard line several times. Rather than run Exekiel Elliott in the short yard situation, they used other plays that failed. Elliott returned from his six game suspension and played well, gaining 97 yards on 24 carries. Russell Wilson had a good game with 2 TDs on passes to Doug Baldwin and Jimmie Graham. He was 14 for 21 for 93 yards. Dak Prescott, the Dallas QB, was 21 for 34 and 182 yards, but had those turnovers which settled the game. Seattle, having beat Dallas, must now beat Arizona in their final game and get an Atlanta loss to make the playoffs.

I felt good about betting New Orleans (10-4) over Atlanta but with a 6 point favorite, the odds seemed poor, so I passed on the bet. New Orleans did beat Atlanta 23-13. So, as predicted, last year's Super Bowl loser, had a weak year and did not make the playoffs. Drew Brees, who became the fastest QB to reach 70,000 yards, was 21 of 28 for 239 in this game, with 1 TD pass to Ginn. Mark Ingram ran for 1 TD. Atlanta's QB, Matt Ryan, was 22 of 36 for 288 yards and 1 TD pass to Coleman. Their top receiver, Julio Jones, carried the team with 7 receptions for 149 yards but that was not enough to win the game. Ryan's 3 interceptions were the game changer. The win clinched a playoff berth for the Saints, but Drew Brees was lackluster, mostly connecting on short passes so they really need star rookie running back Alvin Kamara to do well if they are to win in the playoffs.

In the Christmas games, Pittsburgh (11-3) completely outclassed Houston (4-10) 34-6 to lock up a bye in the first round of the playoffs. Oakland at Philadelphia ...

Houston has a great defense despite the fact that their two biggest stars JJ Watt and Jadeveon Clowney are injured. Watt spent the year raising millions for hurricane relief for poor families in Houston. Houston used 74 players this year because of the many injuries. They are also weak at the QB position. Pittsburgh seems ready for the playoffs and rebounded from the New England loss. This gives star receiver Antonio Brown an extra week to recover from his injury. His presence dramatically changes the opponent's defense as they need to use two players to attempt to guard him. This makes it a lot easier for Ben Roethinsberger to target other receivers. I won my $200 bet at 1.285 for a gain of $57.

Oakland (6-8) at Philadelphia (12-2) was to be a test of QB Nick Foles. In his first game, replacing the injured Carson Wentz, he had 4 TDs and no interceptions and looked very sharp. In his second game, he was less sharp with 19 for 38 completions, 1 TD and 1 interception; but, the Eagles still won 19-10. The Eagles were a 10 point so they did not cover the spread. Derek Carr, the Oakland QB, had 1 TD and 2 interceptions, Marshan Lynch gained 95 yards on 25 carries. Philadelphia had a balanced attack with Jay Ajayi gaining 52 yards rushing and Ertz had 9 receptions for 81 yards. Oakland needs to be restructured and the hiring of John Gruden for $100 million over 10 years is likely to improve them as they move to Las Vegas.

The Sunday December 24th games plus the Christmas games eliminated Detroit, Miami, Oakland and Dallas from the playoffs.

## Week 17 Highlights

| | |
|---|---|
| Dallas (8-7) -3.0 | **PHILADELPHIA (13-2) +3.0** |
| **Washington (7-8) -3.0** | NY GIANTS (2-13) +3.0 |
| Chicago (5-10) +11.5 | **MINNESOTA (12-3) -11.5** |
| Green Bay (7-8) +7.0 | **DETROIT (8-7) -7.0** |
| **Houston (4-11) +5.5** | INDIANAPOLIS (3-12) -5.5 |
| NY Jets (5-10) +15.0 | **NEW ENGLAND (12-3) -15.0** |
| Cleveland (0-15) +6.5 | **PITTSBURGH (12-3) -6.5** |
| Arizona (7-8) +8.5 | **SEATTLE (9-6) -8.5** |
| **New Orleans (11-4) -5.5** | TAMPA BAY (4-11) +5.5 |
| Carolina (11-4) +4.0 | **ATLANTA (9-6) -4.0** |
| **San Francisco (5-10) -4.0** | LA RAMS (11-4) +4.0 |
| Buffalo (8-7) -2.0 | **MIAMI (6-9) +2.0** |
| Cincinnati (6-9) +8.0 | **BALTIMORE (9-6) -8.0** |
| Jacksonville (10-5) +2.5 | **TENNESSEE (8-7) -2.5** |
| **Kansas City (9-6) +4.5** | DENVER (5-10) -4.5 |
| Oakland (6-9) +7.0 | **LA CHARGERS (8-7) -7.0** |

- Philadelphia (12-3/ elo 1061.8) at home spread is +3 in favor of Dallas (8-7, elo 1002.8): a meaningless game as Philadelphia has clinched home field advantage throughout the playoffs. I bet $100 at 2.44 and not surprisingly they lost 0-6.

- Minnesota (12-3, elo 1052.4) at home spread -11.5 versus Chicago (5-10, elo 979. I bet $326.80 at 1.153 to win $50. They won 23-11.

- New Orleans (11-4, elo 1051.4) at Tampa Bay (4-11, elo 962.9). I bet $150 at 1.415 and lost it.

- Kansas City (9-6, elo 1021.7) at Denver (5-10, elo 959.4). I bet $100 at 3.01 and won $201.

- Pittsburgh (12-3, elo 1046) at home favored by 6.5 points against Cleveland (0-15, elo 917). Pittsburgh did not play their top players. I bet $200 at 1.384 and won $76.80. The score was 28-24.

- Carolina (11-4, elo 1029.9) at Atlanta (9-6, elo 1016.9) favored by 4. I bet $100 at 2.79 on Carolina and they lost 10-22.

- Baltimore (9-6, elo 1030.2) an 8 point favorite at home against Cincinnati (6-9, elo 972.8). I bet $200 at 1.25 and I lost. The score was 27-31.

- New England (12-3, elo 1054) a 15 point favorite at home against NY Jets (5-10, elo 966.7). I bet $602.41 at 1.083 to win $50.

Net gain $227.80.

| Week | Games | Picked Winner | Beat Spread |
|---|---|---|---|
| 1 | 15 | 10 | 8 |
| 2 | 16 | 10 | 8 |
| 3 | 16 | 7 | 3 |
| 4 | 16 | 12 | 9 |
| 5 | 14 | 7 | 7 |
| 6 | 14 | 5 | 3 |
| 7 | 15 | 12 | 9 |
| 8 | 13 | 9 | 6 |
| 9 | 13 | 7 | 6 |
| 10 | 14 | 8 | 5 |
| 11 | 14 | 11 | 9 |
| 12 | 16 | 11 | 9 |
| 13 | 16 | 10 | 7 |
| 14 | 16 | 6 | 2 |
| 15 | 15 | 12 | 7 |
| 16 | 16 | 13 | 9 |
| 17 | 16 | 11 | 8 |
| Total | 255 | 161 | 115 |

Thus, the percent of games correctly predicted by the Radcliffe Rebels is $161/255 = 63.1\%$ and $115/255 = 45;1\%$ is the percent of time they beat the Las Vegas spread. This shows that the Radcliffe Rebels were able to correctly predict the majority of the games but not beat the spread therefore it would not be a winning system for betting. Again showing that the Las Vegas spread odds are essentially an efficient market and it requires another approach to actually win such as the mean reversion risk arbitrage that we propose in this book.

The spreads are in the weekly Radcliffr Rebel as shown week by week. The scores for the season are below:

| Week 1 | Week 2 | Week 3 | Week 4 | Week 5 | Week 6 |
|---|---|---|---|---|---|
| BUF 21, NYJ 12 | HOU 13, CIN 9 | LAR 41, SF 39 | GB 35, CHI 14 | NE 19, TB 14 | PHI 28, CAR 23 |
| ATL 23, CHI 17 | ARI 16, IND 13 (OT) | JAX44, Bal 7 | NO 20, MIA 0 | CIN 20, BUF 16 | MIA 20, ATL 17 |
| BAL 20, CIN 0 | KC 27, PHI 20 | BUF 26, DEN 16 | BUF 23, ATL 17 | NYJ 17, CLE 14 | MIN 23, GB 10 |
| PIT 21, CLE 18 | NE 36, NO 20 | CHI 23, PIT 24 (OT) | CIN 31, CLE 7 | CAR 27, DET 24 | NE 24, NYJ 17 |
| DET 35, ARI 23 | PIT 26, MIN 9 | ATL 30, DET 26 | LAR 35, DAL 30 | IND 26, SF 23 (OT) | WSH 26, SF 24 |
| OAK 26, TEN 16 | TB 29, CHI 7 | IND 31, CLE 28 | DET 14, MIN 7 | MIA 16, TEN 10 | CHI 27, BAL 24 (OT) |
| PHI 30, WSH 17 | CAR 9, BUF 3 | MIN 34, TB 17 | CAR 33, NE 30 | LAC 27, NYG 22 | HOU 33, CLE 17 |
| JAX 29, HOU 7 | TEN 37, JAX 16 | NE 36, HOU 33 | NYJ 23, JAX 20 (OT) | PHI 34, ARI 7 | ARI 38, TB 33 |
| LAR 46, IND 9 | BAL 24, CLE 10 | NYJ 20, MIA 6 | PIT 26, BAL 9 | JAX 30, PIT 9 | LAR 27, JAX 17 |
| GB 17, SEA 9 | OAK 45, NYJ 20 | PHI 27, NYG 24 | HOU 57, TEN 14 | SEA 16, LAR 10 | PIT 19, KC 13 |
| CAR 23, SF 3 | MIA 19, LAC 17 | NO 34, CAR 13 | ARI 18, SF 15 (OT) | GB 35, DAL 31 | LAC 17, OAK 16 |
| DAL 19, NYG 3 | DEN 42, DAL 17 | TEN 33, SEA 27 | PHI 26, LAC 24 | KC 42, HOU 34 | NYG 23, DEN 10 |
| Postponed | WSH 27, LAR 20 | GB 27, CIN 24 (OT) | TB 25, NYG 23 | MIN 20, CHI 17 | TEN 36, IND 22 |
| MIN 29, NO 19 | SEA 12, SF 9 | KC 24, LAC 10 | DEN 16, OAK 10 | | |
| DEN 24, LAC 21 | ATL 34, GB 23 | WSH 27, OAK 10 | SEA 46, IND 18 | | |
| KC 42, NE 27 | DET 24, NYG 10 | DAL 28, ARI 17 | KC 29, WSH 20 | | |

| Week 7 | Week 8 | Week 9 | Week 10 | Week 11 | Week 12 |
|---|---|---|---|---|---|
| OAK 31, KC 30 | BAL 40, MIA 0 | NYJ 34, BUF 21 | NO 47, BUF 10 | PIT 40, TEN 17 | MIN 30, DET 23 |
| BUF 30, TB 27 | MIN 33, CLE 16 | TEN 23, BAL 20 | GB 23, CHI 16 | DET 27, CHI 24 | LAC 28, DAL 6 |
| CHI 17, CAR 3 | BUF 34, OAK 14 | NO 30, TB 10 | DET 38, CLE 24 | JAX 19, CLE 7 | WSH 20, NYG 10 |
| TEN 12, CLE 9 (OT) | CIN 24, IND 23 | LAR 51, NYG 17 | TEN 24, CIN 20 | BAL 23, GB 0 | ATL 34, TB 20 |
| NO 26, GB 17 | NE 21, LAC 13 | PHI 51, DEN 23 | PIT 20, IND 17 | TB 30, MIA 20 | CIN 30, CLE 16 |
| JAX 27, IND 0 | NO 20, CHI 12 | CAR 20, ATL 17 | TB 15, NYJ 10 | MIN 24, LAR 7 | TEN 20, IND 16 |
| LAR 33, ARI 0 | ATL 25, NYJ 20 | JAX 23, CIN 7 | MIN 38, WSH 30 | NO 34, WSH 31 (OT) | BUF 16, KC 10 |
| MIA 31, NYJ 28 | PHI 33, SF 10 | IND 20, HOU 14 | JAX 20, LAC 17 (OT) | NYG 12, KC 9 (OT) | NE 35, MIA 17 |
| MIN 24, BAL 16 | CAR 17, TB 3 | ARI 20, SF 10 | LAR 33, HOU 7 | HOU 31, ARI 21 | CAR 35, NYJ 27 |
| DAL 40, SF 10 | SEA 41, HOU 38 | WSH 17, SEA 14 | ATL 27, DAL 7 | LAC 54, BUF 24 | PHI 31, CHI 3 |
| SEA 24, NYG 7 | DAL 33, WSH 19 | DAL 28, KC 17 | SF 31, NYG 21 | CIN 20, DEN 17 | SEA 24, SF 13 |
| PIT 29, CIN 14 | PIT 20, DET 15 | OAK 27, MIA 24 | NE 41, DEN 16 | NE 33, OAK 8 | OAK 21, DEN 14 |
| LAC 21, DEN 0 | KC 29, DEN 19 | DET 30, GB 17 | CAR 45, MIA 21 | PHI 37, DAL 9 | LAR 26, NO 20 |
| NE 23, ATL 7 | | | | ATL 34, SEA 31 | ARI 27, JAX 24 |
| PHI 34, WSH 24 | | | | | PIT 31, GB 28 |
| | | | | | BAL 23, HOU 16 |

| Week 13 | Week 14 | Week 15 | Week 16 | Week 17 | |
|---|---|---|---|---|---|
| DAL 38, WSH 14 | ATL 20, NO 17 | DEN 25, IND 13 | BAL 23, IND 16 | DET 35, GB 11 | |
| MIN 14, ATL 9 | BUF 13, IND 7 (OT) | DET 20, CHI 10 | MIN 16, GB 0 | IND 22, HOU 13 | |
| NE 23, BUF 3 | CHI 33, CIN 7 | KC 30, LAC 13 | CHI 20, CLE 3 | MIN 23, CHI 10 | |
| SF 15, CHI 14 | GB 27, CLE 21 (OT) | BUF 24, MIA 16 | CIN 26, DET 17 | NE 26, NYJ 6 | |
| GB 26, TB 20 (OT) | KC 26, OAK 15 | BAL 27, CLE 10 | LAR 27, TEN 23 | NYG 18, WSH 10 | |
| TEN 24, HOU 13 | DAL 30, NYG 10 | MIN 34, CIN 7 | KC 29, MIA 13 | DAL 6, PHI 0 | |
| MIA 35, DEN 9 | DET 24, TB 21 | NO 31, NYJ 19 | NE 37, BUF 16 | PIT 28, CLE 24 | |
| NYJ 38, KC 31 | CAR 31, MIN 24 | PHI 34, NYG 29 | NO 23, ATL 13 | ATL 22, CAR 10 | |
| JAX 30, IND 10 | SF 26, HOU 16 | WSH 20, ARI 15 | LAC 14, NYJ 7 | KC 27, DEN 24 | |
| BAL 44, DET 20 | DEN 23, NYJ 0 | CAR 31, GB 24 | WSH 27, DEN 11 | TEN 15, JAX 10 | |
| LAC 19, CLE 10 | ARI 12, TEN 7 | JAX 45, HOU 7 | CAR 22, TB 19 | SF 34, LAR 13 | |
| OAK 24, NYG 17 | LAC 30, WSH 13 | LAR 42, SEA 7 | SF 44, JAX 33 | BUF 22, MIA 16 | |
| NO 31, CAR 21 | PHI 43, LAR 35 | NE 27, PIT 24 | SEA 21, DAL 12 | LAC 30, OAK 10 | |
| LAR 32, ARI 16 | JAX 30, SEA 24 | SF 25, TEN 23 | ARI 23, NYG 0 | ARI 26, SEA 24 | |
| SEA 24, PHI 10 | PIT 39, BAL 38 | DAL 20, OAK 17 | PIT 34, HOU 6 | TB 31, NO 24 | |
| PIT 23, CIN 20 | MIA 27, NE 20 | ATL 24, TB 21 | PHI 19, OAK 10 | CIN 31, BAL 27 | |

## The evolution of the Elo over the season

We compare the two versions of the Elo: the 538-type which starts the season with the final Elos mean reverted from the previous year's final elos and Swetye's which begins the season with all teams starting at 1000.

The Patriots have a 1080 rating if this season picks up where last year left off. They have a 1054 rating if all teams start the season with 1000.

The teams ranked 2 through 5 have fairly close elos when their ratings are made both ways.

|  | all at 1000 | prior standings |
|---|---|---|
| Philadelphia Eagles | 1061.8 | 1063 |
| Los Angeles Rams | 1056.9 | 1037 |
| New England Patriots | 1054.0 | 1080 |
| Minnesota Vikings | 1052.4 | 1049 |
| New Orleans Saints | 1051.4 | 1050 |
| Pittsburgh Steelers | 1045.0 | 1058 |

Which will prove to be more accurate?

Swetye says:

> I have noticed that teams that do better this year compared to last year are not as strong as teams who have a foundation built over several seasons.

> The Denver Broncos won two Super Bowls in a row. In the second Super Bowl they played Atlanta who had a very good season, but did not have a foundation built over a few seasons. Denver won easily.

> A good analogy is the KY Derby. It has been since 1881, when Apollo won, that a horse has won the Derby without having raced as a 2 year old. Derby horses need a strong foundation of conditioning in order to run well at a long distance at a sustained pace so early in their third year.

> It would be hard for me to bet against the Patriots in the playoffs.

# Chapter 16

# The 2017-2018 Playoffs and the Super Bowl

## The Playoff Picture

The final standings after week 17 are:

### AFC Playoff Standings

1. New England Patriots (13-3)
2. Pittsburgh Steelers (13-3)
3. Jacksonville Jaguars (10-6)
4. Kansas City Chiefs (10-6)
5. Tennessee Titans (9-7)
6. Buffalo Bills (9-7)

### NFC Playoff Standings

1. Philadelphia Eagles (13-3)
2. Minnesota Vikings (13-3)
3. Los Angeles Rams (11-5)
4. New Orleans Saints (11-5)
5. Carolina Panthers (11-5)
6. Atlanta Falcons (10-6)

Swetye's Elos and the 538 type Elos computed by Swetye are in Tables 16.1 and 16.2.

Table 16.1: Final Swetye Elo Ratings, 2018

| Team | week 1 | week 2 | week 3 | week 4 | week 5 | week 6 | week 7 | week 8 | week 9 | week 10 | week 11 | week 12 | week 13 | week 14 | week 15 | week 16 | week 17 |
|---|---|---|---|---|---|---|---|---|---|---|---|---|---|---|---|---|---|
| Arizona Cardinals | 992.81 | 996.99 | 989.75 | 993.71 | 982.87 | 988.05 | 976.54 | 1,002.18 | 982.18 | 977.62 | 971.46 | 977.18 | 971.34 | 977.04 | 971.97 | 980.21 | 984.72 |
| Atlanta Falcons | 1,005.31 | 1,011.85 | 1,016.59 | 1,010.74 |  | 1,005.62 | 997.40 | 1,004.66 | 997.88 | 1,008.28 | 1,012.94 | 1,019.12 | 1,014.52 | 1,019.49 | 1,022.63 | 1,016.95 | 1,024.30 |
| Baltimore Ravens | 1,009.69 | 1,016.47 | 999.95 | 991.09 | 999.04 | 993.89 | 988.57 | 1,019.79 | 1,010.81 | 996.79 | 1,010.59 | 1,015.40 | 1,025.33 | 1,023.04 | 1,027.43 | 1,030.24 | 1,023.84 |
| Buffalo Bills | 1,005.93 | 1,000.73 | 1,007.50 | 1,013.09 | 1,007.84 |  | 1,011.61 |  |  | 996.79 | 983.48 | 989.70 | 982.52 | 986.65 | 991.92 | 985.02 | 989.70 |
| Carolina Panthers | 1,009.69 | 1,014.62 | 1,002.41 | 1,006.82 | 1,011.39 | 1,006.36 | 997.45 | 985.43 |  | 996.79 | 975.92 | 968.85 | 1,016.50 | 1,022.80 | 1,027.19 | 1,029.88 | 1,022.16 |
| Chicago Bears | 994.42 | 1,014.44 | 990.34 | 981.04 | 976.94 | 981.86 | 990.38 | 991.44 | 984.46 | 979.77 | 984.29 | 989.84 | 965.92 | 978.84 | 973.13 | 979.03 | 974.52 |
| Cincinnati Bengals | 989.82 | 984.88 | 980.85 | 991.96 | 996.98 |  | 989.48 | 951.11 | 978.18 | 980.19 | 941.43 | 935.51 | 986.41 | 972.91 | 965.39 | 972.80 | 978.99 |
| Cleveland Browns | 995.40 | 988.23 | 983.66 | 971.99 | 968.01 | 961.20 | 957.37 | 1,012.42 | 1,019.52 | 945.63 | 998.28 | 959.75 | 931.87 | 928.00 | 923.27 | 916.96 | 915.22 |
| Dallas Cowboys | 1,008.01 | 996.51 | 1,003.40 | 998.36 | 993.79 | 1,003.37 | 1,004.88 | 987.05 | 1,012.42 | 1,008.63 | 998.28 | 987.70 | 998.42 | 1,005.52 | 1,009.33 | 1,002.78 | 1,009.83 |
| Denver Broncos | 1,004.15 | 1,015.08 | 1,007.98 | 1,014.51 |  | 1,001.73 | 992.52 | 996.92 | 978.18 | 969.21 | 964.89 | 959.75 | 947.99 | 960.55 | 967.21 | 959.36 | 956.29 |
| Detroit Lions | 1,006.82 | 1,013.95 | 1,008.97 | 1,012.98 | 1,009.72 | 1,007.70 | 1,001.33 |  | 1,004.62 | 1,009.74 | 1,013.37 | 987.56 | 989.18 | 1,001.50 | 1,006.88 | 999.17 | 1,008.48 |
| Green Bay Packers | 1,005.64 | 998.75 | 1,002.55 | 1,011.35 | 1,015.69 | 1,008.32 |  | 996.92 | 993.26 | 998.63 | 994.12 | 984.32 | 982.52 | 992.80 | 988.13 | 982.05 | 972.19 |
| Houston Texans | 989.16 | 993.87 | 989.65 | 1,007.54 | 1,001.92 | 970.10 | 960.50 | 958.41 | 997.24 | 988.29 | 987.56 | 989.03 | 951.94 | 974.46 | 964.65 | 955.77 | 949.83 |
| Indianapolis Colts | 985.00 | 980.60 | 984.94 | 973.32 | 977.59 | 1,012.66 | 1,021.69 |  | 965.09 | 961.90 | 994.12 | 957.85 | 987.56 | 947.56 | 940.54 | 937.52 | 944.14 |
| Jacksonville Jaguars | 1,010.31 | 998.82 | 1,014.58 | 1,009.63 | 1,031.09 | 1,024.70 | 1,021.71 | 1,026.86 | 1,028.26 | 1,031.56 | 1,035.45 | 1,029.54 | 1,035.03 | 1,039.88 | 1,049.02 | 1,038.99 | 1,032.64 |
| Kansas City Chiefs | 1,008.13 | 1,013.44 | 1,020.29 | 1,025.77 | 985.93 | 988.54 | 998.88 | 993.59 | 1,019.41 | 990.07 | 1,013.50 | 1,007.01 | 1,000.61 | 1,006.68 | 1,015.80 | 1,021.68 | 1,024.55 |
| Los Angeles Chargers | 995.63 | 991.78 | 984.54 | 981.05 | 1,009.74 | 1,027.52 |  |  | 1,037.32 | 1,045.71 | 1,002.73 | 1,012.78 | 1,016.16 | 1,022.77 | 1,013.22 | 1,017.51 | 1,024.42 |
| Los Angeles Rams | 1,014.24 | 1,007.62 | 1,010.90 | 1,015.68 | 990.03 | 994.92 | 999.06 | 982.16 | 977.63 | 1,041.44 | 1,036.06 | 1,041.44 | 1,046.89 | 1,040.78 | 1,053.74 | 1,056.87 | 1,041.98 |
| Miami Dolphins | 1,006.23 | 1,003.66 | 994.93 | 984.82 | 1,011.97 | 1,011.97 | 1,016.69 | 1,022.85 | 982.16 | 968.64 | 962.12 | 956.86 | 968.03 | 975.93 | 970.35 | 964.07 | 959.13 |
| Minnesota Vikings | 991.46 | 997.39 | 1,006.30 |  | 1,004.36 | 994.92 | 1,016.99 | 1,022.75 | 1,027.88 | 1,027.88 | 1,037.09 | 1,041.95 | 1,046.29 | 1,039.71 | 1,046.72 | 1,052.42 | 1,056.61 |
| New England Patriots | 993.44 | 1,000.00 | 1,003.99 | 999.36 | 1,009.95 | 1,011.97 | 1,017.75 | 1,024.11 | 1,030.96 | 1,031.18 | 1,039.74 | 1,044.63 | 1,051.36 | 1,043.22 | 1,047.57 | 1,054.02 | 1,058.83 |
| New Orleans Saints | 991.56 | 984.48 | 996.19 | 976.79 | 1,004.47 | 1,009.95 | 1,019.45 | 1,022.75 | 1,044.23 | 1,044.23 | 1,037.09 | 1,044.63 | 1,046.97 | 1,041.78 | 1,046.05 | 1,051.41 | 1,043.15 |
| New York Giants | 993.75 | 984.04 | 980.11 | 996.39 | 980.91 | 980.91 | 973.16 | 1,024.11 | 962.70 | 955.51 | 1,047.10 | 955.66 | 950.96 | 943.39 | 941.08 | 932.32 | 939.79 |
| New York Jets | 1,006.56 | 983.33 | 991.66 | 1,008.90 | 994.38 | 980.91 | 990.02 | 984.97 | 993.59 | 988.01 | 961.23 | 982.77 | 988.89 | 975.81 | 971.23 | 966.66 | 961.47 |
| Oakland Raiders | 1,007.50 | 1,016.42 | 1,006.77 | 1,001.49 | 990.43 | 994.38 | 993.30 | 984.63 | 988.94 | 955.51 | 979.82 | 984.68 | 989.10 | 982.68 | 978.66 | 975.09 | 967.73 |
| Philadelphia Eagles | 1,004.38 | 1,001.90 | 1,005.60 | 1,015.02 | 993.16 | 1,023.92 | 1,029.44 | 1,035.50 | 1,043.81 | 1,024.96 | 1,053.56 | 1,036.81 | 1,050.53 | 1,056.34 | 1,058.48 | 1,061.79 | 1,054.51 |
| Pittsburgh Steelers | 989.82 | 1,012.77 | 1,006.60 | 977.90 | 1,004.20 | 1,010.33 | 1,017.42 | 1,021.97 | 1,015.57 | 952.91 | 1,033.77 | 948.08 | 1,040.03 | 1,042.19 | 1,037.62 | 1,044.97 | 1,046.57 |
| San Francisco 49ers | 994.06 | 985.55 | 982.09 | 1,003.99 | 973.41 | 970.27 | 958.54 | 952.02 | 952.02 | 1,019.88 | 1,019.51 | 978.28 | 950.88 | 958.62 | 963.03 | 972.78 | 987.27 |
| Seattle Seahawks |  | 998.11 | 992.98 | 1,003.23 | 1,009.66 | 1,009.66 | 1,016.97 | 1,020.91 | 973.33 | 1,019.88 | 1,014.99 | 1,019.51 | 1,028.73 | 1,023.61 | 1,009.93 | 1,016.15 | 1,011.46 |
| Tampa Bay Buccaneers |  | 1,009.46 | 1,000.10 | 990.21 | 997.87 | 992.44 | 988.45 | 980.64 | 978.66 | 978.66 | 984.84 | 978.28 | 973.16 | 969.18 | 965.83 | 962.94 | 970.97 |
| Tennessee Titans | 993.10 | 1,004.09 | 1,008.95 |  | 991.83 | 991.83 | 995.44 | 999.82 | 999.82 | 1,003.86 | 994.52 | 998.34 | 1,004.50 | 998.55 | 993.96 | 990.61 | 996.72 |
| Washington Redskins | 992.12 | 998.46 | 1,007.66 | 1,001.87 | 984.73 | 1,004.82 | 998.98 | 991.04 | 996.16 | 990.83 | 987.76 | 993.00 | 981.73 | 974.69 | 979.50 | 986.92 | 979.17 |

Table 16.2: Final 538 Elo Ratings, 2018

| Mean Reversion | week 1 | week 2 | week 3 | week 4 | week 5 | week 6 | week 7 | week 8 | week 9 | week 10 | week 11 | week 12 | week 13 | week 14 | week 15 | week 16 | week 17 |
|---|---|---|---|---|---|---|---|---|---|---|---|---|---|---|---|---|---|
| Arizona Cardinals | 973.80 | 977.13 | 970.56 | 974.46 | 968.18 | 972.91 | 965.47 | 1,014.75 | 970.87 | 966.81 | 959.97 | 966.40 | 962.21 | 967.84 | 962.93 | 969.49 | 974.38 |
| Atlanta Falcons | 1,021.12 | 1,026.39 | 1,030.63 | 1,023.91 | 1,021.77 | 1,017.81 | 1,011.17 | 1,022.57 | 1,017.20 | 1,020.23 | 1,024.73 | 1,029.46 | 1,025.55 | 1,031.01 | 1,033.44 | 1,028.43 | 1,036.07 |
| Baltimore Ravens | 1,036.83 | 1,039.68 | 1,023.92 | 1,015.92 | 1,021.77 | 1,015.70 | 1,011.05 |  |  | 1,026.06 | 1,029.56 | 1,038.61 | 1,036.55 | 1,038.85 | 1,040.67 | 1,033.66 |  |
| Buffalo Bills | 990.30 | 986.37 | 992.30 | 998.76 | 993.16 | 1,015.70 | 996.57 | 1,004.42 | 994.92 | 985.23 | 973.67 | 980.67 | 975.54 | 978.84 | 983.76 | 978.72 | 983.08 |
| Carolina Panthers | 1,036.50 | 1,040.18 | 1,029.43 | 1,034.43 | 1,038.26 | 1,038.26 | 1,043.60 | 1,023.15 | 1,032.02 | 1,037.89 | 963.47 | 1,041.35 | 1,035.98 | 1,042.75 | 1,046.27 | 1,046.27 | 1,040.19 |
| Chicago Bears | 974.60 | 963.60 | 971.27 | 962.16 | 959.58 | 965.46 | 965.30 | 975.85 | 962.27 | 967.03 | 962.31 | 958.93 | 955.90 | 968.01 | 962.71 | 966.86 | 963.71 |
| Cincinnati Bengals | 965.94 | 960.42 | 956.62 | 964.58 | 969.95 |  | 1,002.26 | 967.02 |  | 958.26 | 962.31 | 966.42 | 964.17 | 951.47 | 946.79 | 954.83 | 961.66 |
| Cleveland Browns | 915.19 | 912.10 | 908.13 | 889.64 | 896.66 | 891.60 | 889.10 | 886.72 |  | 883.55 | 881.65 | 877.23 | 875.25 | 872.63 | 870.11 | 865.63 | 864.83 |
| Dallas Cowboys | 1,007.61 | 993.65 | 999.88 | 996.21 | 991.26 | 1,002.46 | 1,000.96 | 1,008.40 | 1,016.41 | 1,006.40 | 998.83 | 988.85 | 999.18 | 1,004.21 | 1,007.63 | 1,001.44 | 1,009.34 |
| Denver Broncos | 964.95 | 978.36 | 972.10 | 977.47 |  | 967.05 | 959.05 | 955.42 | 950.74 | 945.61 | 941.33 | 936.38 | 924.90 | 937.37 | 943.50 | 936.59 | 934.27 |
| Detroit Lions | 1,005.21 | 1,009.73 | 1,005.26 | 1,012.42 | 1,008.38 | 1,002.46 | 990.30 | 998.66 | 1,005.80 | 1,008.71 | 1,012.06 | 1,008.08 | 998.48 | 1,001.70 | 1,006.68 | 998.36 | 1,007.29 |
| Green Bay Packers | 988.84 | 983.23 | 986.82 | 995.42 | 1,000.13 | 994.69 | 982.78 |  | 982.78 | 988.08 | 978.69 | 976.32 | 980.75 | 983.18 | 979.41 | 974.98 | 965.50 |
| Houston Texans | 950.57 | 955.67 | 953.51 | 974.17 | 970.37 | 975.08 | 971.91 | 964.72 | 964.72 | 959.43 | 965.94 | 962.19 | 956.31 | 948.56 | 941.82 | 936.75 | 929.30 |
| Indianapolis Colts | 931.46 | 927.92 | 931.67 | 924.43 | 929.38 | 923.55 | 918.38 | 916.54 | 923.49 | 921.81 | 1,012.06 | 918.53 | 915.07 | 911.53 | 905.05 | 903.06 | 910.20 |
| Jacksonville Jaguars | 1,044.76 | 1,030.91 | 1,045.90 | 1,039.51 | 1,050.41 | 1,043.60 | 1,048.37 | 1,046.07 | 1,052.78 | 1,055.79 | 1,057.53 | 1,050.93 | 1,054.11 | 1,058.57 | 1,064.78 | 1,053.80 | 1,046.80 |
| Kansas City Chiefs | 1,031.30 | 1,037.77 | 1,044.20 | 1,048.55 | 1,052.09 | 1,046.26 | 1,042.71 | 1,005.55 | 1,037.73 |  | 1,030.61 | 1,023.37 | 1,015.69 | 1,020.50 | 1,029.31 | 1,033.89 | 1,036.04 |
| Los Angeles Chargers | 1,011.72 | 1,006.79 | 999.97 | 997.31 | 1,000.17 | 1,002.26 | 1,009.77 |  | 1,002.34 | 1,002.34 | 1,013.25 | 1,022.71 | 1,024.52 | 1,030.53 | 1,021.28 | 1,024.67 | 1,030.47 |
| Los Angeles Rams | 1,062.45 | 1,054.17 | 1,056.11 | 1,059.54 | 1,052.59 | 1,059.07 | 1,065.97 | 1,068.03 | 1,070.40 | 1,075.28 | 1,065.98 | 1,071.43 | 1,075.31 | 1,069.39 | 1,080.57 | 1,082.86 | 1,066.33 |
| Miami Dolphins | 1,058.61 | 968.83 | 960.22 | 954.58 | 960.41 | 966.32 | 970.44 | 958.16 | 953.71 | 947.39 | 940.77 | 937.60 | 948.49 | 957.60 | 952.39 | 947.46 | 942.83 |
| Minnesota Vikings | 1,044.00 | 1,049.25 | 1,054.05 | 1,046.62 | 1,049.02 | 1,054.12 | 1,058.48 | 1,060.66 |  | 1,064.31 | 1,073.17 | 1,076.90 | 1,080.56 | 1,073.53 | 1,077.83 | 1,081.94 | 1,084.85 |
| New England Patriots | 1,044.89 | 1,052.48 | 1,054.48 | 1,049.27 | 1,052.15 | 1,055.26 | 1,061.50 | 1,065.44 | 1,077.07 | 1,070.19 |  | 1,078.40 | 1,083.15 | 1,073.87 | 1,078.18 | 1,082.85 | 1,085.86 |
| New Orleans Saints | 927.13 | 1,035.98 | 1,046.22 | 1,051.47 | 1,057.01 | 1,061.11 | 1,064.11 | 1,068.03 | 915.48 | 1,079.18 | 1,073.46 | 1,078.51 | 1,072.84 | 1,075.46 | 1,080.15 | 1,070.83 |  |
| New York Giants | 961.07 | 922.28 | 920.78 | 918.03 | 914.96 | 925.04 | 920.30 | 956.89 | 966.03 | 909.41 | 916.39 | 912.27 | 908.36 | 902.93 | 901.80 | 894.76 | 903.21 |
| New York Jets | 982.24 | 951.19 | 959.39 | 965.60 | 963.39 | 965.05 | 960.71 | 972.12 | 968.02 | 960.55 |  | 956.84 | 964.27 | 951.28 | 948.43 | 944.79 | 941.51 |
| Oakland Raiders | 991.57 | 951.19 | 982.75 | 956.21 | 970.89 | 968.68 | 972.12 | 963.79 | 1,084.46 | 960.55 | 962.30 | 966.96 | 970.62 | 965.49 | 961.86 | 959.56 | 953.35 |
| Philadelphia Eagles | 1,066.25 | 1,059.51 | 1,060.88 | 1,063.37 | 1,069.18 | 1,073.30 | 1,076.87 | 1,080.15 |  | 1,058.78 | 1,091.51 | 1,095.69 | 1,084.84 | 1,090.45 | 1,091.48 | 1,093.59 | 1,085.50 |
| Pittsburgh Steelers | 1,046.60 | 1,055.51 | 1,047.62 | 1,055.18 | 1,043.78 | 1,049.35 | 1,053.67 | 1,057.24 |  | 1,058.78 | 1,065.01 | 1,067.20 | 1,069.29 | 1,071.23 | 1,066.70 | 1,066.70 | 1,072.11 |
| San Francisco 49ers | 965.71 | 962.41 | 960.32 | 956.21 | 951.04 | 948.20 | 937.88 | 934.31 | 928.58 | 934.32 |  | 930.32 | 933.23 | 940.66 | 945.21 | 955.96 | 972.19 |
| Seattle Seahawks | 1,009.07 | 1,012.16 | 1,006.38 | 1,013.11 | 1,019.81 |  | 1,024.21 | 1,027.18 | 1,021.55 | 1,025.36 | 1,020.63 | 1,024.35 | 1,034.86 | 1,030.13 | 1,018.25 | 1,024.11 | 1,019.05 |
| Tampa Bay Buccaneers | 983.13 | 973.42 | 968.26 | 970.83 | 967.74 | 962.75 | 959.13 | 953.72 | 949.48 | 954.70 | 960.98 | 955.92 | 951.23 | 947.80 | 945.19 | 943.11 | 952.27 |
| Tennessee Titans | 982.14 | 996.54 | 1,002.06 | 980.58 |  | 979.94 | 982.27 | 987.43 | 987.43 | 991.21 | 984.52 | 987.58 | 993.12 | 987.24 | 982.51 | 980.04 | 986.82 |
| Washington Redskins |  | 990.20 | 998.57 | 993.92 | 974.48 | 996.59 | 992.75 | 984.91 | 990.33 | 986.41 | 984.13 | 987.97 | 977.09 | 970.67 | 975.34 | 981.83 | 973.15 |

## Divisional Playoffs

The Divisional Playoffs had four games. Atlanta at Philadelphia; Tennessee at New England, Jacksonville at Pittsburgh, and New Orleans at Minnesota.

## Atlanta at Philadelphia

The Falcons (10-6, elo 1024.30) were a 3.5 point favorites against the Eagles (13-3, elo 1054.51). The bookmakers favored the Falcons, the most experienced team with MVP QB Matt Ryan. Ryan had an ok year with 20 TDs and 12 interceptions, a 91.4 rating and 4095 yards gained. He was very strong in his last few games, hence the rating. Despite that, the Pinnacle odds on Atlanta were 2.28:1. So I bet $200 on Atlanta.

Philadelphia had a very strong running game led by Le Garrette Blount who was traded from the Patriots where he had 18 TDs last year, and Ajayi who was traded from Miami this year. Both of them had near 1000 yards gained. The QB Nick Foles, while he was a backup, was actually 27 TDs and 2 interceptions in 2014 when he was a starting QB before he was injured. Still, the feeling was that Ryan was more experienced for the playoffs.

The game see-sawed and was a very good one for mean reversion risk arbitrage. My second bet was $100 Philadelphia at 3.18 made near half time. My third bet in the 3rd quarter when the score was 10-9 Atlanta leading, was $100 on Atlanta at 1.625. That bet was intended to have a risk arbitrage with the 2nd bet. Later, at the start of the 4th quarter, I bet $100 on Philadelphia when the score was 12-10 in favor of Philadelphia. Late in the 4th quarter I bet $100 Atlanta at 2.14. My final bet was $50 on Philadelphia and they got a field goal to win the game 15-10.

To summarize my six bets gained $232.20. This was a very good example of winning the bets on the game even though the team you picked to win lost the game. Philadelphia won the game because of their strong defense, failrly good play by QB Foles, and 3 field goals by their kicker Jake Elliott who actually missed one extra point. Foles guarded the team well but is not considered to be as spectacular a QB as Carson Wentz who is in the MVP conversation with Tom Brady, Aaron Donald, Russell Wilson and Antonio Brown.

## Tennessee at New England

Tennessee (10-7, elo 996.72) against New England (13-3, elo 1043.16). Coming into the game, the Patriots were huge favorites with a spread of 13.5. I bet $500 at 1.117 giving me a potential gain of $58.50. Throughout the season, Brady had 32 TDs and 8 interceptions and a 102.8 rating and a league leading 4577 yards passing. The Patriots have a very balanced attack: running they got 6 TDs from Dion Lewis, 5 more from Mike Gillislee, and 5 more from Rex Burkhead. Together they gained about 1500 yards. New England is noted for Brady's passing and he through 8 TDs to Gronkowski, 7 to Brandon Cooks each of whom gained over 1000 yards and over 60 receptions. So did Amendola who also had over 60 receptions and added 2 TDs. Chris Hogan had 5 TDs and James White, Burkhead, and Lewis each had 3 more.

The Titans are led by Hawaiian (University of Oregon) QB Marcus Mariota who is a scrambler and had 13 TDs but 15 interceptions. Mariota scored 5 TDs and was the third leading runner. Their top runners Henry and Murray had 5 and 6 TDsew.

New England is 17-3 in home playoff games and are nearly invincible in Foxoboro. Tennessee started the game with the first TD to lead 7-0. After that it was all New England, who scored the next 35 points. Mariota threw a second TD to close the gap to the final score of 35-14. I won my bet and Brady became at 40, the oldest QB to win a playoff game.

## Jacksonville at Pittsburgh

Jacksonville (10-6) at Pittsburgh (13-3).

Jacksonville had gotten 3 TDs from rookie running back Leonard Fornette, starting with 2 in the first quarter to make it 14-0. In this game Fornette had 25 carries for 109 yards.

Down 28-14 at halftime, the Steelers got within 7 points in the 4th quarter.

With 9:05 left in the 4th quarter, Big Ben connected with Antonio Brown for a 43 yard TD to make it 35-28. Blake Bortles had a 14 yard TD pass to Tommy Bohanan to make it 42-28. Pittsburgh then got a clever play from Big Ben who ran towards the end zone and appeared stopped. Then he threw a backward pass to LéVeon Bell, who ran to score a TD to make it 42-35. With 2:18 left, the Steelers failed on an onside kick. Jacksonville recovered and got a field goal to make it 45-35. The Steelers got the ball back with 1:45 left and scored a TD to make it 45-42. Another Pittsburgh onside kick failed. The game ended 45-42.

Big Ben had 5 TD passes in a losing cause and had a 110.5 rating. Antonio Brown caught 7 passes for 132 yards and 2 TDs. Vance McDonald caught 10 passes for 112. Pittsburgh had many great plays in the game but fell slightly short to win the game.

## New Orleans at Minnesota

Minnesota (13-3, elo 1056.87) has a 4 point favorite against New Orleans (11-5, elo 1043.15) was a game for the ages. In addition to four lead changes in the final three minutes, the game had a spectacular finish. Throughout these three minutes, it seemed that one team had the game won only to have it slip away and then reverse and then reverse again. Each time the score changed, the odds changed dramatically. So that one theoretically could get good mean reversion bets to create profitable hedges, but the Pinnacle site, where I was betting, is a cumbersome one. The bets appear and you must ask quickly otherwise these bets disappear from the screen. Then the screen is blank for a long time with no available bets. So one needs technique that is super fast luck to get the bets you want. Betfair, which is no longer allowed in Canada, was superior.

The game pitted the #2 offense of the Saints against the NFL's top ranked defense. I favored New Orleans because they seemed to be the better team and had better odds. The Vikings led 17-0 in the first half. Drew Brees had a weak first half with two interceptions, however, in the second half he showed his future Hall of Fame form. Most of the action was in the last 3.01 minutes of the fourth quarter. Brees threw 3 TD passes. At 1.29 minutes to go, Kai Forbath hit a 53 yard field goal to put them in the lead 22-21. Then, with 25 seconds to go, New Orleans got a 43 yard TD pass from Brees to Will Lutz to make the score 24-22 in favor of New Orleans. Then with 10 seconds to go, and the odds that Minnesota would win rising by the second past 6-1 however I could not get the bet on. The QB Case Keenan, who was up and down all the game, threw a long pass caught by Stefan Diggs. Since he was in bounds, it looked like the game was over but he ran to score the winning TD to create a Minnesota 29-24 victory. Minnesota now plays Philadelphia for the NFC championship.

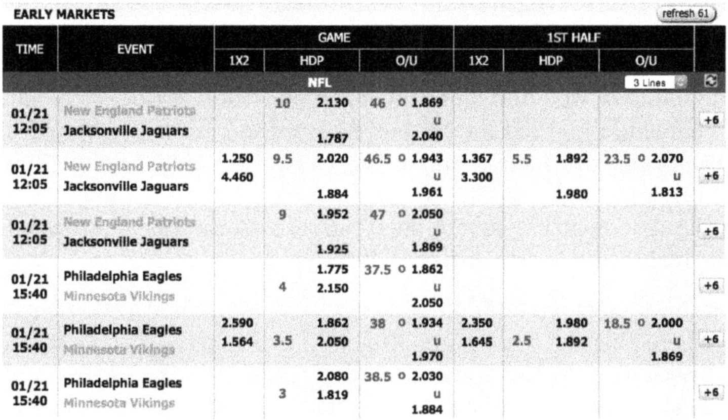

EARLY MARKETS refresh 61

| TIME | EVENT | GAME 1X2 | GAME HDP | GAME O/U | 1ST HALF 1X2 | 1ST HALF HDP | 1ST HALF O/U | |
|---|---|---|---|---|---|---|---|---|
| NFL | | | | | | | 3 Lines | |
| 01/21 12:05 | New England Patriots<br>Jacksonville Jaguars | | 10 2.130<br>1.787 | 46 o 1.869<br>u<br>2.040 | | | | +6 |
| 01/21 12:05 | New England Patriots<br>Jacksonville Jaguars | 1.250<br>4.460 | 9.5 2.020<br>1.884 | 46.5 o 1.943<br>u<br>1.961 | 1.367<br>3.300 | 5.5 1.892<br>1.980 | 23.5 o 2.070<br>u<br>1.813 | +6 |
| 01/21 12:05 | New England Patriots<br>Jacksonville Jaguars | | 9 1.952<br>1.925 | 47 o 2.050<br>u<br>1.869 | | | | +6 |
| 01/21 15:40 | Philadelphia Eagles<br>Minnesota Vikings | | 1.775<br>4 2.150 | 37.5 o 1.862<br>u<br>2.050 | | | | +6 |
| 01/21 15:40 | Philadelphia Eagles<br>Minnesota Vikings | 2.590<br>1.564 | 1.862<br>3.5 2.050 | 38 o 1.934<br>u<br>1.970 | 2.350<br>1.645 | 1.980<br>2.5 1.892 | 18.5 o 2.000<br>u<br>1.869 | +6 |
| 01/21 15:40 | Philadelphia Eagles<br>Minnesota Vikings | | 2.080<br>3 1.819 | 38.5 o 2.030<br>u<br>1.884 | | | | +6 |

Figure 16.1: Early odds for week 4 of the playoffs

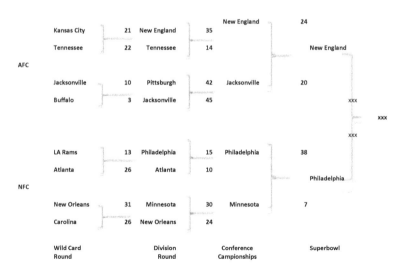

Figure 16.2: The 2018 playoffs and Super Bowl. Source: Wikipedia

## Conference Championships

### AFC Championship: the impossible is routine for Brady

It was a mean-reversion risk arbitrage betting situation designed to have betting gains no matter whether the New England Patriots or the Jacksonville Jaguars won the game. Once again the Patriots were in a hole quite far behind and outplayed, but a case where Tom Brady and his cast of receivers and the defense came back from a large deficit to win the game. Brady has repeatedly shown that no matter how far behind the Patriots are in the 3rd and 4th quarters, they can rally to win the game even though it looks like the opponent has it locked up.

I started out betting $200 on New England at 1.25 and another $200 at 1.281 where this bet was made after it was disclosed that Brady had injured his right thumb. It was New England's 7th consecutive conference championship game and their 12th overall. Tom Brady cut his right thumb on a minor collision in practice with running back Rex Burkhead. When he came onto the field he was wearing a glove on his throwing hand for the first time in 15 years; however, in the game, he did not actually use it.

New England is 18-3 in home playoff games and they are 5-0 in AFC championship game when they are the #1 seed as they are this year. Jacksonville had the best pass defense in the NFL and New England the best offensive team focusing on passing.

Tom Coughlin, who was the NY Giants head coach when they beat New England twice in the Super Bowl, is now director of football operations for the Jaguars and gets a lot of credit for rebuilding.

The game started with Jacksonville winning the coin toss and deferring to the 2nd half. Brady started out 6 for 6, so his passing looked fine and the injury did not seem to bother him. New England got to the 10 but could not score the TD but got a field goal to make in 3-0.

Leonard Fornette has become a top rusher and gained 1040 yards this year for the Jaguars. He was strong early in this game. After several Fornette runs, Jacksonville scored on a TD pass to Mercedes Lewis to make it 7-3. New England tried to retaliate but could not score. After a 4th down punt, Fornette led Jacksonville to another TD to make it 14-3. New England had the ball again but could not score, so when Jacksonville got the punt, I bet $200 more on New England, but now got very good 2.76:1 odds. At the 2 minute warning the odds were 2.58:1 as New England was charging. Brady passed to his favorite receiver Rob Gronkowski who was unable to catch the pass. But the defender, Barry Church, purposively head butted Gronkowski and knocked him out of the game with a concussion. There was a penalty for unnecessary roughness, but the loss of New England's 2nd best player and top receiver who is worth over 10 extra points per game on average when he plays, was devastating to New England. They have a way of regrouping after trouble. They did score a TD on a Brady pass to James White to make it 14-10. I then hedged my New England bet by going long Jacksonville $200 at 2.2 and the 1st half ended.

The Jaguar's QB Blake Bortles was the equal or better than Brady and had 12 straight completions so far. A Jacksonville field goal early in the 2nd half made it 17-10. Fornette continued his good running and Jacksonville got another field goal to make it 20-10. Their field goal kicker has made all but one of his field goal tries this year. New England made 2 trick plays including a double hand off pass to Lewis which ended up with a large gain but he fumbled. Jacksonville got the ball again. New England then held them and then they drove towards the end zone and Danny Amendola caught a TD pass from Brady to make it 20-17. New England coach Bill Belichick is well known to be NFL's best coach at making half time adjustments to help his team. They contained Fornette and Jacksonville was unable to get a first down and had to punt. The Jaguars were backed up closed to their end zone so their punt was short going only to the 50th yard line and Amendola ran it 20 more yards to the Jaguars 30. James White got it to the 15 and then New England scored on a Lewis run to make it 24-20 in favor of New England.

Legendary 39 year old, 2008 defensive player of the year, James Harrison, who was cut this year from Pittsburgh and picked up by New England, excelled on defense with good tackles and sacks in the game.

New England had, through Brady's passing and other good plays, come back once again from a large deficit to win. Brady was 26-34 for 290 yards, 2 TDs, no interceptions and a 108.4 rating. Amendola scored 2 TDs, had 7 receptions and was named MVP. Bortles was 23 of 36 for 293 yards and 1 TD. Fornette had 24 carries for 76 yards, mostly in the first half. The betting showed a gain of $238.20 because the first bet gained 50, the 2nd 56.20 and the 3rd 352.00 and the two Jacksonville hedge bets lost 250.

### NFC Championship

This game between the Philadelphia Eagles and Minnesota Vikings favored the visiting Vikings by 3 points. Their elo's were similar so even though the Eagles were the #1 seed and at home, it looked like a tossup. Swetye's

1000 start elos were Minnesota 1084, Philadlephia 1085. The 538-type elos were Minnesota 1056, Philadelphia 1054. I favored Philadelphia with two strong running backs and a QB who had 27 TDs and 2 interceptions before he was injured in 2014. Nick Foles was the better QB in my view, even though he was the Philadelphia backup and got the starting position when Carson Wentz was injured. The Vikings had the best defense and were strong on offense but Philadelphia seemed a notch better. So I bet $100 Eagles +3 at 1.884 to win 88.40 or lose 100 and $100 Eagles at 2.36 to win 126 or lose 100.

Minnesota scored to make it 7-0 and looked sharp. Then the Eagles defense got a Pick 6 to tie the game at 7. Philadelphia then quickly took over the game with a Blount TD to make it 14-7 and another TD to make if 21-7 near half time. I hedged the Philadelphia long bet to create a winning risk arbitrage by going long Minnesota 100 at 2.51:1 and 100 at 2.26:1. A field goal made it 24-7 Philadelphia. I then added to the Minnesota bet by adding 100 at 4.33:1 to win 333 or lose 100. All the while, Foles was sharp and by then had a 113.4 rating. The Eagles got the ball to start the second half, a flea-flicker trick led to a long Foles TD to make it 37-7. The Pinnacle site creates new bets as the score evolves in these games. At 24-7 they offered the bet Philadelphia -17.5 at 2.21:1, so you win 121 or lose 100 with a bet of 100. I passed on this bet. Notice that this bet is clever. If the team that is behind and gets a TD and a 1 point extra, you would lose the bet.

Philadelphia continued to score and at 24-7 the straight odds were Philadelphia 1.02:1, Minnesota 17.22:1. A bet Eagles -19.5 was now offered with the scored 31-7. I passed on this bet as well which was designed to create losses for people who bet on Minnesota.

Foles now had 324 yards passng, 8-10 on 3rd down, 2 TDs and 4 completions of 35+ yards. The game continued. There was an illegal hands to the face of Zach Ertz. With 32 seconds left in the 3rd quarter, Philadelphia was on the 5. Ajaji ran it to the 1. The 3rd quarter ended. The bet offered now was Philadelphia -25.5 was 2.01:1 Philadelphia which moved to 2.03 and 2.14. Meanwhile the respective Minnesota odds were 1.87:1, 1.833:1 and 1.751:1.

Philadelphia scored the TD to make the score 38-7. There was a fight on the field with unnecessary roughness against a Minnesota player. Now Minnesota needs 2 TDs to win the -17.5 bet. The offered bet was Philadelphia -16.5 giving 1.704:1 and 2.221:1 for Minnesota. I did not understand why they offered this bet.

Keenum had a run of 8 but was short of the first down. In the game he had had 2 interceptions, 1 fumble picked up by Chris Long that led to a field goal. He was 28 of 48 for 271 in a losing cause. Fletcher Cox, the outstanding Philadelphia defender was strong all the game. Foles ended 26 of 33 for 352 yards with 2 TDs, 1 to Alshon Jeffrey and the other Torrey Smith. He had a 141 rating. Ajayi had 18 carries for 17 yards. Ertz had 8 receptions for 93 yards. Philadelphia scored one more TD to make it 38-7, 31 points ahead. They offered the following bet: Philadelphia -30.5 giving them 1.6171:1 and Minnesota 2.23:1. I pondered as to why they offered this bet rather than Philadelphia -31.5. The game ended 38-7. My two long Eagles gained 88.40 and won 36, my Philadelphia -17.5 bet gained 121 for a total of 345.40 subtracting the three Minnesota 100 bets gave a net profit of 45.40. This was a case where the risk management hedging lowered the net profit because there was a huge trend with one team completely dominating the other team. Foles now received a 100 plus rating in his first 3 post season games, an accomplishment only Troy Aikman has done before.

**Super Bowl 52**

The Super Bowl was with New England against Philadelphia, which was held the US Bank Stadium in Minneapolis. At 40 years of age, Tom Brady, MVP for the third time, led the Patriots. He had 32 TDs and 8 interceptions.

The best news for the Patriots was that Rob Gronkowski passed the concussion protocol. On average he is worth more that 10 points per game.

Tom Brady's second favorite receiver, Julian Edelman, was out for an injury. He was replaced by Danny Amendola for the short passes. Long passes are reserved for Gronkowski and others. I noticed right away a huge Belichick blunder, in my opinion, not giving LaGarrette Blount the same salary as last year when he scored 18 TDs and was a great help in New England winning the Super Bowl. Asked to take a pay cut after a brilliant season Blount opted for free agency and he wound up on Philadelphia. So a great asset was now a liability as he was on the other team. We see below that I was right in this analysis.

The next dubious move by Belichick was to bench star defensive back Malcolm Butler, who played almost none of the Super Bowl. It shows the extreme rigor of the way Belichick runs the team. Players come and go in rapid fashion and minor infractions lead to players not being used. The greatest example was Gray who scored 4 TDs and over 200 yards in one game and then was late for a practice and never played again. But somehow, Belichick style leads to a very high level of performance.

I made the following bets on New England who were slightly favored:

- $200 @ 1.507:1; returning 101.40 if they win and -200 if they lose

- $200 on New England + 3.5 points @ 1.303:1 to win 60.60 or -200 if they lose

- New England + 7.5 @ 1.181:1, that's bet $276.24 to win 50

- $ 400 on New England + 10.5 @ 1.125:1 to win 50

Both teams had 13-3 records and led their divisions with a top QB in the MPV discussion. For Philadelphia, Nick Foles replaced the injured Carson Wentz. Wentz in his second season had a 101.9 rating with 3296 yards, 33 TDs and 7 interceptions. The running duo of Blount and Ajayi who came from Miami, added to their powerful offense. The management of Philadelphia who had a weak prior season rebuilt the team to be very strong on both offense and defense.

New England led the league with 6307 yards and was second in points with 458. Their defense allowed a lot of yards gained being 29th of the 32 teams, but were fifth best in points allowed with 296.

The game started out with Philadelphia scoring a field goal making it 3-0. The Patriots responded with a similar drive ending with a 28 yard Stephen Gostkowski field goal to make it 3-3.

Then in just 3 plays, the Eagles scored a TD on a short pass to Agholos, a 31 yard Blount run and a 36 yard Foles pass to Jeffrey. They missed the extra point to make it 9-3.

The Patriots then drove to the Eagles 11 yard line, mainly on a 50 yard pass from Brady to Amendola. Then Gostkowski missed the 26 yard field goal attempt when holder Allen could not handle the snap.

The Eagles then got the ball to their 35 and got a 19 yard to Ertz and a 22 yarder to Jeffrey. Then Blount ran it in for a 21 yard TD that made it 15-3 for Philadelphia when the 2 point extra try failed.

Brady was sharp and had a 46 yard pass to Berkhart but the drive stalled and Gostkowski got a 45 yard field goal to make the score 15-6.

Then with 7:24 to go in the second quarter, Ajaji got them in scoring position position with a 26 yard run. New England safety Harmon got an interception on a Foles pass that bounced off Jeffrey who tried to make a Odell Beckham Jr style pass. New England got the ball on their 10 yard line and went the whole 90 yards to score a TD making the score 15-12. The key plays were a 43 yard pass to Hogan and a 26 yard TD romp by White. Again Gostkowski failed to get the extra point.

The Eagles Barner returned the kickoff 27 yards to their 30 as the game got to the 2 minute warning. Then Clement ran 55 yards on a pass to the New England 8 yard line and he got it to the 2 yard line. Then on 4th and 1 with 38 seconds to go they attempted a trick play. Foles moved to the running back position and Clement took the snap and threw the ball to Foles who caught it and scored a TD. That was the first QB to ever catch a TD pass in a Super Bowl game. The extra point was good this time so the half ended 22-12. Both QBs had over 200 yards gained with 276 for Brady and 215 for Foles, an NFL record.

The Patriots got the ball in the 2nd half and Brady went to Gronkowski five separate times, finally, with the TD from 5 yards away so the narrowed the score to 22-19.

The Eagles then responded with an 85 yard 11 play drive with 3 straight 3rd down completions by Foles. Clement scored the TD on a controversial play of the variety "did he actually catch the ball in play without hitting the ground?" Elliott got the extra point to make it 29-19.

The mean reversion up-down pattern continued with Brady hitting 3 straight passes for 61 yards, the last to Hogan who scored a 26 yard TD to make the score close at 29-26. The third quarter ended with the Eagles driving to the New England 6th yard line. They got a field goal to start the 4th quarter to extend their lead to 32-26.

Brady then led a 75 yard drive with a 30 yard pass to Amendola and a 4 yard Gronkowski TD, his second of the game. The Patriots then led, for the first time, 33-32. The Eagles came back with runs by Ajai and Blount, 3 third down completions to Agholor and the 9 yard TD to Ertz with 2:21 to go. Again, the TD was controversial but the Eagles got the decision in their favor that Ertz was in the end zone legally. Then they missed the 2 point extra try.

The Eagles had a 5 point lead, 38-33 and New England got the ball and were charging but a strip of Brady by Eagles defensive end Brandon Graham late in the 4th quarter was crucial. That was the only sack of the game. This helped the Eagles get a field goal by Elliott to now lead by 8 points, 41-33. The game ended when Brady's "hail Mary" pass from the 49 yard line with 9 seconds left failed and time ran out.

The final score remained 41-33. The 33 points set a record for a losing team. There were other records set as well such as the 1151 yards for both teams. There was only one punt. Foles completed 28 of 43 passes for 3 TDs and 1 interception and he caught the 1 yard pass for another TD so was the game's MVP. The Eagles won their first Vince Lombardi Trophy and their first championship since 1960.

I won the largest bet with the Patriots plus 10.5 points but I decided not to hedge the other three bets at various times in the game because I assumed that the Patriots would win in the end. They did not so I lost those three bets.

# Chapter 17

# ELO Team Strength Ratings: Predicting Win Probabilities and Point Spreads in NFL Games in 2017-2018

## Win Probability in Games

A NFL season is a tournament of games between teams, with each game having a win/loss outcome. If $X_{ij}$ is the outcome of a game between team $i$ and team $j$, then consider $X_{ij} = 1$ if team $i$ wins and $X_{ij} = 0$ if team $j$ wins. The score $S_i = \sum_{j \neq i} X_{ij}$ defines the performance of team $i$ against other teams. The outcome of a game is uncertain, so consider $p_{ij} = Prob\left[X_{ij} = 1\right]$. Considering that the team standings in a season depend only on $\{S_i, i = 1, ..., N\}$ for $N$ teams, then the outcome probabilities can be defined by

$$p_{ij} = \frac{1}{1 + e^{-(\theta_i - \theta_j)}},$$

for parameters $\theta_i$ and $\theta_j$ for teams $i$ and $j$. (Buhlmann and Huber, 1963.) Of course the values for the parameters $\theta_i$ and $\theta_j$ in a head to head competition are unknown. If the parameters reflect the relative strengths of the teams, then elements of team composition, strategy and management would factor into competitiveness. In this chapter the ELO method of estimating team strength will be described and applied to games in the 2017 NFL season.

## Competitor Ratings — the ELO system

Without accounting for the talents of individual players and coaches, the pattern of wins and losses to date indicate the relative strengths of teams heading into a match. A strength rating based on wins/losses is the ELO rating system pioneered by Arpad Elo, a Hungarian-born American physicist. The rating evolves as games are completed. Following a match, the rating for each competitor is adjusted up or down depending on the outcome. Victories over strong opponents increase one's rating the most. The amount one's rating improves with a victory depends on the way the system is tuned.

If a game between team $i$ and team $j$ is scheduled to commence at time $t, t = 1, ..., T$ we assume the teams have up to date ratings of $\theta_i(t)$ and $\theta_j(t)$, respectively. Also suppose heading into the competition team $i$ has a prior chance of winning against team $j$ of $p_{ij}(t)$. So $p_{ij}(t) + p_{ji}(t) = 1$. If there is no basis for favoring one team then $p_{ij}(t) = p_{ji}(t) = 0.50$. The outcome of the game is $x_{ij}(t)$ , where $x_{ij}(t) = 1$ for a win and $x_{ij}(t) = 0$ for a loss. The formula for updating team ratings based on the game result is

$$\theta_i(t + 1) = \theta_i(t) + \alpha(x_{ij}(t) - p_{ij}(t)).$$

The change in rating is $\alpha(x_{ij}(t) - p_{ij}(t))$, which weights the difference in actual and expected outcome by the smoothing parameter $\alpha$. The sensitivity parameter $\alpha$ determines how much the most recent game result contributes to the revision of the rating.

With the revised (posterior) values of the strength parameters the probabilities for the games in the next week, $t + 1$, are calculated as

$$p_{ij}(t + 1) = \frac{1}{1 + e^{-(\theta_i(t+1) - \theta_j(t+1))}}.$$

The initial value of the parameter $\theta$ and the $\alpha$ are to be determined. If the teams are evenly matched, with $\theta_i(t) - \theta_j(t) = 0$ and $p_{ij}(t) = 0.5$, and team $i$ wins: $x_{ij}(t) = 1$, then $\theta_i(t + 1) - \theta_j(t + 1) = \alpha$ and $p_{ij}(t + 1) = \frac{1}{1+e^{-\alpha}}$. Each additional unit of 0.01 added to $\alpha$ adds 0.0025 to $p_{ij}(t + 1)$. A single win shouldn't move the probability very much, so a reasonable choice is $\alpha = .02$.

# FiveThirtyEight ELO NFL Ratings

FiveThirtyEight, sometimes referred to as 538, is a website that focuses on opinion poll analysis, politics, economics, and sports blogging. The website, which takes its name from the number of electors in the United States electoral college. FiveThirtyEight's NFL coverage uses Elo ratings. As indicated teams gain and lose ground based on the final score of each game and how unexpected the result was in the eyes of the pregame ratings. Under Elo, teams pick up where they left off in the previous season.

The scale of the 538 ELO ratings is magnified by a factor of 400, so we will use notation $R_i$ for team strength. The benchmark rating is 1500. The initial team ratings for 2017 are by definition the same as last season's end-of-year ratings, but are more compressed because of reversion toward the mean — each team's rating is shrunk to the mean by one-third, with the league average team clocking in slightly above 1500. The updating equation is

$$R_i(t+1) = R_i(t) + K(X_{ij}(t) - p_{ij}(t)),$$

where the sensitivity parameter $K$ is scaled appropriately.

In calculating win probabilities for the game between team $i$ and team $j$, 538 uses a base 10, and the formula is

$$p_{ij}(t+1) = \frac{1}{1 + 10^{-\frac{1}{400}(R_i(t+1)-R_j(t+1))}}.$$

Since $10^{-a} = e^{-(log_{10}e) \times a}$ the sensitivity factor is $K = 20 \approx \frac{400 \times .02}{(log_{10}e)}$

Based on these equations the NFL ELO Ratings by Week for 2017 are provided in the weekly tables discussed below. A summary of the the NFL ELO Ratings by team by week for the 2017 season are provided in Table 17.17 at the end of the chapter.

The dynamics of the ELO rating for each team in 2017 is shown in Figure 17.1. Teams with consistently increasing ratings shown in Figure 17.2 are: Carolina, Jacksonville, LA Chargers, LA Rams,Minnesota, New England, New Orleans, Philadelphia, and Pittsburgh. Teams with consistently decreasing ratings shown in Figure 17.3 are: Arizona, Cleveland, Denver, Green Bay, Houston, Indianapolis, NY Giants, and Tampa Bay.

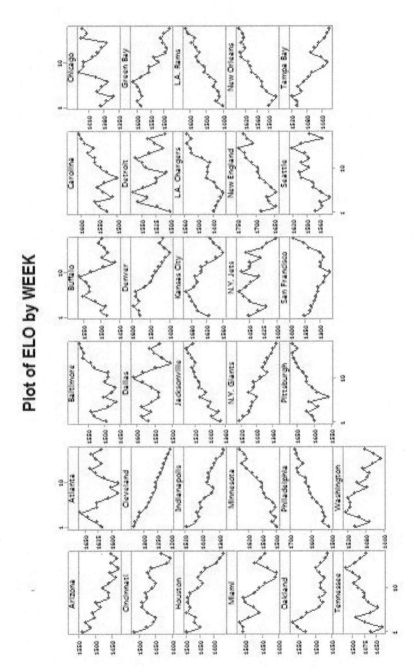

Figure 17.1: Plot of Elo by team week by week, 2017 season

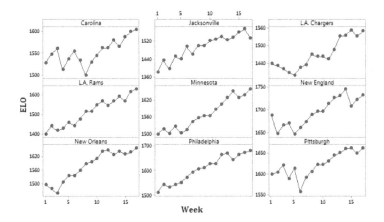

Figure 17.2: Plot of Elo increasing teams, 2017 season

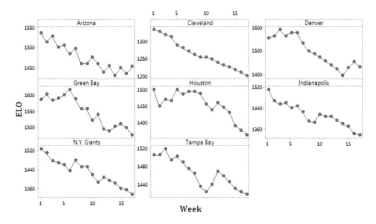

Figure 17.3: Plot of Elo by team decreasing teams, 2017 season

It appears that the ingredients of truly strong/weak teams (players, coaches) are present throughout the football season. There are also up and down teams, where in season dynamics alter performance and the ELO rating reverses direction. We will consider the ability to predict game results using the pregame ELO rating for team matchups each week in the 2017 NFL season. There are two aspects of the game outcome we consider: (1) the win/loss, which determines team standings; (2) the difference between winning and losing scores, which is important for betting.

## Point Spread

Betting on NFL games is very popular. Many games are games between strong and weak teams and the uncertainty in the outcome is not attractive for wagers. The Point Spread is a forecast of the number of points by which a stronger team is expected to defeat a weaker one, used for betting purposes. The general purpose of spread betting is to create an active market for both sides of a binary wager, even if the outcome of an event may appear prima facie to be biased towards one side or the other. The point spread is essentially a handicap towards the underdog. There are a variety of spreads each week, depending on the betting site. We will use a simple conversion formula for calculating the expected point spread based on the probability of winning for the favorite from the ELO rating. The formula comes from Betting Talk, which is a news and information site that covers the sports betting industry. The formula is

$$S = -16 + 32 \times P,$$

where $S =$ the expected point spread and $P =$ the win probability for the favorite.

## Testing the ELO Each Week

Table 17.1: Week 1: In 9 of the 15 games the favorite, as determined by the ELO rating, won. In 7 of the games the point differential covered the spread.

| TeamA | TeamH | PA | PH | Favorite | FavP | spread | RESULT_1 | Diff |
|---|---|---|---|---|---|---|---|---|
| N.Y. Jets | Buffalo | 0.454078 | 0.545922 | Buffalo | 0.545921923 | 1.469502 | BUF 21, NYJ 12 | 9 |
| Atlanta | Chicago | 0.792696 | 0.207304 | Atlanta | 0.792696384 | 9.366284 | ATL 23, CHI 17 | 6 |
| Baltimore | Cincinnati | 0.464084 | 0.535916 | Cincinnati | 0.535915927 | 1.14931 | BAL 20, CIN 0 | -20 |
| Pittsburgh | Cleveland | 0.819646 | 0.180354 | Pittsburgh | 0.819645814 | 10.22867 | PIT 21, CLE 18 | 3 |
| Arizona | Detroit | 0.551624 | 0.448376 | Arizona | 0.551623547 | 1.651954 | DET 35, ARI 23 | -12 |
| Oakland | Tennessee | 0.599397 | 0.400603 | Oakland | 0.599396797 | 3.180697 | OAK 26, TEN 16 | 10 |
| Philadelphia | Washington | 0.510072 | 0.489928 | Philadelphia | 0.510072447 | 0.322318 | PHI 30, WSH 17 | 13 |
| Jacksonville | Houston | 0.333861 | 0.666139 | Houston | 0.666139425 | 5.316462 | JAX 29, HOU 7 | -22 |
| Indianapolis | L.A. Rams | 0.659708 | 0.340292 | Indianapolis | 0.659707994 | 5.110656 | LAR 46, IND 9 | -39 |
| Seattle | Green Bay | 0.47699 | 0.52301 | Green Bay | 0.523009587 | 0.736307 | GB 17, SEA 9 | 8 |
| Carolina | San Francisco | 0.731378 | 0.268622 | Carolina | 0.731377858 | 7.404091 | CAR 23, SF 3 | 20 |
| N.Y. Giants | Dallas | 0.444109 | 0.555891 | Dallas | 0.555890961 | 1.788511 | DAL 19, NYG 3 | 16 |
| Tampa Bay | Miami | 0.495683 | 0.504317 | Tampa Bay | 0.50431724 | 0.138152 | Postponed | |
| New Orleans | Minnesota | 0.5 | 0.5 | New Orleans | 0.5 | 0 | MIN 29, NO 19 | 10 |
| L.A. Chargers | Denver | 0.335142 | 0.664858 | Denver | 0.664857979 | 5.275455 | DEN 24, LAC 21 | 3 |
| Kansas City | New England | 0.395087 | 0.604913 | New England | 0.604912902 | 3.357213 | KC 42, NE 27 | -15 |

Table 17.2: Week 2: the favorite team as calculated from the ELO rating won 14 out of 16 games. The winning team covered the spread in 12 games. The outcome of games was quite predictable and the score differentials were larger than anticipated.

| TeamA | TeamH | PA | PH | Fav | FavP | Spread | SCORE | Diff |
|---|---|---|---|---|---|---|---|---|
| Houston | Cincinnati | 0.464084 | 0.535916 | Cincinnati | 0.535916 | 1.14931 | HOU 13, CIN 9 | -4 |
| Arizona | Indianapolis | 0.561568 | 0.438432 | Arizona | 0.561568 | 1.970174 | ARI 16, IND 13 (OT) | 3 |
| Philadelphia | Kansas City | 0.34548 | 0.65452 | Kansas City | 0.65452 | 4.94464 | KC 27, PHI 20 | 7 |
| New England | New Orleans | 0.724538 | 0.275462 | New England | 0.724538 | 7.185224 | NE 36, NO 20 | 16 |
| Minnesota | Pittsburgh | 0.375998 | 0.624002 | Pittsburgh | 0.624002 | 3.968056 | PIT 26, MIN 9 | 17 |
| Chicago | Tampa Bay | 0.318678 | 0.681322 | Tampa Bay | 0.681322 | 5.802299 | TB 29, CHI 7 | 22 |
| Buffalo | Carolina | 0.432771 | 0.567229 | Carolina | 0.567229 | 2.151323 | CAR 9, BUF 3 | 6 |
| Tennessee | Jacksonville | 0.504317 | 0.495683 | Tennessee | 0.504317 | 0.138152 | TEN 37, JAX 16 | 21 |
| Cleveland | Baltimore | 0.239204 | 0.760796 | Baltimore | 0.760796 | 8.345475 | BAL 24, CLE 10 | 14 |
| N.Y. Jets | Oakland | 0.337712 | 0.662288 | Oakland | 0.662288 | 5.19321 | OAK 45, NYJ 20 | 24 |
| Miami | L.A. Chargers | 0.611771 | 0.388229 | Miami | 0.611771 | 3.576656 | MIA 19, LAC 17 | 2 |
| Dallas | Denver | 0.538778 | 0.461222 | Dallas | 0.538778 | 1.240899 | DEN 42, DAL 17 | -25 |
| Washington | L.A. Rams | 0.545922 | 0.454078 | Washington | 0.545922 | 1.469502 | WSH 27, LAR 20 | 7 |
| San Francisco | Seattle | 0.217902 | 0.782098 | Seattle | 0.782098 | 9.027137 | SEA 12, SF 9 | 3 |
| Green Bay | Atlanta | 0.465516 | 0.534484 | Atlanta | 0.534484 | 1.103486 | ATL 34, GB 23 | 11 |
| Detroit | N.Y. Giants | 0.5187 | 0.4813 | Detroit | 0.5187 | 0.598393 | DET 24, NYG 10 | 14 |

Table 17.3: Week 3: Only 9 of the 16 games in week 3 are correctly predicted by the ELO model. The spread was covered in only 3 games.

| TeamA | TeamH | PA | PH | Fav_1 | FavP | Spread | Score | Diff |
|---|---|---|---|---|---|---|---|---|
| L.A. Rams | San Francisco | 0.625351 | 0.374649 | L.A. Rams | 0.62535139 | 4.01124459 | LAR 41, SF 39 | 2 |
| Baltimore | Jacksonville | 0.69491 | 0.30509 | Baltimore | 0.69490971 | 6.23711081 | JAX44, Bal 7 | -37 |
| Denver | Buffalo | 0.645352 | 0.354648 | Denver | 0.64535245 | 4.65127841 | BUF 26, DEN 16 | -10 |
| Pittsburgh | Chicago | 0.817938 | 0.182062 | Pittsburgh | 0.81793763 | 10.1740042 | CHI 23, PIT 17 (OT) | -6 |
| Atlanta | Detroit | 0.625351 | 0.374649 | Atlanta | 0.62535139 | 4.01124459 | ATL 30, DET 26 | 4 |
| Cleveland | Indianapolis | 0.31494 | 0.68506 | Indianapolis | 0.68505961 | 5.92190749 | IND 31, CLE 28 | 3 |
| Tampa Bay | Minnesota | 0.527316 | 0.472684 | Tampa Bay | 0.52731597 | 0.87411114 | MIN 34, TB 17 | -17 |
| Houston | New England | 0.246614 | 0.753386 | New England | 0.75338608 | 8.10835449 | NE 36, HOU 33 | 3 |
| Miami | N.Y. Jets | 0.638738 | 0.361262 | Miami | 0.63873775 | 4.43960797 | NYJ 20, MIA 6 | -14 |
| N.Y. Giants | Philadelphia | 0.424313 | 0.575687 | Philadelphia | 0.57568695 | 2.42198248 | PHI 27, NYG 24 | 3 |
| New Orleans | Carolina | 0.359935 | 0.640065 | Carolina | 0.640065 | 4.48207999 | NO 34, CAR 13 | -21 |
| Seattle | Tennessee | 0.619941 | 0.380059 | Seattle | 0.61994136 | 3.83812349 | TEN 33, SEA 27 | -6 |
| Cincinnati | Green Bay | 0.321183 | 0.678817 | Green Bay | 0.67881692 | 5.72214143 | GB 27, CIN 24 (OT) | 3 |
| Kansas City | L. A. Chargers | 0.802909 | 0.197091 | Kansas City | 0.80290917 | 9.69309344 | KC 24, LAC 10 | 14 |
| Oakland | Washington | 0.603536 | 0.396464 | Oakland | 0.60353632 | 3.31316219 | WSH 27, OAK 10 | -17 |
| Dallas | Arizona | 0.544495 | 0.455505 | Dallas | 0.54449457 | 1.42382634 | DAL 28, ARI 17 | 11 |

Table 17.4: Week 4: The favorite based on ELO rating won 11 of 16 games in week 4, and the favorite spread was covered in 8 games.

| Team A | Team H | PA | PH | Fav | FavP | Spread | Score | Diff |
|--------|--------|-----|-----|-----|------|--------|-------|------|
| Chicago | Green Bay | 0.241305 | 0.758695 | Green Bay | 0.758695 | 8.278228 | GB 35, CHI 14 | 21 |
| New Orleans | Miami | 0.527316 | 0.472684 | New Orleans | 0.527316 | 0.874111 | NO 20, MIA 0 | 20 |
| Buffalo | Atlanta | 0.301441 | 0.698559 | Atlanta | 0.698559 | 6.353876 | BUF 23, ATL 17 | -6 |
| Cincinnati | Cleveland | 0.683816 | 0.316184 | Cincinnati | 0.683816 | 5.882122 | CIN 31, CLE 7 | 25 |
| L.A. Rams | Dallas | 0.284747 | 0.715253 | Dallas | 0.715253 | 6.888088 | LAR 35, DAL 30 | -5 |
| Detroit | Minnesota | 0.521573 | 0.478427 | Detroit | 0.521573 | 0.690347 | DET 14, MIN 7 | 7 |
| Carolina | New England | 0.287098 | 0.712902 | New England | 0.712902 | 6.812869 | CAR 33, NE 30 | -3 |
| Jacksonville | N.Y. Jets | 0.5 | 0.5 | Jacksonville | 0.5 | 0 | NYJ 23, JAX 20 (OT) | -3 |
| Pittsburgh | Baltimore | 0.645352 | 0.354648 | Pittsburgh | 0.645352 | 4.651278 | PIT 26, BAL 9 | 15 |
| Tennessee | Houston | 0.537347 | 0.462653 | Tennessee | 0.537347 | 1.195114 | HOU 57, TEN 14 | -43 |
| San Francisco | Arizona | 0.259672 | 0.740328 | Arizona | 0.740328 | 7.690509 | ARI 18, SF 15 (OT) | 3 |
| Philadelphia | L.A. Chargers | 0.683816 | 0.316184 | Philadelphia | 0.683816 | 5.882122 | PHI 26, LAC 24 | 2 |
| N.Y. Giants | Tampa Bay | 0.465516 | 0.534484 | Tampa Bay | 0.534484 | 1.103486 | TB 25, NYG 23 | 1 |
| Oakland | Denver | 0.464084 | 0.535916 | Denver | 0.535916 | 1.14931 | DEN 16, OAK 10 | 6 |
| Indianapolis | Seattle | 0.392339 | 0.607661 | Seattle | 0.607661 | 3.445154 | SEA 46, IND 18 | 28 |
| Washington | Kansas City | 0.295415 | 0.704585 | Kansas City | 0.704585 | 6.546707 | KC 29, WSH 20 | 9 |

Table 17.5: Week 5: the favorite from the ELO rating won 8 of 14 games. In 4 of the games the favorite spread was covered.

| TeamA | TeamH | PA | PH | Fav | FavP | Spread | Score | Diff |
|-------|-------|-----|-----|-----|------|--------|-------|------|
| New England | Tampa Bay | 0.69491 | 0.30509 | New England | 0.69491 | 6.237111 | NE 19, TB 14 | 5 |
| Buffalo | Cincinnati | 0.604913 | 0.395087 | Buffalo | 0.604913 | 3.357213 | CIN 20, BUF 16 | -4 |
| N.Y. Jets | Cleveland | 0.727972 | 0.272028 | N.Y. Jets | 0.727972 | 7.295088 | NYJ 17, CLE 14 | 3 |
| Carolina | Detroit | 0.458362 | 0.541638 | Detroit | 0.541638 | 1.332406 | CAR 27, DET 24 | -3 |
| San Francisco | Indianapolis | 0.322439 | 0.677561 | Indianapolis | 0.677561 | 5.681939 | IND 26, SF 23 (OT) | 3 |
| Tennessee | Miami | 0.501439 | 0.498561 | Tennessee | 0.501439 | 0.046052 | MIA 16, TEN 10 | -6 |
| L.A. Chargers | N.Y. Giants | 0.407534 | 0.592466 | N.Y. Giants | 0.592466 | 2.958919 | LAC 27, NYG 22 | -3 |
| Arizona | Philadelphia | 0.437015 | 0.562985 | Philadelphia | 0.562985 | 2.015511 | PHI 34, ARI 7 | 27 |
| Jacksonville | Pittsburgh | 0.267493 | 0.732507 | Pittsburgh | 0.732507 | 7.440233 | JAX 30, PIT 9 | -21 |
| Baltimore | Oakland | 0.407534 | 0.592466 | Oakland | 0.592466 | 2.958919 | BAL 30, OAK 17 | -13 |
| Seattle | L.A. Rams | 0.636077 | 0.363923 | Seattle | 0.636077 | 4.354461 | SEA 16, LAR 10 | 6 |
| Green Bay | Dallas | 0.562985 | 0.437015 | Green Bay | 0.562985 | 2.015511 | GB 35, DAL 31 | 4 |
| Kansas City | Houston | 0.74473 | 0.25527 | Kansas City | 0.74473 | 7.831373 | KC 42, HOU 34 | 8 |
| Minnesota | Chicago | 0.666139 | 0.333861 | Minnesota | 0.666139 | 5.316462 | MIN 20, CHI 17 | 3 |

Table 17.6: Week 6: The favorite based on ELO ratings for week 6 only won 4 of the 15 games. The favorite point spread was covered in 2 matches.

| TeamA | TeamH | PA | PH | Fav | FavP | Spread | Score | Diff |
|---|---|---|---|---|---|---|---|---|
| Philadelphia | Carolina | 0.525881 | 0.474119 | Philadelphia | 0.525881 | 0.82819 | PHI 28, CAR 23 | 5 |
| Miami | Atlanta | 0.295415 | 0.704585 | Atlanta | 0.704585 | 6.546707 | MIA 20, ATL 17 | -3 |
| Green Bay | Minnesota | 0.647983 | 0.352017 | Green Bay | 0.647983 | 4.735456 | MIN 23, GB 10 | -13 |
| Detroit | New Orleans | 0.514387 | 0.485613 | Detroit | 0.514387 | 0.46039 | NO 52, DET 38 | -14 |
| New England | N.Y. Jets | 0.749083 | 0.250917 | New England | 0.749083 | 7.970658 | NE 24, NYJ 17 | 7 |
| San Francisco | Washington | 0.231948 | 0.768052 | Washington | 0.768052 | 8.577664 | WSH 26, SF 24 | 2 |
| Chicago | Baltimore | 0.32496 | 0.67504 | Baltimore | 0.67504 | 5.601286 | CHI 27, BAL 24 (OT) | -3 |
| Cleveland | Houston | 0.234005 | 0.765995 | Houston | 0.765995 | 8.511829 | HOU 33, CLE 17 | 16 |
| Tampa Bay | Arizona | 0.508634 | 0.491366 | Tampa Bay | 0.508634 | 0.276283 | ARI 38, TB 33 | -5 |
| L.A. Rams | Jacksonville | 0.42572 | 0.57428 | Jacksonville | 0.57428 | 2.376967 | LAR 27, JAX 17 | -10 |
| Pittsburgh | Kansas City | 0.30509 | 0.69491 | Kansas City | 0.69491 | 6.237111 | PIT 19, KC 13 | -6 |
| L.A. Chargers | Oakland | 0.410316 | 0.589684 | Oakland | 0.589684 | 2.869872 | LAC 17, OAK 16 | -1 |
| N.Y. Giants | Denver | 0.307537 | 0.692463 | Denver | 0.692463 | 6.158829 | NYG 23, DEN 10 | -13 |
| Indianapolis | Tennessee | 0.504317 | 0.495683 | Indianapolis | 0.504317 | 0.138152 | TEN 36, IND 22 | -14 |

Table 17.7: Week 7: the favorite won 10 of the 15 games and the point spread was covered in 9 games.

| TeamA | TeamH | PA | PH | Fav | FavP | Spread | Score | Diff |
|---|---|---|---|---|---|---|---|---|
| Kansas City | Oakland | 0.750163 | 0.249837 | Kansas City | 0.750163 | 8.005231 | OAK 31, KC 30 | -1 |
| Tampa Bay | Buffalo | 0.4201 | 0.5799 | Buffalo | 0.5799 | 2.556792 | BUF 30, TB 27 | 3 |
| Carolina | Chicago | 0.690006 | 0.309994 | Carolina | 0.690006 | 6.080199 | CHI 17, CAR 3 | -14 |
| Tennessee | Cleveland | 0.754454 | 0.245546 | Tennessee | 0.754454 | 8.142529 | TEN 12, CLE 9 (OT) | 3 |
| New Orleans | Green Bay | 0.456934 | 0.543066 | Green Bay | 0.543066 | 1.378128 | NO 26, GB 17 | -9 |
| Jacksonville | Indianapolis | 0.548774 | 0.451226 | Jacksonville | 0.548774 | 1.560779 | JAX 27, IND 0 | 27 |
| Arizona | L.A. Rams | 0.531618 | 0.468382 | Arizona | 0.531618 | 1.011786 | LAR 33, ARI 0 | -33 |
| N.Y. Jets | Miami | 0.43985 | 0.56015 | Miami | 0.56015 | 1.924805 | MIA 31, NYJ 28 | 3 |
| Baltimore | Minnesota | 0.403371 | 0.596629 | Minnesota | 0.596629 | 3.092134 | MIN 24, BAL 16 | 8 |
| Dallas | San Francisco | 0.793641 | 0.206359 | Dallas | 0.793641 | 9.396504 | DAL 40, SF 10 | 30 |
| Seattle | N.Y. Giants | 0.63207 | 0.36793 | Seattle | 0.63207 | 4.22624 | SEA 24, NYG 7 | 17 |
| Cincinnati | Pittsburgh | 0.359935 | 0.640065 | Pittsburgh | 0.640065 | 4.48208 | PIT 29, CIN 14 | 15 |
| Denver | L.A. Chargers | 0.638738 | 0.361262 | Denver | 0.638738 | 4.439608 | LAC 21, DEN 0 | -21 |
| Atlanta | New England | 0.400603 | 0.599397 | New England | 0.599397 | 3.180697 | NE 23, ATL 7 | 16 |
| Washington | Philadelphia | 0.396464 | 0.603536 | Philadelphia | 0.603536 | 3.313162 | PHI 34, WSH 24 | 10 |

Table 17.8: Week 8: The ELO favorite won 12 of 13 games in week 8. The favorite spread was covered in 8 of the 13 games.

| TeamA | TeamH | PA | PH | Fav | FavP | Spread | Score | Diff |
|---|---|---|---|---|---|---|---|---|
| Miami | Baltimore | 0.567229 | 0.432771 | Miami | 0.567229 | 2.151323 | BAL 40, MIA 0 | -40 |
| Minnesota | Cleveland | 0.843782 | 0.156218 | Minnesota | 0.843782 | 11.00103 | MIN 33, CLE 16 | 17 |
| Oakland | Buffalo | 0.424313 | 0.575687 | Buffalo | 0.575687 | 2.421982 | BUF 34, OAK 14 | 20 |
| Indianapolis | Cincinnati | 0.380059 | 0.619941 | Cincinnati | 0.619941 | 3.838123 | CIN 24, IND 23 | 1 |
| L. A. Chargers | New England | 0.218885 | 0.781115 | New England | 0.781115 | 8.995693 | NE 21, LAC 13 | 8 |
| Chicago | New Orleans | 0.283576 | 0.716424 | New Orleans | 0.716424 | 6.925558 | NO 20, CHI 12 | 8 |
| Atlanta | N. Y. Jets | 0.688774 | 0.311226 | Atlanta | 0.688774 | 6.040754 | ATL 25, NYJ 20 | 5 |
| San Francisco | Philadelphia | 0.136807 | 0.863193 | Philadelphia | 0.863193 | 11.62218 | PHI 33, SF 10 | 23 |
| Carolina | Tampa Bay | 0.547349 | 0.452651 | Carolina | 0.547349 | 1.515153 | CAR 17, TB 3 | 14 |
| Houston | Seattle | 0.353331 | 0.646669 | Seattle | 0.646669 | 4.693403 | SEA 41, HOU 38 | 3 |
| Dallas | Washington | 0.572872 | 0.427128 | Dallas | 0.572872 | 2.331912 | DAL 33, WSH 19 | 14 |
| Pittsburgh | Detroit | 0.614501 | 0.385499 | Pittsburgh | 0.614501 | 3.664044 | PIT 20, DET 15 | 5 |
| Denver | Kansas City | 0.285921 | 0.714079 | Kansas City | 0.714079 | 6.850525 | KC 29, DEN 19 | 10 |

Table 17.9: Week 9: The ELO determined favorite won 5 of 13 games in week 9 and the favorite spread was covered in all 5 games.

| TeamA | TeamH | PA | PH | Fav | FavP | Spread | Score | Diff |
|---|---|---|---|---|---|---|---|---|
| Buffalo | N.Y. Jets | 0.67251 | 0.32749 | Buffalo | 0.67251 | 5.520309 | NYJ 34, BUF 21 | -13 |
| Baltimore | Tennessee | 0.530185 | 0.469815 | Baltimore | 0.530185 | 0.96591 | TEN 23, BAL 20 | -3 |
| Tampa Bay | New Orleans | 0.282408 | 0.717592 | New Orleans | 0.717592 | 6.962935 | NO 30, TB 10 | 20 |
| L.A. Rams | N.Y. Giants | 0.584101 | 0.415899 | L.A. Rams | 0.584101 | 2.691231 | LAR 51, NYG 17 | 34 |
| Denver | Philadelphia | 0.330031 | 0.669969 | Philadelphia | 0.669969 | 5.439008 | PHI 51, DEN 23 | 28 |
| Atlanta | Carolina | 0.600778 | 0.399222 | Atlanta | 0.600778 | 3.224904 | CAR 20, ATL 17 | -3 |
| Cincinnati | Jacksonville | 0.474119 | 0.525881 | Jacksonville | 0.525881 | 0.82819 | JAX 23, CIN 7 | 16 |
| Indianapolis | Houston | 0.357287 | 0.642713 | Houston | 0.642713 | 4.566818 | IND 20, HOU 14 | -6 |
| Arizona | San Francisco | 0.735877 | 0.264123 | Arizona | 0.735877 | 7.548078 | ARI 20, SF 10 | 10 |
| Washington | Seattle | 0.319929 | 0.680071 | Seattle | 0.680071 | 5.762262 | WSH 17, SEA 14 | -3 |
| Kansas City | Dallas | 0.615864 | 0.384136 | Kansas City | 0.615864 | 3.707651 | DAL 28, KC 17 | -11 |
| Oakland | Miami | 0.491366 | 0.508634 | Miami | 0.508634 | 0.276283 | OAK 27, MIA 24 | -3 |
| Detroit | Green Bay | 0.428537 | 0.571463 | Green Bay | 0.571463 | 2.28682 | DET 30, GB 17 | -13 |

Table 17.10: Week 10: the favorite won 11 of 14 games and the spread was covered 10 of those wins.

| TeamA | TeamH | PA | PH | Fav | FavP | Spread | Score | Diff |
|---|---|---|---|---|---|---|---|---|
| Seattle | Arizona | 0.651912 | 0.348088 | Seattle | 0.651912 | 4.861185 | SEA 22, ARI 16 | 6 |
| New Orleans | Buffalo | 0.615864 | 0.384136 | New Orleans | 0.615864 | 3.707651 | NO 47, BUF 10 | 37 |
| Green Bay | Chicago | 0.642713 | 0.357287 | Green Bay | 0.642713 | 4.566818 | GB 23, CHI 16 | 7 |
| Cleveland | Detroit | 0.159277 | 0.840723 | Detroit | 0.840723 | 10.90314 | DET 38, CLE 24 | 14 |
| Cincinnati | Tennessee | 0.458362 | 0.541638 | Tennessee | 0.541638 | 1.332406 | TEN 24, CIN 20 | 4 |
| Pittsburgh | Indianapolis | 0.765995 | 0.234005 | Pittsburgh | 0.765995 | 8.511829 | PIT 20, IND 17 | 3 |
| N.Y. Jets | Tampa Bay | 0.56015 | 0.43985 | N.Y. Jets | 0.56015 | 1.924805 | TB 15, NYJ 10 | -5 |
| Minnesota | Washington | 0.591076 | 0.408924 | Minnesota | 0.591076 | 2.914419 | MIN 38, WSH 30 | 8 |
| L.A. Chargers | Jacksonville | 0.418699 | 0.581301 | Jacksonville | 0.581301 | 2.601647 | JAX 20, LAC 17 (OT) | 3 |
| Houston | L.A. Rams | 0.370611 | 0.629389 | L.A. Rams | 0.629389 | 4.140434 | LAR 33, HOU 7 | 26 |
| Dallas | Atlanta | 0.535916 | 0.464084 | Dallas | 0.535916 | 1.14931 | ATL 27, DAL 7 | -20 |
| N.Y. Giants | San Francisco | 0.706975 | 0.293025 | N.Y. Giants | 0.706975 | 6.623209 | SF 31, NYG 21 | -10 |
| New England | Denver | 0.783077 | 0.216923 | New England | 0.783077 | 9.058478 | NE 41, DEN 16 | 25 |
| Miami | Carolina | 0.37735 | 0.62265 | Carolina | 0.62265 | 3.924806 | CAR 45, MIA 21 | 24 |

Starting with week 11 and for all subsequent weeks the teams are listed as W- winner, L- Loser.

Table 17.11: Week 11: the ELO favorite won 9 of the 14 games. The favorite spread was covered in 7 of the wins.

| TeamW | TeamL | PW | PL | Fav | FavP | Spread | Score | Diff |
|---|---|---|---|---|---|---|---|---|
| Pittsburgh | Tennessee | 0.681322 | 0.318678 | Pittsburgh | 0.681322 | 5.802299 | PIT 40, TEN 17 | 23 |
| New Orleans | Washington | 0.722235 | 0.277765 | New Orleans | 0.722235 | 7.111505 | NO 34, WAS 31 | 3 |
| Houston | Arizona | 0.472684 | 0.527316 | Arizona | 0.527316 | 0.874111 | HUS 31, AR 21 | -10 |
| Detroit | Chicago | 0.702183 | 0.297817 | Detroit | 0.702183 | 6.469843 | DET 27, CHI 24 | 3 |
| Minnesota | L.A. Rams | 0.525881 | 0.474119 | Minnesota | 0.525881 | 0.82819 | MIN 24, LAR 7 | 17 |
| Baltimore | Green Bay | 0.421503 | 0.578497 | Green Bay | 0.578497 | 2.511896 | BAL 23, GB 0 | -23 |
| N.Y. Giants | Kansas City | 0.189021 | 0.810979 | Kansas City | 0.810979 | 9.951333 | NYG 12, KC 9 | -3 |
| Jacksonville | Cleveland | 0.831254 | 0.168746 | Jacksonville | 0.831254 | 10.60013 | JAC 19, CLE 7 | 12 |
| Tampa Bay | Miami | 0.502878 | 0.497122 | Tampa Bay | 0.502878 | 0.092102 | TB 30, MIA 20 | 10 |
| L.A. Chargers | Buffalo | 0.442688 | 0.557312 | Buffalo | 0.557312 | 1.833972 | LAC 54, BUF 24 | -30 |
| New England | Oakland | 0.787927 | 0.212073 | New England | 0.787927 | 9.213657 | NE 33, OAK 8 | 25 |
| Cincinnati | Denver | 0.488489 | 0.511511 | Denver | 0.511511 | 0.368349 | CIN 20, DEN 17 | -3 |
| Philadelphia | Dallas | 0.561568 | 0.438432 | Philadelphia | 0.561568 | 1.970174 | PHI 37, DAL 9 | 28 |
| Atlanta | Seattle | 0.514387 | 0.485613 | Atlanta | 0.514387 | 0.46039 | ATL 34, SEA 31 | 3 |

Table 17.12: Week 12: the ELO favorite won 12 of 16 games played, and the favorite spread was covered 11 of those games.

| TeamW | TeamL | PW | PL | Fav | FavP | Spread | Score | DIFF |
|---|---|---|---|---|---|---|---|---|
| Minnesota | Detroit | 0.567229 | 0.432771 | Minnesota | 0.567229 | 1.949222 | MIN 30, DET 23 | 7 |
| L.A. Chargers | Dallas | 0.408924 | 0.591076 | Dallas | 0.591076 | 2.708025 | LAC 28, DAL 6 | -22 |
| Washington | N.Y. Giants | 0.589684 | 0.410316 | Washington | 0.589684 | 2.663729 | WAS 20, NYG 10 | 10 |
| Cincinnati | Cleveland | 0.785997 | 0.214003 | Cincinnati | 0.785997 | 8.910412 | CIN 30, CLE 16 | 14 |
| Tennessee | Indianapolis | 0.607661 | 0.392339 | Tennessee | 0.607661 | 3.235775 | TEN 20, IND 16 | 4 |
| Buffalo | Kansas City | 0.28946 | 0.71054 | Kansas City | 0.71054 | 6.509383 | BUF 16, KC 10 | -6 |
| Philadelphia | Chicago | 0.827999 | 0.172001 | Philadelphia | 0.827999 | 10.24694 | PHIL 31, CHI 3 | 28 |
| Atlanta | Tampa Bay | 0.714079 | 0.285921 | Atlanta | 0.714079 | 6.621991 | ATL 34, TB 20 | 14 |
| Carolina | N.Y. Jets | 0.65452 | 0.34548 | Carolina | 0.65452 | 4.726826 | CAR 35, NYJ 27 | 8 |
| New England | Miami | 0.860451 | 0.139549 | New England | 0.860451 | 11.27956 | NE 35, MIA 17 | 18 |
| Seattle | San Francisco | 0.839951 | 0.160049 | Seattle | 0.839951 | 10.62723 | SEA 24, SF 13 | 11 |
| L.A. Rams | New Orleans | 0.355966 | 0.644034 | New Orleans | 0.644034 | 4.393157 | LAR 26, NO 20 | -6 |
| Arizona | Jacksonville | 0.361262 | 0.638738 | Jacksonville | 0.638738 | 4.224635 | ARI 27, JAC 24 | -3 |
| Oakland | Denver | 0.547349 | 0.452651 | Oakland | 0.547349 | 1.31663 | OAK 21, DEN 14 | 7 |
| Pittsburgh | Green Bay | 0.703385 | 0.296615 | Pittsburgh | 0.703385 | 6.281711 | PIT 31, GB 28 | 3 |
| Baltimore | Houston | 0.598014 | 0.401986 | Baltimore | 0.598014 | 2.928798 | BAL 23, HOU 16 | 7 |

Table 17.13: Week 13: The ELO based favorite won 11 of the 16 games in Week 13. THe spread was covered in 9 games by the winner.

| TeamW | TeamL | PW | PL | Fav | FavP | Spread | SCORE | DIFF |
|---|---|---|---|---|---|---|---|---|
| Dallas | Washington | 0.52301 | 0.47699 | Dallas | 0.52301 | 0.736307 | DAL 38, WAS 14 | 24 |
| New England | Buffalo | 0.794582 | 0.205418 | New England | 0.794582 | 9.426621 | NE 23, BUF 3 | 20 |
| N.Y. Jets | Kansas City | 0.293025 | 0.706975 | Kansas City | 0.706975 | 6.623209 | NYJ 38, KC 31 | -7 |
| Baltimore | Detroit | 0.505756 | 0.494244 | Baltimore | 0.505756 | 0.184199 | BAL 44, DET 20 | 24 |
| San Francisco | Chicago | 0.366592 | 0.633408 | Chicago | 0.633408 | 4.269046 | SF 15, CHI 14 | -1 |
| Miami | Denver | 0.472684 | 0.527316 | Denver | 0.527316 | 0.874111 | MIA 35, DEN 9 | -26 |
| Minnesota | Atlanta | 0.485613 | 0.514387 | Atlanta | 0.514387 | 0.46039 | MIN 14, ATL 9 | -5 |
| Green Bay | Tampa Bay | 0.541638 | 0.458362 | Green Bay | 0.541638 | 1.332406 | GB 26, TB 20 | 6 |
| Jacksonville | Indianapolis | 0.676302 | 0.323698 | Jacksonville | 0.676302 | 5.641653 | JAC 30, IND 10 | 20 |
| Tennessee | Houston | 0.57428 | 0.42572 | Tennessee | 0.57428 | 2.376967 | TEN 24, HOU 13 | 11 |
| L.A. Chargers | Cleveland | 0.847539 | 0.152461 | L.A. Chargers | 0.847539 | 11.12124 | LAC 19, CLE 10 | 9 |
| New Orleans | Carolina | 0.567229 | 0.432771 | New Orleans | 0.567229 | 2.151323 | NO 31, CAR 21 | 10 |
| Oakland | N.Y. Giants | 0.628045 | 0.371955 | Oakland | 0.628045 | 4.097434 | OAK 24, NYG 17 | 7 |
| L.A. Rams | Arizona | 0.658415 | 0.341585 | L.A. Rams | 0.658415 | 5.069265 | LAR 32, ARI 16 | 16 |
| Seattle | Philadelphia | 0.392339 | 0.607661 | Philadelphia | 0.607661 | 3.445154 | SEA 24, PHI 10 | -14 |
| Pittsburgh | Cincinnati | 0.735877 | 0.264123 | Pittsburgh | 0.735877 | 7.548078 | PIT 23, CIN 20 | 3 |

Table 17.14: Week 14: the favorite won 8 of the 16 games,and the winner covered the spread in 5 games.

| TeamW | TeamL | PW | PL | Fav | FavP | Spread | SCORE | DIFF |
|---|---|---|---|---|---|---|---|---|
| Atlanta | New Orleans | 0.462653 | 0.537347 | New Orleans | 0.537347 | 1.195114 | ATL 20, NO 17 | -3 |
| San Francisco | Houston | 0.316184 | 0.683816 | Houston | 0.683816 | 5.882122 | SF 26, HOU 16 | -10 |
| Buffalo | Indianapolis | 0.640065 | 0.359935 | Buffalo | 0.640065 | 4.48208 | BUF 13, IND 7 | 6 |
| Kansas City | Oakland | 0.584101 | 0.415899 | Kansas City | 0.584101 | 2.691231 | KC 26, OAK 15 | 11 |
| Detroit | Tampa Bay | 0.595243 | 0.404757 | Detroit | 0.595243 | 3.047777 | DET 24, TB 21 | 3 |
| Green Bay | Cleveland | 0.830445 | 0.169555 | Green Bay | 0.830445 | 10.57424 | GB 27, CLE 21 | 6 |
| Chicago | Cincinnati | 0.371955 | 0.628045 | Cincinnati | 0.628045 | 4.097434 | CHI 33, CIN 7 | -26 |
| Carolina | Minnesota | 0.375998 | 0.624002 | Minnesota | 0.624002 | 3.968056 | CAR 31, MIN 24 | -7 |
| Dallas | N.Y. Giants | 0.696129 | 0.303871 | Dallas | 0.696129 | 6.276121 | DAL 30, NYG 10 | 20 |
| Denver | N.Y. Jets | 0.41171 | 0.58829 | N.Y. Jets | 0.58829 | 2.825279 | DEN 23, NYJ 0 | -23 |
| L.A. Chargers | Washington | 0.599397 | 0.400603 | L.A. Chargers | 0.599397 | 3.180697 | LAC 30, WAS 13 | 17 |
| Arizona | Tennessee | 0.378703 | 0.621297 | Tennessee | 0.621297 | 3.881495 | ARI 12, TEN 7 | -5 |
| Philadelphia | L.A. Rams | 0.572872 | 0.427128 | Philadelphia | 0.572872 | 2.331912 | PHI 43, LAR 35 | 8 |
| Jacksonville | Seattle | 0.37735 | 0.62265 | Seattle | 0.62265 | 3.924806 | JAC 30, SEA 24 | -6 |
| Pittsburgh | Baltimore | 0.63073 | 0.36927 | Pittsburgh | 0.63073 | 4.183369 | PIT 39, BAL 38 | 1 |
| Miami | New England | 0.141635 | 0.858365 | New England | 0.858365 | 11.46767 | MIA 27, NE 20 | -7 |

Table 17.15: Week 15: The ELO favorite won 13 of the 16 games in week 15. The favorite covered the spread in 11 of the wins.

| TeamW | TeamL | PW | PL | Fav | FavP | Spread | SCORE | DIFF |
|---|---|---|---|---|---|---|---|---|
| Denver | Indianapolis | 0.582702 | 0.417298 | Denver | 0.582702 | 2.64646 | DEN 25, IND 13 | 12 |
| Detroit | Chicago | 0.645352 | 0.354648 | Detroit | 0.645352 | 4.651278 | DET 20, CHI 10 | 10 |
| Kansas City | L.A. Chargers | 0.531618 | 0.468382 | Kansas City | 0.531618 | 1.011786 | KC 30, LAC 13 | 17 |
| Washington | Arizona | 0.495683 | 0.504317 | Arizona | 0.504317 | 0.138152 | WAS 45, ARI 15 | -5 |
| Jacksonville | Houston | 0.721078 | 0.278922 | Jacksonville | 0.721078 | 7.074504 | JAC 45, HOU 7 | 38 |
| Buffalo | Miami | 0.527316 | 0.472684 | Buffalo | 0.527316 | 0.874111 | BUF 24, MIA 16 | 8 |
| New Orleans | N.Y. Jets | 0.763925 | 0.236075 | New Orleans | 0.763925 | 8.44559 | NO 31, NYJ 19 | 11 |
| Baltimore | Cleveland | 0.879317 | 0.120683 | Baltimore | 0.879317 | 12.13815 | BAL 27, CLE 10 | 17 |
| Minnesota | Cincinnati | 0.777153 | 0.222847 | Minnesota | 0.777153 | 8.868899 | MIN 34, CIN 7 | 27 |
| Philadelphia | N.Y. Giants | 0.851948 | 0.148052 | Philadelphia | 0.851948 | 11.26235 | PHI 34, NYG 29 | 5 |
| Carolina | Green Bay | 0.607661 | 0.392339 | Carolina | 0.607661 | 3.445154 | CAR 31, GB 24 | 7 |
| L.A. Rams | Seattle | 0.452651 | 0.547349 | Seattle | 0.547349 | 1.515153 | LAR 42, SEA 7 | -35 |
| San Francisco | Tennessee | 0.285921 | 0.714079 | Tennessee | 0.714079 | 6.850525 | SF 25, TEN 23 | -2 |
| New England | Pittsburgh | 0.5644 | 0.4356 | New England | 0.5644 | 2.060816 | NE 27, PIT 24 | 3 |
| Dallas | Oakland | 0.595243 | 0.404757 | Dallas | 0.595243 | 3.047777 | DAL 20, OAK 17 | 3 |
| Atlanta | Tampa Bay | 0.756581 | 0.243419 | Atlanta | 0.756581 | 8.210579 | ATL 24, TB 21 | 3 |

Table 17.16: Week 16: the ELO favorite won 13 of 16 games, with the winner covering the spread in 10 of the games.

| TeamW | TeamL | PW | PL | Fav | FavP | Spread | SCORE | DIFF |
|---|---|---|---|---|---|---|---|---|
| Baltimore | Indianapolis | 0.788887 | 0.211113 | Baltimore | 0.788887 | 9.244386 | BAL 23, IND 16 | 7 |
| Minnesota | Green Bay | 0.691236 | 0.308764 | Minnesota | 0.691236 | 6.119557 | MIN 16, GB 0 | 16 |
| Chicago | Cleveland | 0.759747 | 0.240253 | Chicago | 0.759747 | 8.311902 | CHI 20, CLE 3 | 17 |
| New Orleans | Atlanta | 0.502878 | 0.497122 | New Orleans | 0.502878 | 0.092102 | NO 23, ATL 13 | 10 |
| Carolina | Tampa Bay | 0.732507 | 0.267493 | Carolina | 0.732507 | 7.440233 | CAR 22, TB 19 | 3 |
| L.A. Rams | Tennessee | 0.683816 | 0.316184 | L.A. Rams | 0.683816 | 5.882122 | LAR 27, TEN 23 | 4 |
| Washington | Denver | 0.510072 | 0.489928 | Washington | 0.510072 | 0.322318 | WAS 27, DEN 11 | 16 |
| L.A. Chargers | N.Y. Jets | 0.65452 | 0.34548 | L.A. Chargers | 0.65452 | 4.94464 | LAC 14, NYJ 7 | 7 |
| New England | Buffalo | 0.777153 | 0.222847 | New England | 0.777153 | 8.868899 | NE 37, BUF 16 | 21 |
| Kansas City | Miami | 0.690006 | 0.309994 | Kansas City | 0.690006 | 6.080199 | KC 29, MIA 13 | 16 |
| Cincinnati | Detroit | 0.3137 | 0.6863 | Detroit | 0.6863 | 5.961608 | CIN 26, DET 17 | -9 |
| San Francisco | Jacksonville | 0.221852 | 0.778148 | Jacksonville | 0.778148 | 8.900751 | SF 44, JAC 33 | -11 |
| Seattle | Dallas | 0.485613 | 0.514387 | Dallas | 0.514387 | 0.46039 | SEA 21, DAL 12 | -9 |
| Arizona | N.Y. Giants | 0.613137 | 0.386863 | Arizona | 0.613137 | 3.620378 | ARI 23, NYG 0 | 23 |
| Pittsburgh | Houston | 0.826354 | 0.173646 | Pittsburgh | 0.826354 | 10.44331 | PIT 34, HOU 6 | 28 |
| Philadelphia | Oakland | 0.763925 | 0.236075 | Philadelphia | 0.763925 | 8.44559 | PHI 19, OAK 10 | 9 |

Table 17.18: Week 17: The ELO favorite won 8 of 16 games in week 17. The winner covered the spread in 6 games.

| TeamW | TeamL | PW | PL | Fav | FavP | Spread | SCORE | DIFF |
|---|---|---|---|---|---|---|---|---|
| Minnesota | Chicago | 0.800162 | 0.199838 | Minnesota | 0.800162 | 9.605186 | MIN 23, CHI 10 | 13 |
| Indianapolis | Houston | 0.462653 | 0.537347 | Houston | 0.537347 | 1.195114 | IND 22, HOU 13 | -9 |
| New England | N.Y. Jets | 0.8705 | 0.1295 | New England | 0.8705 | 11.85601 | NE 26, NYJ 6 | 20 |
| Detroit | Green Bay | 0.547349 | 0.452651 | Detroit | 0.547349 | 1.515153 | DET 35, GB 11 | 24 |
| Dallas | Philadelphia | 0.302655 | 0.697345 | Philadelphia | 0.697345 | 6.315043 | DAL 6, PHI 0 | -6 |
| Pittsburgh | Cleveland | 0.93424 | 0.06576 | Pittsburgh | 0.93424 | 13.8957 | PIT 28, CLE 24 | 4 |
| N.Y. Giants | Washington | 0.301441 | 0.698559 | Washington | 0.698559 | 6.353876 | NYG 18, WAS 10 | -8 |
| Kansas City | Denver | 0.731378 | 0.268622 | Kansas City | 0.731378 | 7.404091 | KC 27, DEN 24 | 3 |
| L.A. Chargers | Oakland | 0.621297 | 0.378703 | L.A. Chargers | 0.621297 | 3.881495 | LAC 30, OAK 10 | 20 |
| Buffalo | Miami | 0.578497 | 0.421503 | Buffalo | 0.578497 | 2.511896 | BUF 22, MIA 16 | 6 |
| Tennessee | Jacksonville | 0.410316 | 0.589684 | Jacksonville | 0.589684 | 2.869872 | TEN 15, JAC 10 | -5 |
| Cincinnati | Baltimore | 0.301441 | 0.698559 | Baltimore | 0.698559 | 6.353876 | CIN 31, BAL 27 | -4 |
| Atlanta | Carolina | 0.520137 | 0.479863 | Atlanta | 0.520137 | 0.644375 | ATL 22, CAR 10 | 12 |
| San Francisco | L.A. Rams | 0.201685 | 0.798315 | L.A. Rams | 0.798315 | 9.546072 | SF 34, LAR 13 | -21 |
| Arizona | Seattle | 0.321183 | 0.678817 | Seattle | 0.678817 | 5.722141 | ARI 26, SEA 24 | -3 |
| Tampa Bay | New Orleans | 0.201685 | 0.798315 | New Orleans | 0.798315 | 9.546072 | TB 31, NO 24 | -7 |

So, how did ELO perform in the 2017 season? The weekly predictions are given in table 17.19.

Table 17.17: Team ELO's by week — 2017 season

| Team | ELO1 | ELO2 | ELO3 | ELO4 | ELO5 | ELO6 | ELO7 | ELO8 | ELO9 | ELO10 | ELO11 | ELO12 | ELO13 | ELO14 | ELO15 | ELO16 | ELO17 |
|---|---|---|---|---|---|---|---|---|---|---|---|---|---|---|---|---|---|
| Arizona | 1537 | 1514 | 1529 | 1501 | 1506 | 1484 | 1498 | 1460 | 1460 | 1460 | 1459 | 1439 | 1454 | 1430 | 1450 | 1435 | 1453 |
| Atlante | 1617 | 1627 | 1645 | 1660 | 1627 | 1627 | 1603 | 1586 | 1600 | 1586 | 1612 | 1629 | 1639 | 1617 | 1629 | 1637 | 1618 |
| Baltimore | 1491 | 1531 | 1539 | 1485 | 1460 | 1498 | 1475 | 1462 | 1497 | 1485 | 1485 | 1530 | 1542 | 1567 | 1564 | 1572 | 1578 |
| Buffalo | 1484 | 1500 | 1487 | 1514 | 1548 | 1531 | 1531 | 1540 | 1559 | 1528 | 1493 | 1462 | 1496 | 1480 | 1490 | 1506 | 1497 |
| Carolina | 1527 | 1547 | 1560 | 1512 | 1536 | 1554 | 1533 | 1499 | 1529 | 1544 | 1561 | 1561 | 1580 | 1564 | 1587 | 1599 | 1604 |
| Chicago | 1384 | 1374 | 1360 | 1392 | 1382 | 1371 | 1394 | 1428 | 1419 | 1419 | 1401 | 1391 | 1383 | 1373 | 1423 | 1411 | 1420 |
| Cincinnati | 1516 | 1476 | 1455 | 1449 | 1474 | 1491 | 1491 | 1476 | 1480 | 1459 | 1448 | 1465 | 1473 | 1464 | 1413 | 1403 | 1432 |
| Cleveland | 1336 | 1330 | 1321 | 1315 | 1290 | 1281 | 1272 | 1263 | 1255 | 1255 | 1250 | 1239 | 1232 | 1227 | 1219 | 1211 | 1202 |
| Dallas | 1569 | 1589 | 1560 | 1588 | 1557 | 1539 | 1539 | 1557 | 1585 | 1611 | 1585 | 1549 | 1504 | 1528 | 1550 | 1564 | 1535 |
| Denver | 1556 | 1562 | 1591 | 1564 | 1578 | 1578 | 1533 | 1499 | 1489 | 1473 | 1456 | 1439 | 1424 | 1396 | 1428 | 1454 | 1432 |
| Detroit | 1501 | 1524 | 1556 | 1541 | 1565 | 1547 | 1525 | 1525 | 1508 | 1544 | 1550 | 1560 | 1538 | 1513 | 1527 | 1539 | 1510 |
| Green Bay | 1587 | 1603 | 1585 | 1591 | 1601 | 1619 | 1589 | 1558 | 1558 | 1521 | 1540 | 1495 | 1489 | 1503 | 1511 | 1499 | 1477 |
| Houston | 1502 | 1451 | 1472 | 1468 | 1501 | 1487 | 1496 | 1496 | 1489 | 1458 | 1440 | 1461 | 1448 | 1432 | 1392 | 1378 | 1364 |
| Indianapo | 1514 | 1471 | 1456 | 1462 | 1443 | 1449 | 1427 | 1391 | 1387 | 1417 | 1409 | 1409 | 1394 | 1380 | 1370 | 1343 | 1338 |
| Jacksonvil | 1382 | 1433 | 1396 | 1450 | 1439 | 1494 | 1461 | 1498 | 1498 | 1519 | 1527 | 1538 | 1522 | 1536 | 1557 | 1571 | 1533 |
| Kansas Cit | 1613 | 1654 | 1664 | 1677 | 1687 | 1701 | 1668 | 1658 | 1667 | 1641 | 1641 | 1618 | 1584 | 1557 | 1573 | 1594 | 1606 |
| L.A. Charg | 1437 | 1430 | 1420 | 1407 | 1398 | 1424 | 1434 | 1468 | 1462 | 1462 | 1453 | 1485 | 1530 | 1534 | 1551 | 1530 | 1548 |
| L.A. Rams | 1399 | 1441 | 1418 | 1428 | 1460 | 1442 | 1476 | 1514 | 1514 | 1550 | 1550 | 1546 | 1568 | 1592 | 1569 | 1617 | 1630 |
| Miami | 1509 | 1509 | 1519 | 1489 | 1460 | 1476 | 1500 | 1509 | 1474 | 1457 | 1439 | 1410 | 1405 | 1433 | 1471 | 1455 | 1442 |
| Minnesot | 1498 | 1517 | 1501 | 1526 | 1502 | 1513 | 1543 | 1556 | 1564 | 1564 | 1586 | 1607 | 1629 | 1652 | 1630 | 1639 | 1661 |
| N.Y. Giant | 1530 | 1511 | 1479 | 1471 | 1463 | 1437 | 1481 | 1455 | 1455 | 1419 | 1388 | 1410 | 1396 | 1384 | 1362 | 1355 | 1337 |
| N.Y. Jets | 1452 | 1436 | 1420 | 1450 | 1461 | 1470 | 1458 | 1448 | 1434 | 1466 | 1450 | 1450 | 1431 | 1458 | 1427 | 1419 | 1401 |
| New Engl | 1687 | 1647 | 1666 | 1670 | 1646 | 1660 | 1673 | 1689 | 1696 | 1696 | 1713 | 1726 | 1731 | 1746 | 1708 | 1723 | 1732 |
| New Orle | 1498 | 1479 | 1460 | 1508 | 1537 | 1537 | 1559 | 1589 | 1598 | 1610 | 1644 | 1649 | 1627 | 1643 | 1631 | 1639 | 1658 |
| Oakland | 1530 | 1553 | 1569 | 1539 | 1525 | 1487 | 1477 | 1487 | 1468 | 1485 | 1485 | 1472 | 1487 | 1498 | 1483 | 1469 | 1462 |
| Philadelph | 1511 | 1543 | 1532 | 1541 | 1550 | 1572 | 1593 | 1607 | 1612 | 1628 | 1628 | 1664 | 1671 | 1643 | 1666 | 1673 | 1680 |
| Pittsburgh | 1599 | 1605 | 1621 | 1589 | 1614 | 1558 | 1591 | 1606 | 1623 | 1623 | 1631 | 1645 | 1651 | 1660 | 1663 | 1649 | 1663 |
| San Franc | 1333 | 1333 | 1329 | 1319 | 1314 | 1308 | 1305 | 1287 | 1282 | 1266 | 1297 | 1297 | 1288 | 1298 | 1338 | 1353 | 1391 |
| Seattle | 1571 | 1555 | 1559 | 1538 | 1557 | 1575 | 1575 | 1601 | 1601 | 1585 | 1602 | 1585 | 1595 | 1623 | 1602 | 1554 | 1583 |
| Tampa Ba | 1506 | 1506 | 1520 | 1495 | 1503 | 1490 | 1475 | 1466 | 1436 | 1424 | 1441 | 1470 | 1460 | 1446 | 1432 | 1424 | 1419 |
| Tennessee | 1460 | 1436 | 1474 | 1494 | 1461 | 1446 | 1467 | 1476 | 1476 | 1488 | 1499 | 1485 | 1500 | 1516 | 1497 | 1483 | 1470 |
| Washingt | 1504 | 1473 | 1496 | 1526 | 1516 | 1516 | 1520 | 1506 | 1477 | 1500 | 1478 | 1473 | 1488 | 1464 | 1447 | 1461 | 1483 |

Table 17.19: The weekly predictions of the ELO in the 2017 season

| Week | Games | Correct Predictions | Beat the Spread |
|------|-------|---------------------|-----------------|
| 1 | 15 | 9 | 7 |
| 2 | 16 | 14 | 12 |
| 3 | 16 | 9 | 3 |
| 4 | 16 | 11 | 8 |
| 5 | 14 | 8 | 4 |
| 6 | 15 | 4 | 2 |
| 7 | 15 | 10 | 9 |
| 8 | 13 | 12 | 8 |
| 9 | 13 | 5 | 5 |
| 10 | 14 | 11 | 10 |
| 11 | 14 | 9 | 7 |
| 12 | 16 | 12 | 11 |
| 13 | 16 | 11 | 9 |
| 14 | 16 | 8 | 5 |
| 15 | 16 | 13 | 11 |
| 16 | 16 | 13 | 10 |
| 17 | 16 | 8 | 6 |
| ALL | 257 | 167 | 127 |

## Conclusion

The ELO rating of NFL teams when applied to the logistic model predicts the win probability of competing teams in the weekly games during a season. Although the rating doesn't directly incorporate player and coach strengths, since it is based on team performance in games leading up to the forecast week it indirectly considers the components of a team. Clearly there is a level of unpredictability in performance and combined with the balance of teams generated by the player draft, the outcome of games is difficult to forecast. That fact makes the games each week exciting and of considerable interest to sports gambling.

A summary of the the NFL ELO Ratings by team by week for the 2017 season are provided in Table 17.17.

We see that 65% of the outcomes of games are correctly predicted. In terms of beating the spread the percent is 49.5%, which is basically an efficient market.

# Chapter 18

# Changes for the 2018-2019 Season

It is customary, after the regular season ends, to determine the MVP and other awards and to fire and hire new coaches and assistants and for players to change teams through free agency and other maneuvers. We start this chapter with the awards for the previous season. First there is the forecast of the winners and then a list of the actual winners. The rest of the chapter discusses coaches and players, free agencies, injuries, and the preseason draft plus the 25 greatest players for 2018-2019 season. We also do a case study of the Seattle Seahawks after the famous interception on the one yard line in Super Bowl 49.

**NFL Awards 2017-18**

*Forecasts*

An important award is the MVP of the league based on the regular season. To get a forecast of who might be in the running or win, twelve analysts were asked to vote as follows: 5 points for first, 4 points for second, 3 for third, 2 for fourth and 1 for fifth. The results of the voting were:

| Player | Points | Votes |
|---|---|---|
| Tom Brady | 59 | 11 (1 second) |
| Todd Gurley | 46 | 1 |
| Carson Wentz | 22 | 0 |
| Case Keenum | 15 | 0 |
| Drew Brees | 12 | 0 |

Brady led the NFL in passing yards, was third in QB rating and TDs, was fifth in completion percentage and yards gained per attempt and led his team to appear in the Super Bowl at 13-3.

Gurley got 1 first place vote, 9 seconds, a third and a fourth. He led the league with 2093 yards rushing and 19 TDs.

Wentz had 2 seconds, 3 thirds, 1 fourth, 3 fifths. He was second in TD passes and first in QB rating.

Case Keenum was second in QB rating, second in completion percentage, had one fewer interceptions than Brady, led his team to a 13-3 record. He was twelfth in passing yards and TDs.

Drew Brees threw for a league leading 4334 yards, had 23 TDs against only 8 interceptions. He was first in yards per attempt where he set the single season record. He was second in QB rating and his 72% was first in completion percentage.

The NFL awards ceremony was hosted by 23 year Marine veteran Robb Riggle. These are listed in Table 18.1.

Two coaches have left. Bruce Arians, who was the Arizona Cardinals coach, has retired. He is past 65 so this is not unexpected. His team was 8-8 and did not make the playoffs. In 2012 and 2014 he was the NFL coach of the year. Arians was replaced by Carolina Panthers' defensive coordinator Steve Wilks.

The Oakland Raiders, who were 12-4 last year and slipped the 6-10 this year and are out of the playoffs, fired their coach Jack Del Rio, who coached for 3 years and had a 4 year extension last year. Oakland convinced Jon Gruden, an ESPN commentator, to become the coach with a $10 million annual salary. He had coached Oakland in 1998-2001. Gruden was coach of the Tampa Bay Buccaneers when they won the 2003 Super Bowl and they were also thought to be pursuing him since he signaled possible interest by discussing with some possible assistant coaches. In the end Gruden signed for 10 years for $100 million to coach the Raiders.

In addition, we also have the following new coaches:

- Mike Vrabel, a former Patriots player is now the head coach of the Tennessee Titans.

- Josh McDaniel was offered to be the head coach of the Indianapolis Colts. He was the offensive coordinator for the Patriots and instrumental in Tom Brady's success. In the end he decided to stay with the Patriots. Frank Reich is now their coach.

- Matt Patricia, the current defensive coordinator of the Patriots, becomes the head coach of the Detroit Lions.

- Seattle, who had a rough year, have brought in two new coaches. Their offensive coordinator will be Brian Schottenheimer and the de-

Table 18.1: NFL Awards

| Award | Player | Position | Team |
|---|---|---|---|
| AP Assistant Coach of the Year | Pat Shurmur | OC | Minnesota Vikings |
| AP Coach of the Year | Sean McVay | HC | Los Angeles Rams |
| AP Comeback Player of the Year | Keenan Allen | WR | Los Angeles Chargers |
| AP Defensive Player of the Year | Aaron Donald | DT | Los Angeles Rams |
| AP Defensive Rookie of the Year | Marshon Lattimore | CB | New Orleans Saints |
| AP MVP | Tom Brady | QB | New England Patriots |
| AP Offensive Player of the Year | Todd Gurley | RB | Los Angeles Rams |
| AP Offensive Rookie of the Year | Alvin Kamara | RB | New Orleans Saints |
| Art Rooney Award | Luke Kuechly | LB | Carolina Panthers |
| Bridgestone Performance Play of the Year | The "Minneapolis Miracle" | | Minnesota Vikings |
| Built Ford Tough Offensive Line of the Year | Halapoulivaati Vaitai | LT | Philadelphia Eagles |
| Built Ford Tough Offensive Line of the Year | Stefen Wisniewski | LG | Philadelphia Eagles |
| Built Ford Tough Offensive Line of the Year | Jason Kelce | C | Philadelphia Eagles |
| Built Ford Tough Offensive Line of the Year | Brandon Brooks | RG | Philadelphia Eagles |
| Built Ford Tough Offensive Line of the Year | Lane Johnson | RT | Philadelphia Eagles |
| Castrol EDGE Clutch Performer of the Year | Drew Brees | QB | New Orleans Saints |
| Celebration of the Year | Philadelphia Eagles Electric Slide | | Philadelphia Eagles |
| Deacon Jones Award | Chandler Jones | OLB | Arizona Cardinals |
| Don Shula NFL High School Coach of the Year Award | Robert Garrett | HC | Crenshaw High School |
| FedEx Air Player of the Year | Carson Wentz | QB | Philadelphia Eagles |
| FedEx Ground Player of the Year | Todd Gurley | RB | Los Angeles Rams |
| Game Changer Award presented by Secret | Samantha Gordon | RB | |
| Greatness on the Road Award | Deshaun Watson | QB | Houston Texans |
| Pepsi NEXT Rookie of the Year | Alvin Kamara | RB | New Orleans Saints |
| Pro Football Hall of Fame Class of 2018 | Bobby Beathard | GM | |
| Pro Football Hall of Fame Class of 2018 | Robert Brazile | LB | |
| Pro Football Hall of Fame Class of 2018 | Brian Dawkins | S | |
| Pro Football Hall of Fame Class of 2018 | Jerry Kramer | G | |
| Pro Football Hall of Fame Class of 2018 | Ray Lewis | LB | |
| Pro Football Hall of Fame Class of 2018 | Randy Moss | WR | |
| Pro Football Hall of Fame Class of 2018 | Terrell Owens | WR | |
| Pro Football Hall of Fame Class of 2018 | Brian Urlacher | LB | |
| Salute to Service Award | Andre Roberts | WR | Atlanta Falcons |
| Walter Payton NFL Man of the Year Award | J. J. Watt | DE | Houston Texans |

fensive coordinator will be Ken Norton Jr, who was the assistant head coach of the San Francisco 49ers.

- Former Kansas City Chief offense coordinator, Matt Nagy, is now coach of the Chicago Bears.

- The NY Giants fired Ben McAdoo because of their weak season and named Minnesota Viking's offensive coordinator Pat Shumer as their next head coach.

The following coaches were fired after weak seasons: John Fox, Chicago Bears, Jim Caldwell, Detroit Lions, Chuck Pagano, Indianapolis Colts. Mike Mularkey, Tennessee Titans, and Jack Delrio, Oakland Raiders.

The following coaches are on teams that did not do well but they have remained in their positions but are candidates to be fired if their teams do not do better: Marvin Lewis, Cincinnati Bengals, Vance Joseph, Denver Broncos, Hue Jackson, Cleveland Browns, Bill O'Brien, Houston Texans, Dirk Koetter, Tampa Bay Buccaneers, and Jay Gruden, Washington Redskins.

The following assistant coaches are candidates for any up and coming coaching opportunities: John De Fillippo, Philadelphia Eagles QB coach, Dave Fipp, Philadelphia Eagles Special Teams Coordinator, Tom Cable, Oakland Raiders Offensive Line coach, Dennis Allen, New Orleans Saints Defensive Coordinator coach, Dan Campbell, New Orleans Saints Tight End and Assistant Head coach.

**We have the following free agents who may change teams:**

- La Garett Blount now with the Philadelphia Eagles He scored 18 TDs for New England and helped them win Super Bowl51. He refused to take a pay cut so then went to Philadelphia where he was an important part of their offense helping them win Super Bowl52. This seems like a gross error by the usually savvy New England coach Belichick, but it is his typical style that has worked to produce winning teams.

- Alex Smith was traded from the Kansas City Chiefs to the Washington Redskins. Smith has always been an excellent QB with a high completion percentage and QB rating. However his teams have never been able to do well in the playoffs. Washington now has Kirk Cousins who is another outstanding QB also at high pay. They can keep him for a year by giving him a franchise tag to keep him at a high price of about $34.6 million. Cousins prefers a long term contract, so likely he will be a free agent going elsewhere.

### Table 18.2: Top Free Agents with $10 million plus contracts

| Player | Position | Age | Current | Future | Years | Total $ |
|---|---|---|---|---|---|---|
| Kirk Cousins | QB | 29 | WAS | MIN | 3 | 84,000,000.00 |
| Trumaine Johnson | CB | 28 | LA | NYJ | 5 | 72,500,000.00 |
| Andrew Norwell | G | 26 | CAR | JAC | 5 | 66,500,000.00 |
| Nate Solder | LT | 30 | NE | NYG | 4 | 62,000,000.00 |
| Malcolm Butler | CB | 28 | NE | TEN | 5 | 61,250,000.00 |
| Star Lotulelei | DT | 28 | CAR | BUF | 5 | 50,000,000.00 |
| Drew Brees | QB | 39 | NO | NO | 2 | 50,000,000.00 |
| Sammy Watkins | WR | 24 | LA | KC | 3 | 48,000,000.00 |
| Weston Richburg | C | 26 | NYG | SF | 5 | 47,500,000.00 |
| Justin Pugh | G | 27 | NYG | ARI | 5 | 45,025,000.00 |
| Anthony Hitchens | ILB | 25 | DAL | KC | 5 | 45,000,000.00 |
| Ryan Jensen | C | 26 | BAL | TB | 4 | 42,000,000.00 |
| Allen Robinson | WR | 24 | JAC | CHI | 3 | 42,000,000.00 |
| Nigel Bradham | OLB | 28 | PHI | PHI | 5 | 40,000,000.00 |
| Paul Richardson | WR | 26 | SEA | WAS | 5 | 40,000,000.00 |
| Chris Hubbard | RT | 27 | PIT | CLE | 5 | 36,500,000.00 |
| Case Keenum | QB | 30 | MIN | DEN | 2 | 36,000,000.00 |
| Aaron Colvin | CB | 26 | JAC | HOU | 4 | 34,000,000.00 |
| Marqise Lee | WR | 26 | JAC | JAC | 4 | 34,000,000.00 |
| Trey Burton | TE | 26 | PHI | CHI | 4 | 32,000,000.00 |
| Travis Carrie | CB | 27 | OAK | CLE | 4 | 31,000,000.00 |
| Jerick McKinnon | RB | 26 | MIN | SF | 4 | 30,000,000.00 |
| Jimmy Graham | TE | 31 | SEA | GB | 3 | 30,000,000.00 |
| Dontari Poe | DT | 27 | ATL | CAR | 3 | 28,000,000.00 |
| Zach Fulton | G | 26 | KC | HOU | 4 | 28,000,000.00 |
| Spencer Long | C | 27 | WAS | NYJ | 4 | 27,400,000.00 |
| Richard Sherman | CB | 30 | SEA | SF | 3 | 27,150,000.00 |
| Prince Amukamara | CB | 28 | CHI | CHI | 3 | 27,000,000.00 |
| Josh Kline | G | 28 | TEN | TEN | 4 | 26,500,000.00 |
| Taylor Gabriel | WR | 27 | ATL | CHI | 4 | 26,000,000.00 |
| Demario Davis | ILB | 29 | NYJ | NO | 3 | 24,000,000.00 |
| Albert Wilson | WR | 25 | KC | MIA | 3 | 24,000,000.00 |
| Vinny Curry | DE | 29 | PHI | TB | 3 | 23,000,000.00 |
| Trent Murphy | OLB | 27 | WAS | BUF | 3 | 22,500,000.00 |
| Avery Williamson | ILB | 26 | TEN | NYJ | 3 | 22,500,000.00 |
| Michael Crabtree | WR | 30 | OAK | BAL | 3 | 21,000,000.00 |
| Zach Brown | ILB | 28 | WAS | WAS | 3 | 21,000,000.00 |
| DaQuan Jones | DE | 26 | TEN | TEN | 3 | 21,000,000.00 |
| Patrick Robinson | CB | 30 | PHI | NO | 4 | 20,000,000.00 |
| Sam Bradford | QB | 30 | MIN | ARI | 1 | 20,000,000.00 |
| Dion Lewis | RB | 27 | NE | TEN | 4 | 19,800,000.00 |
| Tahir Whitehead | OLB | 28 | DET | OAK | 3 | 19,000,000.00 |
| D.J. Hayden | CB | 27 | DET | JAC | 3 | 19,000,000.00 |
| Denico Autry | DE | 27 | OAK | IND | 3 | 17,800,000.00 |
| Devon Kennard | OLB | 26 | NYG | DET | 3 | 17,250,000.00 |
| Kurt Coleman | FS | 29 | CAR | NO | 3 | 16,350,000.00 |
| Nickell Robey-Coleman | CB | 26 | LA | LA | 3 | 15,675,000.00 |
| Carlos Hyde | RB | 26 | SF | CLE | 3 | 15,250,000.00 |
| Mike Pouncey | C | 28 | MIA | LAC | 2 | 15,000,000.00 |
| Patrick Omameh | G | 28 | JAC | NYG | 3 | 15,000,000.00 |
| Todd Davis | ILB | 25 | DEN | DEN | 3 | 15,000,000.00 |
| Kareem Martin | OLB | 26 | ARI | NYG | 3 | 15,000,000.00 |
| Beau Allen | DT | 26 | PHI | TB | 3 | 15,000,000.00 |
| Cody Parkey | K | 25 | MIA | CHI | 4 | 15,000,000.00 |
| Morgan Burnett | SS | 29 | GB | PIT | 3 | 14,350,000.00 |
| Jordy Nelson | WR | 32 | GB | OAK | 2 | 14,200,000.00 |
| Ndamukong Suh | DT | 31 | MIA | LA | 1 | 14,000,000.00 |
| Josh Sitton | G | 31 | CHI | MIA | 2 | 13,500,000.00 |
| Eric Ebron | TE | 25 | DET | IND | 2 | 13,000,000.00 |
| Brandon Fusco | G | 29 | SF | ATL | 3 | 12,750,000.00 |
| Allen Hurns | WR | 26 | JAC | DAL | 2 | 12,000,000.00 |
| Darren Fells | TE | 32 | DET | CLE | 3 | 12,000,000.00 |
| Senio Kelemete | G | 27 | NO | HOU | 3 | 12,000,000.00 |
| Isaiah Crowell | RB | 25 | CLE | NYJ | 3 | 12,000,000.00 |
| Chris Smith | DE | 30 | CIN | CLE | 3 | 12,000,000.00 |
| Danny Amendola | WR | 32 | NE | MIA | 2 | 12,000,000.00 |
| John Sullivan | C | 32 | LA | LA | 2 | 10,750,000.00 |
| Ed Dickson | TE | 30 | CAR | SEA | 3 | 10,700,000.00 |
| Mike Pennel | DE | 26 | NYJ | NYJ | 3 | 10,500,000.00 |
| Mitch Unrein | DE | 31 | CHI | TB | 3 | 10,500,000.00 |
| Tramon Williams | CB | 35 | ARI | GB | 2 | 10,000,000.00 |
| Adrian Clayborn | DE | 29 | ATL | NE | 2 | 10,000,000.00 |
| Johnathan Joseph | CB | 34 | HOU | HOU | 2 | 10,000,000.00 |
| Austin Seferian-Jenkins | TE | 25 | NYJ | JAC | 2 | 10,000,000.00 |
| A.J. McCarron | QB | 27 | CIN | BUF | 2 | 10,000,000.00 |
| Chase Daniel | QB | 31 | NO | CHI | 2 | 10,000,000.00 |
| Terrance Mitchell | CB | 25 | KC | CLE | 3 | 10,000,000.00 |
| Josh McCown | QB | 38 | NYJ | NYJ | 1 | 10,000,000.00 |

## We have the following players under suspension:

- Star running back Ezekiel Elliot of the Dallas Cowboys was suspended six games for alleged spousal abuse.

- Colin Kaepernick, the former San Francisco 49ers QB, is effectively blocked by all the teams from playing because he started the movement to protest against police brutality to blacks.

- Tom Brady, in a dubious move to show power by the NFL commissioner had a four game suspension at the beginning of the 2017 season.

- Mark Ingram of the New Orleans Saints has a four game suspension going into the 2018-19 season.

## There are more and more injuries to key players

There are many types of injuries, however the main conclusion is that they are on the rise. Some players are out for one or two games or even part of one game. Others are out for the season or out into retirement. Injuries can completely change a team's performance. Some examples are:

- Aaron Rodgers, one of the leagues elite QBs and two time MVP, his early season broken collar bone injury basically knocked Green Bay out of the playoffs.

- Rob Gronkowski, New England's star tight end, is worth over 10 points extra per game when he plays. He is very big and strong, but is injury prone and is in and out of the games.

- Carson Wentz, the Philadelphia Eagles QB

- Deshaun Watson Houston QB

- Odell Beckham Jr NY Giants wide receiver, ankle injury

- JJ Watt Houston defensive star, lower leg injury. While injured, he raised many millions to help Houston people affected by the hurricane.

- Whitney Mercilus Houston defensive end

- Richard Sherman Seattle corner back was traded to the SF Fortyniners, achilles injury

- Kam Chancellor Seattle defensive safety, neck injury

- Adrian Peterson New Orleans running back

- Andrew Luck Indianapolis QB, shoulder-lebrum injury

- Ryan Tannehill Miami QB

- Nick Foles Philadelphia QB, was off for injuries for four years but returned to replace Carson Wentz who tore the anterior cruciate ligament in his left knee. Foles led Philadelphia to a win in Super Bowl52.

- Bobby Wagner Seattle middle linebacker, hamstring injury

- Teddy Bridgewater Minnesota QB, knee injury

- Darren Sproles Philadelphia running back, knee ACL injury

- Luke Kuehly Carolina middle linebacker, shoulder-lebrum injury

- Devin McCourty New England defensive back, shoulder injury

- Cam Newton Carolina QB, knee injury

- Julian Edelman New England wide receiver, knee ACL injury

- Dontá Hightower New England middle linebacker, pectoral injury

- Eric Berry Kansas City safety, achilles

- Joey Bosa San Diego linebacker, finger injury

- Devanta Freeman Atlanta running back, knee-MCL injury

- DeAndre Hopkins Houston wide receiver, calf injury

**Concussions are up, especially on Thursday night games**

The number of diagnosed concussions suffered by NFL players increased over 15% in the 2017-18 season. Also there were more injuries in Thursday night games than in other games according to Mark Maske in the *Washington Post*, January 26, 2018. Players suffered 281 concussions during the pre season and regular season versus 243 the previous year. According to league data, there were 261 concussions in 2012, 229 in 2013, 206 in 2014, a significant improvement before rising again in 2015 to 275.

Jeff Miller the NFL's executive VP of health and safety, observed that there was an increase in the number of concussions suffered in the pre season. That was 26 in 2016 and 45 in 2017.

There were 6.9 injuries in Thursday night games versus 6.3 for Saturday, Sunday and Monday games in total. The situation has changed because the injury rate for Thursday used to be lower and was so in the 2014, 2015 and 2016 seasons.

## Seattle Seahawks: Dynasty Potential Dashed

Players and teams which are outliers in the sense that their performance separates them from competitors are a major factor in the enormous interest in sports worldwide. Fans love and hate the stars who lift spirits and break hearts. For sports teams the ultimate designation is to be a dynasty. The criteria for dynastic status are not rigidly defined, but legitimate dynasties are those with won multiple league titles, are blessed with personality, have superstar talent and produce consistent winning seasons. In the NFL there have been a succession of dynasties, largely broken down by decade.

- Cleveland Browns of the 1950s: three NFL championships and six consecutive title game appearances from 1950 to 1955.

- Green Bay Packers of the 1960s: five championships in seven years; including Super Bowls I and II.

- Pittsburgh Steelers of the 70's: four Super Bowl titles in six years, eight straight playoff appearances and seven division titles.

- San Francisco 49ers of the 80's: won four Super Bowl championships and eight division titles.

- Dallas Cowboys of the 90's: won three Super Bowls in four years, 3 conference championships in 4 straight appearances, 5 straight division titles, 6 in total.

- New England Patriots 2001 – present: Five Super Bowl titles in 16 years, including three in four years, three other Super Bowl appearances , twelve AFC title game appearances , and 15 AFC East Division titles.

Actually the Patriots dynasty status was established in the decade 2000-2009. The next decade had some other potential dynasties which didn't pan out. The often discussed case is the Seattle Seahawks and we consider them here.

## The play

There is no doubt that Seattle had built a strong team in the early part of the 2010-2019 decade. They had star players and a character - the defense was dubbed the "Legion of Boom". The team had a dominant win in the 2013 Super Bowl XLVIII. Seattle was in the 2014 Super Bowl and on the way to victory until "the play". Did one play call derail a potential

Seahawks dynasty? Former Seahawks defensive end Cliff Avril says yes. The team began to doubt coach Pete Carroll and his staff after losing Super Bowl XLIX. Consider the critical play and look at Seattle before and after that game.

In Super Bowl XLIX the Patriots led 28 to 24, but with time running down Seattle reached the New England 5 yard line. Superstar running back Marshawn Lynch picked up four yards on a first-down run, but was kept out of the end zone by a nice tackle from Dont'a Hightower. Instead of handing the ball to running back Lynch on second down at the 1-yard line with 25 seconds to play, the Seahawks threw a slant over the middle that was picked off by Malcolm Butler to seal the New England Patriots' win, see Figure 18.1.

Figure 18.1: Butler Intercepts Wilson

Coach Pete Carroll and the Seahawks decided to pass on second down instead of pounding Lynch again, and Malcolm Butler jumped the pass intended for Ricardo Lockette and made the greatest interception in Super Bowl history and the Patriots win. This infamous goal-line meltdown in Super Bowl XLIX apparently had aftershocks, but did it set the team into decline.

The play was practiced by New England but was never used before in an actual game. To defend the coach, it may well be that the probability of winning the game was higher by passing since interceptions there are very rare and the team had two more downs if the pass was incomplete. The running option could have led to a fumble. The general consensus was that it was a coaching error and the majority of the people believe that would three downs Lynch would have gotten the TD to win the game almost surely.

## Seattle Record by Year: 2010–2018

The seasonal performance of Seattle is in Table 18.3. Starting in the 2012 season the team had a consistent record of success, usually at the top of their division and advancing in the playoffs. Clearly the team lost some important games, especially the 2015 Super Bowl. There was a slight dip afterwards, but it is really in the playoffs that progress stalled. The numbers indicate an aftershock from the dramatic play in Super Bowl 49. They did not make the playoffs last year although they did the previous two years when they made the playoffs but were quickly defeated. Tables 18.4, 18.5 and 18.6 show the decline in the defense and the team. They are not rated in the top ten NFL teams as we show below.

Table 18.3: Seattle Record: 2010-2018

| Season | W-L-T | Standing | Playoffs |
|--------|-------|----------|----------|
| 2010-11 | 7-9-0 | 1st NFC West | W Wild Card 41-36 vs Saints |
| | | | L Divisional Round 24-35 vs. Bears |
| 2011-12 | 7-9-0 | 3rd NFC West | DNP |
| 2012-13 | 11-5-0 | 2nd NFC West | W Wild Card 24-14 vs Redskins |
| | | | Lost Divisional Round 28-30 vs. Falcons |
| 2013-14 | 13-3-0 | 1st NFC West | W Divisional Round 23-15 vs Saints |
| | | | W Conference Championship 23-17 vs 49ers |
| | | | W Super Bowl 43-8 vs. Broncos |
| 2014-15 | 12-4-0 | 1st NFC West | W Divisional Round 31-17 vs Panthers |
| | | | W Conference Championship 28-22 vs Packers |
| | | | **L** Super Bowl 24-28 vs. Patriots |
| 2015-16 | 10-6-0 | 2nd NFC West | W Wild Card 10-9 vs Vikings |
| | | | L Divisional Round 24-31 vs. Panthers |
| 2016-17 | 10-5-1 | 1st NFC West | W Wild Card 26-6 vs Lions |
| | | | L Divisional Round 20-36 vs. Falcons |
| 2017-18 | 9-7-0 | 2nd NFC West | did not make the playoffs |

Table 18.4: Team Rank in League

| MEASURE | SQUAD | 2010 | 2011 | 2012 | 2013 | 2014 | 2015 | 2016 | 2017 |
|---------|-------|------|------|------|------|------|------|------|------|
| Points | Offense | 11 | 18 | 4 | 10 | 8 | 9 | 23 | 23 |
| | Defense | 13 | 3 | 1 | 1 | 1 | 1 | 25 | 25 |
| Yards | Offense | 15 | 12 | 4 | 9 | 17 | 17 | 28 | 28 |
| | Defense | 11 | 5 | 2 | 1 | 1 | 4 | 27 | 27 |

Table 18.5: League Ranks: Passing

| MEASURE | SQUAD | 2010 | 2011 | 2012 | 2013 | 2014 | 2015 | 2016 | 2017 |
|---------|-------|------|------|------|------|------|------|------|------|
| Yards | Offense | 14 | 10 | 20 | 27 | 26 | 27 | 19 | 19 |
| | Defense | 6 | 8 | 2 | 1 | 1 | 6 | 27 | 27 |
| TD's | Offense | 2 | 18 | 6 | 22 | 10 | 8 | 28 | 28 |
| | Defense | 7 | 3 | 1 | 2 | 2 | 2 | 29 | 29 |
| INT's | Offense | 11 | 14 | 3 | 3 | 3 | 5 | 23 | 23 |
| | Defense | 13 | 21 | 13 | 18 | 1 | 8 | 25 | 25 |

Table 18.6: League Ranks: Rushing

| MEASURE | SQUAD | 2010 | 2011 | 2012 | 2013 | 2014 | 2015 | 2016 | 2017 |
|---------|-------|------|------|------|------|------|------|------|------|
| Attempts | Offense | 21 | 20 | 3 | 2 | 2 | 1 | 29 | 29 |
| | Defense | 23 | 25 | 2 | 4 | 10 | 2 | 25 | 25 |
| YD's | Offense | 23 | 25 | 3 | 1 | 4 | 3 | 31 | 31 |
| | Defense | 19 | 7 | 1 | 3 | 7 | 10 | 21 | 21 |
| TD's | Offense | 31 | 16 | 18 | 1 | 13 | 9 | 12 | 12 |
| | Defense | 22 | 22 | 10 | 5 | 1 | 5 | 18 | 18 |

## Team Statistics

Seattle was a top team in each of the five seasons from 2012-2017. The most striking aspect of the power of those teams was the defense. Table 18.4 shows the rank of Seattle's offense and defense. While their offense was fine in those five strong seasons, it is the defense which is the real story. The competitive offense and a shut down defense was a winning combination in 2013-2015.

## Passing

If we breakdown the statistics by passing and rushing we find interesting observations. The rank of the passing game was just so-so. That does not imply it was weak, but rather the split between passing and running plays was balanced. Fewer passing plays gives the low ranking on yards and TD's, see Table 18.5. Also the defense was strong against the pass, the preferred attack on most teams.

**Rushing**

The offense was dominant in the running game, see Table 18.6. The quarterback Russell Wilson is a dangerous running option. He is one of the very best scrambling QBs in the NFL Together with Beast Mode (Marshawn Lynch) they created clock chewing drives on the ground. The defense was dominant against the run in the best seasons 2013 and 2014.

In the two seasons following "the play" the run offense was still strong and the defense against the pass and also the run continued to dominate. In 2016 and 2017 the offense and defense both declined substantially in rank. It is rather surprising that the team record in those years is good, and even very good in 2016. Seattle won more than 60% of their games while ranking near the bottom in rushing and passing. It is fair to conclude the team was efficient.

## Personnel Changes

NFL teams have a lot of turnover of players from season to season, with the key pieces are kept in place. Seattle had top players throughout their top seasons from 2012 to 2017 (Table 18.7). Russell Wilson and Doug Baldwin anchored the passing game and until 2015 Lynch was a Pro Bowl running back and effective receiver. Lynch was injured in 2015 and then departed for Oakland in 2016. On the defensive side the stars Sherman, Chancellor, Bennett and Thomas were Pro Bowl players. It is possible that Lynch or another elite running back was the missing ingredient in the playoff losses in 2015 and 2016.

A look at the coaching team during the 2010 to 2018 seasons in Table 18.8 shows stability. Defensive coordinator Dan Quinn left in 2016, but the Seattle defense was good in 2016.

### Table 18.7: Seattle Starters: Offense and Defense

**Offense**

| | 2012 | | 2013 | | 2014 | | 2015 | | 2016 | | 2017 |
|---|---|---|---|---|---|---|---|---|---|---|---|
| QB | Russell Wilson* | QB | Russell Wilson* | QB | Russell Wilson | QB | Russell Wilson* | QB | Russell Wilson | QB | Russell Wilson* |
| RB | Marshawn Lynch* | RB | Marshawn Lynch* | RB | Marshawn Lynch* | WR | Doug Baldwin | WR | Doug Baldwin* | WR | Doug Baldwin* |
| WR | Sidney Rice | WR | Doug Baldwin | WR | Doug Baldwin | WR | Jermaine Kearse | WR | Jermaine Kearse | WR | Tyler Lockett |
| WR | Golden Tate | WR | Golden Tate | WR | Jermaine Kearse | TE | Jimmy Graham | WR | Tyler Lockett | WR | Paul Richardson |
| TE | Zach Miller | TE | Zach Miller | TE | Luke Willson | LT | Russell Okung | TE | Jimmy Graham* | TE | Jimmy Graham* |
| LT | Russell Okung* | LT | Paul McQuistan | LT | Russell Okung | LG | Justin Britt | LT | George Fant | LT | Duane Brown* |
| C | Max Unger*+ | LT | Russell Okung | LG | James Carpenter | C | Patrick Lewis | LG | Mark Glowinski | LG | Luke Joeckel |
| RG | Paul McQuistan | LG | James Carpenter | RG | J.R. Sweezy | RG | J.R. Sweezy | C | Justin Britt | C | Justin Britt |
| RT | Breno Giacomini | C | Max Unger* | RT | Justin Britt | RT | Garry Gilliam | RG | Germain Ifedi | RG | Oday Aboushi |
| | | RG | J.R. Sweezy | | | | | RT | Garry Gilliam | RT | Germain Ifedi |
| | | RT | Breno Giacomini | | | | | | | | |

**Defense**

| | 2012 | | 2013 | | 2014 | | 2015 | | 2016 | | 2017 |
|---|---|---|---|---|---|---|---|---|---|---|---|
| DE | Red Bryant | DE | Red Bryant | DE | Cliff Avril | DE | Cliff Avril | DE | Cliff Avril* | DE | Michael Bennett* |
| DE | Chris Clemons | DE | Chris Clemons | DE | Michael Bennett | DE | Michael Bennett* | DE | Michael Bennett* | DE | Frank Clark |
| LDT | Alan Branch | LDT | Tony McDaniel | LDT | Tony McDaniel | LDT | Ahtyba Rubin | LDT | Ahtyba Rubin | LDT | Jarran Reed |
| RDT | Brandon Mebane | RDT | Brandon Mebane | MLB | Bobby Wagner*+ | RDT | Brandon Mebane | MLB | Bobby Wagner*+ | RDT | Sheldon Richardson |
| MLB | Bobby Wagner | MLB | Bobby Wagner | LB | Bruce Irvin | MLB | Bobby Wagner* | LB | K.J. Wright* | MLB | Bobby Wagner*+ |
| LB | LeRoy Hill | LB | Bruce Irvin | LB | K.J. Wright | LB | Bruce Irvin | LCB | Richard Sherman* | LB | Michael Wilhoite |
| LB | K.J. Wright | LB | Malcolm Smith | LCB | Richard Sherman*+ | LB | K.J. Wright | RCB | DeShawn Shead | LB | K.J. Wright |
| LCB | Richard Sherman+ | LB | K.J. Wright | RCB | Byron Maxwell | LCB | Richard Sherman* | SS | Kam Chancellor | LCB | Richard Sherman |
| RCB | Brandon Browner | LCB | Richard Sherman*+ | SS | Kam Chancellor* | RCB | Cary Williams | FS | Earl Thomas | RCB | Shaquill Griffin |
| SS | Kam Chancellor | RCB | Brandon Browner | PS | Earl Thomas*+ | SS | Kam Chancellor* | | | SS | Kam Chancellor |
| FS | Earl Thomas*+ | SS | Kam Chancellor* | | | FS | Earl Thomas* | | | FS | Earl Thomas* |
| | | FS | Earl Thomas*+ | | | | | | | | |

### Table 18.8: Coaching, 2010-2018

| SEASON | COACH | OFFENSIVE COORDINATOR | DEFENSIVE COORDINATOR |
|---|---|---|---|
| 2010-11 | Pete Carroll | Jeremy Bates | Gus Bradley |
| 2011-12 | Pete Carroll | Darrell Bevel | Gus Bradley |
| 2012-13 | Pete Carroll | Darrell Bevel | Gus Bradley |
| 2013-14 | Pete Carroll | Darrell Bevel | Dan Quinn |
| 2014-15 | Pete Carroll | Darrell Bevel | Dan Quinn |
| 2015-16 | Pete Carroll | Darrell Bevel | Kris Richard |
| 2016-17 | Pete Carroll | Darrell Bevel | Kris Richard |
| 2017-18 | Pete Carroll | Darrell Bevel | Kris Richard |

The Seattle roster between 2012 and 2017 had many changes, particularly in the last year. A list of players were on the roster then but aren't today includes:

WR Paul Richardson
OG Luke Joeckel
OG Oday Aboushi

OL Matt Tobin
TE Jimmy Graham
TE Luke Willson
QB Austin Davis
RB Eddie Lacy
RB Thomas Rawls
DE Michael Bennett
DT Sheldon Richardson
LB Terence Garvin
LB Michael Wilhoite
CB Byron Maxwell
CB Richard Sherman
CB Jeremy Lane
CB DeShawn Shead
DE Cliff Avril
K Blair Walsh

The league leading defense is gone. Star defenders Frank Clark and Bobby Wagner remain, but the defense is much weaker than in the glory days. If Kam Chancellor retires (likely), then Earl Thomas is the last founding member of the Legion of Boom. Thomas wants the type of long term contract that Lynch, Bennett, and Chancellor got though each of them left the team. So Thomas is a question mark. The elite defensive players became expensive and they are in decline, and that motivated the change.

The Seahawks in 2018-19 are focused on Russell Wilson. He had the best 3 year start for any quarterback in history. However, last season he was often running for his life. Now Seattle is building an offensive line that will help them run the ball more effectively, with backs and ends who can provide Wilson protection help on passing plays. The team will have a new character without the confidence and dominance of the Legion of Boom. Seattle is not one of the top ten rated teams. *USA Today* predicted Seattle to be 4-12. We will see if the new approach will work.

Nate Davis writing in the *USA Today* on July 31, 2018, ranked the teams power as follows: 1) Eagles, 2) Patriots, 3) Falcons, 4) Vikings, 5) Rams, 6) Saints, 7) Packers, 8) Jaguars, 9) Chargers, 10) Steelers, 11) Texans, 12) Titans, 13) Panthers, 14) Redskins, 15) Broncos, 16) Raiders, 17) Cowboys, 18) Ravens, 19) Chiefs, 20) 49rs, 21) Cardinals, 22) Bears, 23) Lions, 24) Giants, 25) Bergals, 26) Dolphins, 27) Seahawks, 28) Browns, 29) Buccaneers, 30) Jets, 31) Colts, and 32) Bills.

These are the Las Vegas odds to win Super Bowl 53 as of early August

2018.

| Patriots | 6-1 | Jaguars | 6-1 | Titans | 25-1 | Browns | 80-1 |
|----------|-----|---------|-----|--------|------|--------|------|
| Rams | 10-1 | Chargers | 16-1 | Cowboys | 30-1 | Bengals | 80-1 |
| Vikings | 10-1 | Saints | 18-1 | Seahawks | 40-1 | Dolphins | 80-1 |
| Steelers | 10-1 | Raiders | 18-1 | Broncos | 40-1 | Bills | 80-1 |
| Eagles | 10-1 | 49ers | 20-1 | Panthers | 40-1 | Bears | 80-1 |
| Packers | 14-1 | Chiefs | 20-1 | Redskins | 50-1 | Buccaneers | 80-1 |
| Falcons | 16-1 | Giants | 20-1 | Ravens | 50-1 | Jets | 80-1 |
| Texans | 16-1 | Lions | 25-1 | Colts | 60-1 | Cardinals | 100-1 |

# Conclusion

The Seattle Seahawks were a powerful team during the most recent decade. Were they a near dynasty? The statistical evidence says no. If they succeeded in 2015 at Super Bowl XLIX their rating for the decade would be higher. There are other back to back winners (Denver, 1996-98), and that team is not considered a dynasty. The competition between teams in the current NFL is fierce and the chance of stringing together Super Bowl winning seasons is small. The success of the New England Patriots, a true dynasty, is difficult to fathom considering the revolving door of players on the team. The fixed pieces, Tom Brady and Bill Belichick, seem to be enough. The Patriots have also felt the sting of game changing plays (David Tyree catch) but continued with excellent follow up seasons.

# The top ten teams in 2018-19

The NFL is approaching the 2018-19 season with a similar look to the finish of season last year. The strong teams have improved and the outlook for each of the divisions is somewhat predictable. Of course injuries and the development of young talent can change the fortunes of early favorites. In Table 18.9 the ten leading teams heading into this season are profiled. These are the teams with the best chance (%) of leading their division and reaching the playoffs. Statistics on Football Power Index (FPI), offense rank (O) and defense rank (D) are found on the ESPN website.

The expectations are that the playoff contenders in 2018 will be much the same as in 2017. The top rated teams are New England and Philadelphia in the American and National Conferences, respectively. Philadelphia, who won Super Bowl 52, have the lowest offense + defense rank at 11 versus 19 for New England, despite its number 2 offense.

Table 18.9: The top ten NFL teams with their chance of winning their division, their power rating index and their offensive and defensive rankings

| Team | Div | Comments | % | FPI | O | D |
|---|---|---|---|---|---|---|
| Green Bay | NFC N | Healthy Rogers with tight end Graham and blocker in Lewis / Strengthened the defensive line and the defensive backfield | 41% | 3.3 | 5 | 18 |
| Atlanta | NFC S | Continued progress of young defense / Lethal offense: Ryan , Freeman, Hooper, Jones, Sanu | 32% | 2.7 | 4 | 27 |
| Philadelphia | NFC E | Wentz and Foles at quarterback / Balance at offense and defense | 62% | 4.7 | 6 | 5 |
| L A Rams | NFC W | Return 10 of 11 starters on offense, including Gurley / Added top cornerbacks and defensive lineman | 45% | 3.7 | 10 | 2 |
| Pittsburgh | AFC N | Brown , Bell and Roethlisberger lead top offense / Picked up linebacker Bostic and safety Edmunds. | 65% | 4.7 | 3 | 12 |
| Jacksonville | AFC S | Defense returns 12 players from number 1 unit / Fournette and Bortles anchor a solid offense | 35% | 1.1 | 19 | 4 |
| New England | AFC E | Brady and Gronkowski lead strong offense / Great coaching with Bill Belichick and Josh McDaniels | 83% | 5.0 | 2 | 17 |
| L A Chargers | AFC W | Williams,Lamp and James bolstering a defensive backfield / Rivers reliable but underrated | 37% | 1.7 | 8 | 10 |
| Minnesota | NFC N | Top defense added Richardson and Hughes / Solid at quarterback with Case Keenum and Kirk Cousins | 40% | 3.7 | 20 | 1 |
| New Orleans | NFC S | Depth at linebacker and the secondary / Drew Brees makes any offense a threat | 36% | 3.6 | 1 | 32 |

There are also strong teams in Pittsburgh and Green Bay,with the health of their team leading quarterbacks being critical. Drew Brees is an all time great and the New Orleans offense is rated number 1 by ESPN. However, the defense is suspect, rated last in the NFL. The Saints games will be exciting. On the other side, Minnesota has a competent offense, but its defense is number 1 and could take the Vikings a long way.

Former Dallas QB Tony Romo, now a TV analyst, has predicted Jacksonville and Green Bay in Super Bowl 53. Of course, to get there, they would have to beat New England and other contenders, but it is possible. Both of these teams have offense + defense ranking totaling 23. Other teams like Seattle, Arizona and Denver might surprise, but the forecast is that these are the top ten teams. There are changes occuring daily, so we have tried to be up to date. Please check the NFL, ESPN and other websites for updates throughout the season.

The current 25 greatest players are in Table 18.10.

The 2018 NFL draft was held April 26-28, 2018 at ATT Stadium in Arlington, Texas and the various rounds are in Tables 18.11 to 18.17.

Table 18.10: The current top 25 players going into 2018-19 and their 2017-18 rankings

|    | Name               | Position | Team                | 2017 Rank |
|----|--------------------|----------|---------------------|-----------|
| 1  | Tom Brady          | QB       | New England Patriots | 1        |
| 2  | Antonio Brown      | WR       | Pittsburgh Steelers | 4         |
| 3  | Carson Wentz       | QB       | Philadelphia Eagles | nr        |
| 4  | Julio Jones        | WR       | Atlanta Falcons     | 3         |
| 5  | Lev'veon Bell      | RB       | Pittsburgh Steelers | 9         |
| 6  | Todd Gurley        | RB       | LA Rams             | nr        |
| 7  | Aaron Donald       | DT       | LA Rams             | 15        |
| 8  | Drew Brees         | QB       | New Orleans Saints  | 16        |
| 9  | Von Miller         | LB       | Denver Broncos      | 2         |
| 10 | Aaron Rodgers      | QB       | Green Bay Packers   | 6         |
| 11 | Russell Wilson     | QB       | Seattle             | 24        |
| 12 | Luke Kuechly       | LB       | North Carolina      | 20        |
| 13 | DeAndre Hopkins    | WR       | Houston             | nr        |
| 14 | Calais Campbell    | DE       | Jacksonville        | 83        |
| 15 | Rob Gronkowski     | TE       | New England         | 23        |
| 16 | Khalil Mack        | DE       | Oakland             | 5         |
| 17 | Jalen Ramsey       | CB       | Jacksonville        | nr        |
| 18 | Ben Roethlisberger | QB       | Pittsburgh          | 22        |
| 19 | Everson Griffen    | DE       | Minnesota           | 92        |
| 20 | Alvin Kamara       | RB       | New Orleans         | nr        |
| 21 | Bobby Wagner       | LB       | Seattle             | 39        |
| 22 | A.J. Green         | WR       | Cincinnati          | 17        |
| 23 | Patrick Peterson   | CB       | Arizona             | 19        |
| 24 | Travis Kelce       | TE       | Kanss City          | 26        |
| 25 | Cam Newton         | QB       | North Carolina      | 44        |

Table 18.11: Round 1 had the following players

| No. | Team | Player | Position | School |
|-----|------|--------|----------|--------|
| 1 | Browns | Baker Mayfield | QB | Oklahoma |
| 2 | Giants | Saquon Barkley | RB | Penn State |
| 3 | Jets | Sam Darnold | QB | USC |
| 4 | Browns | Denzel Ward | CB | Ohio State |
| 5 | Broncos | Bradley Chubb | DE | N.C. State |
| 6 | Colts | Quenton Nelson | G | Notre Dame |
| 7 | Bills | Josh Allen | QB | Wyoming |
| 8 | Bears | Roquan Smith | LB | Georgia |
| 9 | 49ers | Mike McGlinchey | OT | Notre Dame |
| 10 | Cardinals | Josh Rosen | QB | UCLA |
| 11 | Dolphins | Minkah Fitzpatrick | DB | Alabama |
| 12 | Buccaneers | Vita Vea | DT | Washington |
| 13 | Redskins | Da'Ron Payne | DL | Alabama |
| 14 | Saints | Marcus Davenport | DE | UTSA |
| 15 | Raiders | Kolton Miller | OT | UCLA |
| 16 | Bills | Tremaine Edmunds | LB | Virginia Tech |
| 17 | Chargers | Derwin James | S | Florida State |
| 18 | Packers | Jaire Alexander | CB | Louisville |
| 19 | Cowboys | Leighton Vander Esch | LB | Boise State |
| 20 | Lions | Frank Ragnow | C/G | Arkansas |
| 21 | Bengals | Billy Price | C | Ohio State |
| 22 | Titans | Rashaan Evans | LB | Alabama |
| 23 | Patriots | Isaiah Wynn | OL | Georgia |
| 24 | Panthers | D.J. Moore | WR | Maryland |
| 25 | Ravens | Hayden Hurst | TE | South Carolina |
| 26 | Falcons | Calvin Ridley | WR | Alabama |
| 27 | Seahawks | Rashaad Penny | RB | San Diego State |
| 28 | Steelers | Terrell Edmunds | S | Virginia Tech |
| 29 | Jaguars | Taven Bryan | DT | Florida |
| 30 | Vikings | Mike Hughes | CB | UCF |
| 31 | Patriots | Sony Michel | RB | Georgia |
| 32 | Ravens | Lamar Jackson | QB | Louisville |

Table 18.12: Round 2 had the following players

| No. | Team | Player | Position | School |
|---|---|---|---|---|
| 33 | Browns | Austin Corbett | OL | Nevada |
| 34 | Giants | Will Hernandez | G | UTEP |
| 35 | Browns | Nick Chubb | RB | Georgia |
| 36 | Colts | Darius Leonard | LB | South Carolina State |
| 37 | Colts | Braden Smith | G | Auburn |
| 38 | Buccaneers | Ronald Jones II | RB | USC |
| 39 | Bears | James Daniels | C | Iowa |
| 40 | Broncos | Courtland Sutton | WR | SMU |
| 41 | Titans | Harold Landry | OLB | Boston College |
| 42 | Dolphins | Mike Gesicki | TE | Penn State |
| 43 | Lions | Kerryon Johnson | RB | Auburn |
| 44 | 49ers | Dante Pettis | WR | Washington |
| 45 | Packers | Josh Jackson | CB | Iowa |
| 46 | Chiefs | Breeland Speaks | DL | Ole Miss |
| 47 | Cardinals | Christian Kirk | WR | Texas A&M |
| 48 | Chargers | Uchenna Nwosu | OLB | USC |
| 49 | Eagles | Dallas Goedert | TE | South Dakota State |
| 50 | Cowboys | Connor Williams | OL | Texas |
| 51 | Bears | Anthony Miller | WR | Memphis |
| 52 | Colts | Kemoko Turay | DE | Rutgers |
| 53 | Buccaneers | M.J. Stewart | CB | North Carolina |
| 54 | Bengals | Jessie Bates III | S | Wake Forest |
| 55 | Panthers | Donte Jackson | CB | LSU |
| 56 | Patriots | Duke Dawson | CB | Florida |
| 57 | Raiders | P.J. Hall | DL | Sam Houston State |
| 58 | Falcons | Isaiah Oliver | CB | Colorado |
| 59 | Redskins | Derrius Guice | RB | LSU |
| 60 | Steelers | James Washington | WR | Oklahoma State |
| 61 | Jaguars | D.J. Chark | WR | LSU |
| 62 | Vikings | Brian O'Neill | OT | Pittsburgh |
| 63 | Buccaneers | Carlton Davis | CB | Auburn |
| 64 | Colts | Tyquan Lewis | DE | Ohio State |

Table 18.13: Round 3 had the following players

| No. | Team | Player | Position | School |
|---|---|---|---|---|
| 65 | Raiders | Brandon Parker | OT | North Carolina A&T |
| 66 | Giants | Lorenzo Carter | OLB | Georgia |
| 67 | Browns | Chad Thomas | DE | Miami (Fla.) |
| 68 | Texans | Justin Reid | S | Stanford |
| 69 | Giants | B.J. Hill | DT | N.C. State |
| 70 | 49ers | Fred Warner | LB | BYU |
| 71 | Broncos | Royce Freeman | RB | Oregon |
| 72 | Jets | Nathan Shepherd | DT | Fort Hays State |
| 73 | Dolphins | Jerome Baker | LB | Ohio State |
| 74 | Redskins | Geron Christian | OT | Louisville |
| 75 | Chiefs | Derrick Ndadi | DT | Florida State |
| 76 | Steelers | Mason Rudolph | QB | Oklahoma State |
| 77 | Bengals | Sam Hubbard | DE | Ohio State |
| 78 | Bengals | Malik Jefferson | OLB | Texas |
| 79 | Seahawks | Rasheem Green | DE | USC |
| 80 | Texans | Martinas Rankin | C | Mississippi State |
| 81 | Cowboys | Michael Gallup | WR | Colorado State |
| 82 | Lions | Tracy Walker | S | Louisiana-Lafayette |
| 83 | Ravens | Orlando Brown | OT | Oklahoma |
| 84 | Chargers | Justin Jones | DT | N.C. State |
| 85 | Panthers | Rashaan Gaulden | CB | Tennessee |
| 86 | Ravens | Mark Andrews | TE | Oklahoma |
| 87 | Raiders | Arden Key | DE | LSU |
| 88 | Packers | Oren Burks | OLB | Vanderbilt |
| 89 | Rams | Joe Noteboom | OT | TCU |
| 90 | Falcons | Deadrin Senat | DT | South Florida |
| 91 | Saints | Tre'Quan Smith | WR | UCF |
| 92 | Steelers | Chukwuma Okorafor | OT | Western Michigan |
| 93 | Jaguars | Ronnie Harrison | S | Alabama |
| 94 | Buccaneers | Alex Cappa | OT | Humboldt State |
| 95 | 49ers | Tarvarius Moore | S | Southern Miss |
| 96 | Bills | Harrison Phillips | DT | Stanford |
| 97 | Cardinals | Mason Cole | C | Michigan |
| 98 | Texans | Jordan Akins | TE | UCF |
| 99 | Broncos | Isaac Yiadom | CB | Boston College |
| 100 | Chiefs | Dorian O'Daniel | OLB | Clemson |

Table 18.14: Round 4 had the following players

| No. | Team | Player | Position | School |
|-----|------|--------|----------|--------|
| 101 | Panthers | Ian Thomas | TE | Indiana |
| 102 | Vikings | Jalyn Holmes | DE | Ohio State |
| 103 | Texans | Keke Coutee | WR | Texas Tech |
| 104 | Colts | Hyheim Hines | RB | N.C. State |
| 105 | Browns | Antonio Callaway | WR | Florida |
| 106 | Broncos | Josey Jewell | LB | Iowa |
| 107 | Jets | Chris Herndon | TE | Miami (Fla.) |
| 108 | Giants | Kyle Lauletta | QB | Richmond |
| 109 | Redskins | Troy Apke | S | Penn State |
| 110 | Raiders | Nick Nelson | CB | Wisconsin |
| 111 | Rams | Brian Allen | C | Michigan State |
| 112 | Bengals | Mark Walton | RB | Miami (Fla.) |
| 113 | Broncos | DaeSean Hamilton | WR | Penn State |
| 114 | Lions | Da'Shawn Hand | DE | Alabama |
| 115 | Bears | Joel Iyiegbuniwe | LB | Western Kentucky |
| 116 | Cowboys | Dorance Armstrong | DE | Kansas |
| 117 | Buccaneers | Jordan Whitehead | S | Pittsburgh |
| 118 | Ravens | Anthony Averett | CB | Alabama |
| 119 | Chargers | Kyzir White | S | West Virginia |
| 120 | Seahawks | Will Dissly | TE | Washington |
| 121 | Bills | Taron Johnson | CB | Weber State |
| 122 | Ravens | Kenny Young | LB | UCLA |
| 123 | Dolphins | Durham Smyth | TE | Notre Dame |
| 124 | Chiefs | Armani Watts | S | Texas A&M |
| 125 | Eagles | Avonte Maddox | CB | Pittsburgh |
| 126 | Falcons | Ito Smith | RB | Southern Miss |
| 127 | Saints | Rick Leonard | OT | Florida State |
| 128 | 49ers | Kentavius Street | DE | N.C. State |
| 129 | Jaguars | Will Richardson | OT | N.C. State |
| 130 | Eagles | Josh Sweat | DE | Florida State |
| 131 | Dolphins | Kalen Ballage | RB | Arizona State |
| 132 | Ravens | Jaleel Scott | WR | New Mexico State |
| 133 | Packers | J'Mon Moore | WR | Missouri |
| 134 | Cardinals | Chase Edmonds | RB | Fordham |
| 135 | Rams | John Franklin-Meyers | DE | Stephen F. Austin |
| 136 | Panthers | Marquis Haynes | OLB | Ole Miss |
| 137 | Cowboys | Dalton Schultz | TE | Stanford |

Table 18.15: Round 5 had the following players

| No. | Team | Player | Position | School |
|-----|------|--------|----------|--------|
| 138 | Packers | Cole Madison | OT | Washington State |
| 139 | Giants | RJ McIntosh | DT | Miami (Fla.) |
| 140 | Raiders | Maurice Hurst | DT | Michigan |
| 141 | Seahawks | Shaquem Griffin | LB | UCF |
| 142 | 49ers | D.J. Reed | CB | Kansas State |
| 143 | Patriots | Ja'Whaun Bentley | LB | Purdue |
| 144 | Buccaneers | Justin Watson | WR | Penn |
| 145 | Bears | Bilal Nichols | DT | Delaware |
| 146 | Seahawks | Tre Flowers | S | Oklahoma State |
| 147 | Rams | Micah Kiser | LB | Virginia |
| 148 | Steelers | Marcus Allen | S | Penn State |
| 149 | Seahawks | Michael Dickson | P | Texas |
| 150 | Browns | Genard Avery | LB | Memphis |
| 151 | Bengals | Davontae Harris | CB | Illinois St. |
| 152 | Titans | Dane Cruikshank | S | Arizona |
| 153 | Lions | Tyrell Crosby | OT | Oregon |
| 154 | Bills | Siran Neal | CB | Jacksonville St. |
| 155 | Chargers | Scott Quessenberry | C | UCLA |
| 156 | Broncos | Troy Fumagalli | TE | Wisconsin |
| 157 | Vikings | Tyler Conklin | TE | Central Michigan |
| 158 | Bengals | Andrew Brown | DE | Virginia |
| 159 | Colts | Daurice Fountain | WR | Northern Iowa |
| 160 | Rams | Ogbonnia Okoronkwo | LB | Oklahoma |
| 161 | Panthers | Jermaine Carter Jr. | LB | Maryland |
| 162 | Ravens | Jordan Lasley | WR | UCLA |
| 163 | Redskins | Tim Settle | DT | Virginia Tech |
| 164 | Saints | Natrell Jamerson | S | Wisconsin |
| 165 | Steelers | Jaylen Samuels | RB | N.C. State |
| 166 | Bills | Wyatt Teller | G | Virginia Tech |
| 167 | Vikings | Daniel Carlson | K | Auburn |
| 168 | Seahawks | Jamarco Jones | OT | Ohio State |
| 169 | Colts | Jordan Wilkins | RB | Ole Miss |
| 170 | Bengals | Darius Phillips | CB | Western Michigan |
| 171 | Cowboys | Mike White | QB | Western Kentucky |
| 172 | Packers | JK Scott | P | Alabama |
| 173 | Raiders | Johnny Townsend | P | Florida |
| 174 | Packers | Marquez Valdes-Scantling | WR | South Florida |

Table 18.16: Round 6 had the following players

| No. | Team | Player | Position | School |
|-----|------|--------|----------|--------|
| 175 | Browns | Damion Ratley | WR | Texas A&M |
| 176 | Rams | John Kelly | RB | Tennessee |
| 177 | Texans | Duke Eliofor | DE | Wake Forest |
| 178 | Patriots | Christian Sam | LB | Arizona State |
| 179 | Jets | Parry Nickerson | CB | Tulane |
| 180 | Jets | Foley Fatukasi | DT | UConn |
| 181 | Bears | Kylie Fitts | DE | Utah |
| 182 | Cardinals | Christian Campbell | CB | Penn State |
| 183 | Broncos | Sam Jones | G | Arizona State |
| 184 | 49ers | Marcell Harris | S | Florida |
| 185 | Colts | Deon Cain | WR | Clemson |
| 186 | Seahawks | Jacob Martin | DE | Temple |
| 187 | Bills | Ray-Ray McCloud | WR | Clemson |
| 188 | Browns | Simeon Thomas | CB | Louisiana |
| 189 | Saints | Kamrin Moore | CB | Boston College |
| 190 | Ravens | DeShon Elliott | S | Texas |
| 191 | Chargers | Dylan Cantrell | WR | Texas Tech |
| 192 | Rams | Jemil Demby | OL | Maine |
| 193 | Cowboys | Chris Covington | OLB | Indiana |
| 194 | Falcons | Russell Gage | WR | LSU |
| 195 | Rams | Sebastian Joseph | DT | Rutgers |
| 196 | Chiefs | Tremon Smith | CB | Central Arkansas |
| 197 | Redskins | Shaun Dion Hamilton | LB | Alabama |
| 198 | Chiefs | Kahlil McKenzie | OL | Tennessee |
| 199 | Titans | Luke Falk | QB | Washington State |
| 200 | Falcons | Foyesade Oluokun | LB | Yale |
| 201 | Saints | Boston Scott | RB | Louisiana Tech |
| 202 | Buccaneers | Jack Cichy | LB | Wisconsin |
| 203 | Jaguars | Tanner Lee | QB | Nebraska |
| 204 | Jets | Trenton Cannon | RB | Virginia St. |
| 205 | Rams | Trevon Young | LB | Louisville |
| 206 | Eagles | Matt Pryor | G | TCU |
| 207 | Packers | Equanimeous St. Brown | WR | Notre Dame |
| 208 | Cowboys | Cedrick Wilson | WR | Boise State |
| 209 | Dolphins | Cornell Armstrong | CB | Southern Miss |
| 210 | Patriots | Braxton Berrios | WR | Miami (Fla.) |
| 211 | Texans | Jordan Thomas | TE | Mississippi State |
| 212 | Ravens | Greg Senat | OT | Wagner |
| 213 | Vikings | Colby Gossett | G | Appalachain State |
| 214 | Texans | Peter Kalambayi | LB | Stanford |
| 215 | Ravens | Bradley Bozeman | C | Alabama |
| 216 | Raiders | Azeem Victor | LB | Washington |
| 217 | Broncos | Keishawn Bierria | LB | Washington |
| 218 | Vikings | Ade Aruna | DE | Tulane |

Table 18.17: Round 7 had the following players

| No. | Team | Player | Position | School |
|-----|------|--------|----------|--------|
| 219 | Patriots | Danny Etling | QB | LSU |
| 220 | Seahawks | Alex McGough | QB | Florida International |
| 221 | Colts | Matthew Adams | LB | Houston |
| 222 | Texans | Jermaine Kelly | DB | San Jose State |
| 223 | 49ers | Jullian Taylor | DT | Temple |
| 224 | Bears | Javon Wims | WR | Georgia |
| 225 | Vikings | Davante Downs | LB | California |
| 226 | Broncos | David Williams | RB | Arkansas |
| 227 | Dolphins | Quentin Poling | LB | Ohio |
| 228 | Raiders | Marcell Ateman | WR | Oklahoma State |
| 229 | Dolphins | Jason Sanders | K | New Mexico |
| 230 | Jaguars | Leon Jacobs | LB | Wisconsin |
| 231 | Rams | Travin Howard | LB | TCU |
| 232 | Packers | James Looney | DE | California |
| 233 | Eagles | Jordan Mailata | OT | Australia |
| 234 | Panthers | Andre Smith | LB | North Carolina |
| 235 | Colts | Zaire Franklin | LB | Syracuse |
| 236 | Cowboys | Bo Scarbrough | RB | Alabama |
| 237 | Lions | Nick Bawden | FB | San Diego State |
| 238 | Ravens | Zach Sieler | DE | Ferris St. |
| 239 | Packers | Hunter Bradley | LS | Mississippi State |
| 240 | 49ers | Richie James | WR | Middle Tennessee |
| 241 | Redskins | Greg Stroman | CB | Virginia Tech |
| 242 | Panthers | Kendrick Norton | DL | Miami (Fla.) |
| 243 | Patriots | Keion Crossman | CB | Western Carolina |
| 244 | Rams | Justin Lawler | DE | SMU |
| 245 | Saints | Will Clapp | C | LSU |
| 246 | Steelers | Joshua Frazier | DT | Alabama |
| 247 | Jaguars | Logan Cooke | P | Mississippi State |
| 248 | Packers | Kendall Donnerson | LB | Southeast Missouri St. |
| 249 | Bengals | Logan Woodside | QB | Toledo |
| 250 | Patriots | Ryan Izzo | TE | Florida State |
| 251 | Chargers | Justin Jackson | RB | Northwestern |
| 252 | Bengals | Rod Taylor | G | Ole Miss |
| 253 | Bengals | Auden Tate | WR | Florida State |
| 254 | Cardinals | Korey Cunningham | OT | Cincinnati |
| 255 | Bills | Austin Proehl | WR | North Carolina |
| 256 | Redskins | Trey Quinn | WR | SMU |

Table 18.18: NFL Draft History: All Time #1

| Year | Player | Pos | School | Team | Yrs,Bowls |
|------|--------|-----|--------|------|-----------|
| 2017 | Myles Garrett | DE | Texas A&M | Cleveland Browns | 1, 0 |
| 2016 | Jared Goff | QB | California | Los Angeles Rams | 2, 1 |
| 2015 | Jameis Winston | QB | Florida St. | Tampa Bay Buccaneers | 3, 1 |
| 2014 | Jadeveon Clowney | DE | South Carolina | Houston Texans | 4, 2 |
| 2013 | Eric Fisher | OT | Central Michigan | Kansas City Chiefs | 5, 0 |
| 2012 | Andrew Luck | QB | Stanford | Indianapolis Colts | 6, 3 |
| 2011 | Cam Newton | QB | Auburn | Carolina Panthers | 7, 3 |
| 2010 | Sam Bradford | QB | Oklahoma | St. Louis Rams | 8, 0 |
| 2009 | Matthew Stafford | QB | Georgia | Detroit Lions | 9, 1 |
| 2008 | Jake Long | OT | Michigan | Miami Dolphins | 10, 4 |
| 2007 | JaMarcus Russell | QB | LSU | Oakland Raiders | 3, 0 |
| 2006 | Mario Williams | DE | N. Carolina State | Houston Texans | 11, 4 |
| 2005 | Alex Smith | QB | Utah | San Francisco 49ers | 13, 3 |
| 2004 | Eli Manning | QB | Mississippi | San Diego Chargers | 14, 4 |
| 2003 | Carson Palmer | QB | Southern Cal. | Cincinnati Bengals | 15, 3 |
| 2002 | David Carr | QB | Fresno State | Houston Texans | 11, 0 |
| 2001 | Michael Vick | QB | Virginia Tech | Atlanta Falcons | 11, 4 |
| 2000 | Courtney Brown | DE | Penn State | Cleveland Browns | 7, 0 |
| 1999 | Tim Couch | QB | Kentucky | Cleveland Browns | 6, 0 |
| 1998 | Peyton Manning | QB | Tennessee | Indianapolis Colts | 16, 11 |
| 1997 | Orlando Pace | OT | Ohio State | St. Louis Rams | 12, 7 |
| 1996 | Keyshawn Johnson | WR | Southern Cal. | New York Jets | 11, 4 |
| 1995 | Ki-Jana Carter | RB | Penn State | Cincinnati Bengals | 8, 0 |
| 1994 | Dan Wilkinson | DT | Ohio State | Cincinnati Bengals | 13, 0 |
| 1993 | Drew Bledsoe | QB | Washington State | New England Patriots | 14, 4 |
| 1992 | Steve Emtman | DT | Washington | Indianapolis Colts | 8, 0 |
| 1991 | Russell Maryland | DT | Miami, (Fla.) | Dallas Cowboys | 10, 1 |
| 1990 | Jeff George | QB | Illinois | Indianapolis Colts | 13, 0 |
| 1989 | *Troy Aikman | QB | UCLA | Dallas Cowboys | 12, 6 |
| 1988 | Aundray Bruce | LB | Auburn | Atlanta Falcons | 11, 0 |
| 1987 | Vinny Testaverde | QB | Miami, (Fla.) | Tampa Bay Buccaneers | 21, 2 |
| 1986 | Bo Jackson | RB | Auburn | Tampa Bay Buccaneers | 4, 1 |
| 1985 | Bruce Smith | DE | Virginia Tech | Buffalo Bills | 18, 11 |
| 1984 | Irving Fryar | WR | Nebraska | New England Patriots | 15, 5 |
| 1983 | *John Elway | QB | Stanford | Baltimore Colts | 16, 10 |
| 1982 | Kenneth Sims | DT | Texas | New England Patriots | 8, 0 |
| 1981 | George Rogers | RB | South Carolina | New Orleans Saints | 7, 2 |
| 1980 | Bill Sims | RB | Oklahoma | Detroit Lions | 5, 3 |
| 1979 | Tom Cousineau | LB | Ohio State | Buffalo Bills | 6, 0 |
| 1978 | *Earl Campbell | RB | Texas | Houston Oilers | 8, 5 |
| 1977 | Ricky Bell | RB | Southern Cal. | Tampa Bay Buccaneers | 6, 0 |
| 1976 | *Lee Roy Selmon | DE | Oklahoma | Tampa Bay Buccaneers | 9, 6 |
| 1975 | Steve Bartkowski | QB | California | Atlanta Falcons | 12, 2 |
| 1974 | Ed 'Too Tall' Jones | DE | Tennessee State | Dallas Cowboys | 15, 3 |
| 1973 | John Matuszak | DE | Tampa | Houston Oilers | 9, 0 |

Table 18.18: (*Continued*)

| Year | Player | Pos | School | Team | Yrs,Bowls |
|------|--------|-----|--------|------|-----------|
| 1972 | Walt Patulski | DT | Notre Dame | Buffalo Bills | 5, 0 |
| 1971 | Jim Plunkett | QB | Stanford | New England Patriots | 15, 0 |
| 1970 | *Terry Bradshaw | QB | Louisiana Tech | Pittsburgh Steelers | 14, 3 |
| 1969 | *O.J. Simpson | RB | Southern Cal. | Buffalo Bills | 11, 6 |
| 1968 | *Ron Yary | OT | Southern Cal. | Minnesota Vikings | 15, 7 |
| 1967 | Bubba Smith | DE | Michigan State | Baltimore Colts | 9, 2 |
| 1966 | Jim Grabowski | RB | Illinois | Miami Dolphins (AFL) | 6, 0 |
| 1966 | Tommy Nobis | LB | Texas | Atlanta Falcons (NFL) | 11, 5 |
| 1965 | Lawrence Elkins | WR | Baylor | Houston Oilers (AFL) | 2, 0 |
| 1965 | T. Frederickson | RB | Auburn | New York Giants (NFL) | 6, 1 |
| 1964 | Jack Concannon | QB | Boston College | Boston Patriots (AFL) | 10, 0 |
| 1964 | Dave Parks | WR | Texas Tech | San Francisco 49ers (NFL) | 10, 3 |
| 1963 | *Buck Buchanan | DT | Grambling | Kansas City Chiefs (AFL) | 13, 8 |
| 1963 | Terry Baker | QB | Oregon State | Los Angeles Rams (NFL) | 3, 0 |
| 1962 | Roman Gabriel | QB | N. Carolina State | Oakland Raiders (AFL) | 16, 4 |
| 1962 | Ernie Davis | RB | Syracuse | Washington Redskins (NFL) | DNP |
| 1961 | Ken Rice | G | Auburn | Buffalo Bills (AFL) | 6, 1 |
| 1961 | Tommy Mason | RB | Tulane | Minnesota Vikings (NFL) | 11, 3 |
| 1960 | Billy Cannon | RB | Louisiana State | Los Angeles Rams | 11, 2 |
| 1959 | Randy Duncan | QB | Iowa | Green Bay Packers | 1, 0 |
| 1958 | King Hill | QB | Rice | Chicago Cardinals | 12, 0 |
| 1957 | *Paul Hornung | HB | Notre Dame | Green Bay Packers | 9, 2 |
| 1956 | Gary Glick | DB | Colorado A&M | Pittsburgh Steelers | 7, 0 |
| 1955 | George Shaw | QB | Oregon | Baltimore Colts | 8, 0 |
| 1954 | Bobby Garrett | QB | Stanford | Cleveland Browns | 1, 0 |
| 1953 | Harry Babcock | E | Georgia | San Francisco 49ers | 3, 3 |
| 1952 | Bill Wade | QB | Vanderbilt | Los Angeles Rams | 13, 2 |
| 1951 | Kyle Rote | HB | SMU | New York Giants | 11, 4 |
| 1950 | Leon Hart | E | Notre Dame | Detroit Lions | 8, 1 |
| 1949 | *Chuck Bednarik | C/LB | Pennsylvania | Philadelphia Eagles | 12, 8 |
| 1948 | Harry Gilmer | QB | Alabama | Washington Redskins | 2, 0 |
| 1947 | Bob Fenimore | HB | Oklahoma State | Chicago Bears | 1, 0 |
| 1946 | Frank Dancewicz | QB | Notre Dame | Boston Yanks | 3, 0 |
| 1945 | *Charley Trippi | HB | Georgia | Chicago Cardinals | 9, 2 |
| 1944 | Angelo Bertelli | QB | Notre Dame | Boston Yanks | 3, 0 |
| 1943 | Frank Sinkwich | HB | Georgia | Detroit Lions | 4, 0 |
| 1942 | *Bill Dudley | HB | Virginia | Pittsburgh Steelers | 9, 3 |
| 1941 | Tom Harmon | HB | Michigan | Chicago Bears | 2, 0 |
| 1940 | George Cafego | HB | Tennessee | Chicago Cardinals | 4, 0 |
| 1939 | Ki Aldrich | C | Texas Christian | Chicago Cardinals | 7, 2 |
| 1938 | Corbett Davis | FB | Indiana | Cleveland Rams | DNP |
| 1937 | Sam Francis | FB | Nebraska | Philadelphia Eagles | 4, 0 |
| 1936 | Jay Berwanger | HB | Chicago | Philadelphia Eagles | DNP |

* Member of the Pro Football Hall of Fame

## Table 18.19: NFL Draft History: All Time #2

| Year | Player | Pos | School | Team | Yrs,Bowls |
|------|--------|-----|--------|------|-----------|
| 2017 | Mitchell Trubisky | QB | North Carolina | Chicago Bears | 1, 0 |
| 2016 | Carson Wentz | QB | North Dakota St. | Philadelphia Eagles | 2, 1 |
| 2015 | Marcus Mariota | QB | Oregon | Tennessee Titans | 3, 0 |
| 2014 | Greg Robinson | OT | Auburn | St. Louis Rams | 4. 0 |
| 2013 | Luke Joeckel | OT | Texas A&M | Jacksonville Jaguars | 5, 0 |
| 2012 | Robert Griffin III | QB | Baylor | Washington Redskins | 5, 1 |
| 2011 | Von Miller | LB | Texas A&M | Denver Broncos | 7, 6 |
| 2010 | Ndamukong Suh | DT | Nebraska | Detroit Lions | 8, 5 |
| 2009 | Jason Smith | OT | Baylor | St. Louis Rams | 4, 0 |
| 2008 | Chris Long | DE | Virginia | St. Louis Rams | 10, 0 |
| 2007 | Calvin Johnson | WR | Georgia Tech | Detroit Lions | 8, 6 |
| 2006 | Reggie Bush | RB | Southern Cal. | New Orleans Saints | 10, 0 |
| 2005 | Ronnie Brown | RB | Auburn | Miami Dolphins | 9, 1 |
| 2004 | Robert Gallery | OT | Iowa | Oakland Raiders | 8, 0 |
| 2003 | Charles Rogers | WR | Michigan State | Detroit Lions | 3, 0 |
| 2002 | Julius Peppers | DE | North Carolina | Carolina Panthers | 16, 9 |
| 2001 | Leonard Davis | OT | Texas | Arizona Cardinals | 11, 3 |
| 2000 | LaVar Arrington | LB | Penn State | Washington Redskins | 7, 3 |
| 1999 | Donovan McNabb | QB | Syracuse | Philadelphia Eagles | 13, 6 |
| 1998 | Ryan Leaf | QB | Washington St. | San Diego Chargers | 3, 0 |
| 1997 | Darrell Russell | DT | Southern Cal. | Oakland Raiders | 5, 2 |
| 1996 | Kevin Hardy | LB | Illinois | Jacksonville Jaguars | 9, 1 |
| 1995 | Tony Boselli | OT | Southern Cal. | Jacksonville Jaguars | 7, 5 |
| 1994 | Marshall Faulk | RB | San Diego St. | Indianapolis Colts | 12, 7 |
| 1993 | Rick Mirer | QB | Notre Dame | Seattle Seahawks | 12, 0 |
| 1992 | Quentin Coryatt | LB | Texas A&M | Indianapolis Colts | 9, 0 |
| 1991 | Eric Turner | DB | UCLA | Cleveland Browns | 9, 2 |
| 1990 | Blair Thomas | RB | Penn State | New York Jets | 6, 0 |
| 1989 | Tony Mandarich | OT | Michigan State | Green Bay Packers | 8, 0 |
| 1988 | Neil Smith | DE | Nebraska | Kansas City Chiefs | 13, 6 |
| 1987 | Cornelius Bennett | LB | Alabama | Indianapolis Colts | 14,5 |
| 1986 | Tony Casillas | DT | Oklahoma | Atlanta Falcons | 12, 0 |
| 1985 | Bill Fralic | G | Pittsburgh | Atlanta Falcons | 9, 4 |
| 1984 | Dean Steinkuhler | G | Nebraska | Houston Oilers | 7, 0 |
| 1983 | *Eric Dickerson | RB | SMU | Los Angeles Rams | 11, 6 |
| 1982 | Johnnie Cooks | LB | Mississippi State | Baltimore Ravens | 10, 0 |
| 1981 | *Lawrence Taylor | LB | North Carolina | New York Giants | 13, 10 |
| 1980 | Johnny 'Lam' Jones | WR | Texas | New York Jets | 5, 0 |
| 1979 | Mike Bell | DE | Colorado St. | Kansas City Chiefs | 12, 0 |
| 1978 | Art Still | DE | Kentucky | Kansas City Chiefs | 13, 4 |
| 1977 | *Tony Dorsett | RB | Pittsburgh | Dallas Cowboys | 12, 4 |
| 1976 | Steve Niehaus | DT | Notre Dame | Seattle Seahawks | 4, 0 |
| 1975 | *Randy White | LB | Maryland | Dallas Cowboys | 14, 9 |
| 1974 | Bo Matthews | RB | Colorado | San Diego Chargers | 8, 0 |
| 1973 | Bert Jones | QB | LSU | Baltimore Colts | 10, 1 |

Table 18.19: (*Continued*)

| Year | Player | Pos | School | Team | Yrs,Bowls |
|------|--------|-----|--------|------|-----------|
| 1972 | Sherman White | DE | California | Cincinnati Browns | 12, 0 |
| 1971 | Archie Manning | QB | Mississippi | New Orleans Saints | 14, 2 |
| 1970 | Mike McCoy | DT | Notre Dame | Green Bay Packers | 11, 0 |
| 1969 | George Kunz | OT | Notre Dame | Atlanta Falcons | 11, 8 |
| 1968 | Bob Johnson | C | Tennessee | Cincinnati Browns | 12, 1 |
| 1967 | Clint Jones | RB | Michigan St. | Minnesota Vikings | 7, 0 |
| 1966 | Rick Norton | QB | Kentucky | Miami Dolphins (AFL) | 5, 0 |
| 1966 | *Tom Mack | OT | Michigan | Los Angeles Rams (NFL) | 13, 11 |
| 1965 | *Joe Namath | QB | Alabama | New York Jets (AFL) | 13, 5 |
| 1965 | Ken Willard | FB | North Carolina | San Francisco 49ers (NFL) | 10. 4 |
| 1964 | Pete Bethard | QB | Southern Cal. | Kansas City Chiefs (AFL) | 10, 0 |
| 1964 | Bob Brown | G | Nebraska | Philadelphia Eagles (NFL) | 10, 6 |
| 1963 | Walt Sweeney | E | Syracuse | San Diego Chargers (AFL) | 11, 9 |
| 1963 | Jerry Stoval | B | LSU | St. Louis Cardinals (NFL) | 9, 3 |
| 1962 | *Merlin Olsen | DT | Utah State | Denver Broncos (AFL) | 15, 14 |
| 1962 | Roman Gabriel | QB | North Carolina State | Los Angeles Rams (NFL) | 16, 4 |
| 1961 | Tom Brown | G | Minnesota | New York Jets (AFL) | DNP |
| 1961 | Norm Snead | QB | Wake Forest | Washington Redskins (NFL) | 16. 3 |
| 1960 | George Izo | B | Notre Dame | Chicago Cardinals | 7, 0 |
| 1959 | Dick Bass | B | Pacific | Los Angeles Rams | 10, 3 |
| 1958 | Dan Currie | C | Michigan State | Green Bay Packers | 9, 1 |
| 1957 | John Brodie | QB | Stanford | San Francisco 49ers | 17, 2 |
| 1956 | Howard Cassady | B | Ohio State | Detroit Lions | 8, 0 |
| 1955 | Alan Ameche | B | Wisconsin | Baltimore Colts | 6, 4 |
| 1954 | Art Hunter | OT | Notre Dame | Green Bay Packers | 11, 1 |
| 1953 | Jack Scarbath | B | Maryland | Washington Redskins | 3, 0 |
| 1952 | *Ollie Matson | B | San Francisco | Chicago Cardinals | 14, 5 |
| 1951 | *Y.A. Tittle | QB | LSU | San Francisco 49ers | 15, 6 |
| 1950 | Chuck Hunsinger | B | Florida | Chicago Bears | 3, 0 |
| 1949 | Johny Rauch | QB | Georgia | Detroit Lions | 3, 0 |
| 1948 | Tony Minisi | B | Penn | New York Giants | 1, 0 |
| 1947 | Fritz Barzliauskas | G | Yale | Boston Yanks | 4, 0 |
| 1946 | Frank Dancewicz | QB | Notre Dame | Boston Yanks | 3, 0 |
| 1945 | Paul Duhart | B | Florida | Pittsburgh Steelers | 2, 0 |
| 1944 | Pat Harder | B | Wisconsin | Chicago Cardinals | 8, 2 |
| 1943 | Joe Muha | B | VMI | Philadelphia Eagles | 5, 0 |
| 1942 | Jack Wilson | B | Baylor | Cleveland Rams | 3, 0 |
| 1941 | John Kimbrough | B | Texas A&M | Chicago Cardinals | 3, 0 |
| 1940 | *George McAfee | B | Duke | Philadelphia Eagles | 8, 1 |
| 1939 | *Sid Luckman | QB | Columbia | Chicago Bears | 12, 3 |
| 1938 | Jim McDonald | B | Ohio State | Philadelphia Eagles | 2, 0 |
| 1937 | Ed Goddard | B | Washington St. | Brooklyn Dodgers | 2, 1 |
| 1936 | Riley Smith | B | Alabama | Boston Redskins | 3, 0 |

* Member of the Pro Football Hall of Fame

# References

Baker, R. D. and I. G. McHale (2013). Forecasting exact scores in National Football League games. *International Journal of Forecasting 29:* 12-130.

Bradley, R. and Terry, M. (1952). Rank analysis of incomplete block designs: I. the method of paired comparisons. *Biometrika*, 39(3/4):324-345.

Buhlmann, H. and P. J. Huber (1963). Pairwise Comparison and Ranking in Tournaments, *Annals of Mathematical Statistics 34*(2): 501-510.

Byrne, Kerry (2011). "QBR: ESPN's Deeply Flawed Made-For-TV Stat" *Cold Hard Football Facts.* Football Nation LLC.

Cain, M., D. Law, and D. A. Peel (2000). Testing for statistical and market efficiency when forecast errors are non-normal: the NFL betting market revisited. *Journal of Forecasting, 19:* 575-586.

Cameron, R. R. (2010). Determinants of Thoroughbred Racehorse Stud Fees. Honors Economics Thesis, Emory University.

Carroll, B., Palmer, P., and Thorn, J. (1988). *The Hidden Game of Football* Warner Books, New York.

Carter, V. and Macholl, R. (1978). *Management Science 24*(6): 1758-1762.

Dare, W. H. and A. S. Holland (2004). Efficiency in the NFL betting market: modifying and consolidating research methods. *Applied Economics, 36:* 9-15.

Elo, A. E. (2008). *Logistic Probability as a Rating Basis: The Rating of Chessplayers, Past & Present*, Bronx NY 10453: ISHI Press International.

Foder A. (2014). Does jet lag create a profitable opportunity for NFL bettors? *The Journal of Gambling, Business and Economics 8:*(1).

Glickman, M. E. and H. S. Stern (1998). A state-space model for National Football League scores. *Journal of the American Statistical Association, 93*(441), 25-35.

Harville, D. (1980). Predictions for National Football League games via linear-model methodology. *Journal of the American Statistical Association, 75*(371), 516-524.

Hausch, D. B. and W. T. Ziemba, W.T., Eds, (2008). *Handbook of Sports and Lottery Markets*, North Holland Handbooks in Finance Series.

Hausch, D. B., V. Lo, and W. T. Ziemba (Eds) (2008). *Efficiency of Racetrack Betting Markets*, World Scientific.

Kahane, L. H. and S. Shmanske, Eds., *The Oxford Handbook of Sports Economics: Volume 1: The Economics of Sports*, Oxford University Press.

Lane, D. and W. T. Ziemba (2004). Jai-Alai Hedging Strategies, *European Journal of Finance*: 353-369.

Levitt, S. D. (2004). Why are gambling markets organized so differently from financial markets? *The Economic Journal, 114*, 223-246.

Lewis, M. (2003). *Moneyball: the art of winning an unfair game*, W. W. Norton.

MacLean, L. C., E. O. Thorp and W. T. Ziemba (2011). *The Kelly capital growth investment criterion: theory and practice.* Handbook in financial economics series. World Scientific.

MacLean, L. C. and W. T. Ziemba (2018). Player Ranking and Team Performance in American Football. Technical Report.

Maske, M. (2017). This NFL season has been all about who isn't playing rather than who is, *Washington Post*, December 15.

Maske, M. (2018). Concussions suffered by NFL players up this season: injuries rate higher for Thursday games, *Washington Post*, January 26.

Negahban, S., Oh, S. and Shah, D. (2012). Iterative ranking from pair-wise comparisons. *NIPS*.

Paine, N. (2015). NFL Elo Ratings Are Back, *FiveThirtyEight*, September 10.

Poundstone, W. (2005). *Fortune's Formula: the untold story of the scientific system to beat casinos and Wall Street*, Hill and Wang, NY.

Quinn, K. (2012). Field position and strategy in American football. *The Oxford Handbook of Sports Economics: Volume 1: The Economics of Sports*, L. H. Kahane and S. Shmanske, Eds., Oxford University Press.

Romer, D. (2006). Do firms maximize? Evidence from professional football. *Journal of Political Economy 114*(2): 340-365.

Sauer, R. D. (1998). The economics of wagering markets. *Journal of Economic Literature, 36:* 2021-2064.

Sauer, R. D., V. Brajer, S. P. Ferris and M. W. Marr (1988). Hold your bets: another look at the efficiency of the market for National Football League games. *Journal of Political Economy, 96:* 206-213.

Shouler, K. (2017). America's game, pro football, *Cigar*.

Silver, N. (2014). Introducing NFL Elo Ratings, *FiveThirtyEight*, September 4.

Simpson, E. (1951). The Interpretation of Interaction in Contingency Tables, *Journal of the Royal Statistical Society 13*: 238-241.

Snowberg, E. and J. Wolfers (2008). Examining explanations of a market anomaly: preferences or perceptions? in Hausch, D. B. and W. T. Ziemba (Eds), *Handbook of Sports and Lottery Markets*, North Holland Handbooks in Finance Series.

Stern, H. (1991). On the probability of winning a football game. *The American Statistician 45*(3), 179-183.

Walker, J., J. L. Risen, T. Gilovich and R. H. Thaler (2018). Force overtime? or go for the win? *Sunday Review*, February 2 based on a forthcoming paper in *Journal of Personality and Social Psychology*.

Ziemba, W. T. (2008). Efficiency of racetrack betting markets, in *Handbook of Sports and Lottery Markets*, D. B. Hausch and W. T. Ziemba (eds) in Handbooks in Finance, North Holland, 183-221.

Ziemba, W. T. (ed) (2016). *Great investment ideas*, World Scientific, Singapore.

Ziemba, W. T. (2017a). *Adventures of a Renaissance Academic in Investing and Gambling*. World Scientific, Singapore.

Ziemba, W. T. (2017b). The Road to Super Bowl 51. *Wilmott 89:* 26-35.

Ziemba, W. T. (2018). *Exotic Betting at the Racetrack,* World Scientific, Singapore, in press.

Ziemba, W. T. and D. B. Hausch (1986). *Betting at the Racetrack,* Norris Strauss, New York.

Zuber, R. A., J. M. Gandar and B. D. Bowers (1985). Beating the spread: testing the efficiency of the gambling market for National Football League games. *Journal of Political Economy, 93:* 800-806.